P9-DZO-653

TAKING SIDES

Clashing Views on Controversial

Legal Issues

TENTH EDITION

Clashing Views on Controversial

Legal Issues

TENTH EDITION

Selected, Edited, and with Introductions by

M. Ethan Katsh
University of Massachusetts–Amherst

and

William Rose
Albion College

McGraw-Hill/Dushkin
A Division of The McGraw-Hill Companies

To Beverly

Photo Acknowledgment
Cover image: © 2002 by PhotoDisc, Inc.

Cover Art Acknowledgment
Charles Vitelli

Copyright © 2002 by McGraw-Hill/Dushkin,
A Division of The McGraw-Hill Companies, Inc., Guilford, Connecticut 06437

Copyright law prohibits the reproduction, storage, or transmission in any form by any means of any portion of this publication without the express written permission of McGraw-Hill/Dushkin and of the copyright holder (if different) of the part of the publication to be reproduced. The Guidelines for Classroom Copying endorsed by Congress explicitly state that unauthorized copying may not be used to create, to replace, or to substitute for anthologies, compilations, or collective works.

Taking Sides ® is a registered trademark of McGraw-Hill/Dushkin

Manufactured in the United States of America

Tenth Edition

123456789BAHBAH5432

Library of Congress Cataloging-in-Publication Data
Main entry under title:
Taking sides: clashing views on controversial legal issues/selected, edited, and with introductions by M. Ethan Katsh and William Rose.—10th ed.
Includes bibliographical references and index.
1. Law—Social aspects—United States. 2. United States—Constitutional law. 3. Justice, Administration of—United States. I. Katsh, M. Ethan, *comp.* II. Rose, William, *comp.*
340'.115
0-07-248040-8
ISSN: 1098-5395

Printed on Recycled Paper

Preface

The study of law should be introduced as part of a liberal education, to train and enrich the mind.... I am convinced that, like history, economics, and metaphysics—and perhaps even to a greater degree than these—the law could be advantageously studied with a view to the general development of the mind.

— Justice Louis D. Brandeis

The general study of law in colleges, universities, and even high schools has grown rapidly during the last 20 years. Accompanying this development has been the publication of new curriculum materials that go beyond the analysis of legal cases and doctrines that make up much of professional law study in law schools. This book is part of the effort to view and study law as an institution that continuously interacts with other social institutions. Law should be examined from an interdisciplinary perspective and be accessible to all students.

This book focuses on a series of controversial issues involving law and the legal system. It is, we believe, an appropriate starting point for law study because controversy and conflict are inherent in law. Law is based on an adversary approach to conflict resolution, in which two advocates representing opposing sides are pitted against each other. Judicial decisions often contain both majority and dissenting opinions, which reveal some of the arguments that went on in the judges' chambers. Perhaps most relevant to a discussion of the place of controversy in the legal system is the First Amendment guaranty of freedom of speech and of the press, which presumes that we all benefit by a vigorous debate of important issues.

Since many of the issues in *Taking Sides* are often in the news, you probably already have opinions on them. What you should remember, however, is that there is usually more to learn about any given issue, and the topics discussed here are best approached with an open mind. You should not be surprised if your views change as you read the selections.

Organization of the book This book contains 38 selections presented in a pro and con format that debate 19 legal issues. Each issue has an issue *introduction*, which sets the stage for the debate as it is argued in the YES and NO selections. Each issue concludes with a *postscript* that makes some final observations, points the way to other questions related to the issue, and provides some *suggestions for further reading* on the issue. Also, the *On the Internet* page that accompanies each part opener contains a list of Internet site addresses (URLs) that should prove useful as starting points for further research. At the back of the book is a listing of all the *contributors to this volume,* which provides information on the legal scholars, commentators, and judges whose views are debated here.

Changes to this edition   In this edition of *Taking Sides,* we continue to focus on law's relationship to the individual, the state, and the community. However, we have also made considerable revisions to this edition. There are seven new issues: *Do "Standardless" Manual Recounts Violate the Equal Protection and Due Process Clauses of the U.S. Constitution?* (Issue 1); *Does the Sharing of Music Files Through Napster Violate Copyright Laws?* (Issue 5); *Do Religious Groups Have a Right to Use Public School Facilities After Hours?* (Issue 8); *Does the Use of High-Technology Thermal Imaging Devices Violate the Fourth Amendment Search and Seizure Guaranty?* (Issue 9); *Is Virtual Child Pornography Legal?* (Issue 10); *Is It Constitutional to Impose the Death Penalty on the Mentally Retarded?* (Issue 11); and *Does the First Amendment Protect an Informational Web Site That May Encourage Violent Acts?* (Issue 15).

A word to the instructor   An *Instructor's Manual With Test Questions* (multiple-choice and essay) is available through the publisher for the instructor using *Taking Sides* in the classroom. A general guidebook, *Using Taking Sides in the Classroom,* which discusses methods and techniques for integrating the pro-con approach into any classroom setting, is also available. An online version of *Using Taking Sides in the Classroom* and a correspondence service for *Taking Sides* adopters can be found at http://www.dushkin.com/usingts/.

Taking Sides: Clashing Views on Controversial Legal Issues is only one title in the Taking Sides series. If you are interested in seeing the table of contents for any of the other titles, please visit the Taking Sides Web site at http://www.dushkin.com/takingsides/.

A note on case citations   Throughout this book you will see references to judicial opinions. The judge's opinion or decision refers to the written statement of reasons the judge provides when making an interpretation of law or deciding a case. These opinions are printed and distributed in books called *reporters,* which can be found in law libraries and many university libraries. There are separate reporters for federal and state cases. When you see a reference to a case, such as *Brown v. Board of Education,* 347 U.S. 483 (1954), it means that the case with that name can be found in volume 347 of the *United States Reports* on page 483 and that the case was decided in 1954. When you see a legal citation with a series of numbers and words, the first number is always the volume number and the last number is the page number.

M. Ethan Katsh
University of Massachusetts–Amherst

William Rose
Albion College

Contents In Brief

Contents

The U.S. Supreme Court, in a *per curium* decision, rules that Florida's manual recounting of ballots in the 2000 presidential election failed to satisfy the basic constitutional requirements of equal treatment and fundamental fairness. Supreme Court justice John Paul Stevens, dissenting from the Court's decision, asserts that the manner by which presidents are elected is the responsibility of each individual state and that Florida's ballot recount was not limited by federal laws.

Supreme Court justice Sandra Day O'Connor upholds a woman's constitutional right to abortion under most circumstances and reaffirms the central holding of *Roe v. Wade.* Supreme Court chief justice William H. Rehnquist argues that Pennsylvania regulations on abortion should be upheld and that it is appropriate to overrule *Roe v. Wade.*

Supreme Court chief justice William H. Rehnquist rules that although patients have the right to refuse life-sustaining treatment, physician-assisted suicide is not constitutionally protected. Judge Stephen Reinhardt argues that forbidding physician-assisted suicide in the cases of competent, terminally ill patients violates the due process clause of the Constitution.

Professor of law and political science Cass Sunstein, writing as fictional Supreme Court justice Monroe, argues that the right to cloning is analogous to established rights of reproductive privacy and autonomy and is therefore constitutionally protected. Sunstein, writing as fictional Supreme Court justice Winston, argues that the constitutional protection of "reproductive choice" does not extend to the decision to replicate oneself.

U.S. Circuit Court judge Robert R. Beezer upholds the ruling that Napster, Inc., by facilitating the copying and distribution of the plaintiffs' music recordings, is liable for contributory copyright infringement. Jessica Litman et al., all professors of American law, argue that the district court in the *Napster* case applied an unduly narrow interpretation of the fair use doctrine and extended copyright law to shut down a useful new technology.

Editor Jonathan Rowe examines the insanity defense as it is now administered and finds that it is most likely to be used by white middle- or upper-class defendants and that its application is unfair and leads to unjust results. Professor of law Richard Bonnie argues that the abolition of the insanity defense would be immoral and would leave no alternative for those who are not responsible for their actions.

Supreme Court justice Antonin Scalia holds that pretextual traffic stops do not violate an individual's Fourth Amendment rights. He argues that the constitutionality of such stops does not depend on the actual motivations of the police officer who makes the stop but on an objective determination of the reasonableness of the stop. David A. Harris, a professor of criminal law and criminal procedure, contends that Scalia's opinion ignores the potential for abuse by the police of general and all-encompassing traffic codes.

PART 2   LAW AND THE STATE   135

Supreme Court justice Clarence Thomas affirms the right of religious groups to use school facilities after the school day ends, maintaining that restricting such use is a violation of free speech rights. Supreme Court justice David Souter, dissenting from the Court's opinion, contends that the use of school facilities by religious groups blurs the line between public classroom instruction and private religious indoctrination and therefore violates the establishment clause of the Constitution.

Supreme Court justice Antonin Scalia maintains that thermal imaging devices reveal information "that would previously have been unknowable without physical intrusion" and that using such devices for surveillance without a warrant constitutes a violation of the Fourth Amendment. Supreme Court justice John Paul Stevens asserts that the Court's application of search and seizure rules to new technology is too broad and that collecting thermal imaging data from outside the home is not a violation of privacy rights.

U.S. District Court judge Donald W. Molloy rules that illicit images that do not involve actual children in their production or depiction, even when they appear to be child pornography, are protected by the First Amendment. U.S. Circuit Court judge Warren J. Ferguson maintains that "virtual child pornography causes real harm to real children" and that, like real child pornography, it is not protected by the First Amendment's free speech guaranty.

Supreme Court justice Sandra Day O'Connor holds that the Constitution does not preclude the execution of a mentally retarded person who is convicted of a capital offense. The American Bar Association, the principal voluntary national membership organization of the legal profession, argues that the Eighth Amendment should be held to exempt people with mental retardation from capital punishment.

Supreme Court justice Clarence Thomas finds that a Kansas law that allows civil commitment of "mentally abnormal" persons is constitutional and does not violate the Constitution's double jeopardy prohibition or its ban on ex post facto lawmaking. Supreme Court justice Stephen G. Breyer finds that the Kansas law was an effort to inflict further punishment upon Leroy Hendricks and that the ex post facto clause should apply since Hendricks committed his crimes prior to its enactment.

Steven B. Duke, a professor of law of science and technology, contends
that the war on drugs has led to an increase in criminal behavior, including
robberies, assaults with guns, and police corruption, and that the financial,
health, and civil rights costs of drug prohibition are enormous. Therefore,
he recommends decriminalization and government regulation of drugs.
Professor of law Gregory A. Loken, directly responding to Duke, asserts
that the war on drugs has successfully reduced crime and that legalization
would have devastating consequences, particularly for children.

Simeon Schopf, a writing and research editor for the *Columbia Journal
of Law and Social Problems*, looks at various constitutional objections to
Megan's Law and concludes that, in the balance of interests, such laws
are constitutional. Bonnie Steinbock, a legal philosopher, focuses on the
moral issues posed by the notification statutes and argues that Megan's
Law fails to serve its ultimate goal—protecting children.

U.S. Circuit Court judge Alex Kozinski rules that Web sites that contain
intimidating but not explicitly threatening content are protected by the First
Amendment. O. Lee Reed, a professor of legal studies, contends that
intimidating speech directed at individuals—even speech that does not
threaten imminent violence—is significantly harmful and should not be
considered protected speech.

Andrew Sullivan, a journalist and magazine editor, seeks to transcend the traditional liberal and conservative terms of the debate over same-sex marriages and argues that all public discrimination against homosexuals should be ended. James Q. Wilson, an emeritus professor of management and public policy, finds unpersuasive the various arguments that Sullivan puts forward.

Issue 17.   Are Public School Officials Liable for Damages in Cases of Student-on-Student Sexual Harassment?   314

Supreme Court justice Sandra Day O'Connor holds that under Title IX of the Education Amendments of 1972, actions for private damages may be brought against school board officials in cases of student-on-student sexual harassment. Supreme Court justice Anthony Kennedy argues that Title IX cannot be read to provide such a cause of action and that to do so opens the gate for the federal government to intrude into state and local educational decision making.

Issue 18.   Should Children With Disabilities Be Provided With Extraordinary Care in Order to Attend Regular Classes in Public Schools?   330

Supreme Court justice John Paul Stevens interprets the Individuals with Disabilities Education Act as requiring public school districts to provide students who have severe physical disabilities with individualized and continuous nursing services during school hours. Supreme Court justice Clarence Thomas argues that such an interpretation will impose serious and unanticipated financial obligations on the states.

Issue 19.   Do Affirmative Action Programs in Public School Admissions Policies Violate the Fourteenth Amendment?   342

U.S. Circuit Court judge Bruce Seyla holds that the admissions policy of the Boston Latin School, which makes race a determining factor in the admission of a specified segment of each year's incoming class, violates the Constitution's guarantee of equal protection. U.S. Circuit Court judge Kermit Lipez finds that the Boston Latin School's admissions policy serves the state's compelling interest in remedying the continuing effects of past discriminatory practices in the Boston public school system.

Introduction

The Role of Law

M. Ethan Katsh

William Rose

Two hundred years ago, Edmund Burke, the influential British statesman and orator, commented that "in no other country, perhaps, in the world, is the law so general a study as it is in the United States." Today, in America, general knowledge about law is at a disappointing level. One study conducted in the late 1970s concluded that "the general public's knowledge of and direct experience with courts is low."[1] Three out of four persons surveyed admitted that they knew either very little or nothing at all about state and local courts. More than half believed that the burden of proving innocence in a criminal trial is on the accused, and 72 percent thought that every decision made by a state could be reviewed by the Supreme Court. In a 1990 study, 59 percent could not name at least one current justice of the Supreme Court.

One purpose of this volume is to provide information about some specific and important legal issues. In your local newspaper today, there is probably at least one story concerning an issue in this book. The quality of your life will be directly affected by how many of these issues are resolved. But affirmative action (Issue 19), the insanity defense (Issue 6), drug legalization (Issue 13), abortion (Issue 2), copyrighted material on the Internet (Issue 5), and other issues in this book are often the subject of superficial, misleading, or inaccurate statements. *Taking Sides* is designed to encourage you to become involved in the public debate on these issues and to raise the level of the discussion on them.

The issues that are debated in this book represent some of the most important challenges our society faces. How they are dealt with will influence what kind of society we will have in the future. While it is important to look at and study them separately, it is equally necessary to think about their relationship to each other and about the fact that there is a tool called "law," which is being called upon to solve a series of difficult conflicts. The study of discrete legal issues should enable you to gain insight into some broad theoretical questions about law. This introduction, therefore, will focus on several basic characteristics of law and the legal process that you should keep in mind as you read this book.

The Nature of Law

The eminent legal anthropologist E. Adamson Hoebel once noted that the search for a definition of law is as difficult as the search for the Holy Grail. Law is certainly complicated, and trying to define it precisely can be frustrating. What follows, therefore, is not a definition of law but a framework or perspective for looking at and understanding law.

Law as a Body of Rules

One of the common incorrect assumptions about law is that it is merely a body of rules invoked by those who need them and then applied by a judge. Under this view, the judge is essentially a machine whose task is simply to find and apply the right rule to the dispute in question. This perspective makes the mistake of equating law with the rules of law. It is sometimes even assumed that there exists somewhere in the libraries of lawyers and judges one book with all the rules or laws in it, which can be consulted to answer legal questions. As may already be apparent, such a book could not exist. Rules alone do not supply the solutions to many legal problems. The late Supreme Court justice William O. Douglas once wrote, "The law is not a series of calculating machines where definitions and answers come tumbling out when the right levers are pushed." As you read the debates about the issues in this book, you will see that much more goes into a legal argument than the recitation of rules.

Law as a Process

A more meaningful way of thinking about law is to look at it as a process or system, keeping in mind that legal rules are one of the elements in the process. This approach requires a considerably broader vision of law: to think not only of the written rules but also of the judges, the lawyers, the police, and all the other people in the system. It requires an even further consideration of all the things that influence these people, such as their values and economic status.

"Law," one legal commentator has stated, "is very like an iceberg; only one-tenth of its substance appears above the social surface in the explicit form of documents, institutions, and professions, while the nine-tenths of its substance that supports its visible fragment leads a sub-aquatic existence, living in the habits, attitudes, emotions and aspirations of men."[2]

In reading the discussions of controversial issues in this book, try to identify what forces are influencing the content of the rules and the position of the writers. Three of the most important influences on the nature of law are economics, moral values, and public opinion.

Law and Economics

Laws that talk about equality, such as the Fourteenth Amendment, which guarantees that no state shall "deny to any person . . . equal protection of the laws," suggest that economic status is irrelevant in the making and application of the law. As Anatole France, the nineteenth-century French satirist, once wrote, however, "The law, in its majestic equality, forbids the rich as well as the poor to sleep under bridges, to beg in streets, and to steal bread." Sometimes the purpose and effect of the law cannot be determined merely from the words of the law.

Critics of law in capitalistic societies assert that poverty results from the manipulation of the law by the wealthy and powerful. It is possible to look at several issues in this book and make some tentative judgments about the influence of economic power on law. For example, what role does economics play in the debate over drug legalization (Issue 13)? Is the controversy over the fight against drugs one of social concerns or one of economics, in that it costs the government billions of dollars each year?

Law and Values

The relationship between law and values has been a frequent theme of legal writers and a frequent source of debate. Clearly, there is in most societies some relationship between law and morality. One writer has summarized the relationship as follows:

1. *There is a moral order in society.* Out of the many different and often conflicting values of the individuals and institutions that make up society may emerge a dominant moral position, a "core" of the moral order. The position of this core is dynamic, and as it changes, the moral order of society moves in the direction of that change.
2. *There is a moral content to the law.* The moral content of law also changes over time, and as it changes, the law moves in the direction of that change.
3. *The moral content of the law and moral order in society are seldom identical.*
4. *A natural and necessary affinity exists between the two "bodies" of law and moral order.*
5. *When there is a gap between the moral order of society and the law, some movement to close the gap is likely.* The law will move closer to the moral order of society, or the moral order will move closer to the law, or each will move toward the other. The likelihood of the movement to close the gap between law and moral order depends upon the size of the gap between the two bodies and the perceived significance of the subject matter concerning which the gap exists.[3]

Law and morality will not be identical in a pluralistic society, but there will also be attempts by dominant groups to insert their views of what is right into the legal code. The First Amendment prohibition against establishment of religion and the guaranty of freedom of religion are designed to protect those whose beliefs are different. Yet there have also been many historical examples of legal restrictions or limitations being imposed on minorities or of laws being ineffective because of the resistance of powerful groups. Prayers in the public schools, for example, which have been forbidden since the early 1960s, are still said in a few local communities.

Of the topics in this book, the insertion of morality into legal discussions has occurred most frequently in the abortion debate (Issue 2). It is probably fair to say that this issue remains high on the agenda of public debate because it involves strongly held values and beliefs. The nature of the debate is also colored by strong feelings that are held by the parties. Although empirical evidence about public health and abortion does exist, the debate is generally more emotional than objective.

Public Opinion and the Law

It is often claimed that the judicial process is insulated from public pressures. Judges are elected or appointed for long terms or for life, and the theory is that they will, therefore, be less subject to the force of public opinion. As a result, the law should be uniformly applied in different places, regardless of the nature of the community. It is fair to say that the judicial process is less responsive to public sentiment than is the political process, but that is not really saying much. What is important is that the legal process is not totally immune from public pressure. The force of public opinion is not applied directly through lobbying, but it would be naive to think that the force of what large numbers of people believe and desire never gets reflected in what happens in court. The most obvious examples are trials in which individuals are tried as much for their dissident beliefs as for their actions. Less obvious is the fact that the outcomes of cases may be determined in some measure by popular will. Judicial complicity in slavery or the internment of Japanese Americans during World War II are blatant examples of this.

Many of the issues selected for this volume are controversial because a large group is opposed to some practice sanctioned by the courts. Does this mean that the judges have taken a courageous stand and ignored public opinion? Not necessarily. Only in a few of the issues have courts adopted an uncompromising position. In most of the other issues, the trend of court decisions reflects a middle-of-the-road approach that could be interpreted as trying to satisfy everyone but those at the extremes. For example, in affirmative action (Issue 19), the *Bakke* decision, while generally approving of affirmative action, was actually won by Bakke and led to the abolition of all such programs that contained rigid quotas.

Assessing Influences on the Law

This summary of what can influence legal decisions is not meant to suggest that judges consciously ask what the public desires when interpretations of law are made. Rather, as members of society and as individuals who read newspapers and magazines and form opinions on political issues, there are subtle forces at work on judges that may not be obvious in any particular opinion but that can be discerned in a line of cases over a period of time. This may be explicitly denied by judges, such as in this statement by Justice Harry A. Blackmun in his majority opinion for the landmark *Roe v. Wade* abortion case: "Our task, of course, is to resolve the issue by constitutional measurement, free of emotion and predilection." However, a reading of that opinion raises the question of whether or not Blackmun succeeds in being totally objective in his interpretation of law and history.

Do these external and internal influences corrupt the system, create injustice, inject bias and discrimination, and pervert the law? Or do these influences enable judges to be flexible, to treat individual circumstances, and to fulfill the spirit of the law? Both of these ends are possible and do occur. What is important to realize is that there are so many points in the legal system where discretion is employed that it is hopeless to think that we could be governed by rules alone. "A government of laws, not men," aside from the sexism of the language, is not a realistic possibility, and it is not an alternative that many would find satisfying either.

On the other hand, it is also fair to say that the law, in striving to get the public to trust in it, must persuade citizens that it is more than the whim of those who are in power. While it cannot be denied that the law may be used in self-serving ways, there are also mechanisms at work that are designed to limit abuses of discretionary power. One quality of law that is relevant to this problem is that the legal process is fundamentally a conservative institution, which is, by nature, resistant to radical change. Lawyers are trained to give primary consideration in legal arguments to precedent—previous cases involving similar facts. As attention is focused on how the present case is similar to or different from past cases, some pressure is exerted on new decisions to be consistent with old ones and on the law to be stable. Thus, the way in which a legal argument is constructed tends to reduce the influence of currently popular psychological, sociological, philosophical, or anthropological theories. Prior decisions will reflect ideologies, economic considerations, and ethical values that were influential when these decisions were made, and, if no great change has occurred in the interim, the law will tend to preserve the status quo, both perpetuating old injustices and protecting traditional freedoms.

Legal Procedure

The law's great concern with the procedure of decision making is one of its more basic and important characteristics. Any discussion of the law that did not note the importance of procedure would be inadequate. Legal standards are often phrased not in terms of results but in terms of procedure. For example, it is not unlawful to convict the innocent if the right procedures are used (and it *is* unlawful to convict the guilty if the wrong procedures are followed). The law feels that it cannot guarantee that the right result will always be reached and that only the guilty will be caught, so it minimizes the risk of reaching the wrong result or convicting the innocent by specifying procedural steps to be followed. Lawyers, more than most people, are satisfied if the right procedures are followed even if there is something disturbing about the outcome. Law, therefore, has virtually eliminated the word *justice* from its vocabulary and has substituted the phrase *due process,* meaning that the proper procedures, such as right to counsel, right to a public trial, and right to cross-examine witnesses, have been followed. This concern with method is one of the pillars upon which law is based. It is one of the characteristics of law that distinguishes it from nonlegal methods of dispute resolution, where the atmosphere will be more informal and there may be no set procedures.

Conclusion

Law is a challenging area of study because many questions may not be amenable to simple solutions. The legal approach to problem solving is usually methodical and often slow. We frequently become frustrated with this process, and, in fact, it may be an inappropriate way to deal with some problems. For the issues in this book, however, an approach that pays careful attention to the many different aspects of these topics will be the most rewarding. Many of the readings provide historical, economic, and sociological data as well as information about law. The issues examined in *Taking Sides* involve basic cultural institutions such as religion, schools, and the family as well as basic cultural values such as privacy, individualism, and equality. While the law takes a narrow approach to problems, reading these issues should broaden your outlook on the problems discussed and, perhaps, encourage you to do further reading on those topics that are of particular interest to you.

Notes

1. Yankelovich, Skelly, and White, Inc., *The Public Image of Courts* (National Center for State Courts, 1978).
2. Iredell Jenkins, *Social Order and the Limits of Law* (Princeton University Press, 1980), p. xi.
3. Wardle, "The Gap Between Law and Moral Order: An Examination of the Legitimacy of the Supreme Court Abortion Decisions," *Brigham Young University Law Review* (1980), pp. 811–835.

Cornell Legal Information Institute

This is a reliable and useful site for primary legal information and documents.

http://www.law.cornell.edu

FindLaw

This is a good place to begin looking for court decisions, statutes, law reviews, and other primary legal resources.

http://www.findlaw.com

American Civil Liberties Union

The American Civil Liberties Union (ACLU) Web site is a significant repository of information related to individual rights.

http://www.aclu.org

Court TV's Legal Survival Guide

Court TV provides this free survival guide to legal issues. Topics covered include the definition of a crime, your basic rights, the procedure of a criminal case, probable cause, talking to the police, getting booked, your right to a phone call, the right to a lawyer, arraignments, pleas and bail, preliminary hearings and grand juries, jury trials and bench trials, reasonable doubt, insanity and other defenses, sentencing, death penalty cases, probation and parole, habeas corpus, victims' rights, the Miranda warning, warrants, and searches and seizures.

http://www.courttv.com/legalhelp/lawguide/criminal/
index.html

PART 1

Law and the Individual

*T*he American legal and political systems are oriented around protection of the individual. The law does not provide absolute protection
for the individual, however, because legitimate state interests are often
recognized as being controlling. This section examines issues that affect
individual choice and the dignity of the individual.

- Do "Standardless" Manual Recounts Violate the Equal Protection
  and Due Process Clauses of the U.S. Constitution?

- Is Abortion Protected by the Constitution?

- Are Restrictions on Physician-Assisted Suicide Constitutional?

- Do People Have a Legal Right to Clone Themselves?

- Does the Sharing of Music Files Through Napster Violate
  Copyright Laws?

- Should the Insanity Defense Be Abolished?

- Are Pretextual Stops by the Police Constitutional?

ISSUE 1

Do "Standardless" Manual Recounts Violate the Equal Protection and Due Process Clauses of the U.S. Constitution?

YES: U.S. Supreme Court, from *Per Curium* Opinion, *George W. Bush et al. v. Albert Gore, Jr., et al.,* U.S. Supreme Court (December 12, 2000)

NO: John Paul Stevens, from Dissenting Opinion, *George W. Bush et al. v. Albert Gore, Jr., et al.,* U.S. Supreme Court (December 12, 2000)

ISSUE SUMMARY

YES: The U.S. Supreme Court, in a *per curium* decision, rules that Florida's manual recounting of ballots in the 2000 presidential election failed to satisfy the basic constitutional requirements of equal treatment and fundamental fairness.

NO: Supreme Court justice John Paul Stevens, dissenting from the Court's decision, asserts that the manner by which presidents are elected is the responsibility of each individual state and that Florida's ballot recount was not limited by federal laws.

America, many have lamented, is an overly litigious society. Early in the nineteenth century, Alexis de Tocqueville captured this quality of American social and political life when he observed that, ultimately, most important political disputes will be resolved by the courts. The continuing relevance of Tocqueville's commentary on American democracy was once again brought to our attention by the events that took place in the final two months of the twentieth century—the presidential election contest between Albert Gore, Jr., and George W. Bush, an election that was ultimately decided by the U.S. Supreme Court.

Any studies of the Supreme Court now written are sure to feature its rulings from December 2000, which decided a presidential election for the first time in U.S. history. These decisions not only put a president in the White House but also set the stage for the selection of the next member(s) of the

Court itself. As noted political journalists E. J. Dionne and William Kristol have observed:

> Our nation has never decided a presidential contest the way it decided the election of 2000. Never before has an election hung on the judgment of the United States Supreme Court, let alone on a decision that split the court into bitter camps and was settled by a single vote. Not in 124 years has a presidential election result been so disputed. Never in all those years have so many Americans believed that the winner of the White House actually lost the election. Nor in all those years has the winning side been so convinced that the losing candidate was intent on "stealing the election." Rarely in our history have Americans been so divided on basic issues of democracy: how the votes should be counted, whether the electoral system was fair, and which legal bodies should decide the winner.

The basic facts of the case, though undoubtedly still fresh in most people's minds, are set forth at the beginning of the Court's *per curium* opinion. They involve Vice President Gore's legal challenge of the results of the Florida presidential vote count. Although Gore won the popular vote, the electoral contest hinged on the outcome of the contest in Florida, which would determine who claimed that state's 25 electoral votes—a number sufficient to give the election to either candidate. Then-governor Bush had initially carried the state by a total of 1,784 votes. The margin of victory was sufficiently close, however, to trigger an automatic recount under Florida law. Although this machine recount failed to change the final outcome of the Florida election, it did narrow Bush's margin of victory to 327 votes. Gore's challenge was originally made within the context of Florida election law and before the Florida state courts. The challenge, in part, sought a limited manual recount in selected Florida counties and was justified by the allegation of a number of factors that might have led to the systematic undercounting of Gore votes. The Florida Supreme Court, interpreting Florida law, granted Vice President Gore's request for a manual recount of ballots in selected counties. Because of the Florida high court's decision, Governor Bush petitioned the U.S. Supreme Court to "stay" the Florida Supreme Court's decision to allow the manual recount to continue. It decided the case on the merits just four days later. What follows is the *per curium* decision of the Court, which held that the manual recount in Florida constituted a violation of the equal protection and due process clauses, and the dissenting opinion of Justice John Paul Stevens.

 **YES**

Per Curium Opinion

Bush *v.* Gore

I

On December 8, 2000, the Supreme Court of Florida ordered that the Circuit Court of Leon County tabulate by hand 9,000 ballots in Miami-Dade County. It also ordered the inclusion in the certified vote totals of 215 votes identified in Palm Beach County and 168 votes identified in Miami-Dade County for Vice President Albert Gore, Jr., and Senator Joseph Lieberman, Democratic Candidates for President and Vice President. The Supreme Court noted that petitioner, Governor George W. Bush, asserted that the net gain for Vice President Gore in Palm Beach County was 176 votes, and directed the Circuit Court to resolve that dispute on remand. The court further held that relief would require manual recounts in all Florida counties where so-called "undervotes" had not been subject to manual tabulation. The court ordered all manual recounts to begin at once. Governor Bush and Richard Cheney, Republican Candidates for the Presidency and Vice Presidency, filed an emergency application for a stay of this mandate. On December 9, we granted the application, treated the application as a petition for a writ of certiorari, and granted certiorari.

... On November 8, 2000, the day following the Presidential election, the Florida Division of Elections reported that petitioner, Governor Bush, had received 2,909,135 votes, and respondent, Vice President Gore, had received 2,907,351 votes, a margin of 1,784 for Governor Bush. Because Governor Bush's margin of victory was less than "one-half of a percent... of the votes cast," an automatic machine recount was conducted under § 102.141(4) of the election code, the results of which showed Governor Bush still winning the race but by a diminished margin. Vice President Gore then sought manual recounts in Volusia, Palm Beach, Broward, and Miami-Dade Counties, pursuant to Florida's election protest provisions. Fla. Stat. § 102.166 (2000). A dispute arose concerning the deadline for local county canvassing boards to submit their returns to the Secretary of State (Secretary). The Secretary declined to waive the November 14 deadline imposed by statute. §§ 102.111, 102.112. The Florida Supreme

From *George W. Bush et al. v. Albert Gore, Jr., et al.,* 531 U.S. ___ (2000).

Court, however, set the deadline at November 26. We granted certiorari and vacated the Florida Supreme Court's decision, finding considerable uncertainty as to the grounds on which it was based. On December 11, the Florida Supreme Court issued a decision on remand reinstating that date.

On November 26, the Florida Elections Canvassing Commission certified the results of the election and declared Governor Bush the winner of Florida's 25 electoral votes. On November 27, Vice President Gore, pursuant to Florida's contest provisions, filed a complaint in Leon County Circuit Court contesting the certification. Fla. Stat. § 102.168 (2000). He sought relief pursuant to § 102.168(3)(c), which provides that "receipt of a number of illegal votes or rejection of a number of legal votes sufficient to change or place in doubt the result of the election" shall be grounds for a contest. The Circuit Court denied relief, stating that Vice President Gore failed to meet his burden of proof. He appealed to the First District Court of Appeal, which certified the matter to the Florida Supreme Court.

Accepting jurisdiction, the Florida Supreme Court affirmed in part and reversed in part. The court held that the Circuit Court had been correct to reject Vice President Gore's challenge to the results certified in Nassau County and his challenge to the Palm Beach County Canvassing Board's determination that 3,300 ballots cast in that county were not, in the statutory phrase, "legal votes."

The [Florida] Supreme Court held that Vice President Gore had satisfied his burden of proof under § 102.168(3)(c) with respect to his challenge to Miami-Dade County's failure to tabulate, by manual count, 9,000 ballots on which the machines had failed to detect a vote for President ("undervotes"). Noting the closeness of the election, the Court explained that "on this record, there can be no question that there are legal votes within the 9,000 uncounted votes sufficient to place the results of this election in doubt." A "legal vote," as determined by the Supreme Court, is "one in which there is a 'clear indication of the intent of the voter. " The court therefore ordered a hand recount of the 9,000 ballots in Miami-Dade County. Observing that the contest provisions vest broad discretion in the circuit judge to "provide any relief appropriate under such circumstances," Fla. Stat. § 102.168(8)(2000), the Supreme Court further held that the Circuit Court could order "the Supervisor of Elections and the Canvassing Boards, as well as the necessary public officials, in all counties that have not conducted a manual recount or tabulation of the undervotes ... to do so forthwith, said tabulation to take place in the individual counties where the ballots are located."_____ So. 2d at _____ (slip. op., at 38).

The Supreme Court also determined that both Palm Beach County and Miami-Dade County, in their earlier manual recounts, had identified a net gain of 215 and 168 legal votes for Vice President Gore. Rejecting the Circuit Court's conclusion that Palm Beach County lacked the authority to include the 215 net votes submitted past the November 26 deadline, the Supreme Court explained that the deadline was not intended to exclude votes identified after that date through ongoing manual recounts. As to Miami-Dade County, the Court concluded that although the 168 votes identified were the result of a partial recount, they were "legal votes [that] could change the outcome of the election."

The Supreme Court therefore directed the Circuit Court to include those totals in the certified results, subject to resolution of the actual vote total from the Miami-Dade partial recount.

The petition presents the following questions: whether the Florida Supreme Court established new standards for resolving Presidential election contests, thereby violating Art. II, § 1, cl. 2, of the United States Constitution and failing to comply with 3 U.S.C. § 5, and whether the use of standardless manual recounts violates the Equal Protection and Due Process Clauses. With respect to the equal protection question, we find a violation of the Equal Protection Clause.

II

A

The closeness of this election, and the multitude of legal challenges which have followed in its wake, have brought into sharp focus a common, if heretofore unnoticed, phenomenon. Nationwide statistics reveal that an estimated 2% of ballots cast do not register a vote for President for whatever reason, including deliberately choosing no candidate at all or some voter error, such as voting for two candidates or insufficiently marking a ballot. See Ho, More Than 2M Ballots Uncounted, AP Online (Nov. 28, 2000); Kelley, Balloting Problems Not Rare But Only In A Very Close Election Do Mistakes And Mismarking Make A Difference, Omaha World-Herald (Nov. 15, 2000). In certifying election results, the votes eligible for inclusion in the certification are the votes meeting the properly established legal requirements.

This case has shown that punch card balloting machines can produce an unfortunate number of ballots which are not punched in a clean, complete way by the voter. After the current counting, it is likely legislative bodies nationwide will examine ways to improve the mechanisms and machinery for voting.

B

The individual citizen has no federal constitutional right to vote for electors for the President of the United States unless and until the state legislature chooses a statewide election as the means to implement its power to appoint members of the Electoral College. U.S. Const., Art. II, § 1. This is the source for the statement in *McPherson v. Blacker*, 146 U.S. 1, 35, 36 L. Ed. 869, 13 S. Ct. 3 (1892), that the State legislature's power to select the manner for appointing electors is plenary; it may, if it so chooses, select the electors itself, which indeed was the manner used by State legislatures in several States for many years after the Framing of our Constitution. *Id.* at 28-33. History has now favored the voter, and in each of the several States the citizens themselves vote for Presidential electors. When the state legislature vests the right to vote for President in its people, the right to vote as the legislature has prescribed is fundamental; and one source of its fundamental nature lies in the equal weight accorded to each vote and the equal dignity owed to each voter. The State, of course, after granting the franchise in the special context of Article II, can take back the power to appoint electors. See *id.,* at 35 ("There is no doubt of the right of the legislature to resume the power [**530] at any time, for it can neither be taken away nor abdicated") (quoting S. Rep. No. 395, 43d Cong., 1st Sess.).

The right to vote is protected in more than the initial allocation of the franchise. Equal protection applies as well to the manner of its exercise. Having once granted the right to vote on equal terms, the State may not, by later arbitrary and disparate treatment, value one person's vote over that of another. See, e.g., *Harper v. Virginia Bd. of Elections,* 383 U.S. 663, 665, 16 L. Ed. 2d 169, 86 S. Ct. 1079 (1966) ("Once the franchise is granted to the electorate, lines may not be drawn which are inconsistent with the Equal Protection Clause of the Fourteenth Amendment"). It must be remembered that "the right of suffrage can be denied by a debasement or dilution of the weight of a citizen's vote just as effectively as by wholly prohibiting the free exercise of the franchise." *Reynolds v. Sims,* 377 U.S. 533, 555, 12 L. Ed. 2d 506, 84 S. Ct. 1362 (1964).

There is no difference between the two sides of the present controversy on these basic propositions. Respondents say that the very purpose of vindicating the right to vote justifies the recount procedures now at issue. The question before us, however, is whether the recount procedures the Florida Supreme Court has adopted are consistent with its obligation to avoid arbitrary and disparate treatment of the members of its electorate.

Much of the controversy seems to revolve around ballot cards designed to be perforated by a stylus but which, either through error or deliberate omission, have not been perforated with sufficient precision for a machine to count them. In some cases a piece of the card—a chad—is hanging, say by two corners. In other cases there is no separation at all, just an indentation.

The Florida Supreme Court has ordered that the intent of the voter be discerned from such ballots. For purposes of resolving the equal protection challenge, it is not necessary to decide whether the Florida Supreme Court had the authority under the legislative scheme for resolving election disputes to define what a legal vote is and to mandate a manual recount implementing that definition. The recount mechanisms implemented in response to the decisions of the Florida Supreme Court do not satisfy the minimum requirement for non-arbitrary treatment of voters necessary to secure the fundamental right. Florida's basic command for the count of legally cast votes is to consider the "intent of the voter." *Gore v. Harris.* This is unobjectionable as an abstract proposition and a starting principle. The problem inheres in the absence of specific standards to ensure its equal application. The formulation of uniform rules to determine intent based on these recurring circumstances is practicable and, we conclude, necessary.

The law does not refrain from searching for the intent of the actor in a multitude of circumstances; and in some cases the general command to ascertain intent is not susceptible to much further refinement. In this instance, however, the question is not whether to believe a witness but how to interpret the marks or holes or scratches on an inanimate object, a piece of cardboard or paper which, it is said, might not have registered as a vote during the machine count. The factfinder confronts a thing, not a person. The search for intent can be confined by specific rules designed to ensure uniform treatment.

The want of those rules here has led to unequal evaluation of ballots in various respects. See *Gore v. Harris,* _____ So. 2d at _____ (slip op., at 51) (Wells, J., dissenting) ("Should a county canvassing board count or not count a 'dimpled chad' where the voter is able to successfully dislodge the chad in every other contest on that ballot? Here, the county canvassing boards disagree"). As seems to have been acknowledged at oral argument, the standards for accepting or rejecting contested ballots might vary not only from county to county but indeed within a single county from one recount team to another.

The record provides some examples. A monitor in Miami-Dade County testified at trial that he observed that three members of the county canvassing board applied different standards in defining a legal vote. 3 Tr. 497, 499 (Dec. 3, 2000). And testimony at trial also revealed that at least one county changed its evaluative standards during the counting process. Palm Beach County, for example, began the process with a 1990 guideline which precluded counting completely attached chads, switched to a rule that considered a vote to be legal if any light could be seen through a chad, changed back to the 1990 rule, and then abandoned any pretense of a per se rule, only to have a court order that the county consider dimpled chads legal. This is not a process with sufficient guarantees of equal treatment.

An early case in our one person, one vote jurisprudence arose when a State accorded arbitrary and disparate treatment to voters in its different counties. *Gray v. Sanders,* 372 U.S. 368, 9 L. Ed. 2d 821, 83 S. Ct. 801 (1963). The Court found a constitutional violation. We relied on these principles in the context of the Presidential selection process in *Moore v. Ogilvie,* 394 U.S. 814, 23 L. Ed. 2d 1, 89 S. Ct. 1493 (1969), where we invalidated a county-based procedure that diluted the influence of citizens in larger counties in the nominating process. There we observed that "the idea that one group can be granted greater voting strength than another is hostile to the one man, one vote basis of our representative government." 394 U.S. at 819.

The State Supreme Court ratified this uneven treatment. It mandated that the recount totals from two counties, Miami-Dade and Palm Beach, be included in the certified total. The court also appeared to hold *sub silentio* that the recount totals from Broward County, which were not completed until after the original November 14 certification by the Secretary of State, were to be considered part of the new certified vote totals even though the county certification was not contested by Vice President Gore. Yet each of the counties used varying standards to determine what was a legal vote. Broward County used a more forgiving standard than Palm Beach County, and uncovered almost three times as many new votes, a result markedly disproportionate to the difference in population between the counties.

In addition, the recounts in these three counties were not limited to so-called undervotes but extended to all of the ballots. The distinction has real consequences. A manual recount of all ballots identifies not only those ballots which show no vote but also those which contain more than one, the so-called overvotes. Neither category will be counted by the machine. This is not a trivial concern. At oral argument, respondents estimated there are as many as 110,000 overvotes statewide. As a result, the citizen whose ballot was not read by a machine because he failed to vote for a candidate in a way readable by a machine may still have his vote counted in a manual recount; on the other hand, the citizen who marks two candidates in a way discernable by the machine will not have the same opportunity to have his vote count, even if a manual exami-nation of the ballot would reveal the requisite indicia of intent. Furthermore, the citizen who marks two candidates, only one of which is discernable by the machine, will have his vote counted even though it should have been read as an invalid ballot. The State Supreme Court's inclusion of vote counts based on these variant standards exemplifies concerns with the remedial processes that were under way.

That brings the analysis to yet a further equal protection problem. The votes certified by the court included a partial total from one county, Miami-Dade. The Florida Supreme Court's decision thus gives no assurance that the recounts included in a final certification must be complete. Indeed, it is re-spondent's submission that it would be consistent with the rules of the recount procedures to include whatever partial counts are done by the time of final cer-tification, and we interpret the Florida Supreme Court's decision to permit this. See _____ So. 2d at _____, n. 21 (slip op., at 37, n. 21) (noting "practical diffi-culties" may control outcome of election, but certifying partial Miami-Dade total nonetheless). This accommodation no doubt results from the truncated contest period established by the Florida Supreme Court in *Bush I*, at respon-dents' own urging. The press of time does not diminish the constitutional concern. A desire for speed is not a general excuse for ignoring equal protection guarantees.

In addition to these difficulties the actual process by which the votes were to be counted under the Florida Supreme Court's decision raises further con-cerns. That order did not specify who would recount the ballots. The county canvassing boards were forced to pull together ad hoc teams comprised of judges from various Circuits who had no previous training in handling and interpreting ballots. Furthermore, while others were permitted to observe, they were prohibited from objecting during the recount.

The recount process, in its features here described, is inconsistent with the minimum procedures necessary to protect the fundamental right of each voter in the special instance of a statewide recount under the authority of a single state judicial officer. Our consideration is limited to the present circumstances, for the problem of equal protection in election processes generally presents many complexities.

The question before the Court is not whether local entities, in the exercise of their expertise, may develop different systems for implementing elections. Instead, we are presented with a situation where a state court with the power to assure uniformity has ordered a statewide recount with minimal proce-dural safeguards. When a court orders a statewide remedy, there must be at least some assurance that the rudimentary requirements of equal treatment and fundamental fairness are satisfied.

Given the Court's assessment that the recount process underway was prob-ably being conducted in an unconstitutional manner, the Court stayed the order directing the recount so it could hear this case and render an expedited decision. The contest provision, as it was mandated by the State Supreme Court, is not well calculated to sustain the confidence that all citizens must have in the outcome of elections. The State has not shown that its procedures include the necessary safeguards. The problem, for instance, of the estimated 110,000 over-votes has not been addressed, although Chief Justice Wells called attention to the concern in his dissenting opinion. See _____ So. 2d at _____, n. 26 (slip op., at 45, n. 26).

Upon due consideration of the difficulties identified to this point, it is obvious that the recount cannot be conducted in compliance with the require-ments of equal protection and due process without substantial additional work. It would require not only the adoption (after opportunity for argument) of ad-equate statewide standards for determining what is a legal vote, and practicable procedures to implement them, but also orderly judicial review of any disputed matters that might arise. In addition, the Secretary of State has advised that the recount of only a portion of the ballots requires that the vote tabulation equip-ment be used to screen out undervotes, a function for which the machines were not designed. If a recount of overvotes were also required, perhaps even a sec-ond screening would be necessary. Use of the equipment for this purpose, and any new software developed for it, would have to be evaluated for accuracy by the Secretary of State, as required by Fla. Stat. § 101.015 (2000).

The Supreme Court of Florida has said that the legislature intended the State's electors to "participate fully in the federal electoral process," as provided in 3 U.S.C. § 5. _____ So. 2d at _____ slip op. at 27); see also *Palm Beach Can-vassing Bd. v. Harris,* 2000 WL 1725434, *13 (Fla. 2000). That statute, in turn, requires that any controversy or contest that is designed to lead to a conclusive selection of electors be completed by December 12. That date is upon us, and there is no recount procedure in place under the State Supreme Court's order that comports with minimal constitutional standards. Because it is evident that any recount seeking to meet the December 12 date will be unconstitutional for the reasons we have discussed, we reverse the judgment of the Supreme Court of Florida ordering a recount to proceed....

⋅⟨⟩⋅

None are more conscious of the vital limits on judicial authority than are the members of this Court, and none stand more in admiration of the Constitu-tion's design to leave the selection of the President to the people, through their legislatures, and to the political sphere. When contending parties invoke the process of the courts, however, it becomes our unsought responsibility to re-solve the federal and constitutional issues the judicial system has been forced to confront.

The judgment of the Supreme Court of Florida is reversed, and the case is remanded for further proceedings not inconsistent with this opinion.

It is so ordered.

Dissenting Opinion of John Paul Stevens

The Constitution assigns to the States the primary responsibility for determining the manner of selecting the Presidential electors. See Art. II, § 1, cl. 2. When questions arise about the meaning of state laws, including election laws, it is our settled practice to accept the opinions of the highest courts of the States as providing the final answers. On rare occasions, however, either federal statutes or the Federal Constitution may require federal judicial intervention in state elections. This is not such an occasion.

The federal questions that ultimately emerged in this case are not substantial. Article II provides that "each State shall appoint, in such Manner as the Legislature *thereof* may direct, a Number of Electors." *Ibid.* (emphasis added). It does not create state legislatures out of whole cloth, but rather takes them as they come—as creatures born of, and constrained by, their state constitutions. Lest there be any doubt, we stated over 100 years ago in *McPherson v. Blacker*, 146 U.S. 1, 25, 36 L. Ed. 869, 13 S. Ct. 3 (1892), that "what is forbidden or required to be done by a State" in the Article II context "is forbidden or required of the legislative power under state constitutions as they exist." In the same vein, we also observed that "the [State's] legislative power is the supreme authority except as limited by the constitution of the State." *Ibid.; cf. Smiley v. Holm*, 285 U.S. 355, 367, 76 L. Ed. 795, 52 S. Ct. 397 (1932). [footnote omitted] The legislative power in Florida is subject to judicial review pursuant to Article V of the Florida Constitution, and nothing in Article II of the Federal Constitution frees the state legislature from the constraints in the state constitution that created it. Moreover, the Florida Legislature's own decision to employ a unitary code for all elections indicates that it intended the Florida Supreme Court to play the same role in Presidential elections that it has historically played in resolving electoral disputes. The Florida Supreme Court's exercise of appellate jurisdiction therefore was wholly consistent with, and indeed contemplated by, the grant of authority in Article II.

It hardly needs stating that Congress, pursuant to 3 U.S.C. § 5, did not impose any affirmative duties upon the States that their governmental branches could "violate." Rather, § 5 provides a safe harbor for States to select electors in contested elections "by judicial or other methods" established by laws prior to the election day. Section 5, like Article II, assumes the involvement of the

From *George W. Bush et al. v. Albert Gore, Jr., et al.*, 531 U.S. _____ (2000).

state judiciary in interpreting state election laws and resolving election disputes under those laws. Neither § 5 nor Article II grants federal judges any special authority to substitute their views for those of the state judiciary on matters of state law.

Nor are petitioners correct in asserting that the failure of the Florida Supreme Court to specify in detail the precise manner in which the "intent of the voter," Fla. Stat. § 101.5614(5) (Supp. 2001), is to be determined rises to the level of a constitutional violation. [footnote omitted] We found such a violation when individual votes within the same State were weighted unequally, see, e.g., *Reynolds v. Sims,* 377 U.S. 533, 568, 12 L. Ed. 2d 506, 84 S. Ct. 1362 (1964), but we have never before called into question the substantive standard by which a State determines that a vote has been legally cast. And there is no reason to think that the guidance provided to the factfinders, specifically the various canvassing boards, by the "intent of the voter" standard is any less sufficient—or will lead to results any less uniform—than, for example, the "beyond a reasonable doubt" standard employed everyday by ordinary citizens in courtrooms across this country. [footnote omitted]

Admittedly, the use of differing substandards for determining voter intent in different counties employing similar voting systems may raise serious concerns. Those concerns are alleviated—if not eliminated—by the fact that a single impartial magistrate will ultimately adjudicate all objections arising from the recount process. Of course, as a general matter, "the interpretation of constitutional principles must not be too literal. We must remember that the machinery of government would not work if it were not allowed a little play in its joints." *Bain Peanut Co. of Tex. v. Pinson,* 282 U.S. 499, 501, 75 L. Ed. 482, 51 S. Ct. 228 (1931) (Holmes, J.). If it were otherwise, Florida's decision to leave to each county the determination of what balloting system to employ—despite enormous differences in accuracy [footnote omitted]—might run afoul of equal protection. So, too, might the similar decisions of the vast majority of state legislatures to delegate to local authorities certain decisions with respect to voting systems and ballot design.

Even assuming that aspects of the remedial scheme might ultimately be found to violate the Equal Protection Clause, I could not subscribe to the majority's disposition of the case. As the majority explicitly holds, once a state legislature determines to select electors through a popular vote, the right to have one's vote counted is of constitutional stature. As the majority further acknowledges, Florida law holds that all ballots that reveal the intent of the voter constitute valid votes. Recognizing these principles, the majority nonetheless orders the termination of the contest proceeding before all such votes have been tabulated. Under their own reasoning, the appropriate course of action would be to remand to allow more specific procedures for implementing the legislature's uniform general standard to be established.

In the interest of finality, however, the majority effectively orders the disenfranchisement of an unknown number of voters whose ballots reveal their intent—and are therefore legal votes under state law—but were for some reason rejected by ballot-counting machines. It does so on the basis of the deadlines set forth in Title 3 of the United States Code. *Ante,* at 11. But, as I have already noted, those provisions merely provide rules of decision for Congress to follow when selecting among conflicting slates of electors. They do not prohibit a State from counting what the majority concedes to be legal votes until a bona fide winner is determined. Indeed, in 1960, Hawaii appointed two slates of electors and Congress chose to count the one appointed on January 4, 1961, well after the Title 3 deadlines. [citation and footnote omitted] Thus, nothing prevents the majority, even if it properly found an equal protection violation, from ordering relief appropriate to remedy that violation without depriving Florida voters of their right to have their votes counted. As the majority notes, "[a] desire for speed is not a general excuse for ignoring equal protection guarantees."

Finally, neither in this case, nor in its earlier opinion in *Palm Beach County Canvassing Bd. v. Harris,* 2000 WL 1725434 (Fla., Nov. 21, 2000), did the Florida Supreme Court make any substantive change in Florida electoral law. Its decisions were rooted in long-established precedent and were consistent with the relevant statutory provisions, taken as a whole. It did what courts do [footnote omitted]— it decided the case before it in light of the legislature's intent to leave no legally cast vote uncounted. In so doing, it relied on the sufficiency of the general "intent of the voter" standard articulated by the state legislature, coupled with a procedure for ultimate review by an impartial judge, to resolve the concern about disparate evaluations of contested ballots. If we assume—as I do—that the members of that court and the judges who would have carried out its mandate are impartial, its decision does not even raise a colorable federal question.

What must underlie petitioners' entire federal assault on the Florida election procedures is an unstated lack of confidence in the impartiality and capacity of the state judges who would make the critical decisions if the vote count were to proceed. Otherwise, their position is wholly without merit. The endorsement of that position by the majority of this Court can only lend credence to the most cynical appraisal of the work of judges throughout the land. It is confidence in the men and women who administer the judicial system that is the true backbone of the rule of law. Time will one day heal the wound to that confidence that will be inflicted by today's decision. One thing, however, is certain. Although we may never know with complete certainty the identity of the winner of this year's Presidential election, the identity of the loser is perfectly clear. It is the Nation's confidence in the judge as an impartial guardian of the rule of law.

I respectfully dissent.

POSTSCRIPT

Do "Standardless" Manual Recounts Violate the Equal Protection and Due Process Clauses of the U.S. Constitution?

Some people have suggested that the U.S. Supreme Court's involvement in the 2000 presidential election could threaten its standing with the American people as an institution that is "above" politics. That is, in the aftermath of *Bush v. Gore,* citizens may no longer think of the Court as an oracle of the law but simply another venue for partisan political contests—albeit contests articulated through a unique vocabulary and pursued according to the Court's own set of rules. Public opinion polls, though inconclusive in their findings, seem to indicate that the high court remains the most respected of America's national political institutions. While none of us knows exactly what the nine justices on the Court were thinking during this amazing period in American history, it is safe to say that most, if not all, of them were concerned with how this intervention—justified or not—would impact the Court's legitimacy. As political scientist David O'Brien has observed, "The Court's influence on American life rests on a paradox. Its political power is at once antidemocratic and countermajoritarian. Yet that power, which flows from giving meaning to the Constitution, truly rests 'solely upon the approval of a free people'." In the aftermath of *Bush v. Gore,* do the American people now believe that the Court has become more partisan, thereby placing the cherished principle of the rule of law in jeopardy? In the short term, at least, such a question remains difficult to answer. However, it is probably the case that should President Bush make a controversial nomination for a vacant seat on the Supreme Court, many of the issues implicated by this case will be revived, and the competing political forces will revisit old arguments with renewed ferocity.

For those who are interested in further study of this case and its related legal and political issues, there are a number of helpful works available. William Kristol and E. J. Dionne, Jr., have collected all the relevant judicial opinions, both state and federal, along with some of the best commentary that was published as these historical events unfolded. That volume, *Bush v. Gore: The Court Cases and the Commentary* (Brookings Institution Press, 2001), is supplemented by a useful Internet site, http://www.brookings.edu, which provides a good deal of additional information. In addition, one might wish to consult Howard Gillman, *The Votes That Counted: How the Court Decided the 2000 Presidential Election* (University of Chicago Press, 2001); Cass Sunstein and Richard Epstein, *The Vote: Bush, Gore, and the Supreme Court* (University of Chicago Press, 2001); Vincent Bugliosi, *The Betrayal of America: How the Supreme Court Undermined the Constitution and Chose Our President* (Thunder's Mouth Press/

Nation Books, 2001); Samuel Issacharoff, Pamela Karlen, and Richard Pildes, *When Elections Go Bad: The Law of Democracy and the Presidential Election of 2000* (Foundation Press, 2001); and *Symposium: "Bush v. Gore"* in the *University of Chicago Law Review* (Summer 2001). Finally, those who wish to listen to the oral arguments before the Supreme Court should go to `http://oyez.nwu.edu`, the Internet site of the Medill School of Journalism at Northwestern University, which supports the "Oyez" project, a U.S. Supreme Court multimedia database.

ISSUE 2

Is Abortion Protected by the Constitution?

YES: Sandra Day O'Connor, from Majority Opinion, *Planned Parenthood of Southeastern Pennsylvania et al. v. Casey et al.,* U.S. Supreme Court (1992)

NO: William H. Rehnquist, from Dissenting Opinion, *Planned Parenthood of Southeastern Pennsylvania et al. v. Casey et al.,* U.S. Supreme Court (1992)

ISSUE SUMMARY

YES: Supreme Court justice Sandra Day O'Connor upholds a woman's constitutional right to abortion under most circumstances and reaffirms the central holding of *Roe v. Wade.*

NO: Supreme Court chief justice William H. Rehnquist argues that Pennsylvania regulations on abortion should be upheld and that it is appropriate to overrule *Roe v. Wade.*

One of the strengths of the American judicial process, lawyers often claim, is that it encourages logical and objective solutions to problems and reduces the influence of emotion and whim. By proceeding slowly, by applying abstract legal rules, by relying on professional lawyers and restricting the layperson's role, it is asserted that impartiality and neutrality will be achieved and that explosive issues will be defused. The legal process works this kind of magic often, but it has clearly failed to do so with regard to the issue of abortion. Abortion remains as newsworthy and important a subject today as it was when the landmark case of *Roe v. Wade* was decided in 1973.

Perceptions of the abortion issue differ. For the courts, it is a constitutional issue, meaning that the focus is on whether or not laws restricting abortion deny a woman due process of law under the Fourteenth Amendment. Part of the reason courts have been unable to defuse the abortion issue is that they have not persuaded the public to see the subject only in these terms. How we define or categorize an issue frequently determines our conclusions about the subject.

For example, do we view abortion as an issue primarily affecting women and thus see outlawing it as an example of sex discrimination? Or do we think firstly of the fetus and thus conclude that abortion is murder? Do we look at abortion from a religious perspective, thinking of how the legal codes of Western religions treat the subject? Or is it a question of privacy and of preventing the state from intruding into the affairs and personal decisions of citizens? Is it a matter of health, of preventing injuries and death to women who undergo illegal abortions? Is it an issue of discrimination against the poor, who may need the state to subsidize abortions, or even of racial discrimination because a higher proportion of poor women are black? How abortion is described can be all-important. Early in the debate, for example, one writer argued, "The real question is not, 'How can we justify abortion?' but, 'How can we justify compulsory childbearing?'" See Cisler, "Unfinished Business: Birth Control and Women's Liberation," in Robin Morgan, ed., *Sisterhood Is Powerful: An Anthology of Writings From the Women's Liberation Movement* (Random House, 1970).

The landmark decision of *Roe v. Wade*, 410 U.S. 113 (1973) was handed down on January 23, 1973. In the majority opinion, Justice Harry A. Blackmun wrote that states may not prohibit abortions during the first trimester, that some abortions may be regulated but not prohibited during the second trimester, and that abortions may be prohibited during the last trimester.

In the years since *Roe v. Wade* there have been many attempts to circumvent, narrow, delay, or avoid the Court's ruling. In *Harris v. McCrae*, 100 S. Ct. 2671 (1980), for example, in a 5–4 decision, the Supreme Court upheld a federal law that prohibited the federal government from reimbursing states for providing Medicaid abortions to women, except under specified circumstances. The majority held that the law did not illegally discriminate against the poor, nor did it violate the doctrines of separation of church and state merely because the restrictions coincided with Roman Catholic religious beliefs. In 1991 further limits on the use of federal funds were approved by the Court in *Rust v. Sullivan*, 111 S. Ct. 1759 (1991). In that case, regulations prohibiting abortion counseling in programs receiving federal funds for family planning were upheld.

Two years before *Rust*, in *Webster v. Reproductive Health Services*, 109 S. Ct. 3040 (1989), the Court refused to overturn *Roe v. Wade*, but it allowed states to impose more restrictions, such as one that required doctors, when a woman is more than 20 weeks pregnant, to perform tests "to determine if the unborn child is viable." The five-member majority included four votes to overturn *Roe*. Justice Sandra Day O'Connor, the critical fifth vote, was unwilling to overturn *Roe* but felt that the Missouri law was constitutional since it did not place an "undue burden" on the woman's abortion rights.

The following selections are from the most recent and, in all likelihood, the most significant abortion decision since *Roe v. Wade*. The majority refused to overturn *Roe* but was willing to allow some Pennsylvania restrictions involving parental notification and waiting periods. It also parted ways with the trimester model of *Roe*. The decision was neither a clear victory nor a clear defeat for either the pro-choice or pro-life movements. And as you read, you should ask whether or not the Court has finally articulated a position that represents an acceptable middle ground.

Majority Opinion

Planned Parenthood *v.* Casey

JUSTICE O'CONNOR, JUSTICE KENNEDY, and JUSTICE SOUTER announced the judgment of the Court.

I

Liberty finds no refuge in a jurisprudence of doubt. Yet 19 years after our holding that the Constitution protects a woman's right to terminate her pregnancy in its early stages, *Roe v. Wade,* 410 U.S. 113 (1973), that definition of liberty is still questioned. Joining the respondents as *amicus curiae,* the United States, as it has done in five other cases in the last decade, again asks us to overrule *Roe.*

At issue in these cases are five provisions of the Pennsylvania Abortion Control Act of 1982 as amended in 1988 and 1989. 18 Pa. Cons. Stat. Sec. 3203–3220 (1990). The Act requires that a woman seeking an abortion give her informed consent prior to the abortion procedure, and specifies that she be provided with certain information at least 24 hours before the abortion is performed. For a minor to obtain an abortion, the Act requires the informed consent of one of her parents, but provides for a judicial bypass option if the minor does not wish to or cannot obtain a parent's consent. Another provision of the Act requires that, unless certain exceptions apply, a married woman seeking an abortion must sign a statement indicating that she has notified her husband of her intended abortion. The Act exempts compliance with these three requirements in the event of a "medical emergency," which is defined in Sec. 3203 of the Act. In addition to the above provisions regulating the performance of abortions, the Act imposes certain reporting requirements on facilities that provide abortion services.

Before any of these provisions took effect, the petitioners, who are five abortion clinics and one physician representing himself as well as a class of physicians who provide abortion services, brought this suit seeking declaratory and injunctive relief. Each provision was challenged as unconstitutional on its face. The District Court entered a preliminary injunction against the enforcement of the regulations, and, after a 3-day bench trial, held all the provisions

From *Planned Parenthood of Southeastern Pennsylvania et al. v. Casey et al.,* 505 U.S. 833, 60 U.S.L.W. 4795 (1992). Some case citations omitted.

at issue here unconstitutional, entering a permanent injunction against Pennsylvania's enforcement of them. 744 F. Supp 1323 (ED Pa. 1990). The Court of Appeals for the Third Circuit affirmed in part and reversed in part, upholding all of the regulations except for the husband notification requirement. 947 F.2d 682 (1991). We granted certiorari.

... [A]t oral argument in this Court, the attorney for the parties challenging the statute took the position that none of the enactments can be upheld without overruling *Roe v. Wade*. We disagree with that analysis; but we acknowledge that our decisions after *Roe* cast doubt upon the meaning and reach of its holding. Further, the Chief Justice admits that he would overrule the central holding of *Roe* and adopt the rational relationship test as the sole criterion of constitutionality. State and federal courts as well as legislatures throughout the Union must have guidance as they seek to address this subject in conformance with the Constitution. Given these premises, we find it imperative to review once more the principles that define the rights of the woman and the legitimate authority of the State respecting the termination of pregnancies by abortion procedures.

After considering the fundamental constitutional questions resolved by *Roe*, principles of institutional integrity, and the rule of *stare decisis*, we are led to conclude this: the essential holding of *Roe v. Wade* should be retained and once again reaffirmed.

It must be stated at the outset and with clarity that *Roe*'s essential holding, the holding we reaffirm, has three parts. First is a recognition of the right of the woman to choose to have an abortion before viability and to obtain it without undue interference from the State. Before viability, the State's interests are not strong enough to support a prohibition of abortion or the imposition of a substantial obstacle to the woman's effective right to elect the procedure. Second is a confirmation of the State's power to restrict abortions after fetal viability, if the law contains exceptions for pregnancies which endanger a woman's life or health. And third is the principle that the State has legitimate interests from the outset of the pregnancy in protecting the health of the woman and the life of the fetus that may become a child. These principles do not contradict one another; and we adhere to each.

II

... Men and women of good conscience can disagree, and we suppose some always shall disagree, about the profound moral and spiritual implications of terminating a pregnancy, even in its earliest stage. Some of us as individuals find abortion offensive to our most basic principles of morality, but that cannot control our decision. Our obligation is to define the liberty of all, not to mandate our own moral code. The underlying constitutional issue is whether the State can resolve these philosophic questions in such a definitive way that a woman lacks all choice in the matter, except perhaps in those rare circumstances in which the pregnancy is itself a danger to her own life or health, or is the result of rape or incest....

Our law affords constitutional protection to personal decisions relating to marriage, procreation, contraception, family relationships, child rearing, and education. *Carey v. Population Services International,* 431 U.S., at 685. Our cases recognize "the right of the *individual,* married or single, to be free from un-warranted governmental intrusion into matters so fundamentally affecting a person as the decision whether to bear or beget a child." *Eisenstadt v. Baird, supra,* at 453. Our precedents "have respected the private realm of family life which the state cannot enter." *Prince v. Massachusetts,* 321 U.S. 158, 166 (1944). These matters, involving the most intimate and personal choices a person may make in a lifetime, choices central to personal dignity and autonomy, are cen-tral to the liberty protected by the Fourteenth Amendment. At the heart of liberty is the right to define one's own concept of existence, of meaning, of the universe, and of the mystery of human life. Beliefs about these matters could not define the attributes of personhood were they formed under compulsion of the State.

These considerations begin our analysis of the woman's interest in termi-nating her pregnancy but cannot end it, for this reason: though the abortion decision may originate within the zone of conscience and belief, it is more than a philosophic exercise. Abortion is a unique act. It is an act fraught with consequences for others: for the woman who must live with the implications of her decision; for the persons who perform and assist in the procedure; for the spouse, family, and society which must confront the knowledge that these procedures exist, procedures some deem nothing short of an act of violence against innocent human life; and, depending on one's beliefs, for the life or po-tential life that is aborted. Though abortion is conduct, it does not follow that the State is entitled to proscribe it in all instances. That is because the liberty of the woman is at stake in a sense unique to the human condition and so unique to the law. The mother who carries a child to full term is subject to anxieties, to physical constraints, to pain that only she must bear. That these sacrifices have from the beginning of the human race been endured by woman with a pride that ennobles her in the eyes of others and gives to the infant a bond of love cannot alone be grounds for the State to insist she make the sacrifice. Her suf-fering is too intimate and personal for the State to insist, without more, upon its own vision of the woman's role, however dominant that vision has been in the course of our history and our culture. The destiny of the woman must be shaped to a large extent on her own conception of her spiritual imperatives and her place in society.

It should be recognized, moreover, that in some critical respects the abor-tion decision is of the same character as the decision to use contraception, to which *Griswold v. Connecticut, Eisenstadt v. Baird,* and *Carey v. Population Ser-vices International,* afford constitutional protection. We have no doubt as to the correctness of those decisions. They support the reasoning in *Roe* relating to the woman's liberty because they involve personal decisions concerning not only the meaning of procreation but also human responsibility and respect for it. As with abortion, reasonable people will have differences of opinion about these matters. One view is based on such reverence for the wonder of creation that any pregnancy ought to be welcomed and carried to full term no matter how difficult it will be to provide for the child and ensure its well-being. Another is that the inability to provide for the nurture and care of the infant is a cruelty to the child and an anguish to the parent. These are intimate views with infinite variations, and their deep, personal character underlay our decisions in *Griswold, Eisenstadt,* and *Carey.* The same concerns are present when the woman confronts the reality that, perhaps despite her attempts to avoid it, she has become pregnant.

It was this dimension of personal liberty that *Roe* sought to protect, and its holding invoked the reasoning and the tradition of the precedents we have discussed, granting protection to substantive liberties of the person. *Roe* was, of course, an extension of those cases and, as the decision itself indicated, the separate States could act in some degree to further their own legitimate interests in protecting prenatal life. The extent to which the legislatures of the States might act to outweigh the interests of the woman in choosing to terminate her pregnancy was a subject of debate both in *Roe* itself and in decisions following it.

While we appreciate the weight of the arguments made on behalf of the State in the case before us, arguments which in their ultimate formulation conclude that *Roe* should be overruled, the reservations any of us may have in reaffirming the central holding of *Roe* are outweighed by the explication of individual liberty we have given combined with the force of *stare decisis.* We turn now to that doctrine.

III
A

... [W]hen this Court reexamines a prior holding, its judgment is customarily informed by a series of prudential and pragmatic considerations designed to test the consistency of overruling a prior decision with the ideal of the rule of law, and to gauge the respective costs of reaffirming and overruling a prior case. Thus, for example, we may ask whether the rule has proved to be intolerable simply in defying practical workability; whether the rule is subject to a kind of reliance that would lend a special hardship to the consequences of overruling and add inequity to the cost of repudiation; whether related principles of law have so far developed as to have left the old rule no more than a remnant of abandoned doctrine; or whether facts have so changed or come to be seen so differently, as to have robbed the old rule of significant application or justification.

So in this case we may inquire whether *Roe*'s central rule has been found unworkable; whether the rule's limitation on state power could be removed without serious inequity to those who have relied upon it or significant damage to the stability of the society governed by the rule in question; whether the law's growth in the intervening years has left *Roe*'s central rule a doctrinal anachronism discounted by society; and whether *Roe*'s premises of fact have so far changed in the ensuing two decades as to render its central holding somehow irrelevant or unjustifiable in dealing with the issue it addressed.

1

Although *Roe* has engendered opposition, it has in no sense proven "unworkable," see *Garcia v. San Antonio Metropolitan Transit Authority,* 469 U.S. 528, 546 (1985), representing as it does a simple limitation beyond which a state law is unenforceable. While *Roe* has, of course, required judicial assessment of state laws affecting the exercise of the choice guaranteed against government infringement, and although the need for such review will remain as a consequence of today's decision, the required determinations fall within judicial competence.

2

... [F]or two decades of economic and social developments, people have organized intimate relationships and made choices that define their views of themselves and their places in society, in reliance on the availability of abortion in the event that contraception should fail. The ability of women to participate equally in the economic and social life of the Nation has been facilitated by their ability to control their reproductive lives. See, e.g., R. Petchesky, Abortion and Woman's Choice 109, 133, n. 7 (rev. ed. 1990). The Constitution serves human values, and while the effect of reliance on *Roe* cannot be exactly measured, neither can the certain cost of overruling *Roe* for people who have ordered their thinking and living around that case be dismissed.

3

No evolution of legal principle has left *Roe*'s doctrinal footings weaker than they were in 1973. No development of constitutional law since the case was decided has implicitly or explicitly left *Roe* behind as a mere survivor of obsolete constitutional thinking.

It will be recognized, of course, that *Roe* stands at an intersection of two lines of decisions, but in whichever doctrinal category one reads the case, the result for present purposes will be the same. The *Roe* Court itself placed its holding in the succession of cases most prominently exemplified by *Griswold v. Connecticut,* 381 U.S. 479 (1965), see *Roe,* 410 U.S., at 152–153. When it is so seen, *Roe* is clearly in no jeopardy, since subsequent constitutional developments have neither disturbed, nor do they threaten to diminish, the scope of recognized protection accorded to the liberty relating to intimate relationships, the family, and decisions about whether or not to beget or bear a child. See, e.g., *Carey v. Population Services International,* 431 U.S. 678 (1977); *Moore v. East Cleveland,* 431 U.S. 678 (1977).

Roe, however, may be seen not only as an exemplar of *Griswold* liberty but as a rule (whether or not mistaken) of personal autonomy and bodily integrity, with doctrinal affinity to cases recognizing limits on governmental power to mandate medical treatment or to bar its rejection. If so, our cases since *Roe* accord with *Roe*'s view that a State's interest in the protection of life falls short of justifying any plenary override of individual liberty claims. . . .

4

We have seen how time has overtaken some of *Roe*'s factual assumptions: advances in maternal health care allow for abortions safe to the mother later in pregnancy than was true in 1973, and advances in neonatal care have advanced viability to a point somewhat earlier. But these facts go only to the scheme of time limits on the realization of competing interests, and the divergences from the factual premises of 1973 have no bearing on the validity of *Roe*'s central holding, that viability marks the earliest point at which the State's interest in fetal life is constitutionally adequate to justify a legislative ban on non-therapeutic abortions. The soundness or unsoundness of that constitutional judgment in no sense turns on whether viability occurs at approximately 28 weeks, as was usual at the time of *Roe,* at 23 to 24 weeks, as it sometimes does today, or at some moment even slightly earlier in pregnancy, as it may if fetal respiratory capacity can somehow be enhanced in the future. Whenever it may occur, the attainment of viability may continue to serve as the critical fact, just as it has done since *Roe* was decided; which is to say that no change in *Roe*'s factual underpinning has left its central holding obsolete, and none supports an argument for overruling it.

5

The sum of the precedential inquiry to this point shows *Roe*'s underpinnings unweakened in any way affecting its central holding. While it has engendered disapproval, it has not been unworkable. An entire generation has come of age free to assume *Roe*'s concept of liberty in defining the capacity of women to act in society, and to make reproductive decisions; no erosion of principle going to liberty or personal autonomy has left *Roe*'s central holding a doctrinal remnant; *Roe* portends no developments at odds with other precedent for the analysis of personal liberty; and no changes of fact have rendered viability more or less appropriate as the point at which the balance of interests tips. Within the bounds of normal *stare decisis* analysis, then, and subject to the considerations on which it customarily turns, the stronger argument is for affirming *Roe*'s central holding, with whatever degree of personal reluctance any of us may have, not for overruling it....

Our analysis would not be complete... without explaining why overruling *Roe*'s central holding would not only reach an unjustifiable result under principles of *stare decisis,* but would seriously weaken the Court's capacity to exercise the judicial power and to function as the Supreme Court of a Nation dedicated to the rule of law. To understand why this would be so it is necessary to understand the source of this Court's authority, the conditions necessary for its preservation, and its relationship to the country's understanding of itself as a constitutional Republic.

The root of American governmental power is revealed most clearly in the instance of the power conferred by the Constitution upon the Judiciary of the United States and specifically upon this Court. As Americans of each succeeding generation are rightly told, the Court cannot buy support for its decisions by spending money and, except to a minor degree, it cannot independently coerce obedience to its decrees. The Court's power lies, rather, in its legitimacy, a product of substance and perception that shows itself in the people's acceptance of the Judiciary as fit to determine what the Nation's law means and to declare what it demands.

The underlying substance of this legitimacy is of course the warrant for the Court's decisions in the Constitution and the lesser sources of legal principle on which the Court draws. That substance is expressed in the Court's opinions, and our contemporary understanding is such that a decision without principled justification would be no judicial act at all. But even when justification is furnished by apposite legal principle, something more is required. Because not every conscientious claim of principled justification will be accepted as such, the justification claimed must be beyond dispute. The Court must take care to speak and act in ways that allow people to accept its decisions on the terms the Court claims for them, as grounded truly in principle, not as compromises with social and political pressures having, as such, no bearing on the principled choices that the Court is obliged to make. Thus, the Court's legitimacy depends on making legally principled decisions under circumstances in which their principled character is sufficiently plausible to be accepted by the Nation.

The need for principled action to be perceived as such is implicated to some degree whenever this, or any other appellate court, overrules a prior case. This is not to say, of course, that this Court cannot give a perfectly satisfactory explanation in most cases. People understand that some of the Constitution's language is hard to fathom and that the Court's Justices are sometimes able to perceive significant facts or to understand principles of law that eluded their predecessors and that justify departures from existing decisions. However upsetting it may be to those most directly affected when one judicially derived rule replaces another, the country can accept some correction of error without necessarily questioning the legitimacy of the Court.

In two circumstances, however, the Court would almost certainly fail to receive the benefit of the doubt in overruling prior cases. There is, first, a point beyond which frequent overruling would overtax the country's belief in the Court's good faith. Despite the variety of reasons that may inform and justify a decision to overrule, we cannot forget that such a decision is usually perceived (and perceived correctly) as, at the least, a statement that a prior decision was wrong. There is a limit to the amount of error that can plausibly be imputed to prior courts. If that limit should be exceeded, disturbance of prior rulings would be taken as evidence that justifiable reexamination of principle had given way to drives for particular results in the short term. The legitimacy of the Court would fade with the frequency of its vacillation.

That first circumstance can be described as hypothetical; the second is to the point here and now. Where, in the performance of its judicial duties, the Court decides a case in such a way as to resolve the sort of intensely divisive controversy reflected in *Roe* and those rare, comparable cases, its decision has a dimension that the resolution of the normal case does not carry. It is the dimension present whenever the Court's interpretation of the Constitution calls the contending sides of a national controversy to end their national division by accepting a common mandate rooted in the Constitution.

The Court is not asked to do this very often, having thus addressed the Nation only twice in our lifetime, in the decisions of *Brown* and *Roe*. But when the Court does act in this way, its decision requires an equally rare precedential force to counter the inevitable efforts to overturn it and to thwart its implementation. Some of those efforts may be mere unprincipled emotional reactions; others may proceed from principles worthy of profound respect. But whatever the premises of opposition may be, only the most convincing justification under accepted standards of precedent could suffice to demonstrate that a later decision overruling the first was anything but a surrender to political pressure, and an unjustified repudiation of the principle on which the Court staked its authority in the first instance. So to overrule under fire in the absence of the most compelling reason to reexamine a watershed decision would subvert the Court's legitimacy beyond any serious question....

The Court's duty in the present case is clear. In 1973, it confronted the already-divisive issue of governmental power to limit personal choice to undergo abortion, for which it provided a new resolution based on the due process guaranteed by the Fourteenth Amendment. Whether or not a new social consensus is developing on that issue, its divisiveness is no less today than in 1973, and pressure to overrule the decision, like pressure to retain it, has grown only more intense. A decision to overrule *Roe*'s essential holding under the existing circumstances would address error, if error there was, at the cost of both profound and unnecessary damage to the Court's legitimacy, and to the Nation's commitment to the rule of law. It is therefore imperative to adhere to the essence of Roe's original decision, and we do so today.

IV

From what we have said so far it follows that it is a constitutional liberty of the woman to have some freedom to terminate her pregnancy. We conclude that the basic decision in *Roe* was based on a constitutional analysis which we cannot now repudiate. The woman's liberty is not so unlimited, however, that from the outset the State cannot show its concern for the life of the unborn, and at a later point in fetal development the State's interest in life has sufficient force so that the right of the woman to terminate the pregnancy can be restricted.

That brings us, of course, to the point where much criticism has been directed at *Roe,* a criticism that always inheres when the Court draws a specific rule from what in the Constitution is but a general standard. We conclude, however, that the urgent claims of the woman to retain the ultimate control over her destiny and her body, claims implicit in the meaning of liberty, require us to perform that function. Liberty must not be extinguished for want of a line that is clear. And it falls to us to give some real substance to the woman's liberty to determine whether to carry her pregnancy to full term.

We conclude the line should be drawn at viability, so that before that time the woman has a right to choose to terminate her pregnancy. We adhere to this principle for two reasons. First, as we have said, is the doctrine of *stare decisis.*

Any judicial act of line-drawing may seem somewhat arbitrary, but *Roe* was a reasoned statement, elaborated with great care. We have twice reaffirmed it in the face of great opposition. See *Thornburgh v. American College of Obstetricians & Gynecologists,* 476 U.S., at 759; *Akron I,* 462 U.S., at 419–420. Although we must overrule those parts of *Thornburgh* and *Akron I* which, in our view, are inconsistent with *Roe*'s statement that the State has a legitimate interest in promoting the life or potential life of the unborn, the central premise of those cases represents an unbroken commitment by this Court to the essential holding of *Roe.* It is that premise which we reaffirm today.

The second reason is that the concept of viability, as we noted in *Roe,* is the time at which there is a realistic possibility of maintaining and nourishing a life outside the womb, so that the independent existence of the second life can in reason and all fairness be the object of state protection that now overrides the rights of the woman. See *Roe v. Wade,* 410 U.S., at 163. Consistent with other constitutional norms, legislatures may draw lines which appear arbitrary without the necessity of offering a justification. But courts may not. We must justify the lines we draw. And there is no line other than viability which is more workable. To be sure, as we have said, there may be some medical developments that affect the precise point of viability, but this is an imprecision within tolerable limits given that the medical community and all those who must apply its discoveries will continue to explore the matter. The viability line also has, as a practical matter, an element of fairness. In some broad sense it might be said that a woman who fails to act before viability has consented to the State's intervention on behalf of the developing child.

The woman's right to terminate her pregnancy before viability is the most central principle of *Roe v. Wade.* It is a rule of law and a component of liberty we cannot renounce.

On the other side of the equation is the interest of the State in the protection of potential life. The *Roe* Court recognized the State's "important and legitimate interest in protecting the potentiality of human life." *Roe, supra,* at 162. The weight to be given this state interest, not the strength of the woman's interest, was the difficult question faced in *Roe.* We do not need to say whether each of us, had we been Members of the Court when the valuation of the State interest came before it as an original matter, would have concluded, as the *Roe* Court did, that its weight is insufficient to justify a ban on abortions prior to viability even when it is subject to certain exceptions. The matter is not before us in the first instance, and coming as it does after nearly 20 years of litigation in *Roe*'s wake we are satisfied that the immediate question is not the soundness of *Roe*'s resolution of the issue, but the precedential force that must be accorded to its holding. And we have concluded that the essential holding of *Roe* should be reaffirmed.

Yet it must be remembered that *Roe v. Wade* speaks with clarity in establishing not only the woman's liberty but also the State's "important and legitimate interest in potential life." *Roe, supra,* at 163. That portion of the decision in *Roe* has been given too little acknowledgement and implementation by the Court in its subsequent cases....

Roe established a trimester framework to govern abortion regulations. Under this elaborate but rigid construct, almost no regulation at all is permitted during the first trimester of pregnancy; regulations designed to protect the woman's health, but not to further the State's interest in potential life, are permitted during the second trimester; and during the third trimester, when the fetus is viable, prohibitions are permitted provided the life or health of the mother is not at stake. *Roe v. Wade, supra,* at 163–166. Most of our cases since *Roe* have involved the application of rules derived from the trimester framework.

The trimester framework no doubt was erected to ensure that the woman's right to choose not become so subordinate to the State's interest in promoting fetal life that her choice exists in theory but not in fact. We do not agree, however, that the trimester approach is necessary to accomplish this objective. A framework of this rigidity was unnecessary and in its later interpretation sometimes contradicted the State's permissible exercise of its powers.

Though the woman has a right to choose to terminate or continue her pregnancy before viability, it does not at all follow that the State is prohibited from taking steps to ensure that this choice is thoughtful and informed. Even in the earliest stages of pregnancy, the State may enact rules and regulations designed to encourage her to know that there are philosophic and social arguments of great weight that can be brought to bear in favor of continuing the pregnancy to full term and that there are procedures and institutions to allow adoption of unwanted children as well as a certain degree of state assistance if the mother chooses to raise the child herself. " '[T]he Constitution does not forbid a State or city, pursuant to democratic processes, from expressing a preference for normal childbirth.' " *Webster v. Reproductive Health Services,* 492 U.S., at 511 (opinion of the Court) (quoting *Poelker v. Doe,* 432 U.S. 519, 521 (1977)). It follows that States are free to enact laws to provide a reasonable framework for a woman to make a decision that has such profound and lasting meaning. This, too, we find consistent with *Roe's* central premises, and indeed the inevitable consequence of our holding that the State has an interest in protecting the life of the unborn.

We reject the trimester framework, which we do not consider to be part of the essential holding of *Roe.* Measures aimed at ensuring that a woman's choice contemplates the consequences for the fetus do not necessarily interfere with the right recognized in *Roe,* although those measures have been found to be inconsistent with the rigid trimester framework announced in that case. A logical reading of the central holding in *Roe* itself, and a necessary reconciliation of the liberty of the woman and the interest of the State in promoting prenatal life, require, in our view, that we abandon the trimester framework as a rigid prohibition on all previability regulation aimed at the protection of fetal life. The trimester framework suffers from these basic flaws: in its formulation it misconceives the nature of the pregnant woman's interest; and in practice it undervalues the State's interest in potential life, as recognized in *Roe.*

As our jurisprudence relating to all liberties save perhaps abortion has recognized, not every law which makes a right more difficult to exercise is, *ipso facto,* an infringement of that right. An example clarifies the point. We have held that not every ballot access limitation amounts to an infringement of the right to vote. Rather, the States are granted substantial flexibility in establishing the framework within which voters choose the candidates for whom they wish to vote. *Anderson v. Celebrezze,* 460 U.S. 780, 788 (1983); *Norman v. Reed,* 502 U.S. ____ (1992).

The abortion right is similar. Numerous forms of state regulation might have the incidental effect of increasing the cost or decreasing the availability of medical care, whether for abortion or any other medical procedure. The fact that a law which serves a valid purpose, one not designed to strike at the right itself, has the incidental effect of making it more difficult or more expensive to procure an abortion cannot be enough to invalidate it. Only where state regulation imposes an undue burden on a woman's ability to make this decision does the power of the State reach into the heart of the liberty protected by the Due Process Clause. . . .

A finding of an undue burden is a shorthand for the conclusion that a state regulation has the purpose or effect of placing a substantial obstacle in the path of a woman seeking an abortion of a nonviable fetus. A statute with this purpose is invalid because the means chosen by the State to further the interest in potential life must be calculated to inform the woman's free choice, not hinder it. And a statute which, while furthering the interest in potential life or some other valid state interest, has the effect of placing a substantial obstacle in the path of a woman's choice cannot be considered a permissible means of serving its legitimate ends. To the extent that the opinions of the Court or of individual Justices use the undue burden standard in a manner that is inconsistent with this analysis, we set out what in our view should be the controlling standard. . . . Understood another way, we answer the question, left open in previous opinions discussing the undue burden formulation, whether a law designed to further the State's interest in fetal life which imposes an undue burden on the woman's decision before fetal viability could be constitutional. The answer is no.

Some guiding principles should emerge. What is at stake is the woman's right to make the ultimate decision, not a right to be insulated from all others in doing so. Regulations which do no more than create a structural mechanism by which the State, or the parent or guardian of a minor, may express profound respect for the life of the unborn are permitted, if they are not a substantial obstacle to the woman's exercise of the right to choose. Unless it has that effect on her right of choice, a state measure designed to persuade her to choose childbirth over abortion will be upheld if reasonably related to that goal. Regulations designed to foster the health of a woman seeking an abortion are valid if they do not constitute an undue burden.

Even when jurists reason from shared premises, some disagreement is inevitable. That is to be expected in the application of any legal standard which must accommodate life's complexity. We do not expect it to be otherwise with respect to the undue burden standard. We give this summary:

1. To protect the central right recognized by *Roe v. Wade* while at the same time accommodating the State's profound interest in potential life, we will employ the undue burden analysis as explained in this opinion.

An undue burden exists, and therefore a provision of law is invalid, if its purpose or effect is to place a substantial obstacle in the path of a woman seeking an abortion before the fetus attains viability.

2. We reject the rigid trimester framework of *Roe v. Wade.* To promote the State's profound interest in potential life, throughout pregnancy the State may take measures to ensure that the woman's choice is informed, and measures designed to advance this interest will not be invalidated as long as their purpose is to persuade the woman to choose childbirth over abortion. These measures must not be an undue burden on the right.

3. As with any medical procedure, the State may enact regulations to further the health or safety of a woman seeking an abortion. Unnecessary health regulations that have the purpose or effect of presenting a substantial obstacle to a woman seeking an abortion impose an undue burden on the right.

4. Our adoption of the undue burden analysis does not disturb the central holding of *Roe v. Wade,* and we reaffirm that holding. Regardless of whether exceptions are made for particular circumstances, a State may not prohibit any woman from making the ultimate decision to terminate her pregnancy before viability.

5. We also reaffirm *Roe's* holding that "subsequent to viability, the State in promoting its interest in the potentiality of human life may, if it chooses, regulate, and even proscribe, abortion except where it is necessary, in appropriate medical judgment, for the preservation of the life or health of the mother." *Roe v. Wade,* 410 U.S., at 164–165.

Dissenting Opinion of William H. Rehnquist

CHIEF JUSTICE REHNQUIST, with whom JUSTICE WHITE, JUSTICE SCALIA, and JUSTICE THOMAS join, concurring in the judgment in part and dissenting in part.

... We believe that *Roe* was wrongly decided, and that it can and should be overruled consistently with our traditional approach to *stare decisis* in constitutional cases. We would adopt the approach of the plurality in *Webster v. Reproductive Health Services,* 492 U.S. 490 (1989), and uphold the challenged provisions of the Pennsylvania statute in their entirety.

I

... In *Roe v. Wade,* the Court recognized a "guarantee of personal privacy" which "is broad enough to encompass a woman's decision whether or not to terminate her pregnancy." 410 U.S., at 152–153. We are now of the view that, in terming this right fundamental, the Court in *Roe* read the earlier opinions upon which it based its decision much too broadly. Unlike marriage, procreation and contraception, abortion "involves the purposeful termination of potential life." *Harris v. McRae,* 448 U.S. 297, 325 (1980). The abortion decision must therefore "be recognized as *sui generis,* different in kind from the others that the Court has protected under the rubric of personal or family privacy and autonomy." *Thornburgh v. American College of Obstetricians and Gynecologists, supra,* at 792 (White, J., dissenting). One cannot ignore the fact that a woman is not isolated in her pregnancy, and that the decision to abort necessarily involves the destruction of a fetus. See *Michael H. v. Gerald D., supra,* at 124, n. 4 (To look "at the act which is assertedly the subject of a liberty interest in isolation from its effect upon other people [is] like inquiring whether there is a liberty interest in firing a gun where the case at hand happens to involve its discharge into another person's body").

Nor do the historical traditions of the American people support the view that the right to terminate one's pregnancy is "fundamental." The common law which we inherited from England made abortion after "quickening" an

From *Planned Parenthood of Southeastern Pennsylvania et al. v. Casey et al.,* 505 U.S. 833, 60 U.S.L.W. 4795 (1992). Notes and some case citations omitted.

offense. At the time of the adoption of the Fourteenth Amendment, statutory prohibitions or restrictions on abortion were commonplace; in 1868, at least 28 of the then-37 States and 8 Territories had statutes banning or limiting abortion. J. Mohr, Abortion in America 200 (1978). By the turn of the century virtually every State had a law prohibiting or restricting abortion on its books. By the middle of the present century, a liberalization trend had set in. But 21 of the restrictive abortion laws in effect in 1868 were still in effect in 1973 when *Roe* was decided, and an overwhelming majority of the States prohibited abortion unless necessary to preserve the life or health of the mother. *Roe v. Wade*, 410 U.S., at 139–140; *id.*, at 176–177, n. 2 (Rehnquist, J., dissenting). On this record, it can scarcely be said that any deeply rooted tradition of relatively unrestricted abortion in our history supported the classification of the right to abortion as "fundamental" under the Due Process Clause of the Fourteenth Amendment.

We think, therefore, both in view of this history and of our decided cases dealing with substantive liberty under the Due Process Clause, that the Court was mistaken in *Roe* when it classified a woman's decision to terminate her pregnancy as a "fundamental right" that could be abridged only in a manner which withstood "strict scrutiny." In so concluding, we repeat the observation made in *Bowers v. Hardwick*, 478 U.S. 186 (1986):

> "Nor are we inclined to take a more expansive view of our authority to discover new fundamental rights imbedded in the Due Process Clause. The Court is most vulnerable and comes nearest to illegitimacy when it deals with judge-made constitutional law having little or no cognizable roots in the language or design of the Constitution." *Id.*, at 194.

We believe that the sort of constitutionally imposed abortion code of the type illustrated by our decisions following Roe is inconsistent "with the notion of a Constitution cast in general terms, as ours is, and usually speaking in general principles, as ours does." *Webster v. Reproductive Health Services*, 492 U.S., at 518 (plurality opinion). The Court in *Roe* reached too far when it analogized the right to abort a fetus to the rights involved in *Pierce, Meyer, Loving*, and *Griswold*, and thereby deemed the right to abortion fundamental.

II

The joint opinion of Justices O'Connor, Kennedy, and Souter cannot bring itself to say that *Roe* was correct as an original matter, but the authors are of the view that "the immediate question is not the soundness of *Roe*'s resolution of the issue, but the precedential force that must be accorded to its holding." Instead of claiming that *Roe* was correct as a matter of original constitutional interpretation, the opinion therefore contains an elaborate discussion of *stare decisis*. This discussion of the principle of *stare decisis* appears to be almost entirely dicta, because the joint opinion does not apply that principle in dealing with *Roe*. *Roe* decided that a woman had a fundamental right to an abortion. The joint opinion rejects that view. *Roe* decided that abortion regulations were to be subjected to "strict scrutiny" and could be justified only in the light of "compelling state interests." The joint opinion rejects that view. *Roe* analyzed abortion regulation under a rigid trimester framework, a framework which has guided this Court's decisionmaking for 19 years. The joint opinion rejects that framework.... In our view, authentic principles of *stare decisis* do not require that any portion of the reasoning in *Roe* be kept intact. "*Stare decisis* is not... a universal, inexorable command," especially in cases involving the interpretation of the Federal Constitution. *Burnet v. Coronado Oil & Gas Co.,* 285 U.S. 393, 405 (1932) (Brandeis, J., dissenting). Erroneous decisions in such constitutional cases are uniquely durable, because correction through legislative action, save for constitutional amendment, is impossible. It is therefore our duty to reconsider constitutional interpretations that "depar[t] from a proper understanding" of the Constitution.... Our constitutional watch does not cease merely because we have spoken before on an issue; when it becomes clear that a prior constitutional interpretation is unsound we are obliged to reexamine the question.

The joint opinion discusses several *stare decisis* factors which, it asserts, point toward retaining a portion of *Roe.* Two of these factors are that the main "factual underpinning" of *Roe* has remained the same, and that its doctrinal foundation is no weaker now than it was in 1973. Of course, what might be called the basic facts which gave rise to *Roe* have remained the same—women become pregnant, there is a point somewhere, depending on medical technology, where a fetus becomes viable, and women give birth to children. But this is only to say that the same facts which gave rise to *Roe* will continue to give rise to similar cases. It is not a reason, in and of itself, why those cases must be decided in the same incorrect manner as was the first case to deal with the question. And surely there is no requirement, in considering whether to depart from *stare decisis* in a constitutional case, that a decision be more wrong now than it was at the time it was rendered. If that were true, the most outlandish constitutional decision could survive forever, based simply on the fact that it was no more outlandish later than it was when originally rendered.

Nor does the joint opinion faithfully follow this alleged requirement. The opinion frankly concludes that *Roe* and its progeny were wrong in failing to recognize that the State's interests in maternal health and in the protection of unborn human life exist throughout pregnancy. But there is no indication that these components of *Roe* are any more incorrect at this juncture than they were at its inception....

The joint opinion thus turns to what can only be described as an unconventional—and unconvincing—notion of reliance, a view based on the surmise that the availability of abortion since *Roe* has led to "two decades of economic and social developments" that would be undercut if the error of *Roe* were recognized. The joint opinion's assertion of this fact is undeveloped and totally conclusory. In fact, one can not be sure to what economic and social developments the opinion is referring. Surely it is dubious to suggest that women have reached their "places in society" in reliance upon *Roe,* rather than as a result of their determination to obtain higher education and compete with men in the job market, and of society's increasing recognition of their ability to fill positions that were previously thought to be reserved only for men.

In the end, having failed to put forth any evidence to prove any true reliance, the joint opinion's argument is based solely on generalized assertions about the national psyche, on a belief that the people of this country have grown accustomed to the *Roe* decision over the last 19 years and have "ordered their thinking and living around" it. As an initial matter, one might inquire how the joint opinion can view the "central holding" of *Roe* as so deeply rooted in our constitutional culture, when it so casually uproots and disposes of that same decision's trimester framework. Furthermore, at various points in the past, the same could have been said about this Court's erroneous decisions that the Constitution allowed "separate but equal" treatment of minorities, see *Plessy v. Ferguson,* 163 U.S. 537 (1896), or that "liberty" under the Due Process Clause protected "freedom of contract." See *Adkins v. Children's Hospital of D. C.,* 261 U.S. 525 (1923); *Lochner v. New York,* 198 U.S. 45 (1905). The "separate but equal" doctrine lasted 58 years after *Plessy,* and *Lochner*'s protection of contractual freedom lasted 32 years. However, the simple fact that a generation or more had grown used to these major decisions did not prevent the Court from correcting its errors in those cases, nor should it prevent us from correctly interpreting the Constitution here.

Apparently realizing that conventional *stare decisis* principles do not support its position, the joint opinion advances a belief that retaining a portion of *Roe* is necessary to protect the "legitimacy" of this Court. Because the Court must take care to render decisions "grounded truly in principle," and not simply as political and social compromises, the joint opinion properly declares it to be this Court's duty to ignore the public criticism and protest that may arise as a result of a decision. Few would quarrel with this statement, although it may be doubted that Members of this Court, holding their tenure as they do during constitutional "good behavior," are at all likely to be intimidated by such public protests....

The joint opinion also agrees that the Court acted properly in rejecting the doctrine of "separate but equal" in *Brown.* In fact, the opinion lauds *Brown* in comparing it to *Roe.* This is strange, in that under the opinion's "legitimacy" principle the Court would seemingly have been forced to adhere to its erroneous decision in *Plessy* because of its "intensely divisive" character. To us, adherence to *Roe* today under the guise of "legitimacy" would seem to resemble more closely adherence to *Plessy* on the same ground. Fortunately, the Court did not choose that option in *Brown,* and instead frankly repudiated *Plessy.* The joint opinion concludes that such repudiation was justified only because of newly discovered evidence that segregation had the effect of treating one race as inferior to another. But it can hardly be argued that this was not urged upon those who decided *Plessy,* as Justice Harlan observed in his dissent that the law at issue "puts the brand of servitude and degradation upon a large class of our fellow-citizens, our equals before the law." *Plessy v. Ferguson,* 163 U.S., at 562 (Harlan, J., dissenting). It is clear that the same arguments made before the Court in *Brown* were made in *Plessy* as well. The Court in *Brown* simply recognized, as Justice Harlan had recognized beforehand, that the Fourteenth Amendment does not permit racial segregation. The rule of *Brown* is not tied to popular opinion about the evils of segregation; it is a judgment that the Equal

Protection Clause does not permit racial segregation, no matter whether the public might come to believe that it is beneficial. On that ground it stands, and on that ground alone the Court was justified in properly concluding that the *Plessy* Court had erred. . . .

There are other reasons why the joint opinion's discussion of legitimacy is unconvincing as well. In assuming that the Court is perceived as "surrender[ing] to political pressure" when it overrules a controversial decision, the joint opinion forgets that there are two sides to any controversy. The joint opinion asserts that, in order to protect its legitimacy, the Court must refrain from overruling a controversial decision lest it be viewed as favoring those who oppose the decision. But a decision to *adhere* to prior precedent is subject to the same criticism, for in such a case one can easily argue that the Court is responding to those who have demonstrated in favor of the original decision. The decision in *Roe* has engendered large demonstrations, including repeated marches on this Court and on Congress, both in opposition to and in support of that opinion. A decision either way on *Roe* can therefore be perceived as favoring one group or the other. But this perceived dilemma arises only if one assumes, as the joint opinion does, that the Court should make its decisions with a view toward speculative public perceptions. If one assumes instead, as the Court surely did in both *Brown* and *West Coast Hotel,* that the Court's legitimacy is enhanced by faithful interpretation of the Constitution irrespective of public opposition, such self-engendered difficulties may be put to one side.

Roe is not this Court's only decision to generate conflict. Our decisions in some recent capital cases, and in *Bowers v. Hardwick,* 478 U.S. 186 (1986), have also engendered demonstrations in opposition. The joint opinion's message to such protesters appears to be that they must cease their activities in order to serve their cause, because their protests will only cement in place a decision which by normal standards of *stare decisis* should be reconsidered. Nearly a century ago, Justice David J. Brewer of this Court, in an article discussing criticism of its decisions, observed that "many criticisms may be, like their authors, devoid of good taste, but better all sorts of criticism than no criticism at all." Justice Brewer on "The Nation's Anchor," 57 Albany L.J. 166, 169 (1898). This was good advice to the Court then, as it is today. Strong and often misguided criticism of a decision should not render the decision immune from reconsideration, lest a fetish for legitimacy penalize freedom of expression.

The end result of the joint opinion's paeans of praise for legitimacy is the enunciation of a brand new standard for evaluating state regulation of a woman's right to abortion—the "undue burden" standard. As indicated above, *Roe v. Wade* adopted a "fundamental right" standard under which state regulations could survive only if they met the requirement of "strict scrutiny." While we disagree with that standard, it at least had a recognized basis in constitutional law at the time *Roe* was decided. The same cannot be said for the "undue burden" standard, which is created largely out of whole cloth by the authors of the joint opinion. It is a standard which even today does not command the support of a majority of this Court. And it will not, we believe, result in the sort of "simple limitation," easily applied, which the joint opinion anticipates. In sum, it is a standard which is not built to last. . . .

The sum of the joint opinion's labors in the name of *stare decisis* and "legitimacy" is this: *Roe v. Wade* stands as a sort of judicial Potemkin Village, which may be pointed out to passers by as a monument to the importance of adhering to precedent. But behind the facade, an entirely new method of analysis, without any roots in constitutional law, is imported to decide the constitutionality of state laws regulating abortion. Neither *stare decisis* nor "legitimacy" are truly served by such an effort. . . .

III
E

Finally, petitioners challenge the medical emergency exception provided for by the Act. The existence of a medical emergency exempts compliance with the Act's informed consent, parental consent, and spousal notice requirements. See 18 Pa. Cons. Stat. sec. 3205(a), 3206(a), 3209(c) (1990). The Act defines a "medical emergency" as

> "[t]hat condition which, on the basis of the physician's good faith clinical judgment, so complicates the medical condition of a pregnant woman as to necessitate the immediate abortion of her pregnancy to avert her death or for which a delay will create serious risk of substantial and irreversible impairment of major bodily function." sec. 3203.

Petitioners argued before the District Court that the statutory definition was inadequate because it did not cover three serious conditions that pregnant women can suffer—preeclampsia, inevitable abortion, and prematurely ruptured membrane. The District Court agreed with petitioners that the medical emergency exception was inadequate, but the Court of Appeals reversed this holding. In construing the medical emergency provision, the Court of Appeals first observed that all three conditions do indeed present the risk of serious injury or death when an abortion is not performed, and noted that the medical profession's uniformly prescribed treatment for each of the three conditions is an immediate abortion. See 947 F.2d, at 700–701. Finding that "[t]he Pennsylvania legislature did not choose the wording of its medical emergency exception in a vacuum," the court read the exception as intended "to assure that compliance with its abortion regulations would not in any way pose a significant threat to the life or health of a woman." *Id.,* at 701. It thus concluded that the exception encompassed each of the three dangerous conditions pointed to by petitioners.

We observe that Pennsylvania's present definition of medical emergency is almost an exact copy of that State's definition at the time of this Court's ruling in *Thornburgh,* one which the Court made reference to with apparent approval. 476 U.S., at 771 ("It is clear that the Pennsylvania Legislature knows how to provide a medical-emergency exception when it chooses to do so"). We find that the interpretation of the Court of Appeals in this case is eminently reasonable, and that the provision thus should be upheld. When a woman is faced with any condition that poses a "significant threat to [her] life or health," she is exempted from the Act's consent and notice requirements and may proceed immediately with her abortion.

IV

For the reasons stated, we therefore would hold that each of the challenged provisions of the Pennsylvania statute is consistent with the Constitution. It bears emphasis that our conclusion in this regard does not carry with it any necessary approval of these regulations. Our task is, as always, to decide only whether the challenged provisions of a law comport with the United States Constitution. If, as we believe, these do, their wisdom as a matter of public policy is for the people of Pennsylvania to decide.

POSTSCRIPT

Is Abortion Protected by the Constitution?

What would be the consequences of a decision overturning *Roe*? The current state of great controversy over abortion would likely increase. The reason for this is that reversing *Roe* would mean that each state could permit or restrict abortion as it wished. The main contention of the justices who wish to overturn *Roe* is not necessarily that abortion should be banned but that this decision should be left to the states, and that it is not a constitutional issue. Such a position means that the political process will have to deal with the issue more than it does now, which is not likely to defuse the issue.

Even without overturning *Roe,* conflict will continue. Courts will be faced with determining whether or not state regulations constitute an "undue burden." Congress will wrestle with federal legislation that would restrict state regulations, such as the Freedom of Choice Act. Technologies such as RU-486, the so-called abortion pill, will raise legal challenges, as will groups, such as Operation Rescue, that employ methods that are at the boundary of permissible protests.

Most recently, the abortion controversy has become entwined with the question of speech on the Internet. In February 1999 antiabortion activists whose controversial Web site "The Nuremberg Files" struck fear in abortion providers have been ordered by a federal jury to pay nearly $100 million in punitive damages to four abortion doctors, Planned Parenthood, and other plaintiffs. The jury found that the Web site was making threats against the doctors and others. The defendants argued that their Web site was protected by the First Amendment. The defendants had listed the names of 12 doctors who provided abortions, as well as their addresses, phone numbers, and other personal information, on wanted-style posters accusing them of "crimes against humanity." About 200 names appeared on "The Nuremberg Files" Web site, with the names of slain doctors crossed out.

Writings about abortion include Ronald M. Dworkin, *Life's Dominion: An Argument About Abortion, Euthanasia, and Individual Freedom* (Alfred A. Knopf, 1993); Laurence H. Tribe, *Abortion: The Clash of Absolutes* (W. W. Norton, 1990); Note, "Judicial Restraint and the Non-Decision in *Webster v. Reproductive Health Services,*" 13 *Harvard Journal of Law and Public Policy* 263 (1990); and Novick, "Justice Holmes and *Roe v. Wade,*" 25 *Trial* 58 (1989). The story of the *Roe* case is recounted in Marian Faux, *Roe v. Wade: The Untold Story of the Landmark Supreme Court Decision That Made Abortion Legal* (NAL, 1988). Information on both sides of the debate can be found on the Internet at http://www.naral.org and http://www.prolifeinfo.org.

ISSUE 3

Are Restrictions on Physician-Assisted Suicide Constitutional?

YES: William H. Rehnquist, from Majority Opinion, *Washington et al. v. Glucksberg et al.*, U.S. Supreme Court (June 26, 1997)

NO: Stephen Reinhardt, from Majority Opinion, *Compassion in Dying v. State of Washington*, U.S. Court of Appeals for the Ninth Circuit (1996)

ISSUE SUMMARY

YES: Supreme Court chief justice William H. Rehnquist rules that although patients have the right to refuse life-sustaining treatment, physician-assisted suicide is not constitutionally protected.

NO: Judge Stephen Reinhardt argues that forbidding physician-assisted suicide in the cases of competent, terminally ill patients violates the due process clause of the Constitution.

In 1990 the Supreme Court issued its landmark ruling in *Cruzan v. Director, Missouri Department of Health*, 497 U.S. 261 (1990). Nancy Beth Cruzan had sustained severe and irreversible injuries in an automobile accident; her condition was one commonly characterized as a "persistent vegetative state." She displayed no discernible cognitive functioning and was kept alive through the use of artificial hydration and feeding equipment. Four years after the accident, Nancy's parents began proceedings in a Missouri state trial court so that they could withdraw all artificial means of life support.

Cruzan was one of an estimated 10,000 persons in the United States in a vegetative state. She had left no explicit directions on whether or not she wanted to continue to be fed and receive treatment if she were ever to be in such a condition. Should her parents have been allowed to make life-and-death decisions under such circumstances? How clear should an incompetent person's wishes be before the parents are allowed to make a decision? The trial court granted the parents' request to withdraw life support. However, the State of Missouri intervened, claiming an "unqualified governmental interest in preserving the sanctity of human life." Although the state recognized the legal validity of "living wills," in which a person indicates what he or she would like done if the individual were no longer able to make treatment decisions, it argued that in the absence of a living will, "clear and convincing" evidence of the patient's wishes was required to authorize the removal of life-sustaining devices. Agreeing with the state, the Missouri Supreme Court reversed the trial court order directing the withdrawal of life-support equipment.

In *Cruzan* the U.S. Supreme Court granted *certiorari* to hear, for the first time, a constitutional question concerning a "right to die." Upholding the constitutionality of Missouri's evidentiary requirements, the decision of the Missouri Supreme Court was affirmed. Chief Justice William H. Rehnquist delivered the opinion of the Court and wrote that while a "right to die" might be exercised by an individual who was able to make his or her own decisions, "clear and convincing" evidence of the individual's wishes was needed before a court could allow parents or someone else to make a decision to stop treatment or care. The postscript to this issue describes what the consequences of this were for Cruzan and her parents.

The issues raised in the *Cruzan* case illustrate a basic distinction made by the law. The law prohibits active euthanasia, in which death results from some positive act, such as a lethal injection. "Mercy killings" fall into this category and can be prosecuted as acts of homicide. The law is more tolerant of passive euthanasia, in which death results from the failure to act or on the removal of life-saving equipment. This distinction is not always easy to apply, however. The activities of Dr. Jack Kevorkian, who has been helping patients to die since 1990, for example, have brought to the public attention the role of physicians in assisting individuals who are mentally competent but have physical problems that interfere with their ability to carry out their wishes.

William H. Rehnquist

 **YES**

Majority Opinion

Washington *v.* Glucksberg

CHIEF JUSTICE REHNQUIST delivered the opinion of the Court.

The question presented in this case is whether Washington's prohibition against "causing" or "aiding" a suicide offends the Fourteenth Amendment to the United States Constitution. We hold that it does not.

It has always been a crime to assist a suicide in the State of Washington. In 1854, Washington's first Territorial Legislature outlawed "assisting another in the commission of self-murder." Today, Washington law provides: "A person is guilty of promoting a suicide attempt when he knowingly causes or aids another person to attempt suicide." Wash. Rev. Code 9A.36.060(1)(1994). "Promoting a suicide attempt" is a felony, punishable by up to five years' imprisonment and up to a $10,000 fine. §§ 9A.36.060(2) and 9A.20.021(1)(c). At the same time, Washington's Natural Death Act, enacted in 1979, states that the "withholding or withdrawal of life-sustaining treatment" at a patient's direction "shall not, for any purpose, constitute a suicide." Wash. Rev. Code § 70.122.070(1).[1]

Petitioners in this case are the State of Washington and its Attorney General. Respondents Harold Glucksberg, M.D., Abigail Halperin, M.D., Thomas A. Preston, M.D., and Peter Shalit, M.D., are physicians who practice in Washington. These doctors occasionally treat terminally ill, suffering patients, and declare that they would assist these patients in ending their lives if not for Washington's assisted-suicide ban. In January 1994, respondents, along with three gravely ill, pseudonymous plaintiffs who have since died and Compassion in Dying, a nonprofit organization that counsels people considering physician-assisted suicide, sued in the United States District Court, seeking a declaration that Wash. Rev. Code 9A.36.060(1) (1994) is, on its face, unconstitutional. *Compassion in Dying v. Washington, 850 F. Supp. 1454, 1459 (WD Wash. 1994).*

The plaintiffs asserted "the existence of a liberty interest protected by the Fourteenth Amendment which extends to a personal choice by a mentally competent, terminally ill adult to commit physician-assisted suicide." Relying primarily on *Planned Parenthood v. Casey, 505 U.S. 833 (1992)*, and *Cruzan v. Director, Missouri Dept. of Health, 497 U.S. 261 (1990)*, the District Court agreed,

From *Washington et al. v. Glucksberg et al.*, 117 S. Ct. 2258, 117 S. Ct. 2302, 1997 U.S. LEXIS 4039, 138 L. Ed. 2d 772 (1997). References, some notes, and some case citations omitted.

850 F. Supp., at 1459–1462, and concluded that Washington's assisted-suicide ban is unconstitutional because it "places an undue burden on the exercise of [that] constitutionally protected liberty interest." The District Court also decided that the Washington statute violated the Equal Protection Clause's requirement that " 'all persons similarly situated ... be treated alike.' "

A panel of the Court of Appeals for the Ninth Circuit reversed, emphasizing that "in the two hundred and five years of our existence no constitutional right to aid in killing oneself has ever been asserted and upheld by a court of final jurisdiction." *Compassion in Dying v. Washington, 49 F.3d 586, 591 (1995).* The Ninth Circuit reheard the case en banc, reversed the panel's decision, and affirmed the District Court. *Compassion in Dying v. Washington, 79 F.3d 790, 798 (1996).* Like the District Court, the en banc Court of Appeals emphasized our Casey and Cruzan decisions. The court also discussed what it described as "historical" and "current societal attitudes" toward suicide and assisted suicide, and concluded that "the Constitution encompasses a due process liberty interest in controlling the time and manner of one's death—that there is, in short, a constitutionally-recognized 'right to die.' " After "weighing and then balancing" this interest against Washington's various interests, the court held that the State's assisted-suicide ban was unconstitutional "as applied to terminally ill competent adults who wish to hasten their deaths with medication prescribed by their physicians." The court did not reach the District Court's equal-protection holding. We granted certiorari, and now reverse.

I

We begin, as we do in all due-process cases, by examining our Nation's history, legal traditions, and practices. In almost every State—indeed, in almost every western democracy—it is a crime to assist a suicide. The States' assisted-suicide bans are not innovations. Rather, they are longstanding expressions of the States' commitment to the protection and preservation of all human life.

More specifically, for over 700 years, the Anglo-American common-law tradition has punished or otherwise disapproved of both suicide and assisting suicide. In the 13th century, Henry de Bracton, one of the first legal-treatise writers, observed that "just as a man may commit felony by slaying another so may he do so by slaying himself." 2 Bracton on Laws and Customs of England 423 (f. 150) (G. Woodbine ed., S. Thorne transl., 1968). The real and personal property of one who killed himself to avoid conviction and punishment for a crime were forfeit to the king; however, thought Bracton, "if a man slays himself in weariness of life or because he is unwilling to endure further bodily pain ... [only] his movable goods [were] confiscated." Thus, "the principle that suicide of a sane person, for whatever reason, was a punishable felony was ... introduced into English common law."

For the most part, the early American colonies adopted the common-law approach. For example, the legislators of the Providence Plantations, which would later become Rhode Island, declared, in 1647, that "self-murder is by all agreed to be the most unnatural, and it is by this present Assembly declared, to be that, wherein he that doth it, kills himself out of a premeditated hatred against his own life or other humor:... his goods and chattels are the king's custom, but not his debts nor lands; but in case he be an infant, a lunatic, mad or distracted man, he forfeits nothing." The Earliest Acts and Laws of the Colony of Rhode Island and Providence Plantations 1647–1719, p. 19 (J. Cushing ed. 1977). Virginia also required ignominious burial for suicides, and their estates were forfeit to the crown. A. Scott, Criminal Law in Colonial Virginia 108, and n.93, 198, and n.15 (1930).

Over time, however, the American colonies abolished these harsh common-law penalties. William Penn abandoned the criminal-forfeiture sanction in Pennsylvania in 1701, and the other colonies (and later, the other States) eventually followed this example. *Cruzan, 497 U.S. at 294* (SCALIA, J., concurring)....

[T]he movement away from the common law's harsh sanctions did not represent an acceptance of suicide; rather, as Chief Justice Swift observed, this change reflected the growing consensus that it was unfair to punish the suicide's family for his wrongdoing. Nonetheless, although States moved away from Blackstone's treatment of suicide, courts continued to condemn it as a grave public wrong.

That suicide remained a grievous, though nonfelonious, wrong is confirmed by the fact that colonial and early state legislatures and courts did not retreat from prohibiting assisting suicide. Swift, in his early 19th century treatise on the laws of Connecticut, stated that "if one counsels another to commit suicide, and the other by reason of the advice kills himself, the advisor is guilty of murder as principal." 2 Z. Swift, A Digest of the Laws of the State of Connecticut 270 (1823). This was the well established common-law view.

And the prohibitions against assisting suicide never contained exceptions for those who were near death. Rather, "the life of those to whom life had become a burden—of those who [were] hopelessly diseased or fatally wounded —nay, even the lives of criminals condemned to death, [were] under the protection of law, equally as the lives of those who [were] in the full tide of life's enjoyment, and anxious to continue to live." *Blackburn v. State, 23 Ohio St. 146, 163 (1872).*

The earliest American statute explicitly to outlaw assisting suicide was enacted in New York in 1828, and many of the new States and Territories followed New York's example. Between 1857 and 1865, a New York commission led by Dudley Field drafted a criminal code that prohibited "aiding" a suicide and, specifically, "furnishing another person with any deadly weapon or poisonous drug, knowing that such person intends to use such weapon or drug in taking his own life." By the time the Fourteenth Amendment was ratified, it was a crime in most States to assist a suicide. The Field Penal Code was adopted in the Dakota Territory in 1877, in New York in 1881, and its language served as a model for several other western States' statutes in the late 19th and early 20th centuries. California, for example, codified its assisted-suicide prohibition in 1874, using language similar to the Field Code's. In this century, the Model Penal Code also prohibited "aiding" suicide, prompting many States to enact or revise their assisted-suicide bans....

Though deeply rooted, the States' assisted-suicide bans have in recent years been reexamined and, generally, reaffirmed. Because of advances in medicine and technology, Americans today are increasingly likely to die in institutions, from chronic illnesses. Public concern and democratic action are therefore sharply focused on how best to protect dignity and independence at the end of life, with the result that there have been many significant changes in state laws and in the attitudes these laws reflect. Many States, for example, now permit "living wills," surrogate health-care decisionmaking, and the withdrawal or refusal of life-sustaining medical treatment. At the same time, however, voters and legislators continue for the most part to reaffirm their States' prohibitions on assisting suicide.

The Washington statute at issue in this case, Wash. Rev. Code § 9A.36.060 (1994), was enacted in 1975 as part of a revision of that State's criminal code. Four years later, Washington passed its Natural Death Act, which specifically stated that the "withholding or withdrawal of life-sustaining treatment . . . shall not, for any purpose, constitute a suicide" and that "nothing in this chapter shall be construed to condone, authorize, or approve mercy killing. . . ." In 1991, Washington voters rejected a ballot initiative which, had it passed, would have permitted a form of physician-assisted suicide. Washington then added a provision to the Natural Death Act expressly excluding physician-assisted suicide.

California voters rejected an assisted-suicide initiative similar to Washington's in 1993. On the other hand, in 1994, voters in Oregon enacted, also through ballot initiative, that State's "Death With Dignity Act," which legalized physician-assisted suicide for competent, terminally ill adults. Since the Oregon vote, many proposals to legalize assisted suicide have been and continue to be introduced in the States' legislatures, but none has been enacted. And just last year, Iowa and Rhode Island joined the overwhelming majority of States explicitly prohibiting assisted suicide. See Iowa Code Ann. §§ 707A.2, 707A.3 (Supp. 1997); R. I. Gen. Laws §§ 11-60-1, 11-60-3 (Supp. 1996). Also, on April 30, 1997, President Clinton signed the Federal Assisted Suicide Funding Restriction Act of 1997, which prohibits the use of federal funds in support of physician-assisted suicide. . . .

Attitudes toward suicide itself have changed since Bracton, but our laws have consistently condemned, and continue to prohibit, assisting suicide. Despite changes in medical technology and notwithstanding an increased emphasis on the importance of end-of-life decisionmaking, we have not retreated from this prohibition. Against this backdrop of history, tradition, and practice, we now turn to respondents' constitutional claim.

II

. . . In a long line of cases, we have held that, in addition to the specific freedoms protected by the Bill of Rights, the "liberty" specially protected by the Due Process Clause includes the rights to marry, *Loving v. Virginia, 388 U.S. 1 (1967)*; to have children, *Skinner v. Oklahoma ex rel. Williamson, 316 U.S. 535 (1942)*; to direct the education and upbringing of one's children, *Meyer v. Nebraska,*

262 U.S. 390 (1923); Pierce v. Society of Sisters, 268 U.S. 510 (1925); to marital privacy, *Griswold v. Connecticut, 381 U.S. 479 (1965);* to use contraception, ibid; *Eisenstadt v. Baird, 405 U.S. 438 (1972)*; to bodily integrity, *Rochin v. California, 342 U.S. 165 (1952)*, and to abortion, *Casey, supra.* We have also assumed, and strongly suggested, that the Due Process Clause protects the traditional right to refuse unwanted lifesaving medical treatment. *Cruzan, 497 U.S. at 278-279.*

But we "have always been reluctant to expand the concept of substantive due process because guideposts for responsible decisionmaking in this unchartered area are scarce and open-ended." *Collins, 503 U.S. at 125.* By extending constitutional protection to an asserted right or liberty interest, we, to a great extent, place the matter outside the arena of public debate and legislative action. We must therefore "exercise the utmost care whenever we are asked to break new ground in this field," ibid, lest the liberty protected by the Due Process Clause be subtly transformed into the policy preferences of the members of this Court, *Moore, 431 U.S. at 502* (plurality opinion).

Our established method of substantive-due-process analysis has two primary features: First, we have regularly observed that the Due Process Clause specially protects those fundamental rights and liberties which are, objectively, "deeply rooted in this Nation's history and tradition," *id., at 503* (plurality opinion); *Snyder v. Massachusetts, 291 U.S. 97, 105 (1934)* ("so rooted in the traditions and conscience of our people as to be ranked as fundamental"), and "implicit in the concept of ordered liberty," such that "neither liberty nor justice would exist if they were sacrificed," *Palko v. Connecticut, 302 U.S. 319, 325, 326 (1937).* Second, we have required in substantive-due-process cases a "careful description" of the asserted fundamental liberty interest. Our Nation's history, legal traditions, and practices thus provide the crucial "guideposts for responsible decisionmaking," that direct and restrain our exposition of the Due Process Clause. As we stated recently in Flores, the Fourteenth Amendment "forbids the government to infringe ... 'fundamental' liberty interests at all, no matter what process is provided, unless the infringement is narrowly tailored to serve a compelling state interest." *507 U.S. at 302.*

JUSTICE SOUTER, relying on Justice Harlan's dissenting opinion in Poe v. Ullman, would largely abandon this restrained methodology, and instead ask "whether [Washington's] statute sets up one of those 'arbitrary impositions' or 'purposeless restraints' at odds with the Due Process Clause of the Fourteenth Amendment," post, at 1 (quoting *Poe, 367 U.S. 497, 543 (1961)* (Harlan, J., dissenting)). In our view, however, the development of this Court's substantive-due-process jurisprudence, described briefly above, has been a process whereby the outlines of the "liberty" specially protected by the Fourteenth Amendment— never fully clarified, to be sure, and perhaps not capable of being fully clarified —have at least been carefully refined by concrete examples involving fundamental rights found to be deeply rooted in our legal tradition. This approach tends to rein in the subjective elements that are necessarily present in due-process judicial review. In addition, by establishing a threshold requirement— that a challenged state action implicate a fundamental right—before requiring more than a reasonable relation to a legitimate state interest to justify the action, it avoids the need for complex balancing of competing interests in every case.

Turning to the claim at issue here, the Court of Appeals stated that "properly analyzed, the first issue to be resolved is whether there is a liberty interest in determining the time and manner of one's death," or, in other words, "is there a right to die?" Similarly, respondents assert a "liberty to choose how to die" and a right to "control of one's final days," and describe the asserted liberty as "the right to choose a humane, dignified death," and "the liberty to shape death." As noted above, we have a tradition of carefully formulating the interest at stake in substantive-due-process cases. For example, although Cruzan is often described as a "right to die" case, see *79 F.3d, at 799; post, at 9* (STEVENS, J., concurring in judgment) (Cruzan recognized "the more specific interest in making decisions about how to confront an imminent death"), we were, in fact, more precise: we assumed that the Constitution granted competent persons a "constitutionally protected right to refuse lifesaving hydration and nutrition." *Cruzan, 497 U.S. at 279; id., at 287* (O'CONNOR, J., concurring) ("[A] liberty interest in refusing unwanted medical treatment may be inferred from our prior decisions"). The Washington statute at issue in this case prohibits "aiding another person to attempt suicide," Wash. Rev. Code § 9A.36.060(1) (1994), and, thus, the question before us is whether the "liberty" specially protected by the Due Process Clause includes a right to commit suicide which itself includes a right to assistance in doing so.

We now inquire whether this asserted right has any place in our Nation's traditions. Here, as discussed above, we are confronted with a consistent and almost universal tradition that has long rejected the asserted right, and continues explicitly to reject it today, even for terminally ill, mentally competent adults. To hold for respondents, we would have to reverse centuries of legal doctrine and practice, and strike down the considered policy choice of almost every State.

Respondents contend, however, that the liberty interest they assert is consistent with this Court's substantive-due-process line of cases, if not with this Nation's history and practice. Pointing to Casey and Cruzan, respondents read our jurisprudence in this area as reflecting a general tradition of "self-sovereignty," and as teaching that the "liberty" protected by the Due Process Clause includes "basic and intimate exercises of personal autonomy" ("It is a promise of the Constitution that there is a realm of personal liberty which the government may not enter"). According to respondents, our liberty jurisprudence, and the broad, individualistic principles it reflects, protects the "liberty of competent, terminally ill adults to make end-of-life decisions free of undue government interference." Brief for Respondents 10. The question presented in this case, however, is whether the protections of the Due Process Clause include a right to commit suicide with another's assistance. With this "careful description" of respondents' claim in mind, we turn to Casey and Cruzan.

In Cruzan, we considered whether Nancy Beth Cruzan, who had been severely injured in an automobile accident and was in a persistive vegetative state, "had a right under the United States Constitution which would require the hospital to withdraw life-sustaining treatment" at her parents' request. We began with the observation that "at common law, even the touching of one person by another without consent and without legal justification was a battery." We then discussed the related rule that "informed consent is generally required for medical treatment." After reviewing a long line of relevant state cases, we concluded that "the common-law doctrine of informed consent is viewed as generally encompassing the right of a competent individual to refuse medical treatment." Next, we reviewed our own cases on the subject, and stated that "the principle that a competent person has a constitutionally protected liberty interest in refusing unwanted medical treatment may be inferred from our prior decisions." Therefore, "for purposes of [that] case, we assumed that the United States Constitution would grant a competent person a constitutionally protected right to refuse lifesaving hydration and nutrition." We concluded that, notwithstanding this right, the Constitution permitted Missouri to require clear and convincing evidence of an incompetent patient's wishes concerning the withdrawal of life-sustaining treatment.

Respondents contend that in Cruzan we "acknowledged that competent, dying persons have the right to direct the removal of life-sustaining medical treatment and thus hasten death," Brief for Respondents 23, and that "the constitutional principle behind recognizing the patient's liberty to direct the withdrawal of artificial life support applies at least as strongly to the choice to hasten impending death by consuming lethal medication." Similarly, the Court of Appeals concluded that "Cruzan, by recognizing a liberty interest that includes the refusal of artificial provision of life-sustaining food and water, necessarily recognized a liberty interest in hastening one's own death." *79 F.3d, at 816.*

The right assumed in Cruzan, however, was not simply deduced from abstract concepts of personal autonomy. Given the common-law rule that forced medication was a battery, and the long legal tradition protecting the decision to refuse unwanted medical treatment, our assumption was entirely consistent with this Nation's history and constitutional traditions. The decision to commit suicide with the assistance of another may be just as personal and profound as the decision to refuse unwanted medical treatment, but it has never enjoyed similar legal protection. Indeed, the two acts are widely and reasonably regarded as quite distinct. In Cruzan itself, we recognized that most States outlawed assisted suicide—and even more do today—and we certainly gave no intimation that the right to refuse unwanted medical treatment could be somehow transmuted into a right to assistance in committing suicide.

Respondents also rely on Casey. There, the Court's opinion concluded that "the essential holding of Roe v. Wade should be retained and once again reaffirmed." *Casey, 505 U.S. at 846.* We held, first, that a woman has a right, before her fetus is viable, to an abortion "without undue interference from the State"; second, that States may restrict post-viability abortions, so long as exceptions are made to protect a woman's life and health; and third, that the State has legitimate interests throughout a pregnancy in protecting the health of the woman and the life of the unborn child. Ibid. In reaching this conclusion, the opinion discussed in some detail this Court's substantive-due-process tradition of interpreting the Due Process Clause to protect certain fundamental rights and "personal decisions relating to marriage, procreation, contraception, family relationships, child rearing, and education," and noted that many of those rights and liberties "involve the most intimate and personal choices a person may make in a lifetime."

The Court of Appeals, like the District Court, found Casey " 'highly instructive' " and " 'almost prescriptive' " for determining " 'what liberty interest may inhere in a terminally ill person's choice to commit suicide' ":

> "Like the decision of whether or not to have an abortion, the decision how and when to die is one of 'the most intimate and personal choices a person may make in a lifetime,' a choice 'central to personal dignity and autonomy.' " *79 F.3d, at 813–814.*

Similarly, respondents emphasize the statement in Casey that:

> "At the heart of liberty is the right to define one's own concept of existence, of meaning, of the universe, and of the mystery of human life. Beliefs about these matters could not define the attributes of personhood were they formed under compulsion of the State." *Casey, 505 U.S. at 851.*

… By choosing this language, the Court's opinion in Casey described, in a general way and in light of our prior cases, those personal activities and decisions that this Court has identified as so deeply rooted in our history and traditions, or so fundamental to our concept of constitutionally ordered liberty, that they are protected by the Fourteenth Amendment. The opinion moved from the recognition that liberty necessarily includes freedom of conscience and belief about ultimate considerations to the observation that "though the abortion decision may originate within the zone of conscience and belief, it is more than a philosophic exercise." *Casey, 505 U.S. at 852....* That many of the rights and liberties protected by the Due Process Clause sound in personal autonomy does not warrant the sweeping conclusion that any and all important, intimate, and personal decisions are so protected, *San Antonio Independent School Dist. v. Rodriguez, 411 U.S. 1, 33–35 (1973),* and Casey did not suggest otherwise.

The history of the law's treatment of assisted suicide in this country has been and continues to be one of the rejection of nearly all efforts to permit it. That being the case, our decisions lead us to conclude that the asserted "right" to assistance in committing suicide is not a fundamental liberty interest protected by the Due Process Clause. The Constitution also requires, however, that Washington's assisted-suicide ban be rationally related to legitimate government interests. See *Heller v. Doe, 509 U.S. 312, 319–320 (1993); Flores, 507 U.S. at 305.* This requirement is unquestionably met here. As the court below recognized, Washington's assisted-suicide ban implicates a number of state interests.

First, Washington has an "unqualified interest in the preservation of human life." *Cruzan, 497 U.S. at 282.* The State's prohibition on assisted suicide, like all homicide laws, both reflects and advances its commitment to this interest. ("The interests in the sanctity of life that are represented by the criminal homicide laws are threatened by one who expresses a willingness to participate in taking the life of another"). This interest is symbolic and aspirational as well as practical:

> "While suicide is no longer prohibited or penalized, the ban against assisted suicide and euthanasia shores up the notion of limits in human relationships. It reflects the gravity with which we view the decision to take one's own life or the life of another, and our reluctance to encourage or promote these decisions." New York Task Force 131–132.

Respondents admit that "the State has a real interest in preserving the lives of those who can still contribute to society and enjoy life." Brief for Respondents 35, n.23. The Court of Appeals also recognized Washington's interest in protecting life, but held that the "weight" of this interest depends on the "medical condition and the wishes of the person whose life is at stake." *79 F.3d, at 817.* Washington, however, has rejected this sliding-scale approach and, through its assisted-suicide ban, insists that all persons' lives, from beginning to end, regardless of physical or mental condition, are under the full protection of the law. See *United States v. Rutherford, 442, U.S. 544, 558 (1979)* (" ... Congress could reasonably have determined to protect the terminally ill, no less than other patients, from the vast range of self-styled panaceas that inventive minds can devise"). As we have previously affirmed, the States "may properly decline to make judgments about the 'quality' of life that a particular individual may enjoy," *Cruzan, 497 U.S. at 282.* This remains true, as Cruzan makes clear, even for those who are near death.

Relatedly, all admit that suicide is a serious public-health problem, especially among persons in otherwise vulnerable groups.

Those who attempt suicide—terminally ill or not—often suffer from depression or other mental disorders. Research indicates, however, that many people who request physician-assisted suicide withdraw that request if their depression and pain are treated. The New York Task Force, however, expressed its concern that, because depression is difficult to diagnose, physicians and medical professionals often fail to respond adequately to seriously ill patients' needs. Thus, legal physician-assisted suicide could make it more difficult for the State to protect depressed or mentally ill persons, or those who are suffering from untreated pain, from suicidal impulses.

The State also has an interest in protecting the integrity and ethics of the medical profession. In contrast to the Court of Appeals' conclusion that "the integrity of the medical profession would [not] be threatened in any way [by physician-assisted suicide]," *79 F.3d, at 827,* the American Medical Association, like many other medical and physicians' groups, has concluded that "physician-assisted suicide is fundamentally incompatible with the physician's role as healer." American Medical Association, Code of Ethics § 2.211 (1994); see Council on Ethical and Judicial Affairs, Decisions Near the End of Life, *267 JAMA 2229, 2233 (1992)* ("The societal risks of involving physicians in medical interventions to cause patients' deaths is too great"); New York Task Force 103–109 (discussing physicians' views). And physician-assisted suicide could, it is argued, undermine the trust that is essential to the doctor-patient relationship by blurring the time-honored line between healing and harming.

Next, the State has an interest in protecting vulnerable groups—including the poor, the elderly, and disabled persons—from abuse, neglect, and mistakes. The Court of Appeals dismissed the State's concern that disadvantaged persons might be pressured into physician-assisted suicide as "ludicrous on its face." *79 F.3d, at 825.* We have recognized, however, the real risk of subtle coercion and undue influence in end-of-life situations. *Cruzan, 497 U.S. at 281.* Similarly, the New York Task Force warned that "legalizing physician-assisted suicide would pose profound risks to many individuals who are ill and vulnerable.... The risk of harm is greatest for the many individuals in our society whose autonomy and well-being are already compromised by poverty, lack of access to good medical care, advanced age, or membership in a stigmatized social group." If physician-assisted suicide were permitted, many might resort to it to spare their families the substantial financial burden of end-of-life health-care costs.

The State's interest here goes beyond protecting the vulnerable from coercion; it extends to protecting disabled and terminally ill people from prejudice, negative and inaccurate stereotypes, and "societal indifference." *49 F.3d, at 592.* The state's assisted-suicide ban reflects and reinforces its policy that the lives of terminally ill, disabled, and elderly people must be no less valued than the lives of the young and healthy, and that a seriously disabled person's suicidal impulses should be interpreted and treated the same way as anyone else's.

Finally, the State may fear that permitting assisted suicide will start it down the path to voluntary and perhaps even involuntary euthanasia. The Court of Appeals struck down Washington's assisted-suicide ban only "as applied to competent, terminally ill adults who wish to hasten their deaths by obtaining medication prescribed by their doctors." *79 F.3d, at 838.* Washington insists, however, that the impact of the court's decision will not and cannot be so limited. If suicide is protected as a matter of constitutional right, it is argued, "every man and woman in the United States must enjoy it."

The Court of Appeals' decision, and its expansive reasoning, provide ample support for the State's concerns. The court noted, for example, that the "decision of a duly appointed surrogate decision maker is for all legal purposes the decision of the patient himself," *79 F.3d, at 832, n.120;* that "in some instances, the patient may be unable to self-administer the drugs and ... administration by the physician ... may be the only way the patient may be able to receive them," *id., at 831;* and that not only physicians, but also family members and loved ones, will inevitably participate in assisting suicide. *Id., at 838, n.140.* Thus, it turns out that what is couched as a limited right to "physician-assisted suicide" is likely, in effect, a much broader license, which could prove extremely difficult to police and contain. Washington's ban on assisting suicide prevents such erosion.

This concern is further supported by evidence about the practice of euthanasia in the Netherlands. The Dutch government's own study revealed that in 1990, there were 2,300 cases of voluntary euthanasia (defined as "the deliberate termination of another's life at his request"), 400 cases of assisted suicide, and more than 1,000 cases of euthanasia without an explicit request. In addition to these latter 1,000 cases, the study found an additional 4,941 cases where physicians administered lethal morphine overdoses without the patients' explicit consent. Physician-Assisted Suicide and Euthanasia in the Netherlands: A Report of Chairman Charles T. Canady, at 12–13 (citing Dutch study). This study suggests that, despite the existence of various reporting procedures, euthanasia in the Netherlands has not been limited to competent, terminally ill adults who are enduring physical suffering, and that regulation of the practice may not have prevented abuses in cases involving vulnerable persons, including severely disabled neonates and elderly persons suffering from dementia. The New York Task Force, citing the Dutch experience, observed that "assisted suicide and euthanasia are closely linked," New York Task Force 145, and concluded that the "risk of... abuse is neither speculative nor distant." Washington, like most other States, reasonably ensures against this risk by banning, rather than regulating, assisting suicide.

We need not weigh exactingly the relative strengths of these various interests. They are unquestionably important and legitimate, and Washington's ban on assisted suicide is at least reasonably related to their promotion and protection. We therefore hold that Wash. Rev. Code § 9A.36.060(1)(1994) does not violate the Fourteenth Amendment, either on its face or "as applied to competent, terminally ill adults who wish to hasten their deaths by obtaining medication prescribed by their doctors." *79 F.3d, at 838.*

Throughout the Nation, Americans are engaged in an earnest and profound debate about the morality, legality, and practicality of physician-assisted suicide. Our holding permits this debate to continue, as it should in a democratic society. The decision of the en banc Court of Appeals is reversed, and the case is remanded for further proceedings consistent with this opinion.

Note

1. Under Washington's Natural Death Act, "adult persons have the fundamental right to control the decisions relating to the rendering of their own health care, including the decision to have life-sustaining treatment withheld or withdrawn in instances of a terminal condition or permanent unconscious condition." Wash. Rev. Code § 70.122.010 (1994). In Washington, "any adult person may execute a directive directing the withholding or withdrawal of life-sustaining treatment in a terminal condition or permanent unconscious condition," § 70.122.030, and a physician who, in accordance with such a directive, participates in the withholding or withdrawal of life-sustaining treatment is immune from civil, criminal, or professional liability. § 70.122.051.

NO ⬅

Stephen Reinhardt

Majority Opinion

Compassion in Dying *v.* State of Washington

I.

This case raises an extraordinarily important and difficult issue. It compels us to address questions to which there are no easy or simple answers, at law or otherwise. It requires us to confront the most basic of human concerns—the mortality of self and loved ones—and to balance the interest in preserving human life against the desire to die peacefully and with dignity. People of good will can and do passionately disagree about the proper result, perhaps even more intensely than they part ways over the constitutionality of restricting a woman's right to have an abortion. Heated though the debate may be, we must determine whether and how the United States Constitution applies to the controversy before us, a controversy that may touch more people more profoundly than any other issue the courts will face in the foreseeable future.

Today, we are required to decide whether a person who is terminally ill has a constitutionally-protected liberty interest in hastening what might otherwise be a protracted, undignified, and extremely painful death. If such an interest exists, we must next decide whether or not the state of Washington may constitutionally restrict its exercise by banning a form of medical assistance that is frequently requested by terminally ill people who wish to die. We first conclude that there is a constitutionally-protected liberty interest in determining the time and manner of one's own death, an interest that must be weighed against the state's legitimate and countervailing interests, especially those that relate to the preservation of human life. After balancing the competing interests, we conclude by answering the narrow question before us: We hold that insofar as the Washington statute prohibits physicians from prescribing life-ending medication for use by terminally ill, competent adults who wish to hasten their own deaths, it violates the Due Process Clause of the Fourteenth Amendment.

From *Compassion in Dying v. State of Washington,* 96 C.D.O.S. 1507 (1996).

II. Preliminary Matters and History of the Case

... The plaintiffs do not challenge Washington statute RCW 9A.36.060 in its entirety. Specifically they do not object to the portion of the Washington statute that makes it unlawful for a person knowingly to cause another to commit suicide. Rather, they only challenge the statute's "or aids" provision. They challenge that provision both on its face and as applied to terminally ill, mentally competent adults who wish to hasten their own deaths with the help of medication prescribed by their doctors. The plaintiffs contend that the provision impermissibly prevents the exercise by terminally ill patients of a constitutionally-protected liberty interest in violation of the Due Process Clause of the Fourteenth Amendment, and also that it impermissibly distinguishes between similarly situated terminally ill patients in violation of the Equal Protection Clause....

III. Overview of Legal Analysis: Is There a Due Process Violation?

In order to answer the question whether the Washington statute violates the Due Process Clause insofar as it prohibits the provision of certain medical assistance to terminally ill, competent adults who wish to hasten their own deaths, we first determine whether there is a liberty interest in choosing the time and manner of one's death—a question sometimes phrased in common parlance as: Is there a right to die? Because we hold that there is, we must then determine whether prohibiting physicians from prescribing life-ending medication for use by terminally ill patients who wish to die violates the patients' due process rights.

The mere recognition of a liberty interest does not mean that a state may not prohibit the exercise of that interest in particular circumstances, nor does it mean that a state may not adopt appropriate regulations governing its exercise. Rather, in cases like the one before us, the courts must apply a balancing test under which we weigh the individual's liberty interests against the relevant state interests in order to determine whether the state's actions are constitutionally permissible....

Defining the Liberty Interest and Other Relevant Terms

... While some people refer to the liberty interest implicated in right-to-die cases as a liberty interest in committing suicide, we do not describe it that way. We use the broader and more accurate terms, "the right to die," "determining the time and manner of one's death," and "hastening one's death" for an important reason. The liberty interest we examine encompasses a whole range of acts that are generally not considered to constitute "suicide." Included within the liberty interest we examine, is for example, the act of refusing or terminating unwanted medical treatment ... a competent adult has a liberty interest in refusing to be connected to a respirator or in being disconnected from one, even if he is terminally ill and cannot live without mechanical assistance. The law does not classify the death of a patient that results from the granting of his wish to decline or discontinue treatment as "suicide." Nor does the law label the acts of those who help the patient carry out that wish, whether by physically disconnecting the respirator or by removing an intravenous tube, as assistance in suicide. Accordingly, we believe that the broader terms—"the right to die," "controlling the time and manner of one's death," and "hastening one's death" —more accurately describe the liberty interest at issue here. . . .

Like the Court in *Roe [v. Wade]*, we begin with ancient attitudes. In Greek and Roman times, far from being universally prohibited, suicide was often considered commendable in literature, mythology, and practice. . . .

While Socrates counseled his disciples against committing suicide, he willingly drank the hemlock as he was condemned to do, and his example inspired others to end their lives. Plato, Socrates' most distinguished student, believed suicide was often justifiable.

He suggested that if life itself became immoderate, then suicide became a rational, justifiable act. Painful disease, or intolerable constraint were sufficient reasons to depart. And this when religious superstitions faded was philosophic justification enough.

Many contemporaries of Plato were even more inclined to find suicide a legitimate and acceptable act. In *Roe,* while surveying the attitudes of the Greeks toward abortion, the Court stated that "only the Pythagorean school of philosophers frowned on the related act of suicide," 410 U.S. at 131; it then noted that the Pythagorean school represented a distinctly minority view. *Id.*

The Stoics glorified suicide as an act of pure rational will. Cato, who killed himself to avoid dishonor when Ceasar crushed his military aspirations, was the most celebrated of the many suicides among the Stoics. Montaigne wrote of Cato: "This was a man chosen by nature to show the heights which can be attained by human steadfastness and constancy. . . . Such courage is above philosophy."

Like the Greeks, the Romans often considered suicide to be acceptable or even laudable.

To live nobly also meant to die nobly and at the right time. Everything depended on a dominant will and a rational choice. . . .

Suicide was a crime under the English common law, at least in limited circumstances, probably as early as the thirteenth century. Bracton, incorporating Roman Law as set forth in Justinian's Digest, declared that if someone commits suicide to avoid conviction of a felony, his property escheats to his lords. Bracton said "[i]t ought to be otherwise if he kills himself through madness or unwillingness to endure suffering." Despite his general fidelity to Roman law, Bracton did introduce a key innovation: "[I]f a man slays himself in weariness of life or because he is unwilling to endure further bodily pain . . . he may have a successor, but his movable goods [personal property] are confiscated. He does not lose his inheritance [real property], only his movable goods." Bracton's innovation was incorporated into English common law, which has thus treated suicides resulting from the inability to "endure further bodily pain" with compassion and understanding ever since a common law scheme was firmly established. . . .

English attitudes toward suicide, including the tradition of ignominious burial, carried over to America where they subsequently underwent a transformation. By 1798, six of the 13 original colonies had abolished all penalties for suicide either by statute or state constitution. There is no evidence that any court ever imposed a punishment for suicide or attempted suicide under common law in post-revolutionary America. By the time the Fourteenth Amendment was adopted in 1868, suicide was generally not punishable, and in only nine of the 37 states is it clear that there were statutes prohibiting assisting suicide.

The majority of states have not criminalized suicide or attempted suicide since the turn of the century. The New Jersey Supreme Court declared in 1901 that since suicide was not punishable it should not be considered a crime. "[A]ll will admit that in some cases it is ethically defensible," the court said, as when a woman kills herself to escape being raped or "when a man curtails weeks or months of agony of an incurable disease." *Campbell v. Supreme Conclave Improved Order Heptasophs,* 66 N.J.L. 274, 49 A. 550, 553 (1901). Today, no state has a statute prohibiting suicide or attempted suicide; nor has any state had such a statute for at least 10 years. A majority of states do, however, still have laws on the books against assisting suicide.

Current Societal Attitudes

Clearly the absence of a criminal sanction alone does not show societal approbation of a practice. Nor is there any evidence that Americans approve of suicide in general. In recent years, however, there has been increasingly widespread support for allowing the terminally ill to hasten their deaths and avoid painful, undignified, and inhumane endings to their lives. Most Americans simply do not appear to view such acts as constituting suicide, and there is much support in reason for that conclusion.

Polls have repeatedly shown that a large majority of Americans—sometimes nearing 90%—fully endorse recent legal changes granting terminally ill patients, and sometimes their families, the prerogative to accelerate their death by refusing or terminating treatment. Other polls indicate that a majority of Americans favor doctor-assisted suicide for the terminally ill. In April, 1990, the Roper Report found that 64% of Americans believed that the terminally ill should have the right to request and receive physician aid-in-dying. Another national poll, conducted in October 1991, shows that "nearly two out of three Americans favor doctor-assisted suicide and euthanasia for terminally ill patients who request it." A 1994 Harris poll found 73% of Americans favor legalizing physician-assisted suicide. Three states have held referenda on proposals to allow physicians to help terminally ill, competent adults commit suicide with somewhat mixed results. In Oregon, voters approved the carefully-crafted referendum by a margin of 51 to 49 percent in November of 1994. In Washington and California where the measures contained far fewer practical safeguards, they narrowly failed to pass.... Accounts of doctors who have helped their patients end their lives have appeared both in professional journals and in the daily press....

Liberty Interest Under Casey

In *[Planned Parenthood v.] Casey,* the Court surveyed its prior decisions affording "constitutional protection to personal decisions relating to marriage, procreation, contraception, family relationships, child rearing, and education," *id.* at 2807 and then said:

> These matters, involving the most intimate and personal choices a person may make in a lifetime, choices central to personal dignity and autonomy, are central to the liberty protected by the Fourteenth Amendment. At the heart of liberty is the right to define one's own concept of existence, of meaning, of the universe, and of the mystery of human life. Beliefs about these matters could not define the attributes of personhood were they formed under compulsion of the State. The district judge in this case found the Court's reasoning in *Casey* "highly instructive" and "almost prescriptive" for determining "what liberty interest may inhere in a terminally ill person's choice to commit suicide." Compassion In Dying, 850 F. Supp. at 1459. We agree.

Like the decision of whether or not to have an abortion, the decision how and when to die is one of "the most intimate and personal choices a person may make in a lifetime," a choice "central to personal dignity and autonomy." A competent terminally ill adult, having lived nearly the full measure of his life, has a strong liberty interest in choosing a dignified and humane death rather than being reduced at the end of his existence to a childlike state of helplessness, diapered, sedated, incontinent. How a person dies not only determines the nature of the final period of his existence, but in many cases, the enduring memories held by those who love him.

Prohibiting a terminally ill patient from hastening his death may have an even more profound impact on that person's life than forcing a woman to carry a pregnancy to term. The case of an AIDS patient treated by Dr. Peter Shalit, one of the physician-plaintiffs in this case, provides a compelling illustration. In his declaration, Dr. Shalit described his patient's death this way:

> One patient of mine, whom I will call Smith, a fictitious name, lingered in the hospital for weeks, his lower body so swollen from oozing Kaposi's lesions that he could not walk, his genitals so swollen that he required a catheter to drain his bladder, his fingers gangrenous from clotted arteries. Patient Smith's friends stopped visiting him because it gave them nightmares. Patient Smith's agonies could not be relieved by medication or by the excellent nursing care he received. Patient Smith begged for assistance in hastening his death. As his treating doctor, it was my professional opinion that patient Smith was mentally competent to make a choice with respect to shortening his period of suffering before inevitable death. I felt that I should accommodate his request. However, because of the statute, I was unable to assist him and he died after having been tortured for weeks by the end-phase of his disease.

For such patients, wracked by pain and deprived of all pleasure, a state-enforced prohibition on hastening their deaths condemns them to unrelieved misery or torture. Surely, a person's decision whether to endure or avoid such an existence constitutes one of the most, if not the most, "intimate and personal choices a person may make in a life-time," a choice that is "central to personal dignity and autonomy." *Casey,* 112 S.Ct. at 2807....

Cruzan stands for the proposition that there is a due process liberty interest in rejecting unwanted medical treatment, including the provision of food and water by artificial means. Moreover, the Court majority clearly recognized that granting the request to remove the tubes through which Cruzan received artificial nutrition and hydration would lead inexorably to her death. *Cruzan,* 497 U.S. at 267–68, 283. Accordingly, we conclude that *Cruzan,* by recognizing a liberty interest that includes the refusal of artificial provision of life-sustaining food and water, necessarily recognizes a liberty interest in hastening one's own death.

Summary

Casey and *Cruzan* provide persuasive evidence that the Constitution encompasses a due process liberty interest in controlling the time and manner of one's death—that there is, in short, a constitutionally recognized "right to die." Our conclusion is strongly influenced by, but not limited to, the plight of mentally competent, terminally ill adults. We are influenced as well by the plight of others, such as those whose existence is reduced to a vegetative state or a permanent and irreversible state of unconsciousness.

Our conclusion that there is a liberty interest in determining the time and manner of one's death does not mean that there is a concomitant right to exercise that interest in all circumstances or to do so free from state regulation. To the contrary, we explicitly recognize that some prohibitory and regulatory state action is fully consistent with constitutional principles.

In short, finding a liberty interest constitutes a critical first step toward answering the question before us. The determination that must now be made is whether the state's attempt to curtail the exercise of that interest is constitutionally justified.

V. Relevant Factors and Interests

To determine whether a state action that impairs a liberty interest violates an individual's substantive due process rights we must identify the factors relevant to the case at hand, assess the state's interests and the individual's liberty interest in light of those factors, and then weigh and balance the competing interests. The relevant factors generally include: 1) the importance of the various state interests, both in general and in the factual context of the case; 2) the manner in which those interests are furthered by the state law or regulation; 3) the importance of the liberty interest, both in itself and in the context in which it is being exercised; 4) the extent to which that interest is burdened by the challenged state action; and, 5) the consequences of upholding or overturning the statute or regulation....

B. The Means by Which the State Furthers Its Interests

In applying the balancing test, we must take into account not only the strength of the state's interests but also the means by which the state has chosen to further those interests.

1. Prohibition—A Total Ban for the Terminally Ill

Washington's statute prohibiting assisted suicide has a drastic impact on the terminally ill. By prohibiting physician assistance, it bars what for many terminally ill patients is the only palatable, and only practical, way to end their lives. Physically frail, confined to wheelchairs or beds, many terminally ill patients do not have the means or ability to kill themselves in the multitude of ways that healthy individuals can. Often, for example, they cannot even secure the medication or devices they would need to carry out their wishes.

Some terminally ill patients stockpile prescription medicine, which they can use to end their lives when they decide the time is right. The successful use of the stockpile technique generally depends, however, on the assistance of a physician, whether tacit or unknowing (although it is possible to end one's life with over-the-counter medication). Even if the terminally ill patients are able to accumulate sufficient drugs, given the pain killers and other medication they are taking, most of them would lack the knowledge to determine what dose of any given drug or drugs they must take, or in what combination. Miscalculation can be tragic. It can lead to an even more painful and lingering death. Alternatively, if the medication reduces respiration enough to restrict the flow of oxygen to the brain but not enough to cause death, it can result in the patient's falling into a comatose or vegetative state.

Thus for many terminally ill patients, the Washington statute is effectively a prohibition. While technically it only prohibits one means of exercising a liberty interest, practically it prohibits the exercise of that interest as effectively as prohibiting doctors from performing abortions prevented women from having abortions in the days before *Roe*.

2. Regulation—A Permissible Means of Promoting State Interests

State laws or regulations governing physician-assisted suicide are both necessary and desirable to ensure against errors and abuse, and to protect legitimate state interests. Any of several model statutes might serve as an example of how these legitimate and important concerns can be addressed effectively.

By adopting appropriate, reasonable, and properly drawn safeguards Washington could ensure that people who choose to have their doctors prescribe lethal doses of medication are truly competent and meet all of the requisite standards. Without endorsing the constitutionality of any particular procedural safeguards, we note that the state might, for example, require: witnesses to ensure voluntariness; reasonable, though short, waiting periods to prevent rash decisions; second medical opinions to confirm a patient's terminal status and also to confirm that the patient has been receiving proper treatment, including adequate comfort care; psychological examinations to ensure that the patient is not suffering from momentary or treatable depression; reporting procedures that will aid in the avoidance of abuse. Alternatively, such safeguards could be adopted by interested medical associations and other organizations involved in the provision of health care, so long as they meet the state's needs and concerns....

E. The Consequences of Upholding or Overturning the Statutory Provision

In various earlier sections of this opinion, we have discussed most of the consequences of upholding or overturning the Washington statutory provision at issue, because in this case those consequences are best considered as part of the discussion of the specific factors or interests. The one remaining consequence of significance is easy to identify: Whatever the outcome here, a host of painful and agonizing issues involving the right to die will continue to confront the courts. More important, these problems will continue to plague growing numbers of Americans of advanced age as well as their families, dependents, and loved ones. The issue is truly one which deserves the most thorough, careful, and objective attention from all segments of society.

VI. Application of the Balancing Test and Holding

Weighing and then balancing a constitutionally-protected interest against the state's countervailing interests, while bearing in mind the various consequences of the decision, is quintessentially a judicial role. Despite all of the efforts of generations of courts to categorize and objectify, to create multi-part tests and identify weights to be attached to the various factors, in the end balancing entails the exercise of judicial judgment rather than the application of scientific or mathematical formulae. No legislative body can perform the task for us. Nor can any computer. In the end, mindful of our constitutional obligations, including the limitations imposed on us by that document, we must rely on our judgment, guided by the facts and the law as we perceive them.

As we have explained, in this case neither the liberty interest in choosing the time and manner of death nor the state's countervailing interests are static. The magnitude of each depends on objective circumstances and generally varies inversely with the other. The liberty interest in hastening death is at its strongest when the state's interest in protecting life and preventing suicide is at its weakest, and vice-versa.

The liberty interest at issue here is an important one and, in the case of the terminally ill, is at its peak. Conversely, the state interests, while equally important in the abstract, are for the most part at a low point here. We recognize that in the case of life and death decisions the state has a particularly strong interest in avoiding undue influence and other forms of abuse. Here, that concern is ameliorated in large measure because of the mandatory involvement in the decision-making process of physicians, who have a strong bias in favor of preserving life, and because the process itself can be carefully regulated and rigorous safeguards adopted. Under these circumstances, we believe that the possibility of abuse, even when considered along with the other state interests, does not outweigh the liberty interest at issue.

The state has chosen to pursue its interests by means of what for terminally ill patients is effectively a total prohibition, even though its most important interests could be adequately served by a far less burdensome measure. The consequences of rejecting the as-applied challenge would be disastrous for the terminally ill, while the adverse consequences for the state would be of a far lesser order. This, too, weighs in favor of upholding the liberty interest.

We consider the state's interests in preventing assisted suicide as being different only in degree and not in kind from its interests in prohibiting a number of other medical practices that lead directly to a terminally ill patient's death. Moreover, we do not consider those interests to be significantly greater in the case of assisted suicide than they are in the case of those other medical practices, if indeed they are greater at all. However, even if the difference were one of kind and not degree, our result would be no different. For no matter how much weight we could legitimately afford the state's interest in preventing suicide, that weight, when combined with the weight we give all the other state's interests, is insufficient to outweigh the terminally ill individual's interest in deciding whether to end his agony and suffering by hastening the time of his death with medication prescribed by his physician. The individual's interest in making that vital decision is compelling indeed, for no decision is more painful, delicate, personal, important, or final than the decision how and when one's life shall end. If broad general state policies can be used to deprive a terminally ill individual of the right to make that choice, it is hard to envision where the exercise of arbitrary and intrusive power by the state can be halted. In this case, the state has wide power to regulate, but it may not ban the exercise of the liberty interest, and that is the practical effect of the program before us. Accordingly, after examining one final legal authority, we hold that the "or aids" provision of Washington statute RCW 9A.36.06 is unconstitutional as applied to terminally ill competent adults who wish to hasten their deaths with medication prescribed by their physicians. . . .

VII. Conclusion

We hold that a liberty interest exists in the choice of how and when one dies, and that the provision of the Washington statute banning assisted suicide, as applied to competent, terminally ill adults who wish to hasten their deaths by obtaining medication prescribed by their doctors, violates the Due Process Clause. We recognize that this decision is a most difficult and controversial one, and that it leaves unresolved a large number of equally troublesome issues that will require resolution in the years ahead. We also recognize that other able and dedicated jurists, construing the Constitution as they believe it must be construed, may disagree not only with the result we reach but with our method of constitutional analysis. Given the nature of the judicial process and the complexity of the task of determining the rights and interests comprehended by the Constitution, good faith disagreements within the judiciary should not surprise or disturb anyone who follows the development of the law. For these reasons, we express our hope that whatever debate may accompany the future exploration of the issues we have touched on today will be conducted in an objective, rational, and constructive manner that will increase, not diminish, respect for the Constitution.

There is one final point we must emphasize. Some argue strongly that decisions regarding matters affecting life or death should not be made by the courts. Essentially, we agree with that proposition. In this case, by permitting the individual to exercise the right to choose we are following the constitutional mandate to take such decisions out of the hands of the government, both state and federal, and to put them where they rightly belong, in the hands of the people. We are allowing individuals to make the decisions that so profoundly affect their very existence—and precluding the state from intruding excessively into that critical realm. The Constitution and the courts stand as a bulwark between individual freedom and arbitrary and intrusive governmental power. Under our constitutional system, neither the state nor the majority of the people in a state can impose its will upon the individual in a matter so highly "central to personal dignity and autonomy," *Casey,* 112 S.Ct. at 2807. Those who believe strongly that death must come without physician assistance are free to follow that creed, be they doctors or patients. They are not free, however, to force their views, their religious convictions, or their philosophies on all the other members of a democratic society, and to compel those whose values differ with theirs to die painful, protracted, and agonizing deaths.

Affirmed.

POSTSCRIPT

Are Restrictions on Physician-Assisted Suicide Constitutional?

Nancy Cruzan died six months after the U.S. Supreme Court's ruling on her right to die. Two months after the Court's decision, the Cruzans asked for a court hearing to present new evidence from three of their daughter's coworkers. At the hearing, the coworkers testified that they recalled her saying she would never want to live "like a vegetable." At the same hearing, Cruzan's doctor called her existence a "living hell" and recommended removal of the tube. Her court-appointed guardian concurred. The judge then ruled that there was clear evidence of Cruzan's wishes and gave permission for the feeding tube to be removed. She died on December 26, 1990.

The fundamental concern of courts in right-to-die cases—indeed in most civil liberties cases—is the fear of what will happen in the next case. In other words, a judge may avoid doing what seems reasonable in one case if his ruling could be used to reach a less desirable result in a future case with slightly different facts. Lawyers refer to this as the "slippery slope." If euthanasia is justified in a case where the patient is conscious and competent, it may be allowed in a later case where, perhaps due to the pain the patient is in, competency is not perfectly clear.

The legal issues involved in assisting suicide are covered in a symposium in the *Ohio Northern Law Review*, p. 559 (vol. 20, 1994). Dr. Jack Kevorkian's case is discussed by his attorney, Geoffrey Fieger, in "The Persecution and Prosecution of Dr. Death and His Mercy Machine," 20 *Ohio Northern Law Review* 659 (1994). Other interesting writings in this area include "Physician-Assisted Suicide and the Right to Die With Assistance," 105 *Harvard Law Review* 2021 (1992); Kamisar, "When Is There a Constitutional 'Right to Die'? When Is There No Constitutional 'Right to Live'?" 25 *Georgia Law Review* 1203 (1991); Robertson, "Assessing Quality of Life: A Response to Professor Kamisar," 25 *Georgia Law Review* 1243 (1991); and A. W. Alschuler, "The Right to Die," 141 *New Law Journal* 1637 (1991).

On the Internet, information about assisted suicide and about Dr. Kevorkian can be found at http://www.rights.org/deathnet/Kevorkian_one.html and http://dailynews.yahoo.com/fc/US/Assisted_Suicide/. As of summer 1999, Dr. Kevorkian is serving a prison sentence of 10–25 years for second-degree murder in the death of Thomas Youk. Kevorkian fatally injected Youk, who had Lou Gehrig's disease. He then provided the CBS TV show *60 Minutes* with a videotape of the event. Kevorkian was charged and convicted of murder in the second degree and with delivery of a controlled substance.

ISSUE 4

Do People Have a Legal Right to Clone Themselves?

YES: Cass Sunstein, from "The Constitution and the Clone," in Martha C. Nussbaum and Cass R. Sunstein, eds., *Clones and Clones: Facts and Fantasies About Human Cloning* (W. W. Norton, 1998)

NO: Cass Sunstein, from "The Constitution and the Clone," in Martha C. Nussbaum and Cass R. Sunstein, eds., *Clones and Clones: Facts and Fantasies About Human Cloning* (W. W. Norton, 1998)

ISSUE SUMMARY

YES: Professor of law and political science Cass Sunstein, writing as fictional Supreme Court justice Monroe, argues that the right to cloning is analogous to established rights of reproductive privacy and autonomy and is therefore constitutionally protected.

NO: Professor of law and political science Cass Sunstein, writing as fictional Supreme Court justice Winston, argues that the constitutional protection of "reproductive choice" does not extend to the decision to replicate oneself.

I n early 1996 the first mammalian clone was born. Scottish scientist Ian Walmut introduced the world to "Dolly," a female sheep that had been cloned, meaning that this sheep was an exact genetic duplicate of another sheep— Dolly's "parent." As might be expected, the revelation of Dolly's birth generated an immediate and generally negative public reaction. The image of unrestrained scientific inquiry provoked an anxious disquiet among ordinary citizens and political leaders alike. A nearly unanimous consensus quickly formed that any effort to extend this research to the area of human reproduction was morally wrong. As Anne Lawton, in "The Frankenstein Controversy: The Constitutionality of a Federal Ban on Cloning," 87 *Kentucky Law Journal* 277 (1998), observed, the specter of human cloning

> tapped into a societal uneasiness about the proper limits of scientific inquiry. Scientific discoveries do not unfold in a vacuum. They play out against

a cultural backdrop in which both fantasy and reality are intertwined. Tampering with the process of creation, whether it be in the form of assisted reproductive technology, genetic testing, or, at its most extreme, cloning, plays on "profound concerns regarding the nature of humankind and its relationship to other aspects of the natural world."

Responding to a groundswell of negative public sentiment, President Bill Clinton acted quickly; he issued an immediate moratorium on the use of federal funds for research leading to the cloning of human beings, and he gave the National Bioethics Advisory Commission three months to prepare a report on the ethical and legal implications of human cloning. Although the American public mobilized quickly to oppose unrestrained scientific research that seemed to threaten the very mysteries of human creation, by the time the commission issued its report in June 1996, much of the public furor had faded away. Nonetheless, in December of the following year, Richard Seed, though lacking adequate funding and the necessary expertise, still managed to shock the world once again when he announced that he intended to seek private funding in order to begin cloning human beings.

Whether or not Seed can be taken seriously, the possibility of human cloning, though morally repugnant to many, holds out the promise of reproductive autonomy to others. That is, cloning might be a viable means of producing a child for those who are otherwise incapable of doing so in more traditional ways. As such, the question emerges whether or not the legal and moral issues surrounding cloning should be subsumed to the well-litigated constitutional terrain of reproductive rights and individual privacy. And although Congress has not yet enacted legislation that would regulate cloning or ban it outright, any anticloning legislation that might appear will clearly implicate a range of important constitutional doctrines.

The readings that follow suggest many of the potential legal questions that will need to be addressed in this debate. Both pieces are written by Cass Sunstein, a professor in the Law School at the University of Chicago. It is important to note that both opinions are purely fictional accounts of how Sunstein believes a future Supreme Court might deal with this issue. Such fictionalizations have a rich tradition in the American legal academy, and Sunstein makes great use of the style to flesh out the full contour of the legal and constitutional questions as seen against the backdrop of currently existing law.

Opinion of Justice Monroe

Martin and Martin et al. *v.* Ballinger et al.

In this case American citizens seeking to clone human beings have challenged federal and state prohibitions on cloning. The plaintiffs are married couples. They argue that these prohibitions violate their right to free reproductive choice.

The plaintiffs make two arguments. They argue, first, that the right to clone is part and parcel of the right of reproductive privacy. They claim that this right is akin to the rights to use contraception and to have an abortion, firmly recognized under our prior cases. They therefore urge that the right to clone qualifies, under the due process clause of the Fifth and Fourteenth Amendments, as a 'fundamental interest', which may be invaded only if the government can satisfy 'strict scrutiny', by showing the most compelling of justifications.

The plaintiffs argue, second, that even if the right to clone does not qualify as a 'fundamental interest', the legal prohibition on cloning is unconstitutional, because the government cannot show a 'rational basis' for the restriction. The plaintiffs claim that the government has no legitimate reason for interfering with private decisions about whether to have a child via cloning.

The government makes several arguments in response. It urges that the right to clone is very different from the right to use contraceptives or to have an abortion, and that it does not qualify as a fundamental right under the Constitution. The government also claims that there are compelling reasons to ban human cloning even if the right to clone does qualify as a fundamental right. Finally, the government insists that there is a 'rational basis' for restricting human cloning, to prevent a wide range of social harms.

We reject the government's arguments and hold today that under the Constitution as it has come to be understood, there is a constitutional right to control reproduction—to decide whether or not to have a child. This right lies at the very heart of the constitutional right of 'privacy'; it is part of the liberty protected by the due process clause of the Fifth and Fourteenth Amendments.

From Cass Sunstein, "The Constitution and the Clone," in Martha C. Nussbaum and Cass R. Sunstein, eds., *Clones and Clones: Facts and Fantasies About Human Cloning* (W. W. Norton, 1998). Copyright © 1998 by Martha C. Nussbaum and Cass R. Sunstein. Reprinted by permission of W. W. Norton & Company, Inc.

To be sure, the government can override that right if it has an extremely good reason for doing so. But in the context of cloning, the government's arguments are far too weak. Certainly the government cannot satisfy the 'strict scrutiny' standard that governs this Court's review of restrictions on fundamental rights. Indeed, we do not believe that the government's interests are strong enough to overcome 'rational basis' review, the most deferential standard the Court now uses.

I

There is an acknowledged constitutional right to some form of individual control over decisions involving reproduction. In *Griswold v. Connecticut,* 381 U.S. 479 (1965), this Court held that a state could not ban a married couple from using contraceptives. In the Court's view, a right of 'privacy' forecloses state interference with that decision. In *Eisenstadt v. Baird,* 405 U.S. 438 (1972), the Court extended *Griswold* to invalidate a law forbidding the distribution of contraceptives to unmarried people. In the key passage of its opinion, the Court said, "If the right of privacy means anything, it is the right of the individual, married or single, to be free from unwarranted governmental intrusion into matters so affecting a person as the decision whether to bear or beget a child." And in *Roe v. Wade,* 410 U.S. 113 (1973), the Court held that there is a constitutional right to have an abortion. This decision the Court strongly reaffirmed in *Casey v. Planned Parenthood,* 505 U.S. 833 (1992).

On the other hand, we have held that there is no general right against government interference with important private choices. Thus in *Washington v. Glucksberg,* 516 U.S. 2021 (1997), we held that under ordinary circumstances, there is no general right to physician-assisted suicide. We emphasized that this right is quite foreign to the traditions of American law and policy, which strongly discourage suicide, assisted or otherwise.

These cases clearly establish a basic principle: The Constitution creates a presumptive individual right to decide whether and when to reproduce. The precise dimensions of this right will inevitably change over time. Of course new technologies are expanding the methods by which reproduction is possible. New technologies have been especially prominent in the last decades, and undoubtedly scientific progress will continue, producing unforeseeable developments. The Constitution provides the basic right, which is itself constant; but the specific content of the right necessarily changes with relevant technology.

We think it very plain that the government would need an exceptionally powerful justification to ban couples with serious fertility problems from using methods other than sexual intercourse to produce a child between husband and wife. It has become quite ordinary for couples to use new methods and technologies, and governments have generally refrained from interfering with individual freedom to choose. A governmental ban on in vitro fertilization, to take one example, would have to be powerfully justified, certainly if the ban prevented couples from having children in the only way they could. Cloning is of course a new technology. But for some couples, including the plaintiffs here, it is the only or the best reproductive option. If the government wishes to limit or restrict that choice, it must come up with an exceptionally strong justification.

II

The closest precedent for our decision today is *Roe v. Wade,* reaffirmed in *Casey v. Planned Parenthood,* and these decisions strongly support a right to clone. In fact the argument for a right to clone is far stronger, in many ways, than the argument for a right to abortion. Cloning produces life where abortion destroys it. Abortion is contested on the ground that it destroys the fetus, which many people consider to be equivalent to, or nearly equivalent to, a human being. If there is a right to abort fetal life, there must be a parallel right to create life. Of course the morality of abortion, like that of cloning, is socially contested. *Roe* demonstrates that the fact that people have moral reservations, whether or not inspired by religion, is by itself an insufficient reason to allow interference with a decision about whether to bear or beget a child.

In any case the right to have an abortion reflects a judgment that the choice about whether to reproduce lies with the individual, not the government. That judgment strongly supports the plaintiffs' claim here.

III

If a ban on cloning is subject to the most stringent forms of constitutional review, it is clear that the ban cannot be upheld. The government's interests are speculative in the extreme. The government notes that there is a risk of psychological harm to the clone, who will know that it is the genetic equivalent of someone else, with a known life; perhaps this knowledge will be hard to bear. We acknowledge that psychological harm may occur. But psychological harm is a risk in many settings, and it is not a reason to allow the government to control reproductive choices, to ban adoption, or (for that matter) to outlaw twins, for whom there is in any case no decisive evidence of trauma.

The government argues that it fears the outcomes of unsuccessful medical experiments; it says that children with various physical defects are likely to occur. This too is possible, especially at the early stages, but it is a reason for regulation, not for prohibition. The government refers as well to the need for a large stock of genetic diversity. The interest in a large gene pool is, we may acknowledge, compelling; but it is utterly implausible to think that the existence of cloning, bound to be a relatively unusual practice, will compromise the genetic diversity of mankind.

Finally, the government attempts to justify its ban with the legal equivalent of tales from science fiction or horror movies—thus, the government refers to dozens or even hundreds of genetically equivalent people, or of clones of especially abhorrent historical figures. The government fears that narcissistic or ill-motivated people will produce armies of 'selves'. We think it plain that these fanciful speculations, far afield from the case at hand, do not justify a total ban. If problems of this kind arise, they should be controllable through more fine-tuned regulations. The government's emphasis on unlikely scenarios of this kind simply confirms our belief that the government has been unable to find a 'compelling' interest to override the presumptive right to control one's reproductive processes.

IV

Even if the right to clone did not qualify as a fundamental interest, we believe that a wholesale ban on cloning would be unconstitutional, because it cannot survive rational basis review. In the end the government's justifications are best understood as a form of unmediated and highly emotional repugnance—produced not by evidence, arguments, or reality, but by the simple novelty of the practice under review.

Repugnance frequently accompanies new technological developments; and repugnance tends to underlie the worst forms of prejudice and irrationality. We need not repeat the details about our nation's long-standing practices of discrimination on the basis of race and sex—now understood to violate our deepest constitutional ideals—in order to establish the point. Nor should it be necessary to stress that the most solemn obligation of this Court is to uphold constitutional principles against popular prejudice and irrationality, which often take the form of 'repugnance'. And to the extent that the ban on cloning has foundations in religious convictions, it should be unnecessary to say that religious convictions, standing alone, are not, in a pluralistic society, a sufficient basis for the coercion of law. It does not deprecate religious conviction to say that its appropriate place is not in the statute books, and to emphasize that religious arguments must have secular equivalents in order to provide the basis for law.

V

Our conclusions are fortified by a simple, widely recognized point: A ban on cloning will simply drive the practice of human cloning both abroad and underground. At this stage in our history, it is altogether clear that prohibitions on cloning will not operate as prohibitions, but will simply force people who are determined to clone to act unlawfully or in other nations. Thus, the prohibition at issue here cannot be supported by the government's justifications, which would lose what little force they have if the prohibition cannot operate in practice as it does on paper.

We hold, in sum, that the right to clone, however novel as a matter of technology, is part and parcel of a time-honored individual right to control the circumstances and event of reproduction; that the government has pointed to no sufficient justification for overriding that fundamental right; and that on inspection, the government's grounds for concern dissolve into a simple statement of repugnance and disgust, lacking scientific or ethical foundations and fed mostly by imaginative literature. Because they invade the right to privacy in its most fundamental form, legal bans on cloning violate the due process clause of the Constitution.

The judgment of the court of appeals is affirmed. IT IS SO ORDERED.

Opinion of Justice Winston

Martin and Martin et al. *v.* Ballinger et al.

In this case a group of American citizens seeking to clone human beings have challenged federal and state prohibitions on cloning. The plaintiffs are married couples. They argue that these prohibitions violate their right to free reproductive choice.

The plaintiffs make two arguments. They argue, first, that the right to clone is part and parcel of the right to reproductive privacy, closely akin to the rights to use contraception and to have an abortion, recognized under our prior cases. They therefore urge that the right to clone qualifies, under the due process clause of the Fifth and Fourteenth Amendments, as a 'fundamental interest', which may be invaded only if the government can satisfy 'strict scrutiny', by showing the most compelling of justifications.

The plaintiffs argue, second, that even if the right to clone does not qualify as a 'fundamental interest', the legal prohibition is unconstitutional, because the government cannot show a 'rational basis' for the restriction. The plaintiffs claim that the government has no legitimate reason for interfering with private decisions about whether to have a child via cloning.

The government makes several arguments in response. It urges that the right to clone is very different from the right to use contraceptives or to have an abortion, and that it does not qualify as a fundamental right under the Constitution. The government also claims that there are compelling reasons to ban human cloning even if the right to clone does qualify as a fundamental right. Finally, the government insists that there is a 'rational basis' for restricting human cloning, to prevent a wide range of social harms.

We accept the government's arguments and hold today that under the Constitution as it is now understood, there is no constitutional right to clone. The Court's cases recognize individual right to control reproduction, as part of the liberty protected by the due process clause of the Fifth and Fourteenth Amendments. But it is facetious, at best, to say that anything in our precedents recognizes an individual right to replicate oneself through the new technology of cloning.

From Cass Sunstein, "The Constitution and the Clone," in Martha C. Nussbaum and Cass R. Sunstein, eds., *Clones and Clones: Facts and Fantasies About Human Cloning* (W. W. Norton, 1998). Copyright © 1998 by Martha C. Nussbaum and Cass R. Sunstein. Reprinted by permission of W. W. Norton & Company, Inc.

To override the individual interest in replicating other human beings, the government needs only a 'rational basis'. But the government has far more than this. We believe that the government has exceptionally powerful grounds for controlling cloning. Indeed, the government's justifications are strong enough to override the individual's interest even if the government needs to overcome 'strict scrutiny', the least deferential standard the Court now uses.

I

There is an acknowledged constitutional right to some form of individual control over decisions involving reproduction. In *Griswold v. Connecticut,* 381 U.S. 479 (1965), this Court held that a state could not ban a married couple from using contraceptives. In the Court's view, a right of 'privacy' forecloses state interference with that decision. In *Eisenstadt v. Baird,* 405 U.S. 438 (1972), the Court extended *Griswold* to invalidate a law forbidding the distribution of contraceptives to unmarried people. In the key passage of its opinion, the Court said, "If the right of privacy means anything, it is the right of the individual, married or single, to be free from unwarranted governmental intrusion into matters so affecting a person as the decision whether to bear or beget a child." And in *Roe v. Wade,* 410 U.S. 113 (1973), the Court held that there is a constitutional right to have an abortion. This decision the Court strongly reaffirmed in *Casey v. Planned Parenthood,* 505 U.S. 833 (1992).

On the other hand, we have held that there is no general right against government interference with important private choices. Thus in *Washington v. Glucksberg,* 516 U.S. 2021(1997), we held that under ordinary circumstances, there is no general right to physician-assisted suicide. We emphasized that this right is quite foreign to the traditions of American law and policy, which strongly discourage suicide, assisted or otherwise.

These cases clearly establish a basic principle: The Constitution creates a presumptive individual right to decide whether and when to reproduce. Thus, government cannot prevent people from choosing not to have a child, and we agree with the plaintiffs that serious issues would also be raised by (for example) a legal requirement of abortion, or a restriction on the number of children a married couple might have. But the constitutional right is far from unbounded. It lies in a specific judgment about *reproduction,* understood by our traditions as a distinctive human interest with a distinctive human meaning.

Our traditions rebel against the idea that the state, rather than the individual, can make the decision whether a person is to bear or beget a child. But it defies common sense to suggest that *replication* falls in the same category. No tradition supports a right to replicate. This is not merely a matter of technological limitations. The human meaning of replication, of creating genetically identical beings, is fundamentally different from that of reproduction, and replication is to many people horrifying. Centuries of culture, of myth and literature, confirm this basic fact. It is not the business of this Court to say whether replication of human beings should or should not be permitted. But when the people of the country, and their elected representatives, conclude that it should be banned, no fundamental right is invaded. We require only a rational justification.

II

The plaintiffs rely most fundamentally on *Roe v. Wade,* but there is an enormous difference between the right to clone and the right to an abortion. The Court has come to see that the decision in *Roe* turned in large part on the interest in equality on the basis of sex. As a matter of history, governments have denied the right to abortion because they seek to preserve women's traditional role. Moreover, the denial of the right to have an abortion tends to fortify that traditional role and thus to undermine equality on the basis of sex. No equality interest supports the right to clone. With respect to sex equality, cloning is a very complex matter—reasonable people have set forth competing views—and we do not believe that it is plausible to argue that the right to clone finds a justification in principles of equality on the basis of sex.

There is a further point. *Roe v. Wade* did not create a general right to decide whether to have a child through whatever technological means may be available. It is far narrower than that: an outgrowth of cases establishing a right to decide whether to reproduce, a time-honored right in Anglo-American law. The right to replicate stands on much weaker ground.

III

Even if the ban on cloning were subject to the most stringent forms of judicial review, it would be upheld. Physical difficulties and even deformities are highly likely. The government has an exceptionally strong interest in protecting young children against disease and disability, and both of these are likely products of experiments in human cloning. The government has pointed to considerable evidence of this risk, and this Court is in no position to second-guess the scientific evidence.

It is highly likely as well that the practice of cloning would have undesirable effects on the 'people' who result. There is some evidence of psychological difficulties faced by human twins; the practice of cloning will inevitably risk far more severe problems from people who know that they are genetic equivalents of people with known lives, including known problems, known successes, and known failures. Similarly, the government reasonably fears that the parent-child relationship, between genetic equivalents, would be unrecognizable, and permeated by difficulties of various sorts. It may well be that especially wealthy people, or especially narcissistic people, would fund large numbers of replications of themselves. Who would rear the resulting children? With what motivations? The government has the strongest possible reasons to fear the outcomes of such a situation.

There is a further consideration. The government has an extremely powerful interest in preserving the stock of biological diversity. Widespread cloning could compromise that interest to the detriment of humanity as a whole. We think that these points confirm our belief that the government has a wide range of compelling interests sufficient to override any presumptive right to clone.

IV

If the decision whether to clone does not qualify as a fundamental right, the only question is whether the government's ban is 'rational'. Certainly it qualifies as such. As we have indicated, the government might reasonably believe that there would be adverse psychological effects on 'clones'. It might believe that the process of cloning human beings would result in physical deformities for the 'products' of the relevant scientific practices. It might even believe that the existence of clones would have adverse psychological effects on many children and even adults who might fear that they would be cloned against their will. All of these speculations are reasonable.

This Court does not sit to second-guess reasonable judgments by the elected representatives of the American people, especially when there is no defect in the system of democratic deliberation that gave rise to the law under review. And it should not be necessary to say that the religious convictions that may underlie legal bans on cloning are not, in a pluralistic society, at all troublesome from the standpoint of constitutional democracy, where everyone's convictions are entitled to count.

Our conclusions are not undermined in the least by the possibility that people determined to defy the law will do so, either here or by seeking refuge abroad. It is not an argument against the criminal law that criminal prohibitions may be violated or circumvented. If bans on human replication do not operate in practice as they do on paper, Congress and the legislatures of the several states are entitled to respond as they choose.

We hold, in sum, that the right to clone has no basis in our constitutional traditions, which involve human reproduction, not replication; that the government has ample grounds for restricting individual choice in light of the novelty of the relevant technology and its unpredictable and potentially damaging effects on the most basic human values and in particular on those involved in the relevant 'experiments'. Because they do not implicate the right to privacy or any other constitutionally protected interest, legal bans on cloning are entirely consistent with the due process clause of the Constitution.

The judgment of the court of appeals is reversed. IT IS SO ORDERED.

POSTSCRIPT

Do People Have a Legal Right to Clone Themselves?

The cloning of Dolly made real for many people what before had seemed the province of science fiction stories. Richard Seed's interventions in this issue have made this reality all the more frightening to many. Certainly there are those who favor continued research on cloning; they do so out of a sense of the tangible benefits it may bring or through their belief in fostering scientific inquiry for its own sake. Opponents of cloning have generally emphasized the negative ethical, religious, and social dimensions attending the possibility (or probability) of abuse. From a more practical perspective, policymakers are confronted with the questions of whether or not cloning should be banned outright and, if so, whether or not such a ban would be effective. Moreover, if cloning research were banned, might such action have negative consequences for related scientific research that poses no such moral dilemmas?

Sunstein approaches the topic from a somewhat different angle and lends a fictional voice to the constitutional dimensions any future discussions of cloning should, and will, take into account. Sunstein firmly locates the framework of analysis of the cloning issue within the doctrinal tradition that has dealt with individual privacy interests relating to reproductive autonomy. Although at first glance the fictional opinions of Justices Monroe and Winston might seem to be replicas of one another—clones if you will—Sunstein's achievement is in demonstrating how the cloning debate will be (and is) embedded in familiar doctrinal terrain. For Sunstein, the language of *Griswold v. Connecticut, Eisenstadt v. Baird, Roe v. Wade,* and *Casey v. Planned Parenthood* provide the vocabulary for discussion of the cloning question.

There is already a voluminous literature on this topic. One place to begin is with Gina Kolata's book *Clone: The Road to Dolly, and the Path Ahead* (William Morrow, 1998). In addition, the legal and moral philosopher Leon R. Kass and political scientist James Q. Wilson have recently produced *The Ethics of Human Cloning* (AEI Press, 1998). In addition to Sunstein's work reprinted here, the volume he edited with Martha Nussbaum, *Clones and Clones: Facts and Fantasies About Human Cloning* (W. W. Norton, 1998), contains a strong selection of essays on cloning from a variety of perspectives. For a more technical discussion of some of the legal questions involved, see Lori B. Andrews, "Is There a Right to Clone? Constitutional Challenges to Bans on Human Cloning," 11 *Harvard Journal of Law and Technology* 643 (1998). The Subcommittee on

Health and the Environment of the U.S. House of Representatives Committee on Commerce has published the proceedings of its hearings on this matter. See *Cloning: Legal, Medical, Ethical, and Social Issues* (1998). Finally, the Human Cloning Foundation maintains their own Web site, which they bill as "the official site in support of human cloning." This site can be found at http://www.humancloning.org.

ISSUE 5

Does the Sharing of Music Files Through Napster Violate Copyright Laws?

YES: Robert R. Beezer, from Majority Opinion, *A&M Records, Inc. v. Napster, Inc.,* U.S. Court of Appeals for the Ninth Circuit (February 12, 2001)

NO: Jessica Litman et al., from Brief Amicus Curiae of Copyright Law Professors in Support of Reversal, *Napster, Inc. v. A&M Records, Inc.* and *Napster, Inc. v. Jerry Leiber et al.,* U.S. Court of Appeals for the Ninth Circuit (August 2000)

ISSUE SUMMARY

YES: U.S. Circuit Court judge Robert R. Beezer upholds the ruling that Napster, Inc., by facilitating the copying and distribution of the plaintiffs' music recordings, is liable for contributory copyright infringement.

NO: Jessica Litman et al., all professors of American law, argue that the district court in the *Napster* case applied an unduly narrow interpretation of the fair use doctrine and extended copyright law to shut down a useful new technology.

$\mathbf{T}$his is the first edition of *Taking Sides: Clashing Views on Controversial Legal Issues* to include an issue involving the law of copyright. When the first edition was published in 1983, it would have been very hard to find a controversial copyright issue and only slightly less difficult to find a suitable issue involving the personal computer.

Copyright law now has the attention of both the legal community and the public at large. The most newsworthy recent case involved Napster, an Internet service that allows one to obtain copies of music that might be stored on a computer in some distant country. Napster was sued by some copyright holders, mostly record companies, who argued that the process established by Napster was violating their copyrights and costing them large sums of money. In the eyes of the plaintiffs, Napster users were thieves—and Napster was providing the means to allow the thievery to take place.

The following selection contains the ruling by the U.S. Court of Appeals, as presented by Judge Robert R. Beezer, in the lawsuit against Napster. In the days before the ruling, over 50 million files were downloaded by Napster users. The Court of Appeals ruled in favor of the plaintiffs, and Napster's future is currently in doubt. Certainly, far fewer files are being downloaded by users and far fewer songs are listed. Yet even if Napster, the software, the company, or the Internet site were to disappear, the issues involved in the Napster litigation would not be dead.

The phenomenon of Napster is that it allows Internet users to obtain copies of files that exist on individual computers located anywhere in the world. Typically, when one "surfs" the Internet, one is only able to look at files located on a machine called a server. If anyone has something they want to make available on the Internet, they must find a server and then find a way to put the file containing the information on that server. Every server, in order to be reachable on the Internet, has an address, such as http://www.dushkin.com or http://128.119.199.27.

Napster made it possible to obtain files that were located on anyone's machine, whether it was a server or not. Obviously, there are many more machines using the Internet and connected to it than there are servers. Thus, Napster greatly increased the number of files available for download. Indeed, Napster at one point had over 50 million users, and many times that number of files were being circulated.

Copyright law is being challenged online because sharing and circulating anything in the online environment occurs differently from the way it occurs offline. Offline, one could make a copy of something one wanted to share, but it is equally likely that sharing involves someone borrowing and taking possession of whatever it is that one wishes to share. Online, every instance of sharing involves copying. Anything "downloaded" is actually a copy of something that continues to reside in its original place, so it is no exaggeration to say that everything you see on your computer screen when you are connected to the Internet is a copy of something residing elsewhere. You may decide not to save the copy on a disk, thus not keeping the copy, but it is through copying that the transfer of information online happens.

While the argument that online copying and file sharing violate the copyright laws probably seems quite reasonable, there is a strong response from the other side. Very simply, not all copying is unlawful, and not all machines that facilitate copying are unlawful. In the second selection, Jessica Litman et al. state that in the mid-1980s, the Supreme Court ruled that the videotape machine does not violate copyright law. The plaintiffs in that case made many of the same arguments that the plaintiffs in the Napster case were making. The copyright laws can be looked at as restrictions on communication and, due to the First Amendment, we should be careful in restricting communication and expression, even when it might involve copying part of someone else's work. Indeed, there is a clear exception in the copyright laws for "fair use" copying, and part of the argument made by Napster is that what was occurring was "fair use."

Majority Opinion

A&M Records *v.* Napster

BEEZER, Circuit Judge:

Plaintiffs are engaged in the commercial recording, distribution and sale of copyrighted musical compositions and sound recordings. The complaint alleges that Napster, Inc. ("Napster") is a contributory and vicarious copyright infringer. On July 26, 2000, the district court granted plaintiffs' motion for a preliminary injunction. The injunction was slightly modified by written opinion on August 10, 2000. *A & M Records, Inc. v. Napster, Inc.,* 114 F. Supp. 2d 896 (N.D. Cal. 2000). The district court preliminarily enjoined Napster "from engaging in, or facilitating others in copying, downloading, uploading, transmitting, or distributing plaintiffs' copyrighted musical compositions and sound recordings, protected by either federal or state law, without express permission of the rights owner." Id. at 927. Federal Rule of Civil Procedure 65(c) requires successful plaintiffs to post a bond for damages incurred by the enjoined party in the event that the injunction was wrongfully issued. The district court set bond in this case at $5 million.

We entered a temporary stay of the preliminary injunction pending resolution of this appeal. We have jurisdiction pursuant to 28 U.S.C. § 1292(a)(1). We affirm in part, reverse in part and remand....

III

Plaintiffs claim Napster users are engaged in the wholesale reproduction and distribution of copyrighted works, all constituting direct infringement. The district court agreed. We note that the district court's conclusion that plaintiffs have presented a prima facie case of direct infringement by Napster users is not presently appealed by Napster. We only need briefly address the threshold requirements.

From *A&M Records, Inc. v. Napster, Inc.,* 239 F.3d 1004 (9th Cir. 2001). Some notes omitted.

A. Infringement

Plaintiffs must satisfy two requirements to present a prima facie case of direct infringement: (1) they must show ownership of the allegedly infringed material and (2) they must demonstrate that the alleged infringers violate at least one exclusive right granted to copyright holders under 17 U.S.C. § 106. *See* 17 U.S.C. § 501(a) (infringement occurs when alleged infringer engages in activity listed in § 106); *see also Baxter v. MCA, Inc.*, 812 F.2d 421, 423 (9th Cir.1987); *see, e.g., S.O.S., Inc. v. Payday, Inc.*, 886 F.2d 1081, 1085 n. 3 (9th Cir.1989) ("The word 'copying' is shorthand for the infringing of any of the copyright owner's five exclusive rights...."). Plaintiffs have sufficiently demonstrated ownership. The record supports the district court's determination that "as much as eighty-seven percent of the files available on Napster may be copyrighted and more than seventy percent may be owned or administered by plaintiffs." *Napster,* 114 F.Supp.2d at 911.

The district court further determined that plaintiffs' exclusive rights under § 106 were violated: "here the evidence establishes that a majority of Napster users use the service to download and upload copyrighted music.... And by doing that, it constitutes—the uses constitute direct infringement of plaintiffs' musical compositions, recordings." *A&M Records, Inc. v. Napster, Inc.*, Nos. 99-5183, 00-0074, 2000 WL 1009483, at *1 (N.D.Cal. July 26, 2000) (transcript of proceedings). The district court also noted that "it is pretty much acknowledged ... by Napster that this is infringement." *Id.* We agree that plaintiffs have shown that Napster users infringe at least two of the copyright holders' exclusive rights: the rights of reproduction, § 106(1); and distribution, § 106(3). Napster users who upload file names to the search index for others to copy violate plaintiffs' distribution rights. Napster users who download files containing copyrighted music violate plaintiffs' reproduction rights.

Napster asserts an affirmative defense to the charge that its users directly infringe plaintiffs' copyrighted musical compositions and sound recordings.

B. Fair Use

Napster contends that its users do not directly infringe plaintiffs' copyrights because the users are engaged in fair use of the material. *See* 17 U.S.C. § 107 ("[T]he fair use of a copyrighted work ... is not an infringement of copyright."). Napster identifies three specific alleged fair uses: sampling, where users make temporary copies of a work before purchasing; space-shifting, where users access a sound recording through the Napster system that they already own in audio CD format; and permissive distribution of recordings by both new and established artists.

The district court considered factors listed in 17 U.S.C. § 107, which guide a court's fair use determination. These factors are: (1) the purpose and character of the use; (2) the nature of the copyrighted work; (3) the "amount and substantiality of the portion used" in relation to the work as a whole; and (4) the effect of the use upon the potential market for the work or the value of the work. *See* 17 U.S.C. § 107. The district court first conducted a general analysis of

Napster system uses under § 107, and then applied its reasoning to the alleged fair uses identified by Napster. The district court concluded that Napster users are not fair users. We agree. We first address the court's overall fair use analysis.

1. Purpose and Character of the Use

This factor focuses on whether the new work merely replaces the object of the original creation or instead adds a further purpose or different character. In other words, this factor asks "whether and to what extent the new work is 'transformative.'" *See Campbell v. Acuff-Rose Music, Inc.,* 510 U.S. 569, 579, 114 S.Ct. 1164, 127 L.Ed.2d 500 (1994).

The district court first concluded that downloading MP3 files does not transform the copyrighted work. *Napster,* 114 F.Supp.2d at 912. This conclusion is supportable. Courts have been reluctant to find fair use when an original work is merely retransmitted in a different medium. *See, e.g., Infinity Broadcast Corp. v. Kirkwood,* 150 F.3d 104, 108 (2d Cir.1998) (concluding that retransmission of radio broadcast over telephone lines is not transformative); *UMG Recordings, Inc. v. MP3.com, Inc.,* 92 F.Supp.2d 349, 351 (S.D.N.Y.) (finding that reproduction of audio CD into MP3 format does not "transform" the work), *certification denied,* 2000 WL 710056 (S.D.N.Y. June 1, 2000) ("Defendant's copyright infringement was clear, and the mere fact that it was clothed in the exotic webbing of the Internet does not disguise its illegality.").

This "purpose and character" element also requires the district court to determine whether the allegedly infringing use is commercial or noncommercial. *See Campbell,* 510 U.S. at 584–85, 114 S.Ct. 1164. A commercial use weighs against a finding of fair use but is not conclusive on the issue. *Id.* The district court determined that Napster users engage in commercial use of the copyrighted materials largely because (1) "a host user sending a file cannot be said to engage in a personal use when distributing that file to an anonymous requester" and (2) "Napster users get for free something they would ordinarily have to buy." *Napster,* 114 F. Supp.2d at 912. The district court's findings are not clearly erroneous.

Direct economic benefit is not required to demonstrate a commercial use. Rather, repeated and exploitative copying of copyrighted works, even if the copies are not offered for sale, may constitute a commercial use. See *Worldwide Church of God v. Philadelphia Church of God,* 227 F.3d 1110, 1118 (9th Cir. 2000) (stating that church that copied religious text for its members "unquestionably profit[ed]" from the unauthorized "distribution and use of [the text] without having to account to the copyright holder"); *American Geophysical Union v. Texaco, Inc.,* 60 F.3d 913, 922 (2d Cir.1994) (finding that researchers at for-profit laboratory gained indirect economic advantage by photocopying copyrighted scholarly articles). In the record before us, commercial use is demonstrated by a showing that repeated and exploitative unauthorized copies of copyrighted works were made to save the expense of purchasing authorized copies. *See Worldwide Church,* 227 F.3d at 1117-18; *Sega Enters. Ltd. v. MAPHIA,* 857 F.Supp. 679, 687 (N.D.Cal.1994) (finding commercial use when individuals downloaded copies of video games "to avoid having to buy video game cartridges"); *see also*

American Geophysical, 60 F.3d at 922. Plaintiffs made such a showing before the district court.

We also note that the definition of a financially motivated transaction for the purposes of criminal copyright actions includes trading infringing copies of a work for other items, "including the receipt of other copyrighted works." *See* No Electronic Theft Act ("NET Act"), Pub.L. No. 105–147, 18 U.S.C. § 101 (defining "Financial Gain").

2. The Nature of the Use

Works that are creative in nature are "closer to the core of intended copyright protection" than are more fact-based works. *See Campbell,* 510 U.S. at 586, 114 S.Ct. 1164. The district court determined that plaintiffs' "copyrighted musical compositions and sound recordings are creative in nature . . . which cuts against a finding of fair use under the second factor." *Napster,* 114 F.Supp.2d at 913. We find no error in the district court's conclusion.

3. The Portion Used

"While 'wholesale copying does not preclude fair use per se,' copying an entire work 'militates against a finding of fair use.'" *Worldwide Church,* 227 F.3d at 1118 (quoting *Hustler Magazine, Inc. v. Moral Majority, Inc.,* 796 F.2d 1148, 1155 (9th Cir. 1986)). The district court determined that Napster users engage in "wholesale copying" of copyrighted work because file transfer necessarily "involves copying the entirety of the copyrighted work." *Napster,* 114 F.Supp.2d at 913. We agree. We note, however, that under certain circumstances, a court will conclude that a use is fair even when the protected work is copied in its entirety. *See, e.g., Sony Corp. v. Universal City Studios, Inc.,* 464 U.S. 417, 449-50, 104 S.Ct. 774, 78 L.Ed.2d 574 (1984) (acknowledging that fair use of time-shifting necessarily involved making a full copy of a protected work).

4. Effect of Use on Market

"Fair use, when properly applied, is limited to copying by others which does not materially impair the marketability of the work which is copied." *Harper & Row Publishers, Inc. v. Nation Enters.,* 471 U.S. 539, 566-67, 105 S.Ct. 2218, 85 L.Ed.2d 588 (1985). "[T]he importance of this [fourth] factor will vary, not only with the amount of harm, but also with the relative strength of the showing on the other factors." *Campbell,* 510 U.S. at 591 n. 21, 114 S.Ct. 1164. The proof required to demonstrate present or future market harm varies with the purpose and character of the use:

> A challenge to a noncommercial use of a copyrighted work requires proof either that the particular use is harmful, or that if it should become widespread, it would adversely affect the potential market for the copyrighted work. . . . *If the intended use is for commercial gain, that likelihood [of market harm] may be presumed. But if it is for a noncommercial purpose, the likelihood must be demonstrated.*

— *Sony,* 464 U.S. at 451, 104 S.Ct. 774 (emphases added).

Addressing this factor, the district court concluded that Napster harms the market in "at least" two ways: it reduces audio CD sales among college students and it "raises barriers to plaintiffs' entry into the market for the digital downloading of music." *Napster,* 114 F.Supp.2d at 913. The district court relied on evidence plaintiffs submitted to show that Napster use harms the market for their copyrighted musical compositions and sound recordings. In a separate memorandum and order regarding the parties' objections to the expert reports, the district court examined each report, finding some more appropriate and probative than others. *A & M Records, Inc. v. Napster, Inc.,* Nos. 99–5183 & 00–0074, 2000 WL 1170106 (N.D. Cal. August 10, 2000). Notably, plaintiffs' expert, Dr. E. Deborah Jay, conducted a survey (the "Jay Report") using a random sample of college and university students to track their reasons for using Napster and the impact Napster had on their music purchases. *Id.* at *2. The court recognized that the Jay Report focused on just one segment of the Napster user population and found "evidence of lost sales attributable to college use to be probative of irreparable harm for purposes of the preliminary injunction motion." *Id.* at *3.

Plaintiffs also offered a study conducted by Michael Fine, Chief Executive Officer of Soundscan, (the "Fine Report") to determine the effect of online sharing of MP3 files in order to show irreparable harm. Fine found that online file sharing had resulted in a loss of "album" sales within college markets. After reviewing defendant's objections to the Fine Report and expressing some concerns regarding the methodology and findings, the district court refused to exclude the Fine Report insofar as plaintiffs offered it to show irreparable harm. *Id.* at *6.

Plaintiffs' expert Dr. David J. Teece studied several issues ("Teece Report"), including whether plaintiffs had suffered or were likely to suffer harm in their existing and planned businesses due to Napster use. *Id.* Napster objected that the report had not undergone peer review. The district court noted that such reports generally are not subject to such scrutiny and overruled defendant's objections. *Id.*

As for defendant's experts, plaintiffs objected to the report of Dr. Peter S. Fader, in which the expert concluded that Napster is *beneficial* to the music industry because MP3 music file-sharing stimulates more audio CD sales than it displaces. *Id.* at *7. The district court found problems in Dr. Fader's minimal role in overseeing the administration of the survey and the lack of objective data in his report. The court decided the generality of the report rendered it "of dubious reliability and value." The court did not exclude the report, however, but chose "not to rely on Fader's findings in determining the issues of fair use and irreparable harm." *Id.* at *8.

The district court cited both the Jay and Fine Reports in support of its finding that Napster use harms the market for plaintiffs' copyrighted musical compositions and sound recordings by reducing CD sales among college students. The district court cited the Teece Report to show the harm Napster use caused in raising barriers to plaintiffs' entry into the market for digital downloading of music. *Napster,* 114 F.Supp.2d at 910. The district court's careful consideration of defendant's objections to these reports and decision to rely on the reports for specific issues demonstrates a proper exercise of discretion in addition to a correct application of the fair use doctrine. Defendant has failed to show any basis for disturbing the district court's findings.

We, therefore, conclude that the district court made sound findings related to Napster's deleterious effect on the present and future digital download market. Moreover, lack of harm to an established market cannot deprive the copyright holder of the right to develop alternative markets for the works. *See L.A. Times v. Free Republic,* 54 U.S.P.Q.2d 1453, 1469–71 (C.D. Cal.2000) (stating that online market for plaintiff newspapers' articles was harmed because plaintiffs demonstrated that "[defendants] are attempting to exploit the market for viewing their articles online"); *see also UMG Recordings,* 92F.Supp.2d at 352 ("Any allegedly positive impact of defendant's activities on plaintiffs' prior market in no way frees defendant to usurp a further market that directly derives from reproduction of the plaintiffs' copyrighted works."). Here, similar to *L.A. Times* and *UMG Recordings,* the record supports the district court's finding that the "record company plaintiffs have already expended considerable funds and effort to commence Internet sales and licensing for digital downloads." 114 F.Supp.2d at 915. Having digital downloads available for free on the Napster system necessarily harms the copyright holders' attempts to charge for the same downloads.

Judge Patel did not abuse her discretion in reaching the above fair use conclusions, nor were the findings of fact with respect to fair use considerations clearly erroneous. We next address Napster's identified uses of sampling and space-shifting.

5. Identified Uses

Napster maintains that its identified uses of sampling and space-shifting were wrongly excluded as fair uses by the district court.

a. Sampling

Napster contends that its users download MP3 files to "sample" the music in order to decide whether to purchase the recording. Napster argues that the district court: (1) erred in concluding that sampling is a commercial use because it conflated a noncommercial use with a personal use; (2) erred in determining that sampling adversely affects the market for plaintiffs' copyrighted music, a requirement if the use is noncommercial; and (3) erroneously concluded that sampling is not a fair use because it determined that samplers may also engage in other infringing activity.

The district court determined that sampling remains a commercial use even if some users eventually purchase the music. We find no error in the district court's determination. Plaintiffs have established that they are likely to succeed in proving that even authorized temporary downloading of individual songs for sampling purposes is commercial in nature. *See Napster,* 114 F.Supp.2d at 913. The record supports a finding that free promotional downloads are highly regulated by the record company plaintiffs and that the companies collect royalties for song samples available on retail Internet sites. *Id.* Evidence relied on by the district court demonstrates that the free downloads provided by the record companies consist of thirty-to-sixty second samples or are full songs programmed to "time out," that is, exist only for a short time on the downloader's computer. *Id.* at 913–14. In comparison, Napster users download a full, free and permanent copy of the recording. *Id.* at 914–15. The determination by the district court as to the commercial purpose and character of sampling is not clearly erroneous.

The district court further found that both the market for audio CDs and market for online distribution are adversely affected by Napster's service. As stated in our discussion of the district court's general fair use analysis: the court did not abuse its discretion when it found that, overall, Napster has an adverse impact on the audio CD and digital download markets. Contrary to Napster's assertion that the district court failed to specifically address the market impact of sampling, the district court determined that "[e]ven if the type of sampling supposedly done on Napster were a non-commercial use, plaintiffs have demonstrated a substantial likelihood that it would adversely affect the potential market for their copyrighted works if it became widespread." *Napster,* 114 F. Supp.2d at 914. The record supports the district court's preliminary determinations that: (1) the more music that sampling users download, the less likely they are to eventually purchase the recordings on audio CD; and (2) even if the audio CD market is not harmed, Napster has adverse effects on the developing digital download market.

Napster further argues that the district court erred in rejecting its evidence that the users' downloading of "samples" increases or tends to increase audio CD sales. The district court, however, correctly noted that "any potential enhancement of plaintiffs' sales . . . would not tip the fair use analysis conclusively in favor of defendant." *Id.* at 914. We agree that increased sales of copyrighted material attributable to unauthorized use should not deprive the copyright holder of the right to license the material. *See Campbell,* 510 U.S. at 591 n. 21, 114 S.Ct 1164 ("Even favorable evidence, without more, is no guarantee of fairness. Judge Leval gives the example of the film producer's appropriation of a composer's previously unknown song that turns the song into a commercial success; the boon to the song does not make the film's simple copying fair."); *see also L.A. Times,* 54 U.S.P.Q.2d at 1471–72. Nor does positive impact in one market, here the audio CD market, deprive the copyright holder of the right to develop identified alternative markets, here the digital download market. *See id.* at 1469–71.

We find no error in the district court's factual findings or abuse of discretion in the court's conclusion that plaintiffs will likely prevail in establishing that sampling does not constitute a fair use.

b. Space-Shifting

Napster also maintains that space-shifting is a fair use. Space-shifting occurs when a Napster user downloads MP3 music files in order to listen to music he already owns on audio CD. *See id.* at 915–16. Napster asserts that we have already held that space-shifting of musical compositions and sound recordings is a fair use. *See Recording Indus. Ass'n of Am. v. Diamond Multimedia Sys., Inc.,* 180 F.3d 1072, 1079 (9th Cir.1999) ("Rio [a portable MP3 player] merely makes copies in order to render portable, or 'space-shift,' those files that already reside on a user's hard drive.... Such copying is a paradigmatic noncommercial personal use."). *See also generally Sony,* 464 U.S. at 423, 104 S.Ct. 774 (holding that "time-shifting," where a video tape recorder owner records a television show for later viewing, is a fair use).

We conclude that the district court did not err when it refused to apply the "shifting" analyses of *Sony* and *Diamond.* Both *Diamond* and *Sony* are inapposite because the methods of shifting in these cases did not also simultaneously involve distribution of the copyrighted material to the general public; the time or space-shifting of copyrighted material exposed the material only to the original user. In *Diamond,* for example, the copyrighted music was transferred from the user's computer hard drive to the user's portable MP3 player. So too *Sony,* where "the majority of VCR purchasers ... did not distribute taped television broadcasts, but merely enjoyed them at home." *Napster,* 114 F. Supp.2d at 913. Conversely, it is obvious that once a user lists a copy of music he already owns on the Napster system in order to access the music from another location, the song becomes "available to millions of other individuals," not just the original CD owner. *See UMG Recordings,* 92F.Supp. 2d at 351–52 (finding space-shifting of MP3 files not a fair use even when previous ownership is demonstrated before a download is allowed); *cf. Religious Tech. Ctr. v. Lerma,* No. 95–1107A, 1996 WL 633131, at *6 (E.D.Va. Oct.4, 1996) (suggesting that storing copyrighted material on computer disk for later review is not a fair use).

c. Other Uses

Permissive reproduction by either independent or established artists is the final fair use claim made by Napster. The district court noted that plaintiffs did not seek to enjoin this and any other noninfringing use of the Napster system, including: chat rooms, message boards and Napster's New Artist Program. *Napster,* 114 F.Supp.2d at 917. Plaintiffs do not challenge these uses on appeal.

We find no error in the district court's determination that plaintiffs will likely succeed in establishing that Napster users do not have a fair use defense. Accordingly, we next address whether Napster is secondarily liable for the direct infringement under two doctrines of copyright law: contributory copyright infringement and vicarious copyright infringement.

IV

We first address plaintiffs' claim that Napster is liable for contributory copyright infringement. Traditionally, "one who, with knowledge of the infringing activity, induces, causes or materially contributes to the infringing conduct of another, may be held liable as a 'contributory' infringer." *Gershwin Publ'g Corp. v. Columbia Artists Mgmt., Inc.,* 443 F.2d 1159, 1162 (2d Cir. 1971); *see also Fono-visa, Inc. v. Cherry Auction, Inc.,* 76 F.3d 259, 264 (9th Cir. 1996). Put differently, liability exists if the defendant engages in "personal conduct that encourages or assists the infringement." *Matthew Bender & Co. v. West Publ'g Co.,* 158 F.3d 693, 706 (2d Cir.1998).

The district court determined that plaintiffs in all likelihood would establish Napster's liability as a contributory infringer. The district court did not err; Napster, by its conduct, knowingly encourages and assists the infringement of plaintiffs' copyrights.

A. Knowledge

Contributory liability requires that the secondary infringer "know or have reason to know" of direct infringement. *Cable/Home Communication Corp. Network Prods., Inc.*, 902 F.2d 829, 845 & 846 n. 29 (11th Cir. 1990); *Religious Tech. Ctr. v. Netcom On-Line Communication Servs., Inc.*, 907 F.Supp. 1361, 1373-74 (N.D. Cal.1995) (framing issue as "whether Netcom knew or should have known of" the infringing activities). The district court found that Napster had both actual and constructive knowledge that its users exchanged copyrighted music. The district court also concluded that the law does not require knowledge of "specific acts of infringement" and rejected Napster's contention that because the company cannot distinguish infringing from noninfringing files, it does not "know" of the direct infringement. 114 F.Supp.2d at 917.

It is apparent from the record that Napster has knowledge, both actual and constructive,[1] of direct infringement. Napster claims that it is nevertheless protected from contributory liability by the teaching of *Sony Corp. v. Universal City Studios, Inc.*, 464 U.S. 417, 104 S.Ct. 774, 78 L.Ed.2d 574 (1984). We disagree. We observe that Napster's actual, specific knowledge of direct infringement renders Sony's holding of limited assistance to Napster. We are compelled to make a clear distinction between the architecture of the Napster system and Napster's conduct in relation to the operational capacity of the system.

The *Sony* Court refused to hold the manufacturer and retailers of video tape recorders liable for contributory infringement despite evidence that such machines could be and were used to infringe plaintiffs' copyrighted television shows. *Sony* stated that if liability "is to be imposed on petitioners in this case, it must rest on the fact that *they have sold equipment with constructive knowledge of the fact that their customers may use that equipment to make unauthorized copies* of copyrighted material." *Id.* at 439, 104 S.Ct. 774 (emphasis added). The *Sony* Court declined to impute the requisite level of knowledge where the defendants made and sold equipment capable of both infringing and "substantial noninfringing uses." *Id.* at 442 (adopting a modified "staple article of commerce" doctrine from patent law). *See also Universal City Studios, Inc. v. Sony Corp.*, 480 F.Supp. 429, 459 (C.D.Cal.1979) ("This court agrees with defendants that their knowledge was insufficient to make them contributory infringers."), *rev'd*, 659 F.2d 963 (9th Cir.1981), *rev'd*, 464 U.S. 417, 104 S.Ct. 774,78 L.Ed.2d 574 (1984); Alfred C. Yen, *Internet Service Provider Liability for Subscriber Copyright Infringement, Enterprise Liability, and the First Amendment*, 88 Geo. L.J. 1833, 1874 & 1893 n.210 (2000) (suggesting that, after *Sony*, most Internet service providers lack "the requisite level of knowledge" for the imposition of contributory liability).

We are bound to follow *Sony*, and will not impute the requisite level of knowledge to Napster merely because peer-to-peer file sharing technology may be used to infringe plaintiffs' copyrights. *See* 464 U.S. at 436, 104 S.Ct.

774 (rejecting argument that merely supplying the " 'means' to accomplish an infringing activity" leads to imposition of liability). We depart from the reasoning of the district court that Napster failed to demonstrate that its system is capable of commercially significant noninfringing uses. *See Napster,* 114 F. Supp.2d at 916, 917–18. The district court improperly confined the use analysis to current uses, ignoring the system's capabilities. See *generally Sony,* 464 U.S. at 442–43, 104 S.Ct. 774 (framing inquiry as whether the video tape recorder is *"capable* of commercially significant noninfringing uses") (emphasis added). Consequently, the district court placed undue weight on the proportion of current infringing use as compared to current and future noninfringing use. *See generally Vault Corp. v. Quaid Software Ltd.,* 847 F.2d 255, 264–67 (5th Cir.1988) (single noninfringing use implicated *Sony*). Nonetheless, whether we might arrive at a different result is not the issue here. *See Sports Form, Inc. v. United Press Int'l, Inc.,* 686 F.2d 750, 752 (9th Cir. 1982). The instant appeal occurs at an early point in the proceedings and "the fully developed factual record may be materially different from that initially before the district court...." *Id.* at 753. Regardless of the number of Napster's infringing versus noninfringing uses, the evidentiary record here supported the district court's finding that plaintiffs would likely prevail in establishing that Napster knew or had reason to know of its users' infringement of plaintiffs' copyrights.

This analysis is similar to that of *Religious Technology Center v. Netcom On-Line Communication Services, Inc.,* which suggests that in an online context, evidence of actual knowledge of specific acts of infringement is required to hold a computer system operator liable for contributory copyright infringement. 907 F.Supp. at 1371. *Netcom* considered the potential contributory copyright liability of a computer bulletin board operator whose system supported the posting of infringing material. *Id.* at 1374. The court, in denying Netcom's motion for summary judgment of noninfringement and plaintiff's motion for judgment on the pleadings, found that a disputed issue of fact existed as to whether the operator had sufficient knowledge of infringing activity. *Id.* at 1374–75.

The court determined that for the operator to have sufficient knowledge, the copyright holder must "provide the necessary documentation to show there is likely infringement." 907 F.Supp. at 1374; cf. *Cubby, Inc. v. Compuserve, Inc.,* 776 F. Supp. 135, 141 (S.D.N.Y. 1991) (recognizing that online service provider does not and cannot examine every hyperlink for potentially defamatory material). If such documentation was provided, the court reasoned that Netcom would be liable for contributory infringement because its failure to remove the material "and thereby stop an infringing copy from being distributed worldwide constitutes substantial participation" in distribution of copyrighted material. *Id.*

We agree that if a computer system operator learns of specific infringing material available on his system and fails to purge such material from the system, the operator knows of and contributes to direct infringement. *See Netcom,* 907 F.Supp. at 1374. Conversely, absent any specific information which identifies infringing activity, a computer system operator cannot be liable for contributory infringement merely because the structure of the system allows for the exchange of copyrighted material. *See Sony,* 464 U.S. at 436, 442-43. To enjoin simply because a computer network allows for infringing use would, in our opinion, violate *Sony* and potentially restrict activity unrelated to infringing use.

We nevertheless conclude that sufficient knowledge exists to impose contributory liability when linked to demonstrated infringing use of the Napster system. *See Napster,* 114 F.Supp.2d at 919 (*"Religious Technology Center* would not mandate a determination that Napster, Inc. lacks the knowledge requisite to contributory infringement."). The record supports the district court's finding that Napster has *actual* knowledge that *specific* infringing material is available using its system, that it could block access to the system by suppliers of the infringing material, and that it failed to remove the material. *See Napster,* 114 F. Supp.2d at 918, 920-21.

B. Material Contribution

Under the facts as found by the district court, Napster materially contributes to the infringing activity. Relying on *Fonovisa,* the district court concluded that "[w]ithout the support services defendant provides, Napster users could not find and download the music they want with the ease of which defendant boasts." *Napster,* 114 F.Supp.2d at 919-20 ("Napster is an integrated service designed to enable users to locate and download MP3 music files."). We agree that Napster provides "the site and facilities" for direct infringement. *See Fonovisa,* 76 F.3d at 264; *cf. Netcom,* 907 F.Supp. at 1372 ("Netcom will be liable for contributory infringement since its failure to cancel [a user's] infringing message and thereby stop an infringing copy from being distributed worldwide constitutes substantial participation."). The district court correctly applied the reasoning in *Fonovisa,* and properly found that Napster materially contributes to direct infringement.

We affirm the district court's conclusion that plaintiffs have demonstrated a likelihood of success on the merits of the contributory copyright infringement claim....

The district court correctly recognized that a preliminary injunction against Napster's participation in copyright infringement is not only warranted but required. We believe, however, that the scope of the injunction needs modification in light of our opinion. Specifically, we reiterate that contributory liability may potentially be imposed only to the extent that Napster: (1) receives reasonable knowledge of specific infringing files with copyrighted musical compositions and sound recordings; (2) knows or should know that such files are available on the Napster system; and (3) fails to act to prevent viral distribution of the works. *See Netcom,* 907 F. Supp. at 1374–75. The mere existence of the Napster system, absent actual notice and Napster's demonstrated failure to remove the offending material, is insufficient to impose contributory liability. *See Sony,* 464 U.S. at 442–43, 104 S.Ct. 774.

Conversely, Napster may be vicariously liable when it fails to affirmatively use its ability to patrol its system and preclude access to potentially infringing files listed in its search index. Napster has both the ability to use its search function to identify infringing musical recordings and the right to bar participation of users who engage in the transmission of infringing files.

The preliminary injunction which we stayed is overbroad because it places on Napster the entire burden of ensuring that no "copying, downloading, uploading, transmitting, or distributing" of plaintiffs' works occur on the system. As stated, we place the burden on plaintiffs to provide notice to Napster of copyrighted works and files containing such works available on the Napster system before Napster has the duty to disable access to the offending content. Napster, however, also bears the burden of policing the system within the limits of the system. Here, we recognize that this is not an exact science in that the files are user named. In crafting the injunction on remand, the district court should recognize that Napster's system does not currently appear to allow Napster access to users' MP3 files.

Based on our decision to remand, Napster's additional arguments on appeal going to the scope of the injunction need not be addressed. We, however, briefly address Napster's First Amendment argument so that it is not reasserted on remand. Napster contends that the present injunction violates the First Amendment because it is broader than necessary. The company asserts two distinct free speech rights: (1) its right to publish a "directory" (here, the search index) and (2) its users' right to exchange information. We note that First Amendment concerns in copyright are allayed by the presence of the fair use doctrine. *See* 17 U.S.C. § 107; *see generally Nihon Keizai Shimbun v. Comline Business Data, Inc.,* 166 F.3d 65, 74 (2d Cir.1999); *Netcom,* 923 F.Supp. at 1258 (stating that the Copyright Act balances First Amendment concerns with the rights of copyright holders). There was a preliminary determination here that Napster users are not fair users. Uses of copyrighted material that are not fair uses are rightfully enjoined. *See Dr. Seuss Enters. v. Penguin Books USA, Inc.,* 109 F.3d 1394, 1403 (9th Cir.1997) (rejecting defendants' claim that injunction would constitute a prior restraint in violation of the First Amendment).

Note

1. The district court found actual knowledge because: (1) a document authored by Napster co-founder Sean Parker mentioned "the need to remain ignorant of users' real names and IP addresses 'since they are exchanging pirated music'"; and (2) the Recording Industry Association of America ("RIAA") informed Napster of more than 12,000 infringing files, some of which are still available. 114 F.Supp.2d at 918. The district court found constructive knowledge because: (a) Napster executives have recording industry experience; (b) they have enforced intellectual property rights in other instances; (c) Napster executives have downloaded copyrighted songs from the system; and (d) they have promoted the site with "screen shots listing infringing files." *Id.* at 919.

Jessica Litman et al.

 **NO**

Brief Amicus Curiae of Copyright Law Professors in Support of Reversal

I. Interests of Amici

This brief is submitted by 18 American law professors who teach and write about copyright law. Amici are deeply concerned with the integrity of copyright law, and with assuring that enforcement of copyright owners' rights is consistent with, rather than in conflict with, the copyright laws' goals of promoting innovation and encouraging the broad dissemination of protected works. This case raises a number of important issues, several of them issues of first impression. We believe that this case will have a critical impact on the application of copyright law to the Internet....

II. Summary of Argument

Napster's peer-to-peer file sharing system is an example of an enormously promising technology that gives individual consumers enhanced control over the information they find, save and transmit over the Internet. The district court, concerned about the use of Napster to infringe copyrights in recorded music, entered a sweeping injunction that would have the effect of shutting Napster down. It would be impractical for any peer-to-peer file sharing system to operate within the constraints imposed by the district court's view of the law. In reaching this result, the district court misread the Supreme Court's decision in *Sony Corp. of America v. Universal City Studios,* 464 U.S. 417, 447 (1984), and applied an unduly narrow interpretation of the fair use privilege.

III. Argument

A. Copyright Law Should Not Be Extended to Disable New Technologies

United States history has seen the introduction of a variety of new technologies that could and did facilitate massive copyright infringement. The development

From Brief Amicus Curiae of Copyright Law Professors in Support of Reversal, *Napster, Inc. v. A&M Records, Inc.* and *Napster, Inc. v. Jerry Leiber et al.,* Appeal Nos. 00-16401 and 00-16403 (9th Cir. 2001). Some notes omitted.

of radio, television, photocopiers, analog audio and video tape recorders, cable television, fax, communications satellites, computers, digital audio, digital video and the Internet all permitted new methods of copyright infringement and piracy. *See, e.g., Sony Corp. of America v. Universal City Studios,* 464 U.S. 417, 447 (1984); *Teleprompter Corp. v. Columbia Broadcasting System,* 415 U.S. 394 (1974); *Buck v. Jewell-LaSalle Realty Co,* 283 U.S. 191(1931); *Williams & Wilkins v. United States,* 487 F.2d 1345 (Ct. Cl. 1973), *aff'd by an equally divided Court,* 420 U.S. 376 (1975). Courts responded cautiously to claims that new technologies should be shut down because they facilitate copyright infringement, and rightly so. The Constitution empowers Congress to enact copyright laws in order to "promote the Progress of Science and useful Arts...." U.S. Const. Art. 1, § 8, cl. 8. Outlawing a useful technology merely because many people use it as a tool for infringement will rarely promote the progress of science and the useful arts. Only when the technology is not capable of legitimate uses does it make sense to outlaw it.

In this case, it is common ground that Napster is not directly infringing Plaintiffs' copyrights. It does not in any way reproduce, adapt, distribute to the public, publicly perform or publicly display works controlled by the Plaintiffs. That is uncontested. Rather, Napster is a tool. Plaintiffs argued, and the district court held, that an injunction should issue against Napster on the ground that [1] ordinary users were infringing Plaintiffs' copyrights when they shared music files; and [2] Napster was the tool that facilitated those infringing acts.

The Supreme Court has spoken directly to the question of when an injunction may issue against the supplier of a technology purely because of infringing acts by the technology's users. In *Sony Corp. of America v. Universal City Studios,* 464 U.S. 417, 447 (1984), copyright owners sought to enjoin the sale of VCRs because consumers used them to engage in unauthorized copying of copyright-protected programming. Plaintiffs argued that the manufacturer was liable for the unauthorized copies made by consumers. The Supreme Court disagreed. Where a technology functioned as a tool for infringement but was capable of significant non-infringing uses, the Court held, supplying the technology to consumers does not violate the law. *Id.* at 442. Allowing an injunction to issue in such a case, it continued, would disserve the public interest in access to the technology. *Id.*

Napster is the best-known example of a new technology deploying what has come to be called peer-to-peer networking, a system in which individuals can search for and share files that reside on the hard drives of other personal computers connected to the Internet. *A&M Records, Inc. v. Napster,* No. C 99-5183 MHP (Aug. 10, 2000), slip op. at 4. See David Streitfeld, *The Web's Next Step: Unraveling Itself; Software Threatens Search Engines,* Washington Post, July 18, 2000, at A01. Peer-to-peer file sharing allows individuals to bypass central providers of content and to find and exchange material with one another. The decentralized model of peer-to-peer networking poses a significant challenge to sectors of the entertainment and information businesses that follow a model of centralized control over content distribution. However, this is not the sort of challenge that copyright law is designed to redress. The district court's ruling would ban a new technology in order to protect existing business models, and would invoke copyright to stifle innovation, not to promote it.

Peer-to-peer file sharing may hold solutions for a number of problems plaguing the Internet. The majority of individuals search for content on the Internet using search engines. *See* Steve Lawrence and Lee Giles, *Accessibility and Distribution of Information on the Web,* 400 Nature 107 (1999). Current search engines, however, are imperfect, indexing only a small fraction of available websites. The design of web-based search engines, moreover, tends to favor commercial sites over non-commercial ones, popular sites over more marginal ones, and U.S.-based sites over sites in other countries. *See id.*; Helen Nissenbaum and Lucas Introna, *Sustaining the Public Good Vision of the Internet: The Politics of Search Engines* (Princeton University Center for the Arts and Cultural Policy Studies Working Paper #9, 1999). Current search engines have a massive task to complete in order to maintain a current record of even a small fraction of the Internet, and their indexes are notoriously out of date. *See* Lawrence and Giles, *supra.* Peer-to-peer networking enables individuals to locate material available over the Internet that most search engines do not find, by searching among computers of groups of individuals likely to have the content or know where to find it.

Peer-to-peer file sharing systems have significant advantages over conventional web-based distribution for individuals who want to make content available as well as for those who seek content. Distribution over a peer-to-peer network does not require access to a web server, nor the ability to translate the content into HTML code. Further, it is unnecessary to cause the content to be indexed by a search engine, or to encourage the search engine to list it prominently in relevant search results. Peer-to-peer file sharing systems have the potential to change the architecture of the Internet. *See, e.g.,* Amy Kover, *Napster: The Hot Idea of the Year,* Fortune, June 26, 2000, at 128.

Peer-to-peer technology, finally, holds promise as a potential method to relieve network congestion. Because file transfers need not be routed through central control points (and need not even be hosted at central locations), the ability to share files using peer-to-peer technology does not depend on the level of traffic at a host server. Thus, the technology ultimately may deliver greatly increased efficiency in the operation of the Internet.

The injunction issued by the district court is so sweeping that it would be impractical for any peer-to-peer file sharing application to operate under its strictures. As the district court recognized, the key feature of peer-to-peer file sharing systems is that the individual users control the transfer of files. *Napster,* slip op. at 17. The court's injunction required that Napster reconfigure its system to ensure that users could not share files without the copyright owner's authorization. To comply with such an injunction, Napster, or any other peer-to-peer file sharing system, would need to disable users from controlling the selection and transfer of files, lest they choose to engage in unauthorized transfers. The effect of the injunction is to brand an enormously promising technological innovation as illegal. Copyright law does not, and in our view quite plainly should not, authorize this result. Copyright owners' interests in maintaining control over their works are very important, but not so important that society must forego useful technology capable of substantial non-infringing uses in order to protect those interests. That is the lesson of the Supreme Court's decision in *Sony*.

B. The District Court Should Not Have Imposed Contributory Liability on a Technology Capable of Substantial Non-Infringing Use

In *Sony*, copyright owners argued that the producer of videocassette recorders should be held contributorily liable for consumers' unauthorized copies of copyrighted programming. The Supreme Court's response was two-fold. First, the Court held, liability for copyright infringement should not be imposed on the basis of the sale of a device that was widely used for legitimate purposes. "Indeed, it need merely be *capable* of substantial noninfringing uses." *Sony*, 464 U.S. at 442 (emphasis added). Second, the Court recognized, unauthorized uses are not necessarily illegitimate or unlawful uses.*Id.* at 447. The district court's opinion misunderstood both points.

1. The Court's "Ongoing Control" Exception Is Groundless
The district court acknowledged the controlling effect of *Sony* with respect to a claim of contributory infringement based on a tool that facilitates unauthorized copying. *See Napster*, slip op. at 17. Judge Patel nonetheless held the *Sony* test to be inapplicable because "Napster exercises ongoing control over its service," *id.* at 25, although she did not find that Napster exercised any control over the selection and transmission of files shared by its subscribers. She postulated that perhaps Napster could write software that would inventory users' hard drives when they log on, and allow only the sharing of "authorized music." *Id.* at 33. The nub of this reasoning is that the supplier of a technology should be liable for infringements committed by the technology's users whenever it might be able to redesign or retrofit the technology to eliminate the possibility of infringement. The lessor of a photocopy machine, thus, would be liable for the infringing copies made by its lessee because it continued to maintain and service the equipment, and might be able (in theory) to design and install different technology that publishers would prefer.

Yet that is precisely the approach rejected by the Supreme Court in *Sony*. The Court in *Sony* did not hold that when ordinary people use a new technology to engage in copyright infringement, the supplier of that technology must come up with ways to stop the infringement or stand enjoined. Rather, the Court held the opposite: Notwithstanding that a technological tool facilitates copyright infringement, the "Progress of Science and the useful Arts" precludes an injunction so long as the tool is capable of substantial noninfringing uses. The balance rests on the side of permitting new technology, not of stifling it.

In any event, the record does not show that Napster, as a practical matter, could ensure that only non-infringing file sharing took place while continuing to offer a peer-to-peer network system. Quite the contrary: Peer-to-peer file sharing systems vest control over the transfer of files in the individual users. From users' standpoint, that is their most compelling feature. If the proprietors of peer-to-peer file sharing systems are required to control the content of all files on the system, the technology will lose much of its value for a host of legitimate information-sharing applications.

2. The District Court Incorrectly Treated All Unauthorized Use as Infringing

The district court's opinion is incorrect for a second, independent reason: The court classed a large category of potentially legitimate uses as infringing. The judge took the view that *all* unauthorized copying and distribution of copyright-protected material by Napster subscribers was illegal. Because Plaintiffs had not licensed Napster, the judge concluded that any files shared by Napster users containing copyrighted material constituted infringement:

> For the reasons set forth below, the court finds that any potential non-infringing use of the Napster service is minimal or connected to the infringing activity, or both. The substantial or commercially significant use of the service was, and continues to be, the unauthorized downloading and uploading of popular music, most of which is copyrighted.

> — *Napster,* slip op. at 18.[1]

Thus, she issued a broad injunction prohibiting Napster from facilitating any "copying, downloading, uploading, transmitting or distributing Plaintiffs' copyrighted musical compositions or sound recordings, protected by either federal or state law, without express permission of the rights owner." Yet this too flies in the face of the Supreme Court's opinion in *Sony.*

Copyright law has never given copyright owners control over all uses of their works. Rather, it gives copyright owners exclusive rights and expressly subjects those rights to a host of exceptions. *See* 17 U.S.C. §§ 106–122, 1008. Of particular relevance here, the law allows unauthorized copies, downloads, uploads, transmissions or distributions that might be fair use under § 107, lawful noncommercial consumer copies under § 1008, or private performances and transmissions over which the statute gives the copyright owner no control. *Sony* makes plain that facilitation of such unauthorized but lawful uses is sufficient as a matter of law to constitute the capability for substantial non-infringing use. *Sony,* 464 U.S. at 447.[1]

The district court rejected Napster's arguments that some or all of its users' file trading activity might be permitted under 17 U.S. C. § 1008 or the fair use doctrine codified in 17 U.S. C. § 107. Yet the issue whether and when individual consumers may be liable under the copyright act for making noncommercial copies of recorded music for their personal use is a difficult one, requiring careful and thoughtful analysis. It seems evident that if individuals may legally engage in massive free copying of recorded music, a potential source of copyright owners' revenue may be undermined. It seems equally clear, however, that the exercise of a statutory privilege does not become illegal merely because many people engage in it.

3. The District Court Applied an Inappropriately Narrow View of Fair Use

The district court's analysis of fair use gave the doctrine unduly limited scope in the online context.[3] Individual users who use Napster to share MP3 files for their personal use are engaging in consumptive rather than transformative use, but are also engaging in noncommercial personal use, which has traditionally been within the core of uses considered to be fair. *See* Alan Latman, *Fair Use of Copyrighted Works,* Study No. 14, Copyright Law Revision, Studies Prepared for the Subcommittee on Patents, Trademarks and Copyrights, Senate Judiciary Committee 11–12 (1958). The district court was unwilling to consider Napster users' activities to be personal or private use, both because files were transmitted over the Internet and because of the "vast scale of Napster use." *See Napster,* slip op. at 19. The court's reluctance is understandable, but problematic.

Most Internet-related activity involves the transfer of files over the Internet. The use of the Internet is growing at an extraordinary pace. There is a very real possibility that within our lifetimes, the Internet will become a dominant if not the dominant medium for both personal and commercial communication in the U.S. *See Reno v. ACLU,* 521 U.S. 844, 885 (1997). Because individual consumers' activities over digital networks can be tracked and recorded, a whole realm of personal uses that were essentially undetectable in the offline world become a matter of record when conducted online. Moreover, the nature of digital technology means that many activities analogous to non-infringing acts in the offline world become at least technical infringements when conducted over the Internet. Traditionally, loaning or giving a book or record to a friend infringed no rights under copyright; the distribution came within the first sale doctrine. *See* 17 U.S.C. § 109. On the Internet, however, the analysis is different. Under current technology, one cannot share material over the Internet without both reproducing it multiple times and transmitting it. The need for a balanced fair use privilege in the online world is at least as crucial as it is in the offline world.

4. The Court Disregarded Concededly Non-Infringing Uses

Finally, the district judge reasoned that her injunction did not offend *Sony* because it permits Napster to operate so long as it is used only for the narrow set of activities that the opinion deems noninfringing: "chat rooms, message boards, the new artist program or any distribution authorized by rights holders." Napster, under the injunction, remains free to operate so long as it can ensure that no unauthorized uploading or downloading of major label recordings takes place. Slip op. at 26. Yet this, again, turns *Sony* on its head. The district court's analysis is tantamount to a holding that Sony could market VCRs only if it could ensure that the VCRs were never used to commit infringement. The point of *Sony* is that copyright law does not give copyright owners control over new technologies with legitimate uses, even though consumers can use those technologies to enjoy copyrighted works without authorization. It is clear why copyright owners might want such protection, but Congress has not given it to them.

C. This Court Should Reverse the District Court's Decision

To paint Napster as an outlaw, the district court detailed at great length Plaintiffs' plans to venture into online distribution. Slip op. at 15–17. But by focusing on Plaintiffs' hoped-for but still inchoate profits before finding a cognizable wrong, the court erred. Absent a showing of contributory infringement, copyright law was not intended to insulate Plaintiffs' business plans from the course of technological development. Having to change business plans in response to evolving technologies is what competition is all about. The development of peer-to-peer networking technologies may cause Plaintiffs to rethink their plans for online distribution. However, that is a setback for which current copyright law provides no cure. If Plaintiffs want copyright law extended to allow the suppression of new technologies, they must make their case to Congress. The core copyright principle recognized in the *Sony* opinion is that intellectual property owners are not entitled to prohibit or exercise monopoly control over new technologies that incidentally (or even not so incidentally) threaten their established business models. Evolving technologies create new opportunities for lawful competition and, as a result, copyright owners must sometimes change their business methods.

Notes

1. The district court repeatedly referred to the fact that most of the files downloaded and uploaded on Napster contain music that is copyrighted. *See, e.g., id.,* at 5 ("The evidence shows that virtually all Napster users download or upload copyrighted files and that the vast majority of the music available on Napster is copyrighted."). It would be surprising if any of the music available on Napster were not subject to copyright protection. Since copyright vests automatically in all original works fixed in tangible form, and lasts for a term now lasting for approximately 95 years, *see* 17 U.S.C. §§ 201, 302, 304, almost all music except that written before 1923 and recorded before Congress extended copyright protection to sound recordings in 1971 is protected by copyright. That of course includes the music in Napster's New Artist Program, and the music files authorized for upload and download as well as the material controlled by the major record labels.

2. The Court wrote:

   > Even unauthorized uses of a copyrighted work are not necessarily infringing. An unlicensed use of the copyright is not an infringement unless it conflicts with one of the specific exclusive rights conferred by the copyright statute. *Twentieth Century Music Corp. v. Aiken,* 422 U.S., at 154–155. Moreover, the definition of exclusive rights in § 106 of the present Act is prefaced by the words "subject to sections 107 through 118." Those sections describe a variety of uses of copyrighted material that "are not infringements of copyright" "notwithstanding the provisions of section 106." The most pertinent in this case is § 107, the legislative endorsement of the doctrine of "fair use."

   > — 464 U.S. at 447.

3. In evaluating whether consumers' use of Napster qualifies as fair use, moreover, Judge Patel gave no weight to this Court's conclusion in *RIAA v. Diamond Multimedia,* 180 F.3d 1072 (9th Cir. 1999), that the copyright law permits consumers to make noncommercial personal MP3 files of major label music. Her opinion assumes without analysis that individual consumers should be liable under the statute when a pattern of unauthorized copying threatens to displace a sale. That assumption seems highly questionable. Congress has twice turned its attention

to consumer home copying of recorded music. Both times it concluded that consumers should not be individually liable for noncommercial reproduction of music for personal use. *See* Audio Home Recording Act, Pub. L. No. 102-563, 106 Stat. 4237 (1992); H. R. Rep. No. 102-873, pt. 1 (1992); Act of Oct. 15, 1971, Pub. L. No. 92-104, 85 Stat. 391; H. R. Rep. No. 92-487, at 7 (1971). In neither case, of course, was Congress envisioning the Internet. It may be that the nature of the Internet will persuade Congress to revisit the issue of individual liability for noncommercial copying of recorded music. For now, the courts have the difficult task of applying the current statute to circumstances Congress did not consider.

POSTSCRIPT

Does the Sharing of Music Files Through Napster Violate Copyright Laws?

As this is being written, the future of Napster does not look promising. If the ruling declaring that Napster was engaged in a violation of copyright laws is not overturned on appeal, Napster will try to change its model for sharing software or go out of business altogether. Yet whatever happens to Napster will not put an end to the issues and disputes involving the Internet and copyright that will arise, and the resulting arguments will almost assuredly be made again in contexts slightly different from Napster.

Napster highlighted the opportunities for and ease of copying online. What should be remembered is that while all this copying was going on, Napster itself was not really copying anything. The company was making copying possible by others, and Napster ran into particular trouble because it made and employed an index of songs that could be copied. The Court was troubled by how involved Napster was in facilitating copying, but others may figure out ways to allow file "sharing" without using indexes or other mechanisms that link them directly with users who copy the files.

Is copying simple theft, as many copyright owners argue? Or is copying merely part of the creative process, something that we all do and need to do in order to foster progress? Copyright is specifically mentioned in the U.S. Constitution. Article I, Section 8, states that the purpose of copyright is "to promote the progress of science and useful arts, by securing for limited times to authors and inventors the exclusive right to their respective writings and discoveries." Copyright, therefore, is for the benefit of society, and rewarding authors and creators is the means to achieve this. But it should be kept in mind that there will always be tension between encouraging the use and processing of information and discouraging it. Too little control might negatively affect a creative activity. But too much control and too many restrictions on copying might also interfere with creative activity.

Interesting readings about copyright in a digital age are Jessica Litman, *Digital Copyright: Protecting Intellectual Property on the Internet* (Prometheus Books, 2001); Robert P. Merges, Peter S. Menell, and Mark A. Lemley, *Intellectual Property in the New Technological Age,* 2d ed. (Panel, 2000); Paul Edward Geller, "Copyright History and the Future: What's Culture Got to Do With It?" 47 *Journal of the Copyright Society of the U.S.A.* 209, 264 (2000); and Jonathan Zittrain, "What the Publisher Can Teach the Patient: Intellectual Property and Privacy in an Era of Trusted Privication," 52 *Stanford Law Review* 1201 (2000).

ISSUE 6

Should the Insanity Defense
Be Abolished?

YES: Jonathan Rowe, from "Why Liberals Should Hate the Insanity Defense," *The Washington Monthly* (May 1984)

NO: Richard Bonnie, from Statement Before the Committee on the Judiciary, U.S. Senate (August 2, 1982)

ISSUE SUMMARY

YES: Editor Jonathan Rowe examines the insanity defense as it is now administered and finds that it is most likely to be used by white middle- or upper-class defendants and that its application is unfair and leads to unjust results.

NO: Professor of law Richard Bonnie argues that the abolition of the insanity defense would be immoral and would leave no alternative for those who are not responsible for their actions.

There is rarely a year in which the insanity defense is not raised in a high-profile case. When a crime is committed that raises questions about humanity and responsibility, defense lawyers may raise (or threaten to raise) the insanity defense. The success rate of such a defense strategy is quite low, and it is certainly lower than the public believes it to be. Yet the insanity defense remains a controversial issue.

In 1843 Daniel McNaughtan, suffering from delusions of persecution, fired a shot at a man he believed was British prime minister Robert Peel. Actually, the victim was the prime minister's secretary and the bullet killed him. Englishmen were outraged because three other attempted assassinations of political officials had recently taken place, and Queen Victoria was prompted to send her husband, Prince Albert, to the trial as an observer. When McNaughtan was found not guilty by reason of insanity, Victoria sent a letter to the House of Lords, complaining that McNaughtan and the other assassins were "perfectly conscious and aware of what they did." The Lords summoned 15 judges who, after considering the matter, pronounced the McNaughtan rule (commonly referred to as the M'Naghten rule) as the most appropriate formulation of the insanity defense. This test requires that a jury must find that the defendant, when the act was committed, did not know the nature and quality of the act or that he or she could not tell right from wrong.

One of the problems with the insanity defense is in defining insanity. If one argues in favor of the defense, one should be able to define insanity with reasonable precision and in a way that can be applied consistently. The great difficulty in providing a definition is the basic argument against the insanity defense. The insanity defense issue has caused great controversy between lawyers and psychiatrists over the meaning of insanity and mental illness and over the ability of psychiatrists to reliably diagnose the problems of defendants.

A frequent objection to the M'Naghten rule was that there were individuals who could distinguish between good and evil but still could not control their behavior. One response to this critique was the "irresistible impulse" test. Using this standard, a defendant would be relieved of responsibility for his or her actions even if he or she could distinguish right from wrong but, because of mental disease, could not avoid the action in question. A somewhat broader and more flexible version of the combined M'Naghten–irresistible impulse test was recommended by the American Law Institute in 1962. Under this formulation, people are not responsible for criminal conduct if they lack *substantial capacity* to appreciate the criminality of their conduct or to conform their conduct to the requirements of the law.

The most noteworthy and radical experiment with the reformulation of the insanity defense occurred in *Durham v. United States,* 214 F.2d 862 (1954). The District of Columbia Court of Appeals ruled that an accused was not criminally responsible if his or her act was the product of mental disease or defect. The effect of this rule was to increase the amount of expert psychiatric testimony presented in court about whether or not mental disease was present and whether or not the act was a product of the disease. Although welcomed by many because it allowed for a more complete psychiatric picture to be presented to the jury, the rule proved to be too vague and led to too much power being given to psychiatric experts. As a result, in *United States v. Brawner,* 471 F.2d 969 (1972), the Durham experiment was abandoned.

Examination of the insanity defense opens up some extremely important issues of law. For example, what are the purposes of punishment? What assumptions does the law make about human nature, free will, and personal responsibility? What should be the role of the jury, and what authority should be given medical and psychiatric experts in evaluating deviant behavior? How should we deal with the often competing goals of rehabilitation, retribution, and deterrence? These are among the questions raised in the following arguments presented by Jonathan Rowe and Richard Bonnie on the need for reforming or abolishing the insanity defense.

Jonathan Rowe

 **YES**

Why Liberals Should Hate the Insanity Defense

It's the fallacy of your legal system," said Gary Trapnell, a bank robber who not long afterwards would hijack a TWA 707 flying from Los Angeles to New York. "Either the man falls under this antiquated psychiatric scheme of things, or he doesn't." Trapnell was talking about the insanity defense, which he had used with great acumen to avoid jail for his innumerable crimes over the years. "I have no right to be on the streets," he added.

The insanity defense has been much in the news of late. We read cases such as that of the Michigan ex-convict who pleaded insanity after seven killings, won an acquittal, but returned to the streets two months later when he was declared sane. In a month, he was charged with murdering his wife. Or take the 23-year-old Connecticut man who left the state hospital three months after an insanity acquittal for stabbing a man. The acquittee's mother pleaded to have him recommitted, but to no avail. Shortly thereafter, he repeatedly stabbed a man whose home he was burglarizing. Once again he was declared not guilty by reason of insanity.

It sounds like the warmup for a right-wing tirade against the coddlers of criminals. But the much publicized trials of John Hinckley and others have cast the issue in a somewhat different light. In a strange way, by jumbling liberal and conservative loyalties, these have made debate on the subject not only necessary, but possible as well. Take the "Twinkie Defense," which enabled former San Francisco City Supervisor Dan White to get off with a light eight-year sentence after shooting, with obvious deliberation, San Francisco Mayor George Moscone and his city administrator, Harvey Milk. As Milk was both liberal and openly homosexual, thousands who probably never before identified with the cause of law and order were outraged that this brutal act of (at least symbolic) homophobia should go lightly punished. John Hinckley, for his part, was the son of a wealthy upper-middle-class family, and not the sort of fellow who evoked sympathies usually reserved for the downtrodden. His trial prompted even *The Nation,* which rarely concedes the cops an inch, to suggest some mild reforms in the insanity defense.

From Jonathan Rowe, "Why Liberals Should Hate the Insanity Defense," *The Washington Monthly,* vol. 16, no. 4 (May 1984). Copyright © 1984 by The Washington Monthly Company, 1611 Connecticut Avenue, NW, Washington, DC 20009; (202) 462–0128. Reprinted by permission of *The Washington Monthly.*

In the wake of the Hinckley trial, a number of reforms have been suggested. *The Nation,* along with many others, advocates that we put the burden of proof upon the defendant. (In the Hinckley case, the prosecutors actually had to prove him sane, which is no mean feat.) Others have called for a tighter legal definition of insanity itself. Such changes might be helpful, but they amount to fiddling. The only way to resolve the injustices of the insanity defense is to do away with it entirely. This may sound cruel, but it is not. Nor is it a proposal to "lock 'em up and throw away the key." To the contrary, the injustices of this defense go much deeper than a few criminals getting off the hook. They go close to the core of our current practices regarding punishment and correction. Getting rid of the insanity defense would help to make us confront the need for humane reform in the way we sentence and confine those who break the law.

Such a Deal

The insanity defense looms a good deal larger in our minds than it does in actual life. Somewhere between 1,000 and 2,000 criminals make use of it each year, or about 1 percent to 2 percent of felonies that go to trial (over 90 percent in many jurisdictions are plea-bargained before trial). The issue is important not because it arises frequently, but because it tends to arise in the most serious crimes: think of Son of Sam, for example, or the Hillside Strangler. Such people tend to be dangerous, and their trials attract so much publicity that they put our entire system of justice to a test. What single event of the last two years affected your view of the criminal justice system more than the Hinckley trial did?

It is hard to read about such trials without getting the impression that something is fundamentally wrong. Take the case of Robert H. Torsney, the New York City policeman who shot a 15-year-old black youth in the head from two feet away in November of 1978. In an article in the *Journal of Legal Medicine,* Abraham Halpern, director of psychiatry at the United Hospital, Port Chester, New York, tells the case in salient detail.

At first, Torsney's lawyer resisted any suggestion of psychological observation or treatment for his client. Such treatment for an officer who was only acting in the line of duty was "worse than putting him in the electric chair," the attorney said. As public indignation rose, however, and acquittal became more and more unlikely, the attorney decided that Torsney might have deep-seated psychological problems after all. At a hearing on Torsney's insanity defense, his paid psychiatrist explained the policeman's errant account of the incident, which was contradicted by other witnesses as an "involuntary retrospective falsification." Not a lie, mind you. The psychiatrist went on to explain that Torsney shot the kid because of an "organic psychomotor seizure" arising from a "mental defect."

The jury found Torsney not guilty by reason of insanity. After a year, however, the staff at the mental hospital recommended that he be released because they could find nothing wrong with him. When the lower court balked—such hasty releases are unseemly if nothing else—Torsney's attorney indignantly filed an appeal. "It can't be seriously argued," he wrote, "that the record in this case establishes that Mr. Torsney is either seriously mentally ill or presently dangerous. At most he may be said to have a personality flaw, which certainly does not distinguish him from the rest of society."

What really distinguished Torsney, it seemed, was that he had shot somebody and deserved to be punished. That such simple observations can become so obscured is largely the result of the wholesale invasion of psychiatry into the courtroom that has been underway since the 1950s. Back then, the stars of psychiatry and psychoactive drugs were shining bright. To many, we were on the threshold of a new age, in which psychiatrists could measure such things as responsibility and mental disease down to minute calibrations and effect cures with the precision of engineers. If only we could let these new wizards into the courtroom, to bring their expertise to bear upon the processes of justice.

The main opening came in 1954, when federal appeals Judge David Bazelon, of the Washington, D.C., District Court, declared the so-called "Durham Rule." Under the old "M'Naghten Rule," a criminal could be judged insane only if he or she didn't know right from wrong. This crimped the psychiatrists somewhat, since they tend to shrug their shoulders on questions of values. In the *Durham* case Judge Bazelon set them free, declaring that henceforth in the District of Columbia an accused was not criminally responsible "if his unlawful act was the product of mental disease or defect." Bazelon received a special award from the American Psychiatric Association, but not everyone was that enthused. The American Law Institute (ALI) produced a sort of compromise, declaring that a person wouldn't be responsible for a misdeed if he couldn't appreciate the wrongfulness of it or if he "lacked a substantial capacity ... to conform his conduct to the requirements of the law." Though somewhat stiffer on paper, this ALI rule didn't vary from the Durham Rule in practice all that much. Adopted by a majority of the states, its various permutations have given the psychiatrists virtual free rein in the courtroom ever since.

The Hinckley trial demonstrated what the heavenly city of courtroom psychiatry has become. Three teams of psychiatrists—11 in all—picked over Hinckley's mind for hours in an exercise that 200 years from now will no doubt seem much the way that the heated debates over the medieval heresies seem to us today. The resulting trial dragged on for 52 excruciating days. One defense psychiatrist, Thomas C. Goldman, told the jury with a straight face that Hinckley saw actress Jody Foster as an "idealized mother who is all-giving and endowed with magical power," while President Reagan was an "all evil prohibitive figure who hates him, seeks to destroy him, and deny access to the idealized mother figure." No wonder he tried to shoot the man.

Or take the comments of Richard Delman, a psychiatrist who testified for the defense in the Dan White trial. As Lee Coleman, also a psychiatrist, tells it in his new book, *The Reign of Error,* Delman concluded on the basis of inkblot and other tests that it was White's deep concern for others that led him to sneak into San Francisco City Hall through a window rather than walk in through the front door. "He didn't want to embarrass the officer who was operating the metal detector [and would have discovered his gun]," Delman said.

On at least one occasion this kind of analysis has been more than even the defendant could take. Coleman cites the case of Inez Garcia, who was raped by two men in Soledad, California; afterwards, she went home, got a rifle, and shot one of her attackers. At her trial she sat listening to defense psychiatrist Jane Olden go on and on about her "reactive formations" and her self-image as a "saint-like idealized virgin." "If you trigger her negative feelings, which would be provoked by such an act as rape," Olden explained, "being a hysterical person who was striving always to express this sensuality and aggression, then you could indeed throw her into a state where she is emotionally relating to her own conflict."

Garcia stood up and yelled at the judge, "I killed [him] because I was raped and I'd kill him again."

If you smell a fish in such psychologizing, it is with good reason. There is a cadre of so-called "forensic psychiatrists," who show up in these insanity trials again and again, plying their offensive or defensive specialties. Dr. Alan Stone of Harvard, former head of the American Psychiatric Association, describes the kind of trial that results as a "three-ring circus, in which lawyers are the ring-masters and the psychiatric witnesses are the clowns, and if they are carefully trained, then they will be trained clowns." Another Harvard psychiatrist, David Baer, was a defense witness in the Hinckley trial but does not regularly partic-ipate in these affairs, and he revealed some of the details to a reporter from *Harper's*. He spent, he said, at least 20 to 25 hours rehearsing his testimony with the lawyers, who admonished him, among other things, not to "weaken your answers with all the qualifications you think you ought to make." They said, "Oh, don't mention the exploding bullets. My God, that's so damaging to the case," he recalls. Baer, who was paid $35,000 for his efforts, added that he was "determined never to tell a lie."

That may be. But what happens to most psychiatrists who resist the "train-ing" of the defense lawyers? "If a man doesn't testify the right way, he is not rehired," said one defense attorney in a study published in the *Rutgers Law Jour-nal*. (Section 6 of the "Principles of Medical Ethics" of the American Psychiatric Association, by the way, reads: "A physician should not dispose of his services under terms or conditions which tend to interfere with or impair the free and complete exercise of his medical judgment.")

Did You Hear Voices?

The theory behind our "adversary" system is that when you pit one group of experts like these against another the truth will somehow emerge. When the hired-gun psychiatrists do their act, however, the result is not information, but confusion. "None of them had the same conclusion," complained Nathalia Brown, a shop mechanic at the local electric utility and a Hinckley juror. "All of them said he had this illness, that illness, so how are we to know what illness he has? I felt on the brink of insanity myself going through this, you know."

This, of course, is precisely what defense lawyers seek. As far back as 1945, Julian Carroll, the New York attorney who handled poet Ezra Pound's famous insanity defense against treason charges, wrote a friend that insanity trials are a "farce" in which the "learned medicos for each side squarely contradict each other and completely befuddle the jury." What was true then is even more true today, and all it took was confusion and nagging doubts in the minds of the jurors to gain Hinckley's acquittal.

In the nation's prisons, fooling the shrinks is getting to be a science. Inkblot tests offer fertile ground for displays of psychosis, and inmates who have successfully pleaded insanity have instructed their cohorts on what to see —sexual acts, genitalia, and the like. Ken Bianchi, the Hillside Strangler, studied books on psychology and hypnosis before convincing a number of psychiatrists he had a dual personality, and only an especially alert one found him out. An experiment at Stanford University suggested that conning these psychiatrists may not be all that hard. Eight subjects, all without any record of mental illness, feigned hearing voices and thereby gained admission to 12 different mental hospitals. They did not falsify any details of their lives other than that they heard voices. Eleven of the 12 were diagnosed as "schizophrenic" while the 12th was diagnosed "manic depressive."

"I probably know more about psychiatry... than your average resident psychiatrist," boasted Gary Trapnell, who had some justification for his claim. "I can bullshit the hell out of one in ten minutes."

It's not that psychiatry has nothing to tell us, nor that many of its practitioners are not dedicated to helping others. The problem is the way this specialty is used in insanity trials: the endeavor itself is in many ways absurd. These psychiatrists are interviewing criminals who know that if they come off seeming a little bananas, they might get off the hook. The notion that something resembling scientific data will always result from such subjective encounters is, well, a little bananas itself. On top of that, the courtroom psychiatrists are not purporting to inform us of a defendant's *present* mental state, though even that can be elusive enough. They are claiming to divine the defendant's mental state when he committed the crime, which probably was months before. "I can't even tell you what *I* was thinking about a week ago, or a year ago, let alone what someone else was thinking," says criminal psychologist Stanton Samenow, author of *Inside the Criminal Mind,* whose eight years working at St. Elizabeths hospital in Washington made him deeply skeptical of traditional attempts to understand and catalogue criminals according to Freudian concepts. Indeed, how would you begin to *prove* an assertion such as the one that John Hinckley tried to shoot Reagan because he saw the president as an "all evil prohibitive figure"? This is not evidence. It is vaporizing. Coleman testifies at criminal trials with delightful iconoclasm that psychiatrists such as himself have no more ability than anyone else to inform the jury as to what was going on in a criminal's mind at any given time.

Poor Relations

But one should not conclude that the only thing wrong with the insanity defense is that it lets the felons free on the basis of recondite psychiatric excuses. The injustice goes much deeper. Some psychiatrists, for example, lend their courtroom aura and mantle of expertise to the prosecution. Jim Grigson, the so-called "Hanging Shrink" of Texas, will tell a jury after a 90-minute inter-view with a defendant that this individual "has complete disregard for another human being's life" and that "no treatment, no medicine, nothing is going to change this behavior." Psychiatric opinionizing can cut both ways.

There's the further problem that psychiatrists, the gatekeepers of this de-fense, have their greatest rapport with the problems of those closest to their own social status. A few years ago, Dr. Daniel Irving, a psychiatrist in Washington, demonstrated this attitude in an article Blain Harden wrote for *The Washing-ton Post.* "I hate to say this," Irving confided, "but I don't like to work with poor people.... They are talking about stuff that doesn't interest me particu-larly. They are the kind of people who don't interest me." Over 95 percent of all psychiatric patients are white, and James Collins, a black psychiatrist who is chairman of the Howard University Medical School Department of Psychiatry, told Harden that "[the] biggest problem is that many psychiatrists cannot relate to poor people."

In fact, the insanity defense itself can be weighted heavily towards those who are well-off. This is not just because a Hinckley family can muster upwards of a million dollars to mount a prodigious legal and psychiatric defense. On a subtler level, someone from a "nice" upper-middle-class background who com-mits a heinous crime is more readily seen as off his rocker than is someone from a poorer background in which crime is closer to the norm (or is at least perceived to be). During the Hinckley trial the jury witnessed his family sitting behind him, the "perfect couple," as one observer said later. "Hinckley's father was sitting there with a pondering look on his face; his mother was wearing red, white, and blue outfits; and his sister was a former cheerleader and home-coming queen. Real Americans." Surely there must be something wrong with a young man who could enjoy such advantages and still go out and shoot a president. It was the sort of tableau that a black felon from, say, East St. Louis, might have some trouble assembling.

Such considerations may help explain why Henry Steadman of the New York State Department of Mental Hygiene found that while whites account for only 31 percent of the prison population in his state, they were a full 65 percent of those found not guilty by reason of insanity. "Racial discrimination favoring whites in successful insanity defenses is strongly suggested by these figures," writes Abraham Halpern.

This in turn points to something even more fundamentally unjust about the insanity defense: the way it draws arbitrary and culture-bound distinctions between defendants with different kinds of life burdens and afflictions. A John Hinckley may well harbor anger against his parents and anguish at his unre-quited love for actress Jody Foster. Such problems can be very real for those who go through them. But they are no *more* real, no *more* inclined to affect behavior, than are the problems of a teenager of lesser means, who may be ugly, or kept back in school two or three times, or whose parents may not love him and who may have been "passed around" among relatives and older siblings for as long as he can remember, or who may find doors closed to him because he is not blond and blue-eyed the way Hinckley is. If a Hinckley merits our compassion, then surely those with hard life circumstances do also. Under the insanity defense, we absolve Hinckley totally of responsibility, while we label his hypothetical counterpart a bad person and send him to jail.

So arbitrary is the line that the insanity defense invites us to draw that all sorts of prejudices and vagaries can enter, of which racial and class bias are just two. "The actual psychological state of the defendant may be a rather minor factor" in the decision even to use the insanity defense, writes C. R. Jeffrey in his book, *Criminal Responsibility and Mental Disease*. Rather, this decision is based on such factors as "the economic position of the defendant, the nature of the criminal charges, the medical facilities in the community," and the like.

Big Difference

This is not to say that you won't find any poor people or non-Caucasians in the maximum-security hospitals in which insanity acquittees are kept. You will, but it's important to understand how they got there. It probably wasn't through the kind of circus trial that John Hinckley could afford. Very likely, it was a plea bargain, in which a prosecutor decided it was better to put a dangerous person away, even if just for a short time, than to devote scarce resources to a trial that he or she might lose. One study, published in the *Rutgers Law Review*, found at least two jurisdictions in which the prosecutors actually raised the insanity defense more frequently than the defense attorney did. "Clearly the prosecutor saw the [insanity] defense as a means to lock defendants up without having their guilt proved beyond a reasonable doubt," the study concludes.

Given such realities, it should not be surprising that there is often not much difference between those who end up in maximum security mental hospitals and those who end up in their penal counterparts. "Lots of people could have ended up in either one or the other," says E. Fuller Torrey, a psychiatrist at St. Elizabeths mental hospital in Washington. Samenow goes further. On the basis of his own experience studying insanity acquittees at St. Elizabeths, he declares flatly that "neither [his colleague Dr. Samuel] Yochelson nor I found that any of the men we evaluated were insane unless one took tremendous liberties with that word."

That may be a bit of an exaggeration. But the similarities between criminals we call "insane," and those we call simply "criminals," cannot be dismissed. Take recidivism. There is evidence that criminals released from mental hospitals tend to repeat their crimes with about the same frequency as their counterparts released from prison. This point is crucial because the purpose of a criminal justice system is not just to punish offenders; it is to protect the rest of us from dangerous people as well. Through the insanity defense, we go to lengths that are often ridiculous to make a distinction that in many cases is without a difference.

Sometimes the experts are the last to see what needs to be done. Listen to Lawrence Coffey, one of the Hinckley jurors who was unhappy with the verdict for which he himself voted. "I think it [the law] should be changed," he told a Senate hearing, "in some way where the defendant gets mental help enough that where he's not harmful to himself and society, and then be punished for what he has done wrong." Maryland Copelin, also one of the jurors, agreed. "I think they [defendants] should get the help they need and also punishment for the act they did." In other words, Hinckley needed treatment, but he deserved punishment, too. Who could argue with that? Well, the law, for one. It said that Hinckley was either guilty or not guilty by reason of insanity. "We could not do any better than what we did," Copelin said, "on account of your forms," which gave the jury only these two options.

In short, the insanity defense cuts the deck the wrong way. It makes no provision for the vast middle ground in which offenders have problems but should bear responsibility too. Instead of persisting in making this artificial distinction between "normal" criminals (whatever that means) and "insane" ones, we should ask first a very simple question: did the individual commit the crime? That established in a trial, we should then, in a sentencing phase, take all relevant factors into account in deciding what combination of punishment and treatment is appropriate. "Either you did it or you didn't do it," says Samenow, who supports the abolition of the insanity defense. "I think we should try the criminal first, and then worry about treatment." In other words, don't expect the jury to make Talmudic distinctions on which even the experts cannot agree. Get the psychiatrists out of the courtroom, where they cause confusion, and put them into the sentencing and treatment process, where they may be able to help.

In this sentencing phase, which would take on a new importance, Hinckley's infatuation with Jody Foster, and Dan White's overindulgence in junk food, would be given due regard. So too would the incapacity of one who was totally deranged. The crucial difference from current practice is that the examination would be done by court-appointed psychiatrists (or other professionals) instead of by hired guns proffered by either side. Since psychiatrists are as human as the rest of us, this system would not be perfect. It would, however, be better than what we have today.

In almost all cases, some punishment would be in order. You don't have to believe that retribution is the whole purpose of the law to acknowledge that something very basic in us requires that when someone causes serious harm to someone else, he should pay. This approach would eliminate perhaps the most dangerous absurdity of the present insanity defense. When a criminal wins acquittal on this ground, the criminal justice system has no more claim on him. The only way he can be kept in confinement is if he is declared insane and committed to a mental institution through a totally separate procedure. (Some states require an automatic confinement for one or two months, ostensibly to "observe" the acquittee.) No Problem, you say. They've just been declared insane. The problem is, *that* insanity was at the time of the crime, which may have been a year or more before. By the time of the commitment hearing, the old problem may have miraculously cleared up. The commitment authorities are then faced with two bad options. Either they tell the truth and let a dangerous person out or they fill a bed in a crowded mental hospital with someone who will be there not for treatment, but only to be kept off the streets. Eliminating the insanity defense would eliminate such charades.

Once punishment is completed, the question of danger to society would come to the fore. First offenders committing nonviolent crimes generally pose little such threat, and in most cases could be safely paroled. At the other extreme, violent repeat offenders would be locked up for a very long time. While reform is always possible, the sad fact is that most repeat offenders will keep on repeating until they reach a "burn-out" period sometime after they reach age 40. Since the recidivism rates cut across the categories we call "normal" and "insane" criminality, the insanity defense simply doesn't help us deal with reality in this regard.

Hot-blooded crimes, such as the Dan White shooting, should be seen for what they are. Such people generally don't pose a great threat because the circumstances of their crime are not likely to happen again. It costs between $10,000 and $20,000 a year to keep a prisoner in jail, and that money would be better spent on those for whom it's really needed. In other words, White's eight-year sentence was not necessarily wrong. The wrong was in the psychiatric speculation through which that result was justified. We can achieve justice in such cases through simpler and more honest means.

What a Time

But isn't the insanity defense necessary to protect the infirm? "People who are mentally ill deserve treatment," says Flora Rheta Schreiber, whose book *The Shoemaker* details the sad story of a troubled murderer. "They don't deserve to be locked up in prison."

Fair enough. The trouble is, virtually all criminals have mental problems. The difference between a bank robber and yourself is not in your shirt size or the shape of your hands. Is there any such thing as a "sane" rape or a "sane" axe murder? If anyone did such deeds with calm and rational deliberation, would that individual not be the most insane—and dangerous—of all? Samenow, moreover, says that for the vast majority of criminals, the kind of treatment that might be effective is pretty much the same. The secret scandal of the insanity defense is the way it justifies our atrocious penal system by purporting to show kindness for one group that is selected arbitrarily in the first place. We deny treatment to the many under the pretext of providing it for a few.

And a pretext it often is. Talk to someone who has visited a maximum-security hospital for the criminally insane. To be sure, there are good ones here and there. But in his book *Beating the Rap,* Henry Steadman describes a reality that is probably more common than not. Such hospitals in his state are "prisonlike," he writes, with "locked wards, security officers, and barbed wire fences.... There is a substantial level of patient-patient assault; homosexuality, both consenting and nonconsenting, is common, and guards are sometimes unnecessarily brutal ... *It is simply doing time in a different setting.*" (Emphasis added.) Barbara Weiner, who heads a special outpatient program for insanity acquittees in Chicago—one of the few programs of its kind in the country— told a Senate hearing that "few states have specialized programs for treating mentally ill offenders." (Those of means, of course, can often arrange a transfer to private facilities at which conditions are more genteel.)

So averse are American psychiatrists to helping people in life's lower stations that over half the staffs of this country's public mental hospitals are graduates of foreign medical schools, where standards may not be awfully high.

In 11 states, including Illinois and Ohio, the figure is over 70 percent. Just try to imagine a psychiatrist from, say, India, trying to understand a felon from the South Bronx. Torrey cites a psychiatrist who left the Illinois state hospital system telling of a colleague in charge of prescribing drugs who did not know that .8 and .80 were the same number.

Much of the problem is that most of us prefer to keep a comfortable arm's length from such realities. The people who run our criminal justice system are no exception. After observing a year's worth of mental incompetency hearings in New York, Steadman observed that "of about 35 judges, 12 attorneys, six district attorneys, and 12 psychiatrists, not one had ever seen or been inside either of the two facilities to which incompetent defendants are committed." A former public defender in Washington, D.C., who had pleaded before the Supreme Court the case of an insanity-acquittee who was trying to get out of St. Elizabeths, told me he had never met the individual for whose release he was pleading.

Getting rid of the insanity defense would help to break the spell and make us confront the deficiencies in our correctional systems. No longer could we congratulate ourselves that we are being humane and just when we are being neither. If eliminating the defense would help get a few dangerous felons off the street, so much the better. But a great deal more is at stake.

Richard Bonnie

 **NO**

Statement of Richard Bonnie

The effect of most of the proposals now before you would be to abolish the insanity defense as it has existed for centuries in Anglo-American criminal law. I urge you to reject these sweeping proposals. The insanity defense should be retained, in modified form, because some defendants afflicted by severe mental disorder cannot justly be blamed for their criminal conduct and do not, therefore, deserve to be punished. The defense, in short, is essential to the moral integrity of the criminal law.

I realize that the figure of John Hinckley looms before us today. Doubts about the moral accuracy of the jurors' verdict in this sad case have now been turned on the insanity defense itself. I do not want to second guess the verdict in the Hinckley case, but I do urge you to keep the case in proper perspective.

The highly visible insanity claim, pitting the experts in courtroom battle, is the aberrational case. The plea is raised in no more than 2% of felony cases and the defense is rarely successful when the question is contested in a jury trial. Most psychiatric dispositions in the criminal process are arranged without fanfare, without disagreement among the experts, and without dissent by the prosecution. In short, the exhaustive media coverage of cases like Hinckley's gives the public a distorted picture of the relative insignificance of the insanity defense in the day-to-day administration of justice.

In another way, however, the public debate about the aberrant case is highly to be desired because the trial of insanity claims keeps the community in touch with the moral premises of the criminal law. The legitimacy of the institution of punishment rests on the moral belief that we are all capable of rational choice and therefore deserve to be punished if we choose to do wrong. By acknowledging the exception, we reaffirm the rule. I have no doubt that the Hinckley trial and verdict have exposed the fundamental moral postulates of the criminal law to vigorous debate in every living room in the Nation. Thus, in a sense, whether John Hinckley was or was not legally insane may be less important than the fact that the question was asked at all.

These are the reasons I do not favor abolition of the insanity defense. However, I do not discount or dismiss the possibility that the defense occasionally may be successfully invoked in questionable cases. There is, in fact, some evidence that insanity acquittals have increased in recent years. However, I am

From U.S. Senate. Committee on the Judiciary. *Insanity Defense.* Hearing, August 2, 1982. Washington, DC: Government Printing Office, 1982. (Y4.J89/2:J–97–126.)

persuaded that the possibility of moral mistakes in the administration of the insanity defense can be adequately reduced by narrowing the defense and by placing the burden of proof on the defendant.

The Options

You have basically three options before you.

The Existing (Model Penal Code) Law

One option is to leave the law as it now stands, by judicial ruling, in all of the federal courts (and, parenthetically, as it now stands in a majority of the states). Apart from technical variations, this means the test proposed by the American Law Institute in its Model Penal Code. Under this approach, a person whose perceptual capacities were sufficiently intact that he had the criminal "intent" required in the definition of the offense can nonetheless be found "not guilty by reason of insanity" if, by virtue of mental disease or defect, he lacked substantial capacity *either* to understand or appreciate the legal or moral significance of his actions, *or* to conform his conduct to the requirements of law. In other words, a person may be excused if his thinking was severely disordered —this is the so-called volitional prong of the defense.

Revival of M'Naghten

The second option is to retain the insanity defense as an independent exculpatory doctrine—independent, that is, of mens rea—but to restrict its scope by eliminating the volitional prong. This is the approach that I favor, for reasons I will outline below. Basically, this option is to restore the *M'Naghten* test— although I do not think you should be bound by the language used by the House of Lords in 1843—as the sole basis for exculpation or ground of insanity. Although this is now distinctly the minority position in this country—it is used in less than one third of the states—it is still the law in England.

Abolition: The Mens Rea Approach

The third option is the one I have characterized as abolition of the defense. Technically, this characterization is accurate because the essential substantive effect of the so-called "mens rea" approach (or "elements" approach) would be to eliminate any criterion of exculpation, based on mental disease, which is independent of the elements of particular crimes. To put it another way, the bills taking this approach would eliminate any separate exculpatory doctrine based on proof of mental disease; instead mentally ill (or retarded) defendants would be treated just like everyone else. A normal person cannot escape liability by proving that he did not know or appreciate the fact that his conduct was wrong, and—under the mens rea approach—neither could a psychotic person.

The Case Against the Mens Rea Approach

Most of the bills now before you would adopt the mens rea option, the approach recently enacted in Montana and Idaho. As I have already noted, this change, abolishing the insanity defense, would constitute an abrupt and unfortunate departure from the Anglo-American legal tradition.

If the insanity defense were abolished, the law would not take adequate account of the incapacitating effects of severe mental illness. Some mentally ill defendants may be said to have "intended" to do what they did—that is, their technical guilt can be established—but they nonetheless may have been so severely disturbed that they were unable to appreciate the significance of their actions. These cases do not frequently arise, but when they do, a criminal conviction—signifying the societal judgment that the defendant *deserves* punishment—would offend the basic moral intuitions of the community. Judges and juries would then be forced either to return a verdict which they regard as morally obtuse or to acquit the defendant in defiance of the law. They should be spared such moral embarrassment.

Let me illustrate this point with a real case evaluated at our Institute's Forensic Clinic in 1975. Ms. Joy Baker, a thirty-one-year-old woman, admitted killing her aunt. She had no previous history of mental illness, although her mother was mentally ill and had spent all of Ms. Baker's early years in mental hospitals. Ms. Baker was raised by her grandparents and her aunt in a rural area of the state. After high school graduation Ms. Baker married and had two children. The marriage ended in divorce six years later and Ms. Baker remarried. This second marriage was stressful from the outset. Mr. Baker was a heavy drinker and abusive to his wife. He also was extremely jealous and repeatedly accused his wife of seeing other men.

The night before the shooting Mr. Baker took his wife on a ride in his truck. He kept a gun on the seat between them and stopped repeatedly. At each place he told listeners that his wife was an adultress. He insisted his wife throw her wedding ring from the car, which she did because she was afraid of her husband's anger. The Bakers didn't return home until three in the morning. At that time Ms. Baker woke her children and fed them, then stayed up while her husband slept because she was afraid "something terrible would happen."

During this time and for the three days prior to the day of the shooting Ms. Baker had become increasingly agitated and fearful. Her condition rapidly deteriorated and she began to lose contact with reality. She felt that her dogs were going to attack her and she also believed her children and the neighbors had been possessed by the devil.

On the morning of the shooting, Ms. Baker asked her husband not to leave and told him that something horrible was about to happen. When he left anyway she locked the doors. She ran frantically around the house holding the gun. She made her children sit on the sofa and read the Twenty-Third Psalm over and over. She was both afraid of what they might do and of what she might do but felt that reading the Bible would protect them. Shortly afterwards, Ms. Baker's aunt made an unexpected visit. Ms. Baker told her to go away but the aunt persisted and went to the back door. Ms. Baker was afraid of the dog which was out on the back porch and repeatedly urged her aunt to leave. At this time the aunt seemed to Ms. Baker to be sneering at her.

When her aunt suddenly reached through the screening to unlock the door Ms. Baker said, "I had my aunt over there and this black dog over here, and both of them were bothering me.... And then I had that black dog in front of me and she turned around and I was trying to kick the dog and my aunt was coming in the door and I just—took my hands I just went like this—right through the screen.... I shot her."

Ms. Baker's aunt fell backward into the mud behind the porch. Although she was bleeding profusely from her chest, she did not die immediately. "Why, Joy?" she asked. "Because you're the devil, and you came to hurt me," Joy answered. Her aunt said, "Honey, no, I came to help you." At this point, Ms. Baker said, she saw that her aunt was hurting and became very confused. Then, according to her statement, "I took the gun and shot her again just to relieve the pain she was having because she said she was hurt." Her aunt died after the second shot.

All the psychiatrists who examined Ms. Baker concluded that she was acutely psychotic and out of touch with reality at the time she shot her aunt. The police who arrested her and others in the small rural community concluded that she must have been crazy because there was no other explanation for her conduct. After Ms. Baker was stabilized on anti-psychotic medication, she was permitted to leave the state to live with relatives in a neighboring state. Eventually the case against her was dismissed by the court, with the consent of the prosecution, after a preliminary hearing at which the examining psychiatrists testified. She was never indicted or brought to trial.

It seems clear, even to a layman, that Ms. Baker was so delusional and regressed at the time of the shooting that she did not understand or appreciate the wrongfulness of her conduct. It would be morally obtuse to condemn and punish her. Yet, Ms. Baker had the state of mind required for some form of criminal homicide. If there were no insanity defense, she could be acquitted only in defiance of the law.

Let me explain. The "states of mind" which are required for homicide and other criminal offenses refer to various aspects of conscious awareness. They do not have any qualitative dimension. There is good reason for this, of course. The exclusive focus on conscious perceptions and beliefs enhances predictability, precision and equality in the penal law. If the law tried to take into account degrees of psychological aberration in the definition of offenses, the result would be a debilitating individualization of the standards of criminal liability.

At the time of the first shot, it could be argued that Ms. Baker lacked the "state of mind" required for murder because she did not intend to shoot a "human being" but rather intended to shoot a person whom she believed to be possessed by the devil. At common law, this claim would probably be characterized as a mistake of fact. Since the mistake was, by definition, an unreasonable one—i.e., one that only a crazy person would make—she would most likely be guilty of some form of homicide (at least manslaughter) if ordinary mens rea principles were applied. Even under the modern criminal codes..., she would be guilty of negligent homicide since an ordinary person in her situation would have been aware of the risk that her aunt was a human being. And she possibly could be found guilty of manslaughter since she was probably aware of the risk that her aunt was a human being even though she was so regressed that she disregarded the risk.

It might also be argued that Ms. Baker's first shot would have been justified if her delusional beliefs had been true since she would have been defending herself against imminent annihilation at the hands of the devil. Again, however, the application of ordinary common-law principles of justification . . . would indicate that she was unreasonably mistaken as to the existence of justificatory facts (the necessity for killing to protect oneself) and her defense would fail, although the grade of the offense would probably be reduced to manslaughter on the basis of her "imperfect" justification.

At the time of the second shot, Ms. Baker was in somewhat better contact with reality. At a very superficial level she "knew" that she was shooting her aunt and did so for the non-delusional purpose of relieving her aunt's pain. But euthanasia is no justification for homicide. Thus, if we look only at her legally relevant "state of mind" at the time of the second shot, and we do not take into account her highly regressed and disorganized emotional condition, she is technically guilty of murder.

I believe that Joy Baker's case convincingly demonstrates why, in theoretical terms, the mens rea approach does not take sufficient account of the morally significant aberrations of mental functioning associated with severe mental disorder. I readily concede, however, that these technical points may make little practical difference in the courtroom. If the expert testimony in Joy Baker's case and others like it were admitted to disprove the existence of mens rea, juries may behave as many observers believe they do now—they may ignore the technical aspects of the law and decide, very bluntly, whether the defendant was too crazy to be convicted. However, I do not believe that rational criminal law reform is served by designing rules of law in the expectation that they will be ignored or nullified when they appear unjust in individual cases.

Improving the Quality of Expert Testimony

I have tried to show that perpetuation of the insanity defense is essential to the moral integrity of the criminal law. Yet an abstract commitment to the moral relevance of claims of psychological aberration may have to bend to the need for reliability in the administration of the law.

I fully recognize that the litigation of insanity claims is occasionally imperfect. The defense is sometimes difficult to administer reliably and fairly. In particular, I recognize that we cannot calibrate the severity of a person's mental disability, and it is sometimes hard to know whether the disability was profound enough to establish irresponsibility. Nor can we be confident that every fabricated claim will be recognized. Yet these concerns are not unlike those presented by traditional defenses such as mistake, duress and other excuses which no one is seeking to abolish. Indeed, problems in sorting valid from invalid defensive claims are best seen as part of the price of a humane and just penal law.

Thus, to the extent that the abolitionists would eradicate the insanity defense in response to imperfections in its administration, I would reply that a decent respect for the moral integrity of the criminal law sometimes requires us to ask questions that can be answered only by approximation. Rather than abolishing the defense we should focus our attention on ways in which its administration can be improved.

Some of the abolitionist sentiment among lawyers seems to be responsive to doubts about the competence—and, unfortunately, the ethics—of expert witnesses. The cry for abolition is also raised by psychiatrists and psychologists who believe that the law forces experts to "take sides" and to offer opinions on issues outside their sphere of expertise. These are all legitimate concerns and I have no doubt that the current controversy about the insanity defense accurately reflects a rising level of mutual professional irritation about its administration. However, the correct solution is not to abolish the insanity defense but rather to clarify the roles and obligations of expert witnesses in the criminal process. Some assistance in this effort can be expected from the American Bar Association's Criminal Justice-Mental Health Standards now being drafted by interdisciplinary panels of experts in the field.

A properly trained expert can help the judge or jury to understand aberrations of the human mind. However, training in psychiatry or psychology does not, by itself, qualify a person to be an expert witness in criminal cases. Specialized training in forensic evaluation is necessary, and a major aim of such special training must be to assure that the expert is sensitive to the limits of his or her knowledge.

The Case for Tightening the Defense

I do not favor abolition of the "cognitive" prong of the insanity defense. However, I do agree with those critics who believe the risks of fabrication and "moral mistakes" in administering the defense are greatest when the experts and the jury are asked to speculate whether the defendant had the capacity to "control" himself or whether he could have "resisted" the criminal impulse.

Few would dispute the moral predicate for the control test—that a person who "cannot help" doing what he did is not blameworthy. Unfortunately, however, there is no scientific basis for measuring a person's capacity for self-control or for calibrating the impairment of such capacity. There is, in short, no objective basis for distinguishing between offenders who were undeterrable and those who were merely undeterred, between the impulse that was irresistible and the impulse not resisted, or between substantial impairment of capacity and some lesser impairment. Whatever the precise terms of the volitional test, the question is unanswerable—or can be answered only by "moral guesses." To ask it at all, in my opinion, invites fabricated claims, undermines equal administration of the penal law, and compromises its deterrent effect....

The sole test of legal insanity should be whether the defendant, as a result of mental disease, lacked "substantial capacity to appreciate the wrongfulness of his conduct." This language, drawn from the Model Penal Code, uses clinically meaningful terms to ask the same question posed by the House of Lords in *M'Naghten* 150 years ago. During the past ten years, I have not seen a single case at our Clinic involving a claim of irresponsibility that I personally thought was morally compelling which would not be comprehended by this formulation. Thus, I am convinced that this test is fully compatible with the ethical premises of the penal law, and that results reached by judges and juries in particular cases ordinarily would be congruent with the community's moral sense. In sum, then, I believe that the insanity defense, as I have defined it, should be narrowed, not abandoned, and that the burden of persuasion may properly be shifted to the defendant. Like the mens rea proposal, this approach adequately responds to public concern about possible misuse of the insanity defense. Unlike the mens rea proposal, however, I believe this approach is compatible with the basic doctrines and principles of Anglo-American penal law.

POSTSCRIPT

Should the Insanity Defense Be Abolished?

After the verdict—not guilty by reason of insanity—in the trial of John Hinckley, Jr., for the attempted assassination of President Ronald Reagan in 1981, some changes were made in the federal insanity defense standard. As part of a major anticrime bill passed in 1984, Congress requires the defendant to have the burden of proving that he or she was insane. In the Hinckley trial, the prosecution was required to prove beyond a reasonable doubt that Hinckley was sane. The defendant in such a case must now persuade a jury that, as a result of a severe mental disease or defect, he or she was unable to appreciate the nature and wrongfulness of the act.

In addition to raising questions about the diagnosis of mental illness, the insanity defense also requires consideration of treatment, of sentencing, and of institutionalization. Those advocating its retention argue not only that blameless people should not be punished but also that such individuals need care and treatment for their problems. The fact that many mental institutions have failed to provide adequate treatment or are, by their nature, inappropriate places for some individuals who need help but not institutionalization has been recognized recently in various lawsuits. As a result, the number of people in institutions has been declining. The ineffectiveness of prisons and mental institutions in reducing recidivism or promoting treatment should be considered in the debate over the insanity defense because even those who wish to abolish the defense are willing to take the mental state of the defendant into account at the time of sentencing. There is, in addition, a possible relationship between the increase in the number of defendants invoking the insanity defense and the deinstitutionalization trend. The reason for this is that the insanity defense becomes more appealing as the expectation of a long stay in a mental institution decreases.

Recommended readings on the insanity defense and mental health law include Michael L. Perlin, *The Jurisprudence of the Insanity Defense* (Carolina Academic Press, 1994); Paul S. Appelbaum, *Almost a Revolution: Mental Health Law and the Limits of Change* (Oxford University Press, 1994); Henry J. Steadman, *Before and After Hinckley: Evaluating Insanity Defense Reform* (Guilford Press, 1993); and Richard Moran, *Knowing Right From Wrong: The Insanity Defense of Daniel McNaughtan* (Free Press, 1981), which provides an interesting look at McNaughtan's trial and at the central figure in the history of the insanity defense.

ISSUE 7

Are Pretextual Stops by the Police Constitutional?

YES: Antonin Scalia, from Majority Opinion, *Whren et al. v. United States,* U.S. Supreme Court (June 10, 1996)

NO: David A. Harris, from " 'Driving While Black' and All Other Traffic Offenses: The Supreme Court and Pretextual Traffic Stops," *Journal of Criminal Law and Criminology* (vol. 87, no. 544, 1997)

ISSUE SUMMARY

YES: Supreme Court justice Antonin Scalia holds that pretextual traffic stops do not violate an individual's Fourth Amendment rights. He argues that the constitutionality of such stops does not depend on the actual motivations of the police officer who makes the stop but on an objective determination of the reasonableness of the stop.

NO: David A. Harris, a professor of criminal law and criminal procedure, contends that Scalia's opinion ignores the potential for abuse by the police of general and all-encompassing traffic codes.

On an early summer evening in 1993, plainclothes officers of the District of Columbia's vice squad, while patrolling one of the city's high drug areas, arrested Michael Whren and James Brown for possession of crack cocaine. On the surface, such an arrest might have seemed altogether routine. Nonetheless, the race of the defendants (both are African American) along with the actions of the officers leading up to the arrest, although not uncommon, were highly problematic. Indeed, it is because such police behavior has become, according to some, all too common that this incident became the subject of litigation; the case eventually landed before the U.S. Supreme Court.

At no stage in the criminal process did the defendants ever claim innocence as to the charge of criminal possession of a controlled substance. Rather, Whren and Brown asserted that evidence of the crack cocaine offered at trial was the product of an unlawful search and seizure in violation of their Fourth Amendment guarantee to "be secure in their persons, houses, papers, and effects, against unreasonable searches and seizures." Specifically, Whren and Brown argued that their arrest was the product of an unlawful "pretextual stop." A pretextual stop is one in which police officers exploit a routine traffic violation to stop a motorist in order to investigate other suspected criminal behavior—behavior that the officer lacks the necessary probable cause or reasonable suspicion under which to act. The facts of the case follow.

The vice squad officers had been patrolling certain high drug areas in an unmarked vehicle. They became suspicious of two men—Whren and Brown—operating a late-model sport utility vehicle. As the officers made a pass of the vehicle, they observed that it had temporary license plates and was occupied by two young men. According to Officer Ephraim Soto's testimony, as they crossed the intersection where Whren and Brown had stopped, the officers observed the driver of the vehicle (Brown) looking down into the lap of the passenger (Whren). After the unmarked police vehicle passed, the officers also noted that Whren and Brown continued to wait at the stop sign for an "unusual" length of time. The officers then performed a U-turn and came up behind the suspect's vehicle, whereupon it made a "sudden" right turn and sped off at an "unreasonable speed." The police followed and overtook Brown and Whren's vehicle when it stopped behind traffic at a red light. Officer Soto left his vehicle, approached the driver's side of the suspect's vehicle, and identified himself as a District of Columbia police officer, ostensibly to cite the driver for various traffic violations. From this vantage point, however, Officer Soto observed, on Whren's lap, two large plastic bags containing what appeared to be crack cocaine. Whren and Brown were immediately placed under arrest.

At their pretrial suppression hearing, Whren and Brown challenged the lawfulness of the stop of their vehicle and the ensuing seizure of drugs. Whren and Brown's challenge was grounded in the contention that the initial stop of their vehicle was not based on probable cause or articulable, reasonable suspicion that they were engaged in criminal activity involving a controlled substance. Instead, they argued, the vice squad officers used alleged traffic violations as a pretext to pursue otherwise unsupported suspicions. Moreover, the defendants alleged that their race played no small role in contributing to the officers' suspicions. Although such pretextual stops may objectively appear appropriate, the defendants argued that the court should base its decision on a determination of the subjective intentions of the officers in question.

The district court rejected this argument, concluding that "[t]here was nothing to really demonstrate that the actions of the officers were contrary to a normal traffic stop." The U.S. Court of Appeals affirmed the convictions of Whren and Brown and held that "regardless of whether a police officer subjectively believes that the occupants of an automobile may be engaging in some other illegal behavior, a traffic stop is permissible as long as a reasonable officer in the same circumstances could have stopped the car for the suspected traffic violation." 53 F.3d 371, 374 (C.A.D.C., 1995). The Supreme Court upheld the decisions of the lower courts. The opinion of the Court, which is excerpted in the following selection, was authored by Justice Antonin Scalia. Although Scalia wrote for a unanimous Court, the issues involved continue to generate a tremendous amount of controversy. Some indication of this is given voice by David A. Harris in the second selection.

Antonin Scalia

 **YES**

Majority Opinion

Whren et al. *v.* United States

Petitioners accept that Officer [Ephraim] Soto had probable cause to believe that various provisions of the District of Columbia traffic code had been violated.... They argue, however, that "in the unique context of civil traffic regulations" probable cause is not enough. Since, they contend, the use of automobiles is so heavily and minutely regulated that total compliance with traffic and safety rules is nearly impossible, a police officer will almost invariably be able to catch any given motorist in a technical violation. This creates the temptation to use traffic stops as a means of investigating other law violations, as to which no probable cause or even articulable suspicion exists. Petitioners, who are both black, further contend that police officers might decide which motorists to stop based on decidedly impermissible factors, such as the race of the car's occupants. To avoid this danger, they say, the Fourth Amendment test for traffic stops should be, not the normal one (applied by the Court of Appeals) of whether probable cause existed to justify the stop; but rather, whether a police officer, acting reasonably, would have made the stop for the reason given.

Petitioners contend that the standard they propose is consistent with our past cases' disapproval of police attempts to use valid bases of action against citizens as pretexts for pursuing other investigatory agendas. We are reminded that in *Florida v. Wells,* 495 U.S. 1, 4 (1990), we stated that "an inventory search must not be used as a ruse for a general rummaging in order to discover incriminating evidence"; that in *Colorado v. Bertine,* 479 U.S. 367, 372 (1987), in approving an inventory search, we apparently thought it significant that there had been "no showing that the police, who were following standard procedures, acted in bad faith or for the sole purpose of investigation"; and that in *New York v. Burger,* 482 U.S. 691, 716–717, n. 27 (1987), we observed, in upholding the constitutionality of a warrantless administrative inspection, that the search did not appear to be "a 'pretext' for obtaining evidence of... violation of... penal laws." But only an undiscerning reader would regard these cases as endorsing the principle that ulterior motives can invalidate police conduct that is justifiable on the basis of probable cause to believe that a violation of law has occurred. In each case we were addressing the validity of a search conducted in the *absence* of probable

From *Whren et al. v. United States,* 517 U.S. 806 (1996). Some case citations omitted.

cause. Our quoted statements simply explain that the exemption from the need for probable cause (and warrant), which is accorded to searches made for the purpose of inventory or administrative regulation, is not accorded to searches that are not made for those purposes.

... In *United States v. Robinson*, 414 U.S. 218 (1973), we held that a traffic violation arrest (of the sort here) would not be rendered invalid by the fact that it was "a mere pretext for a narcotics search," and that a lawful post arrest search of the person would not be rendered invalid by the fact that it was not motivated by the officer safety concern that justifies such searches. And in *Scott v. United States*, 436 U.S. 128, 138 (1978), in rejecting the contention that wiretap evidence was subject to exclusion because the agents conducting the tap had failed to make any effort to comply with the statutory requirement that unauthorized acquisitions be minimized, we said that "[s]ubjective intent alone ... does not make otherwise lawful conduct illegal or unconstitutional." We described *Robinson* as having established that "the fact that the officer does not have the state of mind which is hypothecated by the reasons which provide the legal justification for the officer's action does not invalidate the action taken as long as the circumstances, viewed objectively, justify that action."

We think these cases foreclose any argument that the constitutional reasonableness of traffic stops depends on the actual motivations of the individual officers involved. We of course agree with petitioners that the Constitution prohibits selective enforcement of the law based on considerations such as race. But the constitutional basis for objecting to intentionally discriminatory application of laws is the Equal Protection Clause, not the Fourth Amendment. Subjective intentions play no role in ordinary, probable cause Fourth Amendment analysis.

Recognizing that we have been unwilling to entertain Fourth Amendment challenges based on the actual motivations of individual officers, petitioners disavow any intention to make the individual officer's subjective good faith the touchstone of "reasonableness." They insist that the standard they have put forward—whether the officer's conduct deviated materially from usual police practices, so that a reasonable officer in the same circumstances would not have made the stop for the reasons given—is an "objective" one.

But although framed in empirical terms, this approach is plainly and indisputably driven by subjective considerations. Its whole purpose is to prevent the police from doing under the guise of enforcing the traffic code what they would like to do for different reasons. Petitioners' proposed standard may not use the word "pretext," but it is designed to combat nothing other than the perceived "danger" of the pretextual stop, albeit only indirectly and over the run of cases. Instead of asking whether the individual officer had the proper state of mind, the petitioners would have us ask, in effect, whether (based on general police practices) it is plausible to believe that the officer had the proper state of mind.

Why one would frame a test designed to combat pretext in such fashion that the Court cannot take into account *actual and admitted* pretext is a curiosity that can only be explained by the fact that our cases have foreclosed the more sensible option. If those cases were based only upon the evidentiary difficulty of establishing subjective intent, petitioners' attempt to root out subjective vices through objective means might make sense. But they were not based only upon that, or indeed even principally upon that. Their principal basis—which applies equally to attempts to reach subjective intent through ostensibly objective means—is simply that the Fourth Amendment's concern with "reasonableness" allows certain actions to be taken in certain circumstances, whatever the subjective intent. But even if our concern had been only an evidentiary one, petitioners' proposal would by no means assuage it. Indeed, it seems to us somewhat easier to figure out the intent of an individual officer than to plumb the collective consciousness of law enforcement in order to determine whether a "reasonable officer" would have been moved to act upon the traffic violation. While police manuals and standard procedures may sometimes provide objective assistance, ordinarily one would be reduced to speculating about the hypothetical reaction of a hypothetical constable—an exercise that might be called virtual subjectivity.

Moreover, police enforcement practices, even if they could be practicably assessed by a judge, vary from place to place and from time to time. We cannot accept that the search and seizure protections of the Fourth Amendment are so variable, and can be made to turn upon such trivialities. The difficulty is illustrated by petitioners' arguments in this case. Their claim that a reasonable officer would not have made this stop is based largely on District of Columbia police regulations which permit plainclothes officers in unmarked vehicles to enforce traffic laws "only in the case of a violation that is so grave as to pose an *immediate threat* to the safety of others." Metropolitan Police Department—Washington, D. C., General Order 303.1, pt. 1, Objectives and Policies (A)(2)(4) (Apr. 30, 1992), reprinted as Addendum to Brief for Petitioners. This basis of invalidation would not apply in jurisdictions that had a different practice. And it would not have applied even in the District of Columbia, if Officer Soto had been wearing a uniform or patrolling in a marked police cruiser.

Petitioners argue that our cases support insistence upon police adherence to standard practices as an objective means of rooting out pretext. They cite no holding to that effect, and dicta in only two cases. In *Abel v. United States,* 362 U.S. 217 (1960), the petitioner had been arrested by the Immigration and Naturalization Service (INS), on the basis of an administrative warrant that, he claimed, had been issued on pretextual grounds in order to enable the Federal Bureau of Investigation (FBI) to search his room after his arrest. We regarded this as an allegation of "serious misconduct," but rejected Abel's claims on the ground that "[a] finding of bad faith is ... not open to us on th[e] record" in light of the findings below, including the finding that "the proceedings taken by the [INS] differed in no respect from what would have been done in the case of an individual concerning whom [there was no pending FBI investigation]." But it is a long leap from the proposition that following regular procedures is some evidence of lack of pretext to the proposition that failure to follow regular procedures proves (or is an operational substitute for) pretext. Abel, moreover, did not involve the assertion that pretext could invalidate a search or seizure for which there was probable cause—and even what it said about pretext in other contexts here. This is not even a dictum that purports to provide an answer, but merely one that leaves the question open.

In what would appear to be an elaboration on the "reasonable officer" test, petitioners argue that the balancing inherent in any Fourth Amendment inquiry requires us to weigh the governmental and individual interests implicated in a traffic stop such as we have here. That balancing, petitioners claim, does not support investigation of minor traffic infractions by plainclothes police in unmarked vehicles; such investigation only minimally advances the government's interest in traffic safety, and may indeed retard it by producing motorist confusion and alarm—a view said to be supported by the Metropolitan Police Department's own regulations generally prohibiting this practice. And as for the Fourth Amendment interests of the individuals concerned, petitioners point out that our cases acknowledge that even ordinary traffic stops entail "a possibly unsettling show of authority"; that they at best "interfere with freedom of movement, are inconvenient, and consume time" and at worst "may create substantial anxiety." That anxiety is likely to be even more pronounced when the stop is conducted by plainclothes officers in unmarked cars.

It is of course true that in principle every Fourth Amendment case, since it turns upon a "reasonableness" determination, involves a balancing of all relevant factors. With rare exceptions not applicable here, however, the result of that balancing is not in doubt where the search or seizure is based upon probable cause. That is why petitioners must rely upon cases like [*Delaware v. Prouse*, 440 U.S. 648 (1979)] to provide examples of actual "balancing" analysis. There, the police action in question was a random traffic stop for the purpose of checking a motorist's license and vehicle registration, a practice that—like the practices at issue in the inventory search and administrative inspection cases upon which petitioners rely in making their "pretext" claim—involves police intrusion *without the probable cause that is its traditional justification.* Our opinion in *Prouse* expressly distinguished the case from a stop based on precisely what is at issue here: "probable cause to believe that a driver is violating any one of the multitude of applicable traffic and equipment regulations." It noted approvingly that "[t]he foremost method of enforcing traffic and vehicle safety regulations ... is acting upon observed violations," which afford the " 'quantum of individualized suspicion' necessary to ensure that police discretion is sufficiently constrained." What is true of *Prouse* is also true of other cases that engaged in detailed "balancing" to decide the constitutionality of automobile stops....

Where probable cause has existed, the only cases in which we have found it necessary actually to perform the "balancing" analysis involved searches or seizures conducted in an extraordinary manner, unusually harmful to an individual's privacy or even physical interests.... The making of a traffic stop out of uniform does not remotely qualify as such an extreme practice, and so is governed by the usual rule that probable cause to believe the law has been broken "outbalances" private interest in avoiding police contact.

Petitioners urge as an extraordinary factor in this case that the "multitude of applicable traffic and equipment regulations" is so large and so difficult to obey perfectly that virtually everyone is guilty of violation, permitting the police to single out almost whomever they wish for a stop. But we are aware of no principle that would allow us to decide at what point a code of law becomes so expansive and so commonly violated that infraction itself can no longer be the ordinary measure of the lawfulness of enforcement. And even if we could identify such exorbitant codes, we do not know by what standard (or what right) we would decide, as petitioners would have us do, which particular provisions are sufficiently important to merit enforcement.

For the run of the mine case, which this surely is, we think there is no realistic alternative to the traditional common law rule that probable cause justifies a search and seizure.

Here the District Court found that the officers had probable cause to believe that petitioners had violated the traffic code. That rendered the stop reasonable under the Fourth Amendment, the evidence thereby discovered admissible, and the upholding of the convictions by the Court of Appeals for the District of Columbia Circuit correct. *Judgment affirmed.*

NO

David A. Harris

"Driving While Black" and All Other Traffic Offenses

The Supreme Court's decision in *Whren v. United States* could not have surprised many observers of the Court's Fourth Amendment jurisprudence. In *Whren,* police officers used traffic violations as a pretext to stop a car and investigate possible drug offenses; the officers had neither probable cause nor reasonable suspicion to stop the driver for narcotics crimes. In the Supreme Court, the government advocated the "could have" standard: any time the police could have stopped the defendant for a traffic infraction, it does not matter that police actually stopped him to investigate a crime for which the police had little or no evidence. The defense asked the Court to adopt a "would have" rule: a seizure based on a traffic stop would only stand if a reasonable officer would have made this particular stop. The Court sided with the government. If police witness a traffic violation, the Court said, they have the simplest and clearest type of probable cause imaginable for a stop. Requiring more would force lower courts to make post hoc Fourth Amendment judgments based on either the mindset of a reasonable officer or the actual (perhaps ulterior) motives of the arresting officer, neither one of which the Court saw as necessary, useful, or relevant to the task of judging the constitutionality of a seizure. After *Whren,* courts will not ask whether police conducted a traffic stop because officers felt the occupants of the car were involved in some other crime about which they had only a hunch; rather, once a driver commits a traffic infraction, the officer's "real" purpose will make no difference at all.

For the sake of argument, I will concede that the decision in *Whren* makes some sense, at least from the point of view of judicial administration. But examined more carefully, *Whren* does more than opt for a more workable rule: it approves two alarming law enforcement practices. Neither are secret; on the contrary, the law of search and seizure has reflected both for a long time. But both represent profoundly dangerous developments for a free society, especially one dedicated to the equal treatment of all citizens.

First, the comprehensive scope of state traffic codes makes them extremely powerful tools under *Whren.* These codes regulate the details of driving in ways both big and small, obvious and arcane. In the most literal sense, no driver can avoid violating some traffic law during a short drive, even with the most

From David A. Harris, " 'Driving While Black' and All Other Traffic Offenses: The Supreme Court and Pretextual Traffic Stops," *Journal of Criminal Law and Criminology,* vol. 87 (1997). Copyright © 1997 by Northwestern University School of Law. Reprinted by special permission of The Northwestern University School of Law, *The Journal of Criminal Law and Criminology.*

careful attention. Fairly read, *Whren* says that any traffic violation can support a stop, no matter what the real reason for it is; this makes any citizen fair game for a stop, almost any time, anywhere, virtually at the whim of police. Given how important an activity driving has become in American society, *Whren* changes the Fourth Amendment's rule that police must have a reason to forcibly interfere in our business—some basis to suspect wrongdoing that is more than a hunch. Simply put, that rule no longer applies when a person drives a car.

This alone should worry us, but the second police practice *Whren* approves is in fact far worse. It is this: Police will not subject all drivers to traffic stops in the way *Whren* allows. Rather, if past practice is any indication, they will use the traffic code to stop a hugely disproportionate number of African-Americans and Hispanics. We know this because it is exactly what has been happening already, even before receiving the Supreme Court's imprimatur in *Whren*. In fact, the stopping of black drivers, just to see what officers can find, has become so common in some places that this practice has its own name: African-Americans sometimes say they have been stopped for the offense of "driving while black." With *Whren,* we should expect African-Americans and Hispanics to experience an even greater number of pretextual traffic stops. And once police stop a car, they often search it, either by obtaining consent, using a drug-sniffing dog, or by some other means. In fact, searching cars for narcotics is perhaps the major motivation for making these stops.

Under a Constitution that restrains the government vis-à-vis the individual and that puts some limits on what the authorities may do in the pursuit of the guilty, the power of the police to stop any particular driver, at almost any time, seems oddly out of place. And with the words "equal justice under law" carved into the stone of the Supreme Court itself, one might think that the use of police power in one of its rawest forms against members of particular racial or ethnic groups might prompt the Court to show some interest in curbing such abuses. The defendant-petitioners presented both of these arguments—the almost arbitrary power over any driver inherent in the "could have" approach, and the racially biased use of traffic stops—to the Court. Yet the Court paid little attention to these obvious implications of its decision. *Whren* is more than a missed opportunity for the Court to rein in some police practices that strike at the heart of the ideas of freedom and equal treatment; *Whren* represents a clear step in the other direction—toward authoritarianism, toward racist policing, and toward a view of minorities as criminals, rather than citizens....

The real danger of *Whren* [however] is not its use of precedent, its facile logic, or its rejection of one proposed test for another. Rather, *Whren*'s most troubling aspects lie in its implications—the incredible amount of discretionary power it hands law enforcement without any check—and what this means for our everyday lives and our freedom as citizens.

Commentators have criticized the Supreme Court's Fourth Amendment jurisprudence, with considerable justification. As the Court lurches between protecting what it considers bedrock Fourth Amendment values—the sanctity of the home, for example—and the undesirable and distasteful result of suppressing probative evidence of guilt, it has generated a hodgepodge of conflicting rules so technical that law professors—let alone law enforcers—find them difficult to understand. Even so, some basic search and seizure rules seem firmly ensconced in the law. Perhaps this is because they are so fundamental that disturbing them would create an even larger doctrinal mess than the one that already exists; perhaps it is because there is present-day consensus accompanied by historical evidence on these points. Whatever the reason, we can discuss two key rules, secure in the knowledge that they are accepted by the Court.

First, the police must usually have a reason to forcibly stop a person. When I say "forcibly stop," I do not mean the application of force to a suspect, though that may be part of a seizure. And I am not referring to casual encounters with police, in which a citizen is asked whether he or she would mind talking to police. Even though it seems more than just plausible to argue that such encounters always carry with them some element of coercion, I am willing to accept, for the purposes of argument, the idea that such encounters remain consensual. In contrast, a forcible stop is by its nature coercive. When a police officer orders a citizen to halt, questioning, a search of some kind, or even arrest may follow. Police cannot force a citizen to stop and submit in this way without probable cause or at least reasonable suspicion to believe that a crime has been or is about to be committed by the suspect. The Supreme Court reaffirmed this standard just a few years ago in *Minnesota v. Dickerson,* in which Justice White stated clearly that this rule had not changed. The police must still have a reason to force a citizen to stop and submit to their authority, something more than just a hunch.

The other basic rule important to our discussion is this: if police do not have the probable cause or reasonable suspicion necessary for a forcible stop, a citizen may ignore police requests to stop, respond to questions, produce identification, or submit to any further intrusion. The Supreme Court has reiterated this rule in a number of cases stretching over many years. For example, in *Brown v. Texas,* police stopped a man in an area with a "high incidence of drug traffic" because "the situation 'looked suspicious and we had never seen [the] subject in that area before.'" The officers arrested the man under a Texas statute that criminalized any refusal to give police a name and address upon a legitimate stop. The Supreme Court invalidated the statute, and declared that nothing in the facts of the case allowed the officers to make a legitimate stop, even the defendant's presence in an area known for narcotics trafficking. The defendant had every right to walk away and to refuse to produce identification in such a situation, and any law to the contrary did not meet constitutional standards. The Court carried this doctrine forward in *Florida v. Royer,* in which it stated that "[a citizen] may not be detained even momentarily without reasonable, objective grounds for doing so; and his refusal to listen or answer does not, without more, furnish those grounds." And in *Florida v. Bostick,* the Court reaffirmed this principle, declaring that while the police may question a person about whom they have no suspicion, "an individual may decline an officer's request without fearing prosecution."

To be sure, I have not made the mistake of assuming that these legal rules necessarily reflect reality. I know that even though the cases discussed here may guarantee citizens the right to walk away from curious police without interference, the right may exist more in theory than in practice. It may be that the mere appearance of authority—nothing more than the officer's uniform, badge and squad car, to say nothing of her weapon—will cause most people to do what she says or answer her questions. But the point is that even if the law remains more an ideal than anything else, the Court's pronouncements on the subject all point in one direction: the police need at least reasonable suspicion to forcibly interfere with one's movement, and if they do not have it the citizen may walk away.

Whren alters all of this for anyone driving a car. Simply put, it is difficult to imagine a more American activity than driving a car. We use our cars for everything: work (both as transportation to get to and from work and as mobile offices and sales platforms), play, and myriad other activities that make up everyday life. Of course, many Americans do not own cars, and some have even found it unnecessary to learn to drive. But this is not the norm. Most American kids date their emergence from adolescence not from high school graduation or a religious or cultural ceremony, but from something far more central to what they really value: the day they receive their driver's licenses. Americans visiting Europe for the first time often return with the observation that one can get to and from almost any little town entirely on public transportation. Europeans visiting America are often surprised at the lack of public transportation facilities and options outside of major urban centers, and at the sizeable cities that rely entirely on automobile transportation. Despite energy crises, traffic congestion, and the expense of owning a car, most Americans prefer to drive wherever they go. In short, there are few activities more important to American life than driving.

With that in mind, consider traffic codes. There is no detail of driving too small, no piece of equipment too insignificant, no item of automobile regulation too arcane to be made the subject of a traffic offense. Police officers in some jurisdictions have a rule of thumb: the average driver cannot go three blocks without violating some traffic regulation. Reading the codes, it is hard to disagree; the question is how anyone could get as far as three blocks without violating the law.

When we think of traffic offenses, we think of "moving violations"— exceeding the speed limit, crossing dividing lines, and the like. But in fact traffic codes regulate many other aspects of driving-related activity, including some that seem almost wildly hypertechnical. And some of these offenses have nothing to do with driving at all. Rather, they are "equipment violations"—offenses in which driving with incorrect, outdated, or broken equipment constitutes the violation. And then there are catch-all provisions: rules that allow police to stop drivers for conduct that complies with all rules on the books, but that officers consider "imprudent" or "unreasonable" under the circumstances, or that describe the offense in language so broad as to make a violation virtually coextensive with the officer's unreviewable personal judgment. . . . But the existence of powerful and unreviewable police discretion to stop drivers is not the most disturbing aspect of *Whren*. That dubious honor is reserved for the ways in which the police will use this discretion.

Once we understand that *Whren* will permit police to stop anyone driving a car whenever they observe the ever-present violations of the traffic code, the question becomes who the police will stop. At first blush, the question might seem unnecessary. After all, if *Whren* allows the police to stop any driver at virtually any time, everyone faces the risk of a pretextual stop. But while *Whren* certainly makes it possible for the police to stop anyone, the fact is that police will not stop just anyone. In fact, police will use the immense discretionary power *Whren* gives them mostly to stop African-Americans and Hispanics. I say this not to imply that individual officers will act out of racist motivations. Though some will, I believe most will not. Rather, my point is that whatever their motivation, viewed as a whole, pretextual stops will be used against African-Americans and Hispanics in percentages wildly out of proportion to their numbers in the driving population.

It may seem bold that I make this assertion as a fact. In fact, I lack the kind of systematically gathered and analyzed data anyone making such a statement would prefer to have. This is because virtually no one—no individual, no police department, and no other government agency—has ever kept comprehensive statistics on who police stop: basis for the stop, race of suspect, type of police activity after stop (e.g., questioning, search of suspect, search of car, use of drug-sniffing dog, whether consent was given), and the like. Of course, one type of record does follow some percentage of stops: traffic tickets and warnings, and arrest, charging and prosecution records of those suspects police find with contraband. But looking only at the records of those charged and prosecuted can mislead, and says nothing about the many other stops that result in no ticket and yield no contraband.

Even so, information uncovered in the last few years has begun to shed light on the use of pretextual traffic stops. This data reveals several patterns, which African-Americans and Hispanics understand quite well already: police use traffic regulations to investigate many innocent citizens; these investigations, which are often quite intrusive, concern drugs, not traffic; and African-Americans and Hispanics are the targets of choice for law enforcement. So even if we lack systemic data, we now have something that gives us a strong indication of current law enforcement realities and the direction of future trends. We can comfortably predict the effect of *Whren*: police will use the case to justify and expand drug interdiction efforts against people of color....

But perhaps we should examine the issue from another perspective: that of law enforcement. And that outlook would no doubt seem quite different from what I have said so far. In a nutshell, it is this: Stopping a disproportionate number of African-Americans is not racist; it is just plain good police work. After all, African-Americans make up a large share of those arrested, prosecuted and jailed in this country. Police know jails are full of criminals, a substantial portion of whom are black, and that a high percentage of black males are under the control of the criminal justice system in one way or another. The police have no interest in harassing black or Hispanic people; rather, their motivation remains the apprehension of criminals. Race may play a part in law enforcement, but only as a proxy for a higher probability of criminal activity. In other words, racial disparities in stops and searches are nothing more than "an unfortunate byproduct of sound police policies." Lt. Col. Ernest Leatherbury, commander of field operations for the Maryland State Police, puts it this way: "The facts speak for themselves ... When you got a high number of these consent searches resulting in drug arrests do we in law enforcement or the public want to say the state police should discontinue these searches?" In other words, police target blacks and Hispanics because they are the right ones, and this technique gets results. And if it works, we should not let the niceties of search and seizure law get in the way of catching the bad guys.

But this argument contains a flaw, and it is not a small one. Behind the race-neutral reasons police give lies a stark truth. When officers stop disproportionate members of African-Americans because this is "just good police work," they are using race as a proxy for the criminality or "general criminal propensity" of an entire racial group. Simply put, police are targeting all African-Americans because some are criminals. In essence, this thinking predicts that all blacks, as a group, share a general propensity to commit crimes. Therefore, having black skin becomes enough—perhaps along with a minimal number of other factors, perhaps alone—for law enforcement to stop and detain someone. Under this view, all black citizens become probable criminals— suspects the minute they venture out of their homes.

The wrongheadedness and unfairness of treating all members of a group as criminals just because some are seems obvious. But even if not everyone feels this way, treating race as a proxy for criminality suffers from other serious problems. First, implicit in this view is the assumption that blacks are disproportionately more likely than whites and others to be involved with street crimes. Even if this is true, African-Americans being more likely than whites to be involved in street crime is a far cry from any evidence that would strongly support the assertion that any particular black person is committing a crime. Yet that is the way police use this information. Second, even if we accept the assumption of the disproportionate involvement of blacks in street crime, police still greatly overestimate the value of race as a predictor of criminal behavior. Using race as a proxy for criminality may result in "double counting." If, for example, criminal involvement is strongly correlated with poverty, with presence in so-called "high crime areas," or with both, and if African-Americans are disproportionately poor and living in such neighborhoods, race would add little to a police officer's ability to predict criminal involvement beyond what poverty and geography already reveal....

Whren leaves us in an unsatisfactory situation. Any time we use our cars, we can be stopped by the police virtually at their whim because full compliance with traffic laws is impossible. And we can feel relatively certain that past will be prologue: African-Americans and Hispanics will suffer the bulk of this treatment. Whites will not have to endure it very often; if they did, it probably would not happen. And, once police stop drivers, the officers will be able to search almost everyone they want, some with consent and others with dogs. I, for one, feel considerably less than comfortable with this outcome.

We may not always agree on the full contours of the Fourth Amendment, but if nothing else it stands for—indeed, imposes—restraint on the government's power over the individual in the pursuit of crime. At the very least, the police must have a reason—probable cause, or at least reasonable suspicion—to pursue, stop and search citizens. The point is not that the police are powerless until criminals strike, but rather that police cannot treat everyone like a criminal in order that some secretive wrongdoers be caught. From every practical vantage point, *Whren* upends this venerable and sensible principle in the name of the war on drugs. Its implications are clear: everyone is fair game; members of minority groups will pay the largest price, but there are casualties in war, so African-Americans and Hispanics will just have to bear the cost. The Supreme Court could have used *Whren* as an occasion to repudiate the worst of what this tragic and ultimately unwinnable war has brought us. Instead, it increased police power and discretion. We are all the losers for it, but unfortunately some of us—those of us with dark skin—will lose a lot more than the rest. Perhaps police departmental regulation, and further study, can lead us in new directions.

POSTSCRIPT

Are Pretextual Stops by the Police Constitutional?

As Harris indicates, there are few activities that are more central to American life than driving an automobile. Most Americans, however, are probably unaware of the tremendous breadth of traffic codes. More to the point, many would be surprised by the virtually limitless opportunity such codes provide for law enforcement officers to stop motorists travelling on U.S. streets and highways. Some would argue that to use minor traffic violations as a pretext for stopping a motorist in order to investigate the possibility of more serious criminal activity is simply good police work. Others are alarmed by the possibilities such occasions provide for singling out whom to stop based on race and for the serious abuse of discretionary authority by the police.

In *Whren v. United States,* however, the Supreme Court dismissed as constitutionally irrelevant any possible subjective intentions a given police officer might have in stopping a motorist; it held instead that alleged pretextual stops were valid if, objectively, the officer had probable cause to stop the vehicle for either a traffic warning or a citation. Moreover, the Court declined to address the issue that Harris finds most problematic: the contention that far too many police officers use the race of the driver or passengers as a leading factor in their determination of whether or not to stop a vehicle. Scalia suggests that if this is a problem, such arguments should be brought before the courts as equal protection, not Fourth Amendment, claims. But those challenging the use of pretextual stops face a more serious problem—one that Harris readily acknowledges: data to support the assertion that law enforcement agencies utilize pretextual stops in a racially biased manner are simply not available. This is where the matter stands today. Legislation is pending in the U.S. Congress and in various state legislatures that would require all law enforcement agencies to report the race of motorists who are stopped, whether or not a citation or warning was issued.

Those wishing to read the *Traffic Stop Statistics Study Act of 1999* (S.821) —introduced in the U.S. Senate by Senator Frank R. Lautenberg (D-New Jersey) —may find it at Congress's Web site http://thomas.loc.gov. In addition, the American Civil Liberties Union has posted a questionnaire at its Web site to gather information on the "crime of driving while black or brown." See http://www.aclunc.org/dwb-question.html. For further reading, see Randall Kennedy's book *Race, Crime and Law* (Random House, 1997) for a general treatment of the problems of race and the administration of criminal justice and Michael Tonry's *Malign Neglect: Race, Crime, and Punishment in America* (Oxford University Press, 1996). For more specific treatments of the question of pretextual stops, see Angela J. Davis, "Race, Cops, and Traffic Stops," 51 *University of Miami Law Review* 425 (1997); David A. Harris, "Car Wars: The Fourth Amendment's Death on the Highway," 66 *George Washington Law Review* 556 (1998); Tracey Maclin, "Race and the Fourth Amendment," 51 *Vanderbilt Law Review* 333 (1998); and David Slansky, "Traffic Stops, Minority Motorists, and the Future of the Fourth Amendment," 271 *Supreme Court Review* (1997).

Thomas: Legislative Information on the Internet

This site of the Library of Congress provides access to federal statutes, pending legislation, and other legal material.

```
http://thomas.loc.gov
```

FedWorld

FedWorld is a highly comprehensive site with links to other federal agencies and to the reports and information produced by those agencies.

```
http//www.fedworld.gov
```

FedNet

FedNet allows you to listen in on congressional hearings and events and also provides links to archives of previously recorded material.

```
http://www.fednet.net
```

Death Penalty Information Center

The Death Penalty Information Center provides a wealth of information on a variety of topics related to capital punishment, including a history of the death penalty, race issues, and mental retardation and the death penalty.

```
http://www.deathpenaltyinfo.org/index.html
```

PART 2

Law and the State

*T*he use of state power can be seen in various ways, including in the promotion of patriotic and moral values, in efforts to deal with crime, in responses to public opinion, and in choices of policies to be implemented. The majority is not always allowed to rule, and determining when state interests are compelling and legitimate is often difficult. The issues in this section confront some of these challenges.

- Do Religious Groups Have a Right to Use Public School Facilities After Hours?

- Does the Use of High-Technology Thermal Imaging Devices Violate the Fourth Amendment Search and Seizure Guaranty?

- Is Virtual Child Pornography Legal?

- Is It Constitutional to Impose the Death Penalty on the Mentally Retarded?

- Is It Constitutionally Permissible to Detain "Sexually Dangerous" Individuals After They Have Served Their Prison Sentences?

- Should Drug Use Be Legalized?

ISSUE 8

Do Religious Groups Have a Right to Use Public School Facilities After Hours?

YES: Clarence Thomas, from Majority Opinion, *Good News Club et al. v. Milford Central School,* U.S. Supreme Court (June 11, 2001)

NO: David Souter, from Dissenting Opinion, *Good News Club et al. v. Milford Central School,* U.S. Supreme Court (June 11, 2001)

ISSUE SUMMARY

YES: Supreme Court justice Clarence Thomas affirms the right of religious groups to use school facilities after the school day ends, maintaining that restricting such use is a violation of free speech rights.

NO: Supreme Court justice David Souter, dissenting from the Court's opinion, contends that the use of school facilities by religious groups blurs the line between public classroom instruction and private religious indoctrination and therefore violates the establishment clause of the Constitution.

An Easter egg hunt on the White House lawn. Christmas as a national holiday. Prayers opening legislative sessions of state legislatures. If you were a judge and the above practices were challenged as being unconstitutional, how would you rule?

The First Amendment to the Constitution states that "Congress shall make no law respecting an establishment of religion, or prohibiting the free exercise thereof." Interpreting these words and applying them in particular cases has been exceedingly difficult for the courts. What, for example, does "respecting an establishment of religion" mean? Is any governmental involvement or support for religion, direct or indirect, small or great, barred by this phrase?

While the courts have struggled to keep church and state separate, they have also recognized that it would be impossible to have an absolute prohibition on the celebration of religious values and holidays. Therefore, cases continue to be brought, challenging the courts to determine how the words of the Constitution and the standards of prior cases should be applied to the facts of each new case.

The clearest and most well known of the establishment of religion cases are the school prayer decisions. In 1963, in *School District of Abington Township, Pennsylvania v. Schempp*, 374 U.S. 203, the Supreme Court ruled that it was unconstitutional to require students to open the school day by reading biblical passages and reciting the Lord's Prayer. A year earlier, in *Engel v. Vitale*, 370 U.S. 421 (1962), the Supreme Court had ruled that recitation of the New York Regent's Prayer was unconstitutional. This prayer read, "Almighty God, we acknowledge our dependence upon Thee, and we beg thy blessings upon us, our parents, our teachers, and our country."

While banning prayer in the schools, the courts have upheld some questionable practices, such as Sunday closing laws and the loaning of secular textbooks to parochial schools. Yet they have struck down other statutes, such as the Kentucky law that required posting the Ten Commandments in the classroom (see *Stone v. Graham*, 101 S. Ct. 192 [1980]). More generally, the Court has upheld prayers at the beginning of legislative sessions and tuition tax credits for parochial schools. Yet it held unconstitutional a statute requiring a moment of silence in public schools, remedial programs for parochial schools, and a law requiring the teaching of "creation science" whenever evolution is taught.

The many cases involving religion that have been considered by the Supreme Court in the past 25 years indicate that the task of defining precisely what role religion should have in government-sponsored activities is extraordinarily difficult. Religion has not been banned from public life. "In God We Trust" appears on U.S. coins, prayers are said at presidential inaugurations, Christmas is a national holiday, the lighting of the national Christmas tree at the White House is a newsworthy event, and tax exemptions are given to religious institutions. It is probably still accurate, as a Supreme Court justice once wrote, that "we are a religious people whose institutions presuppose a Supreme Being." It is also true, however, that many religious activities may not be sponsored by the government.

The following case is one of the most recent Supreme Court decisions to consider the intersection between the free exercise of religion and the establishment of religion. Justice Clarence Thomas finds that the plaintiff, the Good News Club, has as much a right as anyone else to use school grounds. Justice David Souter dissents.

 **YES**

Majority Opinion

Good News Club *v.* Milford Central School

JUSTICE THOMAS delivered the opinion of the Court.

This case presents two questions. The first question is whether Milford Central School violated the free speech rights of the Good News Club when it excluded the Club from meeting after hours at the school. The second question is whether any such violation is justified by Milford's concern that permitting the Club's activities would violate the Establishment Clause. We conclude that Milford's restriction violates the Club's free speech rights and that no Establishment Clause concern justifies that violation.

I

The State of New York authorizes local school boards to adopt regulations governing the use of their school facilities. In particular, N. Y. Educ. Law §414 (McKinney 2000) enumerates several purposes for which local boards may open their schools to public use. In 1992, respondent Milford Central School (Milford) enacted a community use policy adopting seven of §414's purposes for which its building could be used after school. Two of the stated purposes are relevant here. First, district residents may use the school for "instruction in any branch of education, learning or the arts." Second, the school is available for "social, civic and recreational meetings and entertainment events, and other uses pertaining to the welfare of the community, provided that such uses shall be nonexclusive and shall be opened to the general public."

Stephen and Darleen Fournier reside within Milford's district and therefore are eligible to use the school's facilities as long as their proposed use is approved by the school. Together they are sponsors of the local Good News Club, a private Christian organization for children ages 6 to 12. Pursuant to Milford's policy, in September 1996 the Fourniers submitted a request to Dr. Robert McGruder, interim superintendent of the district, in which they sought permission to hold the Club's weekly afterschool meetings in the school cafeteria. The next month, McGruder formally denied the Fourniers' request on

From *Good News Club et al. v. Milford Central School*, 533 U.S. ___ (2001). Some notes and case citations omitted.

the ground that the proposed use—to have "a fun time of singing songs, hearing a Bible lesson and memorizing scripture,"—was "the equivalent of religious worship." According to McGruder, the community use policy, which prohibits use "by any individual or organization for religious purposes," foreclosed the Club's activities.

In response to a letter submitted by the Club's counsel, Milford's attorney requested information to clarify the nature of the Club's activities. The Club sent a set of materials used or distributed at the meetings and the following description of its meeting:

> "The Club opens its session with Ms. Fournier taking attendance. As she calls a child's name, if the child recites a Bible verse the child receives a treat. After attendance, the Club sings songs. Next Club members engage in games that involve, *inter alia,* learning Bible verses. Ms. Fournier then relates a Bible story and explains how it applies to Club members' lives. The Club closes with prayer. Finally, Ms. Fournier distributes treats and the Bible verses for memorization."

McGruder and Milford's attorney reviewed the materials and concluded that "the kinds of activities proposed to be engaged in by the Good News Club were not a discussion of secular subjects such as child rearing, development of character and development of morals from a religious perspective, but were in fact the equivalent of religious instruction itself." In February 1997, the Milford Board of Education adopted a resolution rejecting the Club's request to use Milford's facilities "for the purpose of conducting religious instruction and Bible study."

In March 1997, petitioners, the Good News Club, Ms. Fournier, and her daughter Andrea Fournier (collectively, the Club), filed an action under 42 U.S.C. §1983 against Milford in the United States District Court for the Northern District of New York. The Club alleged that Milford's denial of its application violated its free speech rights under the First and Fourteenth Amendments, its right to equal protection under the Fourteenth Amendment, and its right to religious freedom under the Religious Freedom Restoration Act of 1993, 107 Stat. 1488, 42 U.S.C. §2000bb *et seq.*

The Club moved for a preliminary injunction to prevent the school from enforcing its religious exclusion policy against the Club and thereby to permit the Club's use of the school facilities. On April 14, 1997, the District Court granted the injunction. The Club then held its weekly afterschool meetings from April 1997 until June 1998 in a high school resource and middle school special education room.

In August 1998, the District Court vacated the preliminary injunction and granted Milford's motion for summary judgment. 21 F. Supp. 2d 147 (NDNY 1998). The court found that the Club's "subject matter is decidedly religious in nature, and not merely a discussion of secular matters from a religious perspective that is otherwise permitted under [Milford's] use policies." Because the school had not permitted other groups that provided religious instruction to use its limited public forum, the court held that the school could deny access to the Club without engaging in unconstitutional viewpoint discrimination. The court also rejected the Club's equal protection claim.

The Club appealed, and a divided panel of the United States Court of Appeals for the Second Circuit affirmed. 202 F. 3d 502 (2000). First, the court rejected the Club's contention that Milford's restriction against allowing religious instruction in its facilities is unreasonable. Second, it held that, because the subject matter of the Club's activities is "quintessentially religious," and the activities "fall outside the bounds of pure 'moral and character development,'" Milford's policy of excluding the Club's meetings was constitutional subject discrimination, not unconstitutional viewpoint discrimination. Judge Jacobs filed a dissenting opinion in which he concluded that the school's restriction did constitute viewpoint discrimination under *Lamb's Chapel v. Center Moriches Union Free School Dist.,* 508 U.S. 384 (1993).

There is a conflict among the Courts of Appeals on the question whether speech can be excluded from a limited public forum on the basis of the religious nature of the speech. Compare *Gentala v. Tucson,* 244 F. 3d 1065 (CA9 2001) (en banc) (holding that a city properly refused National Day of Prayer organizers' application to the city's civic events fund for coverage of costs for city services); *Campbell v. St. Tammany's School Bd.,* 206 F. 3d 482 (CA5 2000) (holding that a school's policy against permitting religious instruction in its limited public forum did not constitute viewpoint discrimination), cert. pending, No. 00–1194; *Bronx Household of Faith v. Community School Dist. No. 10,* 127 F. 3d 207 (CA2 1997) (concluding that a ban on religious services and instruction in the limited public forum was constitutional), with *Church on the Rock v. Albuquerque,* 84 F. 3d 1273 (CA10 1996) (holding that a city's denial of permission to show the film Jesus in a senior center was unconstitutional viewpoint discrimination); and *Good News/Good Sports Club v. School Dist. of Ladue,* 28 F. 3d 1501 (CA8 1994) (holding unconstitutional a school use policy that prohibited Good News Club from meeting during times when the Boy Scouts could meet). We granted certiorari to resolve this conflict. 531 U.S. 923 (2000).

II

The standards that we apply to determine whether a State has unconstitutionally excluded a private speaker from use of a public forum depend on the nature of the forum. See *Perry Ed. Assn. v. Perry Local Educators' Assn.,* 460 U.S. 37, 44 (1983). If the forum is a traditional or open public forum, the State's restrictions on speech are subject to stricter scrutiny than are restrictions in a limited public forum. *Id.,* at 45–46. We have previously declined to decide whether a school district's opening of its facilities pursuant to N. Y. Educ. Law §414 creates a limited or a traditional public forum. See *Lamb's Chapel, supra,* at 391–392. Because the parties have agreed that Milford created a limited public forum when it opened its facilities in 1992, we need not resolve the issue here. Instead, we simply will assume that Milford operates a limited public forum.

When the State establishes a limited public forum, the State is not required to and does not allow persons to engage in every type of speech. The State may be justified "in reserving [its forum] for certain groups or for the discussion of certain topics." *Rosenberger v. Rector and Visitors of Univ. of Va.,* 515 U.S. 819, 829 (1995); see also *Lamb's Chapel, supra,* at 392–393. The State's power to restrict speech, however, is not without limits. The restriction must not discriminate against speech on the basis of viewpoint, *Rosenberger, supra,* at 829, and the restriction must be "reasonable in light of the purpose served by the forum," *Cornelius v. NAACP Legal Defense & Ed. Fund, Inc.,* 473 U.S. 788, 806 (1985).

III

Applying this test, we first address whether the exclusion constituted viewpoint discrimination. We are guided in our analysis by two of our prior opinions, *Lamb's Chapel* and *Rosenberger.* In *Lamb's Chapel,* we held that a school district violated the Free Speech Clause of the First Amendment when it excluded a private group from presenting films at the school based solely on the films' discussions of family values from a religious perspective. Likewise, in *Rosenberger,* we held that a university's refusal to fund a student publication because the publication addressed issues from a religious perspective violated the Free Speech Clause. Concluding that Milford's exclusion of the Good News Club based on its religious nature is indistinguishable from the exclusions in these cases, we hold that the exclusion constitutes viewpoint discrimination. Because the restriction is viewpoint discriminatory, we need not decide whether it is unreasonable in light of the purposes served by the forum.

Milford has opened its limited public forum to activities that serve a variety of purposes, including events "pertaining to the welfare of the community." Milford interprets its policy to permit discussions of subjects such as child rearing, and of "the development of character and morals from a religious perspective." Brief for Appellee in No. 98–9494 (CA2), p. 6. For example, this policy would allow someone to use Aesop's Fables to teach children moral values. Additionally, a group could sponsor a debate on whether there should be a constitutional amendment to permit prayer in public schools, and the Boy Scouts could meet "to influence a boy's character, development and spiritual growth." In short, any group that "promote[s] the moral and character development of children" is eligible to use the school building.

Just as there is no question that teaching morals and character development to children is a permissible purpose under Milford's policy, it is clear that the Club teaches morals and character development to children. For example, no one disputes that the Club instructs children to overcome feelings of jealousy, to treat others well regardless of how they treat the children, and to be obedient, even if it does so in a nonsecular way. Nonetheless, because Milford found the Club's activities to be religious in nature—"the equivalent of religious instruction itself," 202 F. 3d, at 507—it excluded the Club from use of its facilities.

Applying *Lamb's Chapel,*[1] we find it quite clear that Milford engaged in viewpoint discrimination when it excluded the Club from the afterschool forum. In *Lamb's Chapel,* the local New York school district similarly had adopted §414's "social, civic or recreational use" category as a permitted use in its limited public forum. The district also prohibited use "by any group for religious purposes." 508 U.S., at 387. Citing this prohibition, the school district excluded a church that wanted to present films teaching family values from a Christian perspective. We held that, because the films "no doubt dealt with a subject otherwise permissible" under the rule, the teaching of family values, the district's exclusion of the church was unconstitutional viewpoint discrimination. *Id.*, at 394.

Like the church in *Lamb's Chapel* the Club seeks to address a subject otherwise permitted under the rule, the teaching of morals and character, from a religious standpoint. Certainly, one could have characterized the film presentations in *Lamb's Chapel* as a religious use, as the Court of Appeals did, *Lamb's Chapel v. Center Moriches Union Free School Dist.*, 959 F. 2d 381, 388–389 (CA2 1992). And one easily could conclude that the films' purpose to instruct that " 'society's slide toward humanism ... can only be counterbalanced by a loving home where Christian values are instilled from an early age,'" *id.*, at 384, was "quintessentially religious," 202 F. 3d, at 510. The only apparent difference between the activity of Lamb's Chapel and the activities of the Good News Club is that the Club chooses to teach moral lessons from a Christian perspective through live storytelling and prayer, whereas Lamb's Chapel taught lessons through films. This distinction is inconsequential. Both modes of speech use a religious viewpoint. Thus, the exclusion of the Good News Club's activities, like the exclusion of Lamb's Chapel's films, constitutes unconstitutional viewpoint discrimination.

Our opinion in *Rosenberger* also is dispositive. In *Rosenberger,* a student organization at the University of Virginia was denied funding for printing expenses because its publication, Wide Awake, offered a Christian viewpoint. Just as the Club emphasizes the role of Christianity in students' morals and character, Wide Awake " 'challenge[d] Christians to live, in word and deed, according to the faith they proclaim and ... encourage[d] students to consider what a personal relationship with Jesus Christ means.' " 515 U.S., at 826. Because the university "select[ed] for disfavored treatment those student journalistic efforts with religious editorial viewpoints," we held that the denial of funding was unconstitutional. *Id.*, at 831. Although in *Rosenberger* there was no prohibition on religion as a subject matter, our holding did not rely on this factor. Instead, we concluded simply that the university's denial of funding to print Wide Awake was viewpoint discrimination, just as the school district's refusal to allow Lamb's Chapel to show its films was viewpoint discrimination. Given the obvious religious content of Wide Awake, we cannot say that the Club's activities are any more "religious" or deserve any less First Amendment protection than did the publication of Wide Awake in *Rosenberger.*

Despite our holdings in *Lamb's Chapel* and *Rosenberger,* the Court of Appeals, like Milford, believed that its characterization of the Club's activities as religious in nature warranted treating the Club's activities as different in kind from the other activities permitted by the school. See 202 F. 3d, at 510 (the Club "is doing something other than simply teaching moral values"). The "Christian viewpoint" is unique, according to the court, because it contains an "additional layer" that other kinds of viewpoints do not. *Id.*, at 509. That is, the Club "is focused on teaching children how to cultivate their relationship with God through Jesus Christ," which it characterized as "quintessentially religious." *Id.*, at 510. With these observations, the court concluded that, because the Club's activities "fall outside the bounds of pure 'moral and character development,'" the exclusion did not constitute viewpoint discrimination. *Id.*, at 511.

We disagree that something that is "quintessentially religious" or "decidedly religious in nature" cannot also be characterized properly as the teaching of morals and character development from a particular viewpoint. See 202 F. 3d, at 512 (Jacobs, J., dissenting) ("[W]hen the subject matter is morals and character, it is quixotic to attempt a distinction between religious viewpoints and religious subject matters"). What matters for purposes of the Free Speech Clause is that we can see no logical difference in kind between the invocation of Christianity by the Club and the invocation of teamwork, loyalty, or patriotism by other associations to provide a foundation for their lessons. It is apparent that the unstated principle of the Court of Appeals' reasoning is its conclusion that any time religious instruction and prayer are used to discuss morals and character, the discussion is simply not a "pure" discussion of those issues. According to the Court of Appeals, reliance on Christian principles taints moral and character instruction in a way that other foundations for thought or viewpoints do not. We, however, have never reached such a conclusion. Instead, we reaffirm our holdings in *Lamb's Chapel* and *Rosenberger* that speech discussing otherwise permissible subjects cannot be excluded from a limited public forum on the ground that the subject is discussed from a religious viewpoint. Thus, we conclude that Milford's exclusion of the Club from use of the school, pursuant to its community use policy, constitutes impermissible viewpoint discrimination.

IV

Milford argues that, even if its restriction constitutes viewpoint discrimination, its interest in not violating the Establishment Clause outweighs the Club's interest in gaining equal access to the school's facilities. In other words, according to Milford, its restriction was required to avoid violating the Establishment Clause. We disagree.

We have said that a state interest in avoiding an Establishment Clause violation "may be characterized as compelling," and therefore may justify content-based discrimination. *Widmar* v. *Vincent,* 454 U.S. 263, 271 (1981). However, it is not clear whether a State's interest in avoiding an Establishment Clause violation would justify viewpoint discrimination. See *Lamb's Chapel,* 508 U.S., at 394–395 (noting the suggestion in *Widmar* but ultimately not finding an Establishment Clause problem). We need not, however, confront the issue in this case, because we conclude that the school has no valid Establishment Clause interest.

We rejected Establishment Clause defenses similar to Milford's in two previous free speech cases, *Lamb's Chapel* and *Widmar.* In particular, in *Lamb's Chapel,* we explained that "[t]he showing of th[e] film series would not have been during school hours, would not have been sponsored by the school, and would have been open to the public, not just to church members." 508 U.S., at 395. Accordingly, we found that "there would have been no realistic danger that the community would think that the District was endorsing religion or any particular creed." *Ibid.* Likewise, in *Widmar,* where the university's forum was already available to other groups, this Court concluded that there was no Establishment Clause problem. 454 U.S., at 272–273, and n. 13.

The Establishment Clause defense fares no better in this case. As in *Lamb's Chapel,* the Club's meetings were held after school hours, not sponsored by the school, and open to any student who obtained parental consent, not just to Club members. As in *Widmar,* Milford made its forum available to other organizations. The Club's activities are materially indistinguishable from those in *Lamb's Chapel* and *Widmar.* Thus, Milford's reliance on the Establishment Clause is unavailing.

Milford attempts to distinguish *Lamb's Chapel* and *Widmar* by empha-sizing that Milford's policy involves elementary school children. According to Milford, children will perceive that the school is endorsing the Club and will feel coercive pressure to participate, because the Club's activities take place on school grounds, even though they occur during nonschool hours. This argu-ment is unpersuasive.

First, we have held that "a significant factor in upholding governmental programs in the face of Establishment Clause attack is their *neutrality* towards religion." *Rosenberger,* 515 U.S., at 839 (emphasis added). See also *Mitchell v. Helms,* 530 U.S. 793 (2000) (slip op., at 10) (plurality opinion) ("In distinguish-ing between indoctrination that is attributable to the State and indoctrination that is not, [the Court has] consistently turned to the principle of neutrality, up-holding aid that is offered to a broad range of groups or persons without regard to their religion" (emphasis added)); (O'CONNOR, J., concurring in judgment) ("[N]eutrality is an important reason for upholding government-aid programs against Establishment Clause challenges"). Milford's implication that granting access to the Club would do damage to the neutrality principle defies logic. For the "guarantee of neutrality is respected, not offended, when the government, following neutral criteria and evenhanded policies, extends benefits to recipi-ents whose ideologies and viewpoints, including religious ones, are broad and diverse." *Rosenberger, supra,* at 839. The Good News Club seeks nothing more than to be treated neutrally and given access to speak about the same topics as are other groups. Because allowing the Club to speak on school grounds would ensure neutrality, not threaten it, Milford faces an uphill battle in arguing that the Establishment Clause compels it to exclude the Good News Club.

Second, to the extent we consider whether the community would feel coercive pressure to engage in the Club's activities, cf. *Lee v. Weisman,* 505 U.S. 577, 592–593 (1992), the relevant community would be the parents, not the elementary school children. It is the parents who choose whether their children will attend the Good News Club meetings. Because the children cannot attend without their parents' permission, they cannot be coerced into engaging in the Good News Club's religious activities. Milford does not suggest that the parents of elementary school children would be confused about whether the school was endorsing religion. Nor do we believe that such an argument could be reasonably advanced.

Third, whatever significance we may have assigned in the Establishment Clause context to the suggestion that elementary school children are more impressionable than adults, cf., *e.g., Lee, supra,* at 592; *School Dist. of Grand Rapids v. Ball,* 473 U.S. 373, 390 (1985) (stating that "symbolism of a union between church and state is most likely to influence children of tender years, whose experience is limited and whose beliefs consequently are the function of environment as much as of free and voluntary choice"), we have never extended our Establishment Clause jurisprudence to foreclose private religious conduct during nonschool hours merely because it takes place on school premises where elementary school children may be present.

None of the cases discussed by Milford persuades us that our Establishment Clause jurisprudence has gone this far. For example, Milford cites *Lee* v. *Weisman* for the proposition that "there are heightened concerns with protecting freedom of conscience from subtle coercive pressure in the elementary and secondary public schools," 505 U.S., at 592. In *Lee,* however, we concluded that attendance at the graduation exercise was obligatory. *Id.,* at 586. See also *Santa Fe Independent School Dist. v. Doe,* 530 U.S. 290 (2000) (holding the school's policy of permitting prayer at football games unconstitutional where the activity took place during a school-sponsored event and not in a public forum). We did not place independent significance on the fact that the graduation exercise might take place on school premises, *Lee, supra,* at 583. Here, where the school facilities are being used for a nonschool function and there is no government sponsorship of the Club's activities, *Lee* is inapposite.

Equally unsupportive is *Edwards* v. *Aguillard,* 482 U.S. 578 (1987), in which we held that a Louisiana law that proscribed the teaching of evolution as part of the public school curriculum, unless accompanied by a lesson on creationism, violated the Establishment Clause. In *Edwards,* we mentioned that students are susceptible to pressure in the classroom, particularly given their possible reliance on teachers as role models. See *id.,* at 584. But we did not discuss this concern in our application of the law to the facts. Moreover, we did note that mandatory attendance requirements meant that State advancement of religion in a school would be particularly harshly felt by impressionable students. But we did not suggest that, when the school was not actually advancing religion, the impressionability of students would be relevant to the Establishment Clause issue. Even if *Edwards* had articulated the principle Milford believes it did, the facts in *Edwards* are simply too remote from those here to give the principle any weight. *Edwards* involved the content of the curriculum taught by state teachers during the schoolday to children required to attend. Obviously, when individuals who are not schoolteachers are giving lessons after school to children permitted to attend only with parental consent, the concerns expressed in *Edwards* are not present.

Fourth, even if we were to consider the possible misperceptions by schoolchildren in deciding whether Milford's permitting the Club's activities would violate the Establishment Clause, the facts of this case simply do not support Milford's conclusion. There is no evidence that young children are permitted to loiter outside classrooms after the schoolday has ended. Surely even young children are aware of events for which their parents must sign permission forms. The meetings were held in a combined high school resource room and middle school special education room, not in an elementary school classroom. The instructors are not schoolteachers. And the children in the group are not all the same age as in the normal classroom setting; their ages range from 6 to 12. In sum, these circumstances simply do not support the theory that small children would perceive endorsement here.

Finally, even if we were to inquire into the minds of schoolchildren in this case, we cannot say the danger that children would misperceive the endorsement of religion is any greater than the danger that they would perceive a hostility toward the religious viewpoint if the Club were excluded from the public forum. This concern is particularly acute given the reality that Milford's building is not used only for elementary school children. Students, from kindergarten through the 12th grade, all attend school in the same building. There may be as many, if not more, upperclassmen than elementary school children who occupy the school after hours. For that matter, members of the public writ large are permitted in the school after hours pursuant to the community use policy. Any bystander could conceivably be aware of the school's use policy and its exclusion of the Good News Club, and could suffer as much from viewpoint discrimination as elementary school children could suffer from perceived endorsement. Cf. *Rosenberger,* 515 U.S., at 835–836 (expressing the concern that viewpoint discrimination can chill individual thought and expression).

We cannot operate, as Milford would have us do, under the assumption that any risk that small children would perceive endorsement should counsel in favor of excluding the Club's religious activity. We decline to employ Establishment Clause jurisprudence using a modified heckler's veto, in which a group's religious activity can be proscribed on the basis of what the youngest members of the audience might misperceive. Cf. *Capitol Square Review and Advisory Bd. v. Pinette,* 515 U.S. 753, 779–780 (1995) (O'CONNOR, J., concurring in part and concurring in judgment) ("[B]ecause our concern is with the political community writ large, the endorsement inquiry is *not about the perceptions of particular individuals* or saving isolated nonadherents from ... discomfort.... It is for this reason that the reasonable observer in the endorsement inquiry must be deemed aware of the history and context of the community and forum in which the religious [speech takes place]" (emphasis added)). There are countervailing constitutional concerns related to rights of other individuals in the community. In this case, those countervailing concerns are the free speech rights of the Club and its members. Cf. *Rosenberger, supra,* at 835 ("Vital First Amendment speech principles are at stake here"). And, we have already found that those rights have been violated, not merely perceived to have been violated, by the school's actions toward the Club.

We are not convinced that there is any significance in this case to the possibility that elementary school children may witness the Good News Club's activities on school premises, and therefore we can find no reason to depart from our holdings in *Lamb's Chapel* and *Widmar.* Accordingly, we conclude that permitting the Club to meet on the school's premises would not have violated the Establishment Clause.

V

When Milford denied the Good News Club access to the school's limited public forum on the ground that the Club was religious in nature, it discriminated against the Club because of its religious viewpoint in violation of the Free Speech Clause of the First Amendment. Because Milford has not raised a valid Establishment Clause claim, we do not address the question whether such a claim could excuse Milford's viewpoint discrimination.

౭⊚⃝౨

The judgment of the Court of Appeals is reversed, and the case is remanded for further proceedings consistent with this opinion.

It is so ordered.

Note

1. We find it remarkable that the Court of Appeals majority did not cite *Lamb's Chapel*, despite its obvious relevance to the case. We do not necessarily expect a court of appeals to catalog every opinion that reverses one of its precedents. Nonetheless, this oversight is particularly incredible because the majority's attention was directed to it at every turn. See, *e.g.,* 202 F. 3d 502, 513 (CA2 2000) (Jacobs, J., dissenting) ("I cannot square the majority's analysis in this case with *Lamb's Chapel*"); 21 F. Supp. 2d, at 150; App. O9–O11 (District Court stating "that *Lamb's Chapel* and Rosenberger pinpoint the critical issue in this case"); Brief for Appellee in No. 98–9494 (CA2) at 36–39; Brief for Appellants in No. 98–9494 (CA2), pp. 15, 36.

Dissenting Opinion of David Souter

J USTICE SOUTER, with whom JUSTICE GINSBURG joins, dissenting.

The majority rules on two issues. First, it decides that the Court of Appeals failed to apply the rule in *Lambs's Chapel v. Center Moriches Union Free School Dist.*, 508 U.S. 384 (1993), which held that the government may not discriminate on the basis of viewpoint in operating a limited public forum. The majority applies that rule and concludes that Milford violated *Lambs's Chapel* in denying Good News the use of the school. The majority then goes on to determine that it would not violate the Establishment Clause of the First Amendment for the Milford School District to allow the Good News Club to hold its intended gatherings of public school children in Milford's elementary school. The majority is mistaken on both points. The Court of Appeals unmistakably distinguished this case from *Lamb's Chapel*, though not by name, and accordingly affirmed the application of a policy, unchallenged in the District Court, that Milford's public schools may not be used for religious purposes. As for the applicability of the Establishment Clause to the Good News Club's intended use of Milford's school, the majority commits error even in reaching the issue, which was addressed neither by the Court of Appeals nor by the District Court. I respectfully dissent.

I

Lamb's Chapel, a case that arose (as this one does) from application of N. Y. Educ. Law §414 (McKinney 2000) and local policy implementing it, built on the accepted rule that a government body may designate a public forum subject to a reasonable limitation on the scope of permitted subject matter and activity, so long as the government does not use the forum-defining restrictions to deny expression to a particular viewpoint on subjects open to discussion. Specifically, *Lamb's Chapel* held that the government could not "permit school property to be used for the presentation of all views about family issues and child rearing except those dealing with the subject matter from a religious standpoint." 508 U.S., at 393–394.

This case, like *Lamb's Chapel*, properly raises no issue about the reasonableness of Milford's criteria for restricting the scope of its designated public

From *Good News Club et al. v. Milford Central School*, 533 U.S. ___ (2001). Some notes and case citations omitted.

forum. Milford has opened school property for, among other things, "instruction in any branch of education, learning or the arts" and for "social, civic and recreational meetings and entertainment events and other uses pertaining to the welfare of the community, provided that such uses shall be nonexclusive and shall be opened to the general public." App. to Pet. for Cert. D1–D3. But Milford has done this subject to the restriction that "[s]chool premises shall not be used ... for religious purposes." As the District Court stated, Good News did "not object to the reasonableness of [Milford]'s policy that prohibits the use of [its] facilities for religious purposes."

The sole question before the District Court was, therefore, whether, in refusing to allow Good News's intended use, Milford was misapplying its unchallenged restriction in a way that amounted to imposing a viewpoint-based restriction on what could be said or done by a group entitled to use the forum for an educational, civic, or other permitted purpose. The question was whether Good News was being disqualified when it merely sought to use the school property the same way that the Milford Boy and Girl Scouts and the 4-H Club did. The District Court held on the basis of undisputed facts that Good News's activity was essentially unlike the presentation of views on secular issues from a religious standpoint held to be protected in *Lamb's Chapel*, see App. to Pet. for Cert. C29–C31, and was instead activity precluded by Milford's unchallenged policy against religious use, even under the narrowest definition of that term.

The Court of Appeals understood the issue the same way. See 202 F. 3d 502, 508 (CA2 2000) (Good News argues that "to exclude the Club because it teaches morals and values from a Christian perspective constitutes unconstitutional viewpoint discrimination"); *id.,* at 509 ("The crux of the Good News Club's argument is that the Milford school's application of the Community Use Policy to exclude the Club from its facilities is not viewpoint neutral"). The Court of Appeals also realized that the *Lamb's Chapel* criterion was the appropriate measure: "The activities of the Good News Club do not involve merely a religious perspective on the secular subject of morality." 202 F. 3d, at 510. Cf. *Lamb's Chapel, supra,* at 393 (district could not exclude "religious standpoint" in discussion on childrearing and family values, an undisputed "use for social or civic purposes otherwise permitted" under the use policy).[1] The appeals court agreed with the District Court that the undisputed facts in this case differ from those in *Lamb's Chapel,* as night from day. A sampling of those facts shows why both courts were correct.

Good News's classes open and close with prayer. In a sample lesson considered by the District Court, children are instructed that "[t]he Bible tells us how we can have our sins forgiven by receiving the Lord Jesus Christ. It tells us how to live to please Him.... If you have received the Lord Jesus as your Saviour from sin, you belong to God's special group—His family." The lesson plan instructs the teacher to "lead a child to Christ," and, when reading a Bible verse, to "[e]mphasize that this verse is from the Bible, God's Word" and is "important—and true—because God said it." The lesson further exhorts the teacher to "[b]e sure to give an opportunity for the 'unsaved' children in your class to respond to the Gospel" and cautions against "neglect[ing] this responsibility."

While Good News's program utilizes songs and games, the heart of the meeting is the "challenge" and "invitation," which are repeated at various times throughout the lesson. During the challenge, "saved" children who "already believe in the Lord Jesus as their Savior" are challenged to " 'stop and ask God for the strength and the "want" . . . to obey Him.' " *Ibid.* They are instructed that

> "[i]f you know Jesus as your Savior, you need to place God first in your life. And if you don't know Jesus as Savior and if you would like to, then we will —we will pray with you separately, individually. . . . And the challenge would be, those of you who know Jesus as Savior, you can rely on God's strength to obey Him." *Ibid.*

During the invitation, the teacher "invites" the "unsaved" children " 'to trust the Lord Jesus to be your Savior from sin,' " and " 'receiv[e] [him] as your Savior from sin.' " *Id.,* at C21. The children are then instructed that

> "[i]f you believe what God's Word says about your sin and how Jesus died and rose again for you, you can have His forever life today. Please bow your heads and close your eyes. If you have never believed on the Lord Jesus as your Savior and would like to do that, please show me by raising your hand. If you raised your hand to show me you want to believe on the Lord Jesus, please meet me so I can show you from God's Word how you can receive His everlasting life." *Ibid.*

It is beyond question that Good News intends to use the public school premises not for the mere discussion of a subject from a particular, Christian point of view, but for an evangelical service of worship calling children to commit themselves in an act of Christian conversion.[2] The majority avoids this reality only by resorting to the bland and general characterization of Good News's activity as "teaching of morals and character, from a religious standpoint." See *ante,* at 9. If the majority's statement ignores reality, as it surely does, then today's holding may be understood only in equally generic terms. Otherwise, indeed, this case would stand for the remarkable proposition that any public school opened for civic meetings must be opened for use as a church, synagogue, or mosque. . . .

This Court has accepted the independent obligation to obey the Establishment Clause as sufficiently compelling to satisfy strict scrutiny under the First Amendment. See *id.,* at 271 ("[T]he interest of the [government] in complying with its constitutional obligations may be characterized as compelling"); *Lamb's Chapel,* 508 U.S., at 394. Milford's actions would offend the Establishment Clause if they carried the message of endorsing religion under the circumstances, as viewed by a reasonable observer. See *Capitol Square Review and Advisory Bd. v. Pinette,* 515 U.S. 753, 777 (1995) (O'CONNOR, J., concurring). The majority concludes that such an endorsement effect is out of the question in Milford's case, because the context here is "materially indistinguishable" from the facts in *Lamb's Chapel* and *Widmar. Ante,* at 13. In fact, the majority is in no position to say that, for the principal grounds on which we based our Establishment Clause holdings in those cases are clearly absent here.

In *Widmar,* we held that the Establishment Clause did not bar a religious student group from using a public university's meeting space for worship as well as discussion. As for the reasonable observers who might perceive government endorsement of religion, we pointed out that the forum was used by university students, who "are, of course, young adults," and, as such, "are less impressionable than younger students and should be able to appreciate that the University's policy is one of neutrality toward religion." 454 U.S., at 274, n. 14. To the same effect, we remarked that the "large number of groups meeting on campus" negated "any reasonable inference of University support from the mere fact of a campus meeting place." *Ibid.* Not only was the forum "available to a broad class of nonreligious as well as religious speakers," but there were, in fact, over 100 recognized student groups at the University, and an "absence of empirical evidence that religious groups [would] dominate [the University's] open forum." *Id.,* at 274–275; see also *id.,* at 274 ("The provision of benefits to so broad a spectrum of groups is an important index of secular effect"). And if all that had not been enough to show that the university-student use would probably create no impression of religious endorsement, we pointed out that the university in that case had issued a student handbook with the explicit disclaimer that "the University's name will not 'be identified in any way with the aims, policies, programs, products, or opinions of any organization or its members.'" *Id.,* at 274, n. 14.

Lamb's Chapel involved an evening film series on childrearing open to the general public (and, given the subject matter, directed at an adult audience). See 508 U.S., at 387, 395. There, school property "had repeatedly been used by a wide variety of private organizations," and we could say with some assurance that "[u]nder these circumstances . . . there would have been no realistic danger that the community would think that the District was endorsing religion or any particular creed. . . ." *Id.,* at 395.

What we know about this case looks very little like *Widmar* or *Lamb's Chapel.* The cohort addressed by Good News is not university students with relative maturity, or even high school pupils, but elementary school children as young as six.[3] The Establishment Clause cases have consistently recognized the particular impressionability of schoolchildren, see *Edwards v. Aguillard,* 482 U.S. 578, 583–584 (1987), and the special protection required for those in the elementary grades in the school forum, see *County of Allegheny v. American Civil Liberties Union, Greater Pittsburgh Chapter,* 492 U.S. 573, 620, n. 69 (1989). We have held the difference between college students and grade school pupils to be a "distinction [that] warrants a difference in constitutional results," *Edwards v. Aguillard, supra,* at 584, n. 5 (internal quotation marks and citation omitted).

Nor is Milford's limited forum anything like the sites for wide-ranging intellectual exchange that were home to the challenged activities in *Widmar* and *Lamb's Chapel.* See also *Rosenberger,* 515 U.S., at 850, 836–837. In Widmar, the nature of the university campus and the sheer number of activities offered precluded the reasonable college observer from seeing government endorsement in any one of them, and so did the time and variety of community use in the *Lamb's Chapel* case. See also *Rosenberger,* 515 U.S., at 850 ("Given this wide array of nonreligious, antireligious and competing religious viewpoints in the forum supported by the University, any perception that the University endorses one particular viewpoint would be illogical"); *id.,* at 836–837, 850 (emphasizing the array of university-funded magazines containing "widely divergent viewpoints" and the fact that believers in Christian evangelism competed on equal footing in the University forum with aficionados of "Plato, Spinoza, and Descartes," as well as "Karl Marx, Bertrand Russell, and Jean-Paul Sartre"); *Board of Ed. of Westside Community Schools (Dist. 66) v. Mergens,* 496 U.S. 226, 252 (1990) (plurality opinion) ("To the extent that a religious club is merely one of many different student-initiated voluntary clubs, students should perceive no message of government endorsement of religion").

The timing and format of Good News's gatherings, on the other hand, may well affirmatively suggest the *imprimatur* of officialdom in the minds of the young children. The club is open solely to elementary students (not the entire community, as in *Lamb's Chapel*), only four outside groups have been identified as meeting in the school, and Good News is, seemingly, the only one whose instruction follows immediately on the conclusion of the official school day. See Brief for National School Boards Association et al. as *Amici Curiae* 6. Although school is out at 2:56 p.m., Good News apparently requested use of the school beginning at 2:30 on Tuesdays "during the school year," so that instruction could begin promptly at 3:00, at which time children who are compelled by law to attend school surely remain in the building. Good News's religious meeting follows regular school activities so closely that the Good News instructor must wait to begin until "the room is clear," and "people are out of the room," before starting proceedings in the classroom located next to the regular third- and fourth-grade rooms. In fact, the temporal and physical continuity of Good News's meetings with the regular school routine seems to be the whole point of using the school. When meetings were held in a community church, 8 or 10 children attended; after the school became the site, the number went up three-fold.

Even on the summary judgment record, then, a record lacking whatever supplementation the trial process might have led to, and devoid of such insight as the trial and appellate judges might have contributed in addressing the Establishment Clause, we can say this: there is a good case that Good News's exercises blur the line between public classroom instruction and private religious indoctrination, leaving a reasonable elementary school pupil unable to appreciate that the former instruction is the business of the school while the latter evangelism is not. Thus, the facts we know (or think we know) point away from the majority's conclusion, and while the consolation may be that nothing really gets resolved when the judicial process is so truncated, that is not much to recommend today's result.

Notes

1. It is true, as the majority notes, *ante,* at 8, n. 3, that the Court of Appeals did not cite *Lamb's Chapel* by name. But it followed it in substance, and it did cite an earlier opinion written by the author of the panel opinion here, *Bronx Household of Faith v. Community School Dist. No. 10,* 127 F. 3d 207 (CA2 1997), which discussed *Lamb's Chapel* at length.

2. The majority rejects Milford's contention that Good News's activities fall outside the purview of the limited forum because they constitute "religious worship" on

the ground that the Court of Appeals made no such determination regarding the character of the club's program, see *ante,* at 11, n. 4. This distinction is merely semantic, in light of the Court of Appeals's conclusion that "[i]t is difficult to see how the Club's activities differ materially from the 'religious worship' described" in other case law, 202 F. 3d, at 510, and the record below.

JUSTICE STEVENS distinguishes between proselytizing and worship, *ante,* at 1 (dissenting opinion), and distinguishes each from discussion reflecting a religious point of view. I agree with JUSTICE STEVENS that Good News's activities may be characterized as proselytizing and therefore as outside the purpose of Milford's limited forum, *ante,* at 5. Like the Court of Appeals, I also believe Good News's meetings have elements of worship that put the club's activities further afield of Milford's limited forum policy, the legitimacy of which was unchallenged in the summary judgment proceeding.

3. It is certainly correct that parents are required to give permission for their children to attend Good News's classes, see *ante,* at 14, (as parents are often required to do for a host of official school extracurricular activities), and correct that those parents would likely not be confused as to the sponsorship of Good News's classes. But the proper focus of concern in assessing effects includes the elementary school pupils who are invited to meetings, Lodging, Exh. X2, who see peers heading into classrooms for religious instruction as other classes end, and who are addressed by the "challenge" and "invitation."

The fact that there may be no evidence in the record that individual students were confused during the time the Good News Club met on school premises pursuant to the District Court's preliminary injunction is immaterial, cf. Brief for Petitioners 38. As JUSTICE O'CONNOR explained in *Capitol Square Review and Advisory Bd. v. Pinette,* 515 U.S. 753 (1995), the endorsement test does not focus "on the actual perception of individual observers, who naturally have differing degrees of knowledge," but on "the perspective of a hypothetical observer." *Id.,* at 779–780 (opinion concurring in part and concurring in judgment).

POSTSCRIPT

Do Religious Groups Have a Right to Use Public School Facilities After Hours?

Why should church and state be separate? Is there any danger to be feared from public religious displays? It is probably fair to say that behind the debates over this issue and the ongoing controversy over prayer in the schools are differing interpretations of the history of religion. Does religion bring us to a higher level of existence, or is it a system that will oppress dissidents, nonbelievers, and members of minority faiths? Almost everyone has an opinion on this question, and most can find some historical support for their positions. Ironically, the same historical circumstance may even be used to support opposing points of view. For example, at a congressional hearing on school prayer, the following testimony was introduced:

> When I was educated in German public schools, they provided as part of the regular curriculum separate religious instruction for children of the three major faiths. At that time, all children in public schools from the ages of 6 to 18 were required not merely to recite a prayer at the beginning of each school session but to receive religious instruction twice a week. That system continued in the following decades.

> — Statement by Joachim Prinz, quoted in testimony of
> Nathan Dershowitz, Hearings on Prayer in Public Schools
> and Buildings, Committee on the Judiciary, House of
> Representatives, August 19, 1980.

Did that program effectively teach morality to the German people? If it did, it would be difficult to explain the rise of Hitler and the total moral collapse and even depravity of many German people, which resulted in the torture and death of millions of Jews and Christians.

Another witness, however, testifying in support of prayer in the schools, quoted the report of the President's Commission on the Holocaust, which stated,

> The Holocaust could not have occurred without the collapse of certain religious norms; increasing secularity fueled a devaluation of the image of the human being created in the likeness of God.

> — Statement of Judah Glasner, Hearings on Prayer in Public
> Schools and Buildings, Committee on the Judiciary,
> House of Representatives, July 30, 1980.

Relevant cases concerning religion in the public schools are *McCollum v. Board of Education,* 333 U.S. 203 (1948), about religious instruction on school property; *Zorach v. Clauson,* 343 U.S. 306 (1952), regarding free time from school for religious instruction off school property; and *Board of Education of the Westside Community Schools v. Mergens,* 110 S. Ct. 2356 (1990), regarding the use of school premises for an after-school religious club. *Rosenberger v. University of Virginia,* 115 S. Ct. 2510 (1995) involved funding of a student newspaper by a religious group. The pro-prayer lobby has had its greatest failure in cases involving schools or children, the area where it would probably most like to see change. See, for example, *Wallace v. Jaffree,* 105 S. Ct. 2479 (1985), which ruled that the Alabama moment of silence statute was unconstitutional, or *Edwards v. Aquillard,* 107 S. Ct. 2573 (1987), which prohibited the teaching of "creation science."

ISSUE 9

Does the Use of High-Technology Thermal Imaging Devices Violate the Fourth Amendment Search and Seizure Guaranty?

YES: Antonin Scalia, from Majority Opinion, *Danny Lee Kyllo v. United States,* U.S. Supreme Court (June 11, 2001)

NO: John Paul Stevens, from Dissenting Opinion, *Danny Lee Kyllo v. United States,* U.S. Supreme Court (June 11, 2001)

ISSUE SUMMARY

YES: Supreme Court justice Antonin Scalia maintains that thermal imaging devices reveal information "that would previously have been unknowable without physical intrusion" and that using such devices for surveillance without a warrant constitutes a violation of the Fourth Amendment.

NO: Supreme Court justice John Paul Stevens asserts that the Court's application of search and seizure rules to new technology is too broad and that collecting thermal imaging data from outside the home is not a violation of privacy rights.

I n 1991 agent William Elliott of the U.S. Department of the Interior became suspicious that marijuana was being grown in the home of Danny Kyllo. Indoor marijuana growth typically requires high-intensity lamps, and at 3:20 a.m. on January 16, 1992, Elliott scanned Kyllo's home with a thermal imaging device. Such devices can detect infrared radiation, which virtually all objects emit but which is not visible to the naked eye. The imager converts radiation into images based on relative warmth—black is cool, white is hot, and shades of gray connote relative differences.

The scan of Kyllo's home took only a few minutes. It showed that the roof over the garage and a side wall of the home were relatively hot compared to the rest of the home and substantially warmer than neighboring homes. Elliott concluded that Kyllo was using special lamps to grow marijuana in his house.

Based on tips from informants, utility bills, and the thermal imaging, a warrant was issued authorizing a search of Kyllo's home, where the agents found more than 100 plants being grown. Kyllo was indicted on one count of manufacturing marijuana. He unsuccessfully moved to suppress the evidence seized from his home and then entered a conditional guilty plea.

The Fourth Amendment to the Constitution requires authorities to obtain a search warrant before conducting a search. In order to do this, they must first persuade a judge that probable cause exists that a crime has been committed and that the evidence sought will be found in the place to be searched. The warrant requirement is the key constitutional element restricting the power of the police to decide unilaterally to invade the privacy of someone's home.

There are exceptions to this requirement. The Court has held that search warrants are not required for school officials to search school lockers if there are reasonable grounds for believing that the search will reveal evidence of criminal behavior (*New Jersey v. T. L. O., A Juvenile,* 105 S. Ct. 733, [1985]). Nor are search warrants required when a person is searched after an arrest or when the object seized is in plain view. Technological advances, however, are posing new challenges. We are developing technological capabilities to do things at a distance and to obtain information that previously would have required entering a physical location. The *Kyllo* case is a perfect example of this.

The lower court ruled against Kyllo and found that the thermal imager "is a non-intrusive device which emits no rays or beams and shows a crude visual image of the heat being radiated from the outside of the house"; it "did not show any people or activity within the walls of the structure"; "the device used cannot penetrate walls or windows to reveal conversations or human activities"; and "no intimate details of the home were observed." Kyllo appealed to the Court of Appeals and then to the U.S. Supreme Court, which ruled in his favor. The following selections are from the majority and dissenting opinions in the case, as delivered by Justice Antonin Scalia and Justice John Paul Stevens, respectively.

Thermal imaging is only the latest technological challenge to the Fourth Amendment. In *Katz v. United States,* 389 U.S. 347 (1967), the Court held that wiretapping without a warrant could violate the search and seizure clause. It was not necessary for the police to enter someone's property physically to "search" something. Rather, "once it is recognized that the Fourth Amendment protects people—and not simply 'areas'—against unreasonable searches and seizures, it becomes clear that the reach of [the Fourth] Amendment cannot turn upon the presence or absence of a physical intrusion into any given enclosure."

Thermal imaging has been used by law enforcement authorities for some time, and *Kyllo* was not the first case in which a lower court ruled on its use. As it often does, the Supreme Court agreed to hear the *Kyllo* case because various lower courts had come to different conclusions about the constitutionality of using this technology without first obtaining a warrant. As new technological applications that assist law enforcement but also invade privacy are perfected, the opinions covered by the following selections are likely to be referred to often.

 **YES**

Majority Opinion

Kyllo *v.* United States

JUSTICE SCALIA delivered the opinion of the Court....

I

In 1991 Agent William Elliott of the United States Department of the Interior came to suspect that marijuana was being grown in the home belonging to petitioner Danny Kyllo, part of a triplex on Rhododendron Drive in Florence, Oregon. Indoor marijuana growth typically requires high-intensity lamps. In order to determine whether an amount of heat was emanating from petitioner's home consistent with the use of such lamps, at 3:20 a.m. on January 16, 1992, Agent Elliott and Dan Haas used an Agema Thermovision 210 thermal imager to scan the triplex....

II

The Fourth Amendment provides that "[t]he right of the people to be secure in their persons, houses, papers, and effects, against unreasonable searches and seizures, shall not be violated." "At the very core" of the Fourth Amendment "stands the right of a man to retreat into his own home and there be free from unreasonable governmental intrusion." *Silverman v. United States,* 365 U.S. 505, 511 (1961). With few exceptions, the question whether a warrantless search of a home is reasonable and hence constitutional must be answered no. See *Illinois v. Rodriguez,* 497 U.S. 177, 181 (1990); *Payton v. New York,* 445 U.S. 573, 586 (1980).

On the other hand, the antecedent question of whether or not a Fourth Amendment "search" has occurred is not so simple under our precedent. The permissibility of ordinary visual surveillance of a home used to be clear because, well into the 20th century, our Fourth Amendment jurisprudence was tied to common-law trespass.... Visual surveillance was unquestionably lawful because " 'the eye cannot by the laws of England be guilty of a trespass.' " *Boyd v. United States,* 116 U.S. 616, 628 (1886) (quoting *Entick v. Carrington,* 19 How.

From *Danny Lee Kyllo v. United States,* 533 U.S. ____ (2001). Some notes and case citations omitted.

St. Tr. 1029, 95 Eng. Rep. 807 (K. B. 1765)). We have since decoupled violation of a person's Fourth Amendment rights from trespassory violation of his property, see *Rakas v. Illinois,* 439 U.S. 128, 143 (1978), but the lawfulness of warrantless visual surveillance of a home has still been preserved. As we observed in *California v. Ciraolo,* 476 U.S. 207, 213 (1986), "[t]he Fourth Amendment protection of the home has never been extended to require law enforcement officers to shield their eyes when passing by a home on public thoroughfares."

One might think that the new validating rationale would be that examining the portion of a house that is in plain public view, while it is a "search" despite the absence of trespass, is not an "unreasonable" one under the Fourth Amendment. See *Minnesota v. Carter,* 525 U.S. 83, 104 (1998) (BREYER, J., concurring in judgment). But in fact we have held that visual observation is no "search" at all—perhaps in order to preserve somewhat more intact our doctrine that warrantless searches are presumptively unconstitutional. See *Dow Chemical Co. v. United States,* 476 U.S. 227, 234–235, 239 (1986). In assessing when a search is not a search, we have applied somewhat in reverse the principle first enunciated in *Katz v. United States,* 389 U.S. 347 (1967). *Katz* involved eavesdropping by means of an electronic listening device placed on the outside of a telephone booth—a location not within the catalog ("persons, houses, papers, and effects") that the Fourth Amendment protects against unreasonable searches. We held that the Fourth Amendment nonetheless protected Katz from the warrantless eavesdropping because he "justifiably relied" upon the privacy of the telephone booth. *Id.,* at 353. As Justice Harlan's oft-quoted concurrence described it, a Fourth Amendment search occurs when the government violates a subjective expectation of privacy that society recognizes as reasonable. See *id.,* at 361. We have subsequently applied this principle to hold that a Fourth Amendment search does *not* occur—even when the explicitly protected location of a *house* is concerned—unless "the individual manifested a subjective expectation of privacy in the object of the challenged search," and "society [is] willing to recognize that expectation as reasonable." *Ciraolo, supra,* at 211. We have applied this test in holding that it is not a search for the police to use a pen register at the phone company to determine what numbers were dialed in a private home, *Smith v. Maryland,* 442 U.S. 735, 743–744 (1979), and we have applied the test on two different occasions in holding that aerial surveillance of private homes and surrounding areas does not constitute a search, *Ciraolo, supra; Florida v. Riley,* 488 U.S. 445 (1989).

The present case involves officers on a public street engaged in more than naked-eye surveillance of a home. We have previously reserved judgment as to how much technological enhancement of ordinary perception from such a vantage point, if any, is too much. While we upheld enhanced aerial photography of an industrial complex in *Dow Chemical,* we noted that we found "it important that this is *not* an area immediately adjacent to a private home, where privacy expectations are most heightened," 476 U.S., at 237, n. 4 (emphasis in original).

III

It would be foolish to contend that the degree of privacy secured to citizens by the Fourth Amendment has been entirely unaffected by the advance of technology. For example, as the cases discussed above make clear, the technology enabling human flight has exposed to public view (and hence, we have said, to official observation) uncovered portions of the house and its curtilage that once were private. See *Ciraolo, supra,* at 215. The question we confront today is what limits there are upon this power of technology to shrink the realm of guaranteed privacy.

The *Katz* test—whether the individual has an expectation of privacy that society is prepared to recognize as reasonable—has often been criticized as circular, and hence subjective and unpredictable. See 1 W. LaFave, Search and Seizure §2.1(d), pp. 393–394 (3d ed. 1996); Posner, The Uncertain Protection of Privacy by the Supreme Court, 1979 S. Ct. Rev. 173, 188; *Carter, supra,* at 97 (SCALIA, J., concurring). But see *Rakas, supra,* at 143–144, n. 12. While it may be difficult to refine Katz when the search of areas such as telephone booths, automobiles, or even the curtilage and uncovered portions of residences are at issue, in the case of the search of the interior of homes—the prototypical and hence most commonly litigated area of protected privacy—there is a ready criterion, with roots deep in the common law, of the minimal expectation of privacy that *exists,* and that is acknowledged to be *reasonable.* To withdraw protection of this minimum expectation would be to permit police technology to erode the privacy guaranteed by the Fourth Amendment. We think that obtaining by sense-enhancing technology any information regarding the interior of the home that could not otherwise have been obtained without physical "intrusion into a constitutionally protected area," *Silverman,* 365 U.S., at 512, constitutes a search—at least where (as here) the technology in question is not in general public use. This assures preservation of that degree of privacy against government that existed when the Fourth Amendment was adopted. On the basis of this criterion, the information obtained by the thermal imager in this case was the product of a search.[1]

The Government maintains, however, that the thermal imaging must be upheld because it detected "only heat radiating from the external surface of the house," Brief for United States 26. The dissent makes this its leading point, see *post,* at 1, contending that there is a fundamental difference between what it calls "off-the-wall" observations and "through-the-wall surveillance." But just as a thermal imager captures only heat emanating from a house, so also a powerful directional microphone picks up only sound emanating from a house—and a satellite capable of scanning from many miles away would pick up only visible light emanating from a house. We rejected such a mechanical interpretation of the Fourth Amendment in *Katz,* where the eavesdropping device picked up only sound waves that reached the exterior of the phone booth. Reversing that approach would leave the homeowner at the mercy of advancing technology—including imaging technology that could discern all human activity in the home. While the technology used in the present case was relatively crude, the rule we adopt must take account of more sophisticated systems that are already in use or in development.[2] The dissent's reliance on the distinction between "off-the-wall" and "through-the-wall" observation is entirely incompatible with the dissent's belief, which we discuss below, that thermal-imaging observations of the intimate details of a home are impermissible. The most sophisticated thermal imaging devices continue to measure heat "off-the-wall" rather than "through-the-wall"; the dissent's disapproval of those more sophisticated thermal-imaging devices, see *post*, at 10, is an acknowledgement that there is no substance to this distinction. As for the dissent's extraordinary assertion that anything learned through "an inference" cannot be a search, see *post*, at 4–5, that would validate even the "through-the-wall" technologies that the dissent purports to disapprove. Surely the dissent does not believe that the through-the-wall radar or ultrasound technology produces an 8-by-10 Kodak glossy that needs no analysis (*i.e.*, the making of inferences). And, of course, the novel proposition that inference insulates a search is blatantly contrary to *United States v. Karo,* 468 U.S. 705 (1984), where the police "inferred" from the activation of a beeper that a certain can of ether was in the home. The police activity was held to be a search, and the search was held unlawful.[3]

The Government also contends that the thermal imaging was constitutional because it did not "detect private activities occurring in private areas," Brief for United States 22. It points out that in *Dow Chemical* we observed that the enhanced aerial photography did not reveal any "intimate details." 476 U.S., at 238. *Dow Chemical,* however, involved enhanced aerial photography of an industrial complex, which does not share the Fourth Amendment sanctity of the home. The Fourth Amendment's protection of the home has never been tied to measurement of the quality or quantity of information obtained. In *Silverman*, for example, we made clear that any physical invasion of the structure of the home, "by even a fraction of an inch," was too much, 365 U.S., at 512, and there is certainly no exception to the warrant requirement for the officer who barely cracks open the front door and sees nothing but the nonintimate rug on the vestibule floor. In the home, our cases show, *all* details are intimate details, because the entire area is held safe from prying government eyes. Thus, in *Karo, supra,* the only thing detected was a can of ether in the home; and in *Arizona v. Hicks,* 480 U.S. 321 (1987), the only thing detected by a physical search that went beyond what officers lawfully present could observe in "plain view" was the registration number of a phonograph turntable. These were intimate details because they were details of the home, just as was the detail of how warm—or even how relatively warm—Kyllo was heating his residence.[4]

Limiting the prohibition of thermal imaging to "intimate details" would not only be wrong in principle; it would be impractical in application, failing to provide "a workable accommodation between the needs of law enforcement and the interests protected by the Fourth Amendment," *Oliver v. United States,* 466 U.S. 170, 181 (1984). To begin with, there is no necessary connection between the sophistication of the surveillance equipment and the "intimacy" of the details that it observes—which means that one cannot say (and the police cannot be assured) that use of the relatively crude equipment at issue here will always be lawful. The Agema Thermovision 210 might disclose, for example, at what hour each night the lady of the house takes her daily sauna and bath

—a detail that many would consider "intimate"; and a much more sophisticated system might detect nothing more intimate than the fact that someone left a closet light on. We could not, in other words, develop a rule approving only that through-the-wall surveillance which identifies objects no smaller than 36 by 36 inches, but would have to develop a jurisprudence specifying which home activities are "intimate" and which are not. And even when (if ever) that jurisprudence were fully developed, no police officer would be able to know in *advance* whether his through-the-wall surveillance picks up "intimate" details—and thus would be unable to know in advance whether it is constitutional.

The dissent's proposed standard—whether the technology offers the "functional equivalent of actual presence in the area being searched," *post,* at 7—would seem quite similar to our own at first blush. The dissent concludes that *Katz* was such a case, but then inexplicably asserts that if the same listening device only revealed the volume of the conversation, the surveillance would be permissible, *post,* at 10. Yet if, without technology, the police could not discern volume without being actually present in the phone booth, JUSTICE STEVENS should conclude a search has occurred. Cf. *Karo, supra,* at 735 (STEVENS, J., concurring in part and dissenting in part) ("I find little comfort in the Court's notion that no invasion of privacy occurs until a listener obtains some significant information by use of the device.... A bathtub is a less private area when the plumber is present even if his back is turned"). The same should hold for the interior heat of the home if only a person present in the home could discern the heat. Thus the driving force of the dissent, despite its recitation of the above standard, appears to be a distinction among different types of information—whether the "homeowner would even care if anybody noticed," *post,* at 10. The dissent offers no practical guidance for the application of this standard, and for reasons already discussed, we believe there can be none. The people in their houses, as well as the police, deserve more precision.[5]

We have said that the Fourth Amendment draws "a firm line at the entrance to the house," *Payton,* 445 U.S., at 590. That line, we think, must be not only firm but also bright—which requires clear specification of those methods of surveillance that require a warrant. While it is certainly possible to conclude from the videotape of the thermal imaging that occurred in this case that no "significant" compromise of the homeowner's privacy has occurred, we must take the long view, from the original meaning of the Fourth Amendment forward.

> "The Fourth Amendment is to be construed in the light of what was deemed an unreasonable search and seizure when it was adopted, and in a manner which will conserve public interests as well as the interests and rights of individual citizens." *Carroll v. United States,* 267 U.S. 132, 149 (1925).

Where, as here, the Government uses a device that is not in general public use, to explore details of the home that would previously have been unknowable without physical intrusion, the surveillance is a "search" and is presumptively unreasonable without a warrant.

Since we hold the Thermovision imaging to have been an unlawful search, it will remain for the District Court to determine whether, without the evidence it provided, the search warrant issued in this case was supported by probable cause—and if not, whether there is any other basis for supporting admission of the evidence that the search pursuant to the warrant produced.

◦◉◦

The judgment of the Court of Appeals is reversed; the case is remanded for further proceedings consistent with this opinion.

It is so ordered.

Notes

1. The dissent's repeated assertion that the thermal imaging did not obtain information regarding the interior of the home, *post,* at 3, 4 (opinion of STEVENS, J.), is simply inaccurate. A thermal imager reveals the relative heat of various rooms in the home. The dissent may not find that information particularly private or important, see *post,* at 4, 5, 10, but there is no basis for saying it is not information regarding the interior of the home. The dissent's comparison of the thermal imaging to various circumstances in which outside observers might be able to perceive, without technology, the heat of the home—for example, by observing snowmelt on the roof, *post,* at 3—is quite irrelevant. The fact that equivalent information could sometimes be obtained by other means does not make lawful the use of means that violate the Fourth Amendment. The police might, for example, learn how many people are in a particular house by setting up year-round surveillance; but that does not make breaking and entering to find out the same information lawful. In any event, on the night of January 16, 1992, no outside observer could have discerned the relative heat of Kyllo's home without thermal imaging.

2. The ability to "see" through walls and other opaque barriers is a clear, and scientifically feasible, goal of law enforcement research and development. The National Law Enforcement and Corrections Technology Center, a program within the United States Department of Justice, features on its Internet Website projects that include a "Radar-Based Through-the-Wall Surveillance System," "Hand-held Ultrasound Through the Wall Surveillance," and a "Radar Flashlight" that "will enable law officers to detect individuals through interior building walls." www.nlectc.org/techproj/ (visited May 3, 2001). Some devices may emit low levels of radiation that travel "through-the-wall," but others, such as more sophisticated thermal imaging devices, are entirely passive, or "off-the-wall" as the dissent puts it.

3. The dissent asserts, *post,* at 5, n. 3, that we have misunderstood its point, which is not that inference *insulates* a search, but that inference alone is *not* a search. If we misunderstood the point, it was only in a good-faith effort to render the point germane to the case at hand. The issue in this case is not the police's allegedly unlawful inferencing, but their allegedly unlawful thermal-imaging measurement of the emanations from a house. We say such measurement is a search; the dissent says it is not, because an inference is not a search. We took that to mean that, since the technologically enhanced emanations had to be the basis of inferences before anything inside the house could be known, the use of the emanations could not be a search. But the dissent certainly knows better than we what it intends. And if it means only that an inference is not a search, we certainly agree. That has no bearing, however, upon whether hi-tech measurement of emanations from a house is a search.

4. The Government cites our statement in *California v. Ciraolo,* 476 U.S. 207 (1986), noting apparent agreement with the State of California that aerial surveillance of a house's curtilage could become " 'invasive' " if " 'modern technology' " revealed " 'those intimate associations, objects or activities otherwise imperceptible to police or fellow citizens.' " *Id.,* at 215, n. 3 (quoting brief of the State of California). We think the Court's focus in this second-hand dictum was not upon intimacy but upon otherwise-imperceptibility, which is precisely the principle we vindicate today.

5. The dissent argues that we have injected potential uncertainty into the constitutional analysis by noting that whether or not the technology is in general public use may be a factor. See *post,* at 7–8. That quarrel, however, is not with us but with this Court's precedent. See *Ciraolo, supra,* at 215 ("In an age where private and commercial flight in the public airways is routine, it is unreasonable for respondent to expect that his marijuana plants were constitutionally protected from being observed with the naked eye from an altitude of 1,000 feet"). Given that we can quite confidently say that thermal imaging is not "routine," we decline in this case to reexamine that factor.

NO ↵

John Paul Stevens

Dissenting Opinion of John Paul Stevens

JUSTICE STEVENS, with whom THE CHIEF JUSTICE, JUSTICE O'CONNOR, and JUSTICE KENNEDY join, dissenting.

There is, in my judgment, a distinction of constitutional magnitude between "through-the-wall surveillance" that gives the observer or listener direct access to information in a private area, on the one hand, and the thought processes used to draw inferences from information in the public domain, on the other hand. The Court has crafted a rule that purports to deal with direct observations of the inside of the home, but the case before us merely involves indirect deductions from "off-the-wall" surveillance, that is, observations of the exterior of the home. Those observations were made with a fairly primitive thermal imager that gathered data exposed on the outside of petitioner's home but did not invade any constitutionally protected interest in privacy.[1] Moreover, I believe that the supposedly "bright-line" rule the Court has created in response to its concerns about future technological developments is unnecessary, unwise, and inconsistent with the Fourth Amendment.

I

There is no need for the Court to craft a new rule to decide this case, as it is controlled by established principles from our Fourth Amendment jurisprudence. One of those core principles, of course, is that "searches and seizures *inside a home* without a warrant are presumptively unreasonable." *Payton v. New York,* 445 U.S. 573, 586 (1980) (emphasis added). But it is equally well settled that searches and seizures of property in plain view are presumptively reasonable. See *id.,* at 586–587.[2] Whether that property is residential or commercial, the basic principle is the same: " 'What a person knowingly exposes to the public, even in his own home or office, is not a subject of Fourth Amendment protection.' " *California v. Ciraolo,* 476 U.S. 207, 213 (1986) (quoting *Katz v. United States,* 389 U.S. 347, 351 (1967)); see *Florida v. Riley,* 488 U.S. 445, 449–450 (1989); *California v. Greenwood,* 486 U.S. 35, 40–41 (1988); *Dow Chemical Co. v. United States,* 476 U.S. 227, 235–236 (1986); *Air Pollution Variance Bd. of Colo. v. Western Alfalfa Corp.,* 416 U.S. 861, 865 (1974). That is the principle implicated here.

From *Danny Lee Kyllo v. United States,* 533 U.S. ____ (2001). Some notes and case citations omitted.

While the Court "take[s] the long view" and decides this case based largely on the potential of yet-to-be-developed technology that might allow "through-the-wall surveillance," this case involves nothing more than off-the-wall surveillance by law enforcement officers to gather information exposed to the general public from the outside of petitioner's home. All that the infrared camera did in this case was passively measure heat emitted from the exterior surfaces of petitioner's home; all that those measurements showed were relative differences in emission levels, vaguely indicating that some areas of the roof and outside walls were warmer than others. As still images from the infrared scans show, no details regarding the interior of petitioner's home were revealed. Unlike an x-ray scan, or other possible "through-the-wall" techniques, the detection of infrared radiation emanating from the home did not accomplish "an unauthorized physical penetration into the premises," *Silverman v. United States,* 365 U.S. 505, 509 (1961), nor did it "obtain information that it could not have obtained by observation from outside the curtilage of the house," *United States v. Karo,* 468 U.S. 705, 715 (1984).

Indeed, the ordinary use of the senses might enable a neighbor or passerby to notice the heat emanating from a building, particularly if it is vented, as was the case here. Additionally, any member of the public might notice that one part of a house is warmer than another part or a nearby building if, for example, rainwater evaporates or snow melts at different rates across its surfaces. Such use of the senses would not convert into an unreasonable search if, instead, an adjoining neighbor allowed an officer onto her property to verify her perceptions with a sensitive thermometer. Nor, in my view, does such observation become an unreasonable search if made from a distance with the aid of a device that merely discloses that the exterior of one house, or one area of the house, is much warmer than another. Nothing more occurred in this case.

Thus, the notion that heat emissions from the outside of a dwelling is a private matter implicating the protections of the Fourth Amendment (the text of which guarantees the right of people "to be secure *in* their... houses" against unreasonable searches and seizures (emphasis added)) is not only unprecedented but also quite difficult to take seriously. Heat waves, like aromas that are generated in a kitchen, or in a laboratory or opium den, enter the public domain if and when they leave a building. A subjective expectation that they would remain private is not only implausible but also surely not "one that society is prepared to recognize as 'reasonable.'" *Katz,* 389 U.S., at 361 (Harlan, J., concurring).

To be sure, the homeowner has a reasonable expectation of privacy concerning what takes place within the home, and the Fourth Amendment's protection against physical invasions of the home should apply to their functional equivalent. But the equipment in this case did not penetrate the walls of petitioner's home, and while it did pick up "details of the home" that were exposed to the public, *ante,* at 10, it did not obtain "any information regarding the *interior* of the home," *ante,* at 6 (emphasis added). In the Court's own words, based on what the thermal imager "showed" regarding the outside of petitioner's home, the officers "concluded" that petitioner was engaging in illegal activity inside the home. It would be quite absurd to characterize their thought processes as "searches," regardless of whether they inferred (rightly) that petitioner was growing marijuana in his house, or (wrongly) that "the lady of the house [was taking] her daily sauna and bath." In either case, the only conclusions the officers reached concerning the interior of the home were at least as indirect as those that might have been inferred from the contents of discarded garbage, see *California v. Greenwood,* 486 U.S. 35 (1988), or pen register data, see *Smith v. Maryland,* 442 U.S. 735 (1979), or, as in this case, subpoenaed utility records, see 190 F. 3d 1041, 1043 (CA9 1999). For the first time in its history, the Court assumes that an inference can amount to a Fourth Amendment violation.

Notwithstanding the implications of today's decision, there is a strong public interest in avoiding constitutional litigation over the monitoring of emissions from homes, and over the inferences drawn from such monitoring. Just as "the police cannot reasonably be expected to avert their eyes from evidence of criminal activity that could have been observed by any member of the public," *Greenwood,* 486 U.S., at 41, so too public officials should not have to avert their senses or their equipment from detecting emissions in the public domain such as excessive heat, traces of smoke, suspicious odors, odorless gases, airborne particulates, or radioactive emissions, any of which could identify hazards to the community. In my judgment, monitoring such emissions with "sense-enhancing technology," and drawing useful conclusions from such monitoring, is an entirely reasonable public service.

On the other hand, the countervailing privacy interest is at best trivial. After all, homes generally are insulated to keep heat in, rather than to prevent the detection of heat going out, and it does not seem to me that society will suffer from a rule requiring the rare homeowner who both intends to engage in uncommon activities that produce extraordinary amounts of heat, and wishes to conceal that production from outsiders, to make sure that the surrounding area is well insulated. Cf. *United States v. Jacobsen,* 466 U.S. 109, 122 (1984) ("The concept of an interest in privacy that society is prepared to recognize as reasonable is, by its very nature, critically different from the mere expectation, however well justified, that certain facts will not come to the attention of the authorities"). The interest in concealing the heat escaping from one's house pales in significance to the "chief evil against which the wording of the Fourth Amendment is directed," the "physical entry of the home," *United States v. United States Dist. Court for Eastern Dist. of Mich.,* 407 U.S. 297, 313 (1972), and it is hard to believe that it is an interest the Framers sought to protect in our Constitution.

Since what was involved in this case was nothing more than drawing inferences from off-the-wall surveillance, rather than any "through-the-wall" surveillance, the officers' conduct did not amount to a search and was perfectly reasonable.[3]

II

Instead of trying to answer the question whether the use of the thermal imager in this case was even arguably unreasonable, the Court has fashioned a rule that is intended to provide essential guidance for the day when "more sophisticated systems" gain the "ability to 'see' through walls and other opaque barriers." The newly minted rule encompasses "obtaining [1] by sense-enhancing technology [2] any information regarding the interior of the home [3] that could not otherwise have been obtained without physical intrusion into a constitutionally protected area . . . [4] at least where (as here) the technology in question is not in general public use." In my judgment, the Court's new rule is at once too broad and too narrow, and is not justified by the Court's explanation for its adoption. As I have suggested, I would not erect a constitutional impediment to the use of sense-enhancing technology unless it provides its user with the functional equivalent of actual presence in the area being searched.

Despite the Court's attempt to draw a line that is "not only firm but also bright," the contours of its new rule are uncertain because its protection apparently dissipates as soon as the relevant technology is "in general public use." Yet how much use is general public use is not even hinted at by the Court's opinion, which makes the somewhat doubtful assumption that the thermal imager used in this case does not satisfy that criterion.[4] In any event, putting aside its lack of clarity, this criterion is somewhat perverse because it seems likely that the threat to privacy will grow, rather than recede, as the use of intrusive equipment becomes more readily available.

It is clear, however, that the category of "sense-enhancing technology" covered by the new rule is far too broad. It would, for example, embrace potential mechanical substitutes for dogs trained to react when they sniff narcotics. But in *United States v. Place,* 462 U.S. 696, 707 (1983), we held that a dog sniff that "discloses only the presence or absence of narcotics" does "not constitute a 'search' within the meaning of the Fourth Amendment," and it must follow that sense-enhancing equipment that identifies nothing but illegal activity is not a search either. Nevertheless, the use of such a device would be unconstitutional under the Court's rule, as would the use of other new devices that might detect the odor of deadly bacteria or chemicals for making a new type of high explosive, even if the devices (like the dog sniffs) are "so limited in both the manner in which" they obtain information and "in the content of the information" they reveal. If nothing more than that sort of information could be obtained by using the devices in a public place to monitor emissions from a house, then their use would be no more objectionable than the use of the thermal imager in this case.

The application of the Court's new rule to "any information regarding the interior of the home," is also unnecessarily broad. If it takes sensitive equipment to detect an odor that identifies criminal conduct and nothing else, the fact that the odor emanates from the interior of a home should not provide it with constitutional protection. The criterion, moreover, is too sweeping in that information "regarding" the interior of a home apparently is not just information obtained through its walls, but also information concerning the outside of the building that could lead to (however many) inferences "regarding" what might be inside. Under that expansive view, I suppose, an officer using an infrared camera to observe a man silently entering the side door of a house at night carrying a pizza might conclude that its interior is now occupied by someone who likes pizza, and by doing so the officer would be guilty of conducting an unconstitutional "search" of the home.

Because the new rule applies to information regarding the "interior" of the home, it is too narrow as well as too broad. Clearly, a rule that is designed to protect individuals from the overly intrusive use of sense-enhancing equipment should not be limited to a home. If such equipment did provide its user with the functional equivalent of access to a private place—such as, for example, the telephone booth involved in *Katz*, or an office building—then the rule should apply to such an area as well as to a home. See *Katz*, 389 U.S., at 351 ("[T]he Fourth Amendment protects people, not places").

The final requirement of the Court's new rule, that the information "could not otherwise have been obtained without physical intrusion into a constitutionally protected area," *ante*, at 6 (internal quotation marks omitted), also extends too far as the Court applies it. As noted, the Court effectively treats the mental process of analyzing data obtained from external sources as the equivalent of a physical intrusion into the home. As I have explained, however, the process of drawing inferences from data in the public domain should not be characterized as a search.

The two reasons advanced by the Court as justifications for the adoption of its new rule are both unpersuasive. First, the Court suggests that its rule is compelled by our holding in *Katz*, because in that case, as in this, the surveillance consisted of nothing more than the monitoring of waves emanating from a private area into the public domain. Yet there are critical differences between the cases. In *Katz*, the electronic listening device attached to the outside of the phone booth allowed the officers to pick up the content of the conversation inside the booth, making them the functional equivalent of intruders because they gathered information that was otherwise available only to someone inside the private area; it would be as if, in this case, the thermal imager presented a view of the heat-generating activity inside petitioner's home. By contrast, the thermal imager here disclosed only the relative amounts of heat radiating from the house; it would be as if, in Katz, the listening device disclosed only the relative volume of sound leaving the booth, which presumably was discernible in the public domain.[5] Surely, there is a significant difference between the general and well-settled expectation that strangers will not have direct access to the contents of private communications, on the one hand, and the rather theoretical expectation that an occasional homeowner would even care if anybody noticed the relative amounts of heat emanating from the walls of his house, on the other. It is pure hyperbole for the Court to suggest that refusing to extend the holding of *Katz* to this case would leave the homeowner at the mercy of "technology that could discern all human activity in the home." *Ante*, at 8.

Second, the Court argues that the permissibility of "through-the-wall surveillance" cannot depend on a distinction between observing "intimate details" such as "the lady of the house [taking] her daily sauna and bath," and noticing only "the nonintimate rug on the vestibule floor" or "objects no smaller than 36 by 36 inches." *Ante*, at 10–11. This entire argument assumes, of course, that the thermal imager in this case could or did perform "through-the-wall surveillance" that could identify any detail "that would previously have been unknowable without physical intrusion." In fact, the device could not, and did not, enable its user to identify either the lady of the house, the rug on the vestibule floor, or anything else inside the house, whether smaller or larger than 36 by 36 inches. Indeed, the vague thermal images of petitioner's home that are reproduced in the Appendix were submitted by him to the District Court as part of an expert report raising the question whether the device could even take "accurate, consistent infrared images" of the *outside* of his house. Defendant's Exhibit 107, p. 4. But even if the device could reliably show extraordinary differences in the amounts of heat leaving his home, drawing the inference that there was something suspicious occurring inside the residence —a conclusion that officers far less gifted than Sherlock Holmes would readily draw—does not qualify as "through-the-wall surveillance," much less a Fourth Amendment violation.

III

Although the Court is properly and commendably concerned about the threats to privacy that may flow from advances in the technology available to the law enforcement profession, it has unfortunately failed to heed the tried and true counsel of judicial restraint. Instead of concentrating on the rather mundane issue that is actually presented by the case before it, the Court has endeavored to craft an all-encompassing rule for the future. It would be far wiser to give legislators an unimpeded opportunity to grapple with these emerging issues rather than to shackle them with prematurely devised constitutional constraints.

I respectfully dissent.

Notes

1. After an evidentiary hearing, the District Court found:

    "[T]he use of the thermal imaging device here was not an intrusion into Kyllo's home. No intimate details of the home were observed, and there was no intrusion upon the privacy of the individuals within the home. The device used cannot penetrate walls or windows to reveal conversations or human activities. The device recorded only the heat being emitted from the home." Supp. App. to Pet. for Cert. 40.

2. Thus, for example, we have found consistent with the Fourth Amendment, even absent a warrant, the search and seizure of garbage left for collection outside the curtilage of a home, *California v. Greenwood,* 486 U.S. 35 (1988); the aerial surveillance of a fenced-in backyard from an altitude of 1,000 feet, *California v. Ciraolo,* 476 U.S. 207 (1986); the aerial observation of a partially exposed interior of a residential greenhouse from 400 feet above, *Florida v. Riley,* 488 U.S. 445 (1989); the aerial photography of an industrial complex from several thousand feet above, *Dow Chemical Co. v. United States,* 476 U.S. 227 (1986); and the observation of smoke emanating from chimney stacks, *Air Pollution Variance Bd. of Colo. v. Western Alfalfa Corp.,* 416 U.S. 861 (1974).

3. This view comports with that of all the Courts of Appeals that have resolved the issue. See 190 F. 3d 1041 (CA9 1999); *United States v. Robinson,* 62 F. 3d 1325 (CA11 1995) (upholding warrantless use of thermal imager); *United States v. Myers,* 46 F. 3d 668 (CA7 1995) (same); *United States v. Ishmael,* 48 F. 3d 850 (CA5 1995) (same); *United States v. Pinson,* 24 F. 3d 1056 (CA8 1994) (same). But see *United States v. Cusumano,* 67 F. 3d 1497 (CA10 1995) (warrantless use of thermal imager violated Fourth Amendment), vacated and decided on other grounds, 83 F. 3d 1247 (CA10 1996) (en banc).

4. The record describes a device that numbers close to a thousand manufactured units; that has a predecessor numbering in the neighborhood of 4,000 to 5,000 units; that competes with a similar product numbering from 5,000 to 6,000 units; and that is "readily available to the public" for commercial, personal, or law enforcement purposes, and is just an 800-number away from being rented from "half a dozen national companies" by anyone who wants one. App. 18. Since, by virtue of the Court's new rule, the issue is one of first impression, perhaps it should order an evidentiary hearing to determine whether these facts suffice to establish "general public use."

5. The use of the latter device would be constitutional given *Smith v. Maryland,* 442 U.S. 735, 741 (1979), which upheld the use of pen registers to record numbers dialed on a phone because, unlike "the listening device employed in *Katz*... pen registers do not acquire the *contents* of communications."

POSTSCRIPT

Does the Use of High-Technology Thermal Imaging Devices Violate the Fourth Amendment Search and Seizure Guaranty?

Even though Scalia's opinion is a strong statement about the need for protecting privacy in a technological era, there will certainly be more cases in which challenging issues will be presented. Law enforcement's ability to invade privacy at a distance is increasing, and the Supreme Court has not, as it did in this case, always sided with the individual. Indeed, the Court has upheld various novel search techniques in other Fourth Amendment cases. Consider the following:

- *Dow Chemical v. United States,* 476 U.S. 227 (1986)—The Court allowed aerial pictures taken by the Environmental Protection Agency (EPA) even though the company had refused to allow inspectors to enter.
- *Florida v. Riley,* 488 U.S. 445, 450 (1989)—The Court allowed a search in which a police officer in a helicopter looked into a greenhouse from a height of 400 feet and observed through openings in the roof what he thought was marijuana.
- *California v. Ciraolo,* 476 U.S. 207, 213–214 (1986)—The Court held that police officers were not "searching" when they flew over the defendant's property and observed marijuana growing.
- *Smith v. Maryland,* 442 U.S. 735, 742–744 (1979)—The Court allowed the authorities to look at "pen registers," or records of telephone numbers dialed, without a warrant.

Scalia does not mention the use of trained dogs to sniff out the presence of drugs at airports and other public places. The Court, in *United States v. Place,* 462 U.S. 696 (1983), allowed the use of dogs when the sniff "discloses only the presence or absence of narcotics." Stevens raises the interesting question of whether or not "mechanical substitutes for dogs trained to react when they sniff narcotics" would be lawful. Since technology allows information to be obtained at a distance, often without a person feeling that his or her privacy has been invaded, we can expect additional cases in which the lawful use of "mechanical substitutes" is the main issue.

Background information on law enforcement and the drug problem can be found in the Drug Enforcement Administration of the U.S. Department of Justice's *DEA Briefing Book* at http://www.usdoj.gov/dea/briefingbook/.

Additional readings on the thermal imaging issue are Kathleen A. Lomas, "Bad Physics and Bad Law: A Review of the Constitutionality of Thermal Imagery Surveillance After *United States v. Elkins,"* 34 *University of San Francisco Law Review* 799 (2000); Jennifer Murphy, "Trash, Thermal Imagers, and the Fourth Amendment: The New Search and Seizure," 53 *Southern Methodist University Law Review* 1645 (2000); and Jeffrey P. Campisi, "The Fourth Amendment and New Technologies: The Constitutionality of Thermal Imaging," 46 *Villanova Law Review* 241 (2001).

ISSUE 10

Is Virtual Child Pornography Legal?

YES: Donald W. Molloy, from Majority Opinion, *Free Speech Coalition v. Janet Reno,* U.S. Court of Appeals for the Ninth Circuit (March 10, 1998)

NO: Warren J. Ferguson, from Dissenting Opinion, *Free Speech Coalition v. Janet Reno,* U.S. Court of Appeals for the Ninth Circuit (March 10, 1998)

ISSUE SUMMARY

YES: U.S. District Court judge Donald W. Molloy rules that illicit images that do not involve actual children in their production or depiction, even when they appear to be child pornography, are protected by the First Amendment.

NO: U.S. Circuit Court judge Warren J. Ferguson maintains that "virtual child pornography causes real harm to real chldren" and that, like real child pornography, it is not protected by the First Amendment's free speech guaranty.

The growth of the Internet and the World Wide Web is, perhaps, the most significant economic and cultural development of the last decade. Cyberspace is increasingly the "place" where people shop, relax, socialize, learn, etc. It has been equated with such physical places as a library, a shopping mall, a school, a conference center, an arcade, and a casino because we can read, buy, learn, converse, play games, and gamble online.

What cyberspace is *not* is a harmonious place or a problem-free environment. This should not be surprising: there is an enormous amount of activity in cyberspace, a great deal of money is being spent there, and numerous relationships are being formed there. When so much is happening so fast, there will be a demand for law.

Much of what occurs in cyberspace involves activities with which we are familiar. Buying something online, for example, may seem like purchasing an item from a catalog or through the phone. Similarly, e-mail may seem like regular mail. For law, the question is whether or not we need new rules, new frameworks for thinking about traditional rules, and new processes for dealing with disputes that arise online.

This is a difficult question because it is not yet clear what the truly new features of cyberspace are. What we do know is that we can do more things at a distance and we can do them faster than ever before. It is, as a result, harder for the state and other previously powerful entities to exercise control over some online activities.

One area of law that has already attracted a great deal of attention involves pornography and obscenity. Early on, Congress recognized that there were pornographic and obscene sites on the Internet and passed legislation called the Communications Decency Act (CDA) to try to respond to the amount of sexually oriented material online. It was not particularly careful, however, in drafting the legislation, and in *Reno v. ACLU* (http://laws.findlaw.com/US/000/96-511.html), the Supreme Court found that the statute violated First Amendment standards of free speech.

Statutes banning child pornography were found to be constitutional in the case of *New York v. Ferber,* 458 U.S. 747 (1982). The following selections concern an unusual child pornography case that the Supreme Court will decide during its 2001–2002 term. Among the miracles of computers is the ability to create pornographic images of children without using real children. Using the Internet, these images can be distributed instantaneously almost anywhere. In 1996, therefore, Congress passed the Child Pornography Prevention Act of 1996 (CPPA) to combat the evils of virtual child pornography. In the 1996 act Congress wrote that

> "child pornography" means any visual depiction, including any photograph, film, video, picture, or computer, or computer-generated image or picture, whether made or produced by electronic, mechanical, or other means, of sexually explicit conduct, where—
>
> (A) the production of such visual depiction involves the use of a minor engaging in sexually explicit conduct;
> (B) such visual depiction is, or appears to be, of a minor engaging in sexually explicit conduct;
> (C) such visual depiction has been created, adapted, or modified to appear that an identifiable minor is engaging in sexually explicit conduct; or
> (D) such visual depiction is advertised, promoted, presented, described, or distributed in such a manner that conveys the impression that the material is or contains a visual depiction of a minor engaging in sexually explicit conduct.

The "appears to be" language in subsection (8)(B) refers to child pornography that is entirely virtual—"portraying no actual living child."

Should it matter whether real or virtual children are used? Is the harm different or any less when real children are not used? If the harm is less, should the activities of those producing and distributing such material be protected by the First Amendment? These are the issues that are at the heart of the following opinions.

Donald W. Molloy  **YES**

Majority Opinion

Free Speech Coalition *v.* Reno

MOLLOY, District Judge:

I.

The question presented in this case is whether Congress may constitutionally proscribe as child pornography computer images that do not involve the use of real children in their production or dissemination. We hold that the First Amendment prohibits Congress from enacting a statute that makes criminal the generation of images of fictitious children engaged in imaginary but explicit sexual conduct.

II.

In this case, the district court found that the Child Pornography Prevention Act of 1996 ("CPPA" or the "Act") was content-neutral, was not unconstitutionally vague or overbroad, and did not constitute an improper prior restraint of speech. The district court also found that the Child Pornography Prevention Act's affirmative defense did not impermissibly shift the burden of proof to a defendant by virtue of an unconstitutional presumption.

While we agree that the plaintiffs have standing to bring this case and that the Act is not an improper prior restraint of speech, the balance of the district court's analysis does not comport with what we believe is required by the Constitution. We find that the phrases "appears to be" a minor, and "convey[s] the impression" that the depiction portrays a minor, are vague and overbroad and thus do not meet the requirements of the First Amendment. Consequently we hold that while these two provisions of the Act do not pass constitutional muster, the balance of the Child Pornography Prevention Act is constitutional when the two phrases are stricken. Whether the statutory affirmative defense is constitutional is a question that we leave for resolution in a different case.

From *Free Speech Coalition v. Janet Reno,* 198 F.3d 1083 (9th Cir. 1999). Some notes and case citations omitted.

A.

The appellants consist of a group that refers to itself as "The Free Speech Coalition." The Free Speech Coalition is a trade association of businesses involved in the production and distribution of "adult-oriented materials." Bold Type, Inc. is a publisher of a book "dedicated to the education and expression of the ideals and philosophy associated with nudism;" Jim Gingerich is a New York artist whose paintings include large-scale nudes; and Ron Raffaelli is a professional photographer whose works include nude and erotic photographs.

The Free Speech Coalition sought declaratory and injunctive relief by a pre-enforcement challenge to certain provisions of the Child Pornography Prevention Act of 1996. The complaint was filed in the Northern District of California. Both parties moved for summary judgment. The district court determined the CPPA was constitutional and granted the government' s motion for summary judgment. *See The Free Speech Coalition v. Reno,* No. C 97–0281 VSC, 1997 WL 487758, at *7 (N.D. Cal. Aug. 12, 1997). At the same time it denied Free Speech's cross motion for summary judgment. *See id.* After the district court's adverse ruling, Free Speech appealed.

In this appeal, Free Speech argues the district court was mistaken in its determination that the legislation is content neutral. They also argue that the district court was wrong to hold that the Act is not unconstitutionally vague. The argument is that where the statute fails to define "appears to be" and "conveys the impression," it is so vague a person of ordinary intelligence cannot understand what is prohibited. Free Speech also questions the district court's holding that the affirmative defense provided in the Act is constitutional. Finally, Free Speech appeals the lower court's determination that the Act does not impose a prior restraint on protected speech and that it does not create a permanent chill on protected expression.

B.

Child pornography is a social concern that has evaded repeated attempts to stamp it out. State legislatures and Congress have vigorously tried to investigate and enact laws to provide a basis to prosecute those persons involved in the creation, distribution, and possession of sexually explicit materials made by or through the exploitation of children. Our concern is with the most recent federal law enacted as part of the effort to rid society of the exploitation of children for sexual gratification, the Child Pornography Prevention Act of 1996.

1.

The original federal legislation specifically prohibiting the sexual exploitation of children has been amended several times since it was enacted as the Protection of Children Against Sexual Exploitation Act of 1977. *See* Pub. L. No. 95–225, 92 Stat. 7 (1977) (codified as amended at 18 U.S.C. § § 2251–2253). The conduct prohibited by this law criminalized using a minor to engage in sexually explicit conduct for the purpose of producing any visual depiction of such conduct with the knowledge that it was or would be transported in interstate or foreign commerce. . . .

The Protection of Children Against Sexual Exploitation Act was enacted based upon congressional findings that child pornography and prostitution were highly organized, highly profitable, and exploited countless numbers of real children in its production. *See New York v. Ferber,* 458 U.S. 747, 749 n.1, 102 S.Ct. 3348, 73 L.Ed.2d 1113 (1982) (citing S.Rep. No. 95–438, at 5 (1977)). While the Act criminalized the commercial production and distribution of visual depictions of real children under the age of sixteen engaging in sexually explicit conduct, it also extended the prohibitions of the Mann Act, 18 U.S.C. § § 2421–2424, so as to criminalize the interstate transportation of children or juveniles for the purpose of prostitution. See Pub. L. No. 95–225, § 3, 92 Stat. 7 (1977). The Act criminalized a broad range of sexual acts.

2.

The Protection of Children Against Sexual Exploitation Act had its problems. According to the Final Report of the Attorney General's Commission on Pornography, only one person was convicted under the Act's production prohibition. *See* Attorney General's Comm'n On Pornography, *Final Report* 604 (1986) (hereinafter "AG Report"). As a consequence of the law's deficiencies and the Supreme Court's ruling in *Ferber,* Congress enacted the Child Protection Act of 1984. *See* Pub. L. No. 98–292, 98 Stat. 204 (1984) (codified as amended at 18 U.S.C. §§ 2251–2253). The Child Protection Act did away with the earlier requirement that the prohibited material be considered obscene under *Miller v. California,* 413 U.S. 15, 93 S.Ct. 2607, 37 L.Ed.2d 419 (1973), before its production, dissemination, or receipt was criminal. *See id.* § 4. The Child Protection Act also raised the age limit for protecting children involved in the production of sexually explicit material from sixteen years to eighteen years. *See id.* § 5.

When the Child Protection Act of 1984 was enacted Congress recognized that a great deal of pornographic trafficking involving children was not for profit. Thus, the 1984 law also did away with the requirement that the production or distribution of the material be for the purpose of sale. *See id.* §§ 4, 5. The 1984 law also picked up on a key phrase from *Ferber,* where the Supreme Court discussed limits on the classification of child pornography, stating that the "nature of the harm to be combated requires that the state offense be limited to works that visually depict sexual conduct. . . ." *Ferber,* 458 U.S. at 764, 102 S.Ct. 3348. Congress changed the phrase "visual or print medium" in the former law to the phrase "visual depiction." Finally, Congress substituted the word "lascivious" for the word "lewd" in the definition of "sexual conduct" to make it clear that the depiction of children engaged in sexual activity was unlawful even if it did not meet the adult obscenity standard.

3.

In 1986, Congress amended the law once again. The Child Sexual Abuse and Pornography Act of 1986, Public Law No. 99–628, § 2, 100 Stat. 3510 (1986) (codified as amended at 18 U.S.C. § 2251), banned the production and use of advertisements for child pornography. Another statutory change made wrong-doers subject to liability for personal injuries to children resulting from the production of child pornography. *See* Child Abuse Victims' Rights Act of 1986, Pub. L. No. 99–500, 100 Stat. 1783 (1986) (codified as amended at 18 U.S.C. § 2255). By passing these Acts, Congress continued its quest to end "kiddie porn."

4.

The continuing effort to marshal a means of stopping child pornography re-sulted in the passage of the Child Protection and Obscenity Enforcement Act of 1988. *See* Pub. L. No. 100–690, 102 Stat. 4181 (1988) (codified as amended at 18 U.S.C. § § 2251A–2252). This law made it unlawful to use a computer to transport, distribute, or receive child pornography. *See id.* § 7511. It also added a new section to the criminal law that prohibited the buying, selling, or otherwise obtaining of temporary custody or control of children for the purpose of pro-ducing child pornography. The new law required record keeping and imposed disclosure requirements on the producers of certain sexually explicit matter....

The law also mandated restitution for victims of child pornography. *See id.* § 40113.

Throughout the legislative history, Congress has defined the problem of child pornography in terms of real children. Up until 1996 the actual participa-tion and abuse of children in the production or dissemination of pornography involving minors was the *sine qua non* of the regulating scheme. The legislation tracked the decisions of the Supreme Court as well as the swift development of technology and its nearly infinite possibilities. The statutory odyssey was from adult pornography secured or not by the First Amendment, to child pornogra-phy permitted or not, to pseudo child pornography protected or not, until in 1996 the law was amended to prohibit virtual child pornography. The 1996 law, the law at issue here, changed course. The regulation direction shifted from defining child pornography in terms of the harm inflicted upon real children to a determination that child pornography was evil in and of itself, whether it involved real children or not. This shift forms the basis of the constitutional challenge Free Speech makes here.

6.

The Child Pornography Prevention Act of 1996 expanded the law to combat the use of computer technology to produce pornography containing images that look like children. The new law sought to stifle the use of technology for evil purposes. This of course was a marked change in the criminal regulatory scheme. Congress had always acted to prevent harm to real children. In the new law, Congress shifted the paradigm from the illegality of child pornography that involved the use of real children in its creation to forbid a "visual depiction" that "is, or appears to be, of a minor engaging in sexually explicit conduct." *See* 18 U.S.C.A. § 2256(8)(B) (West Supp. 1999).

The premise behind the Child Pornography Prevention Act is the asserted impact of such images on the children who may view them. The law is also based on the notion that child pornography, real as well as virtual, increases the activities of child molesters and pedophiles.

7.

18 U.S.C. § 2256(8) defines child pornography as "any visual depiction, including any photograph, film, video, picture, or computer or computer-generated image or picture, whether made or produced by electronic, mechanical, or other means, of sexually explicit conduct[.]" At issue in this appeal are the definitions contained in subsections (B) and (D) of § 2256(8). Section 2256(8)(B) bans sexually explicit depictions that appear to be minors. Section 2256(8)(D) bans visual depictions that are "advertised, promoted, presented, described or distributed in such a manner that conveys the impression" that they contain sexually explicit depictions of minors.

Because we hold the language at issue is unconstitutional, we do not consider the challenge to the affirmative defense in 18 U.S.C. § 2252A(c)....

1.

The district court held that the contested provisions of the Child Pornography Prevention Act [CPPA] are content-neutral regulations. The district judge reasoned that the law was passed to prevent the secondary effects of the child pornography industry, specifically the exploitation and degradation of children. The court also found that the Act addressed the need to control child pornography because virtual pornography led to the encouragement of pedophilia and the molestation of children. This reasoning was based on a finding that the CPPA is intended "to counteract the effect that [real or virtual child pornography] has on its viewers, on children, and to society as a whole." The lower court expressly found the legislation was not intended to regulate or outlaw the ideas themselves. *See id.*

We do not agree. In *United States v. Hilton,* 167 F.3d 61, 68–69 (1st Cir. 1999), *cert. denied,* _____ U.S. _____, 120 S.Ct. 115, 145 L.Ed.2d 98 (1999), the First Circuit found that the Act at issue was content-based because it expressly aims to curb a particular category of expression, child pornography, by singling out the type of expression based on its content and then banning it. The *Hilton* court's determination that blanket suppression of an entire type of speech is a content-discriminating act is a legal conclusion with which we agree. The child pornography law is at its essence founded upon content-based classification of speech.

The CPPA prohibits any sexually explicit depiction that "appears to be" of a minor or that is distributed or advertised in such a manner as to "convey the impression" that the depiction portrays a minor. Thus, the CPPA distinguishes favored from disfavored speech on the basis of the content of that speech.

Part of the rationale for the Act is the congressional determination that "a major part of the threat to children posed by child pornography is its effects on the viewers of such material[.]" S.Rep. No. 104–358, at 17 (1996). The Congress surmised that "the effect is the same whether the child pornography consists of photographic depictions of actual children or visual depictions produced wholly or in part by computer." One Senator referred to the notion that "[c]omputer imaging technology has given child pornographers a new way to create 'synthetic' child pornography which is virtually indistinguishable from 'traditional' child pornography." This belief was then carried to its logical content-based conclusion that " 'synthetic' child pornography which looks real to the naked eye will have the same effect upon viewers as 'traditional' child pornography."

The government contends the district court was right in finding that the law is content-neutral. The government argues that because Congress enacted the CPPA to address the secondary effects of speech appearing to depict children's sexual activity, this secondary-effects justification for the CPPA hinges upon the effect of pornography seemingly involving children upon its viewers.

When a statute restricts speech by its content, it is presumptively unconstitutional. *See Crawford,* 96 F.3d at 385. As the First Circuit determined in *Hilton:*

> The CPPA fails both tests for substantive neutrality: it expressly aims to curb a particular category of expression (child pornography) by singling out that type of expression based on its content and banning it. Blanket suppression of an entire type of speech is by its very nature a content-discriminating act. Furthermore, Congress has not kept secret that one of its motivating reasons for enacting the CPPA was to counter the primary effect child pornography has on those who view it.
>
> — 167 F.3d at 68–69 (footnote omitted).

The CPPA is not a time, place, or manner regulation.

2.

Under the circumstances, if the CPPA is to survive the constitutional inquiry the government must establish a compelling interest that is served by the statute, and it must show that the CPPA is narrowly tailored to fulfill that interest.

The district court found that even if no children are involved in the production of such materials the devastating secondary effect that sexually explicit materials involving the images of children have on society, and on the well being of children, merits the regulation of such images. This legislative finding supported the lower court's finding of a compelling state interest. We believe this legal determination is wrong.

There are three compelling interests put forward when instituting efforts to curb child pornography using images of actual children. The first interest is that child pornography requires the participation of actual children in sexually explicit situations to create the images. The second interest stems from the belief that dissemination of such pornographic images may encourage more sexual abuse of children because it whets the appetite of pedophiles. The third interest is that such images are morally and aesthetically repugnant.

The Supreme Court has required state statutes criminalizing child pornography to limit the offense to "works that visually depict explicit sexual conduct by children below a specified age." *Ferber,* 458 U.S. at 764, 102 S.Ct. 3348. The *Ferber* Court specifically focused on the harm to children. It also found that distribution of pornographic images is "intrinsically related" to the harm suffered by child victims because the images produced are a permanent record of the child's participation, exacerbated by its dissemination. The Court reasoned that the distribution network for such images needs to be terminated if it is to be effectively controlled. The *Ferber* Court acknowledged that "if it were necessary for literary or artistic value, a person over the statutory age who perhaps looked younger could be utilized."

The language of the statute questioned here can criminalize the use of fictional images that involve no human being, whether that fictional person is over the statutory age and looks younger, or indeed, a fictional person under the prohibited age. Images that are, or can be, entirely the product of the mind are criminalized. The CPPA's definition of child pornography extends to drawings or images that "appear" to be minors or visual depictions that "convey" the impression that a minor is engaging in sexually explicit conduct, whether an actual minor is involved or not. The constitutionality of this definition is not supported by existing case law.

The rationale articulated in *Ferber* and the constitutional permissibility of regulating the category of child pornography as a separate class is not justified by consideration of the effects such images have on others, even if those effects exist. Instead the focus of analysis is on the harm to the children actually used in the production of the materials.[1] Nothing in *Ferber* can be said to justify the regulation of such materials other than the protection of the actual children used in the production of child pornography. The language of the statute criminalizes even those materials that do not involve a recognizable minor. This shift is a significant departure from *Ferber.* While the government is given greater leeway in regulating child pornography, materials or depictions of sexual conduct "which do not involve live performance or photographic or other visual reproduction of live performances, retain[s] First Amendment protection." *Ferber,* 458 U.S. at 765, 102 S.Ct. 3348.

Ferber considered the possibility of simulations of sexually explicit acts involving non-recognizable minors and implicitly found them to be constitutionally protected. The Court also implicitly rejected the regulation of pornography that does not involve minors. Thus, the case law demonstrates that Congress has no compelling interest in regulating sexually explicit materials that do not contain visual images of actual children. Furthermore, to the extent Congress' justification for the CPPA relies upon such pornography's effect on third parties —children victimized by pedophiles who consume sexually explicit depictions that appear to involve minors—the Seventh Circuit has articulated a compelling reason for preventing such third party injury from superseding First Amendment rights.

In *American Booksellers Ass'n, Inc. v. Hudnut,* 771 F.2d 323, 334 (7th Cir. 1985), aff'd, 475 U.S. 1001, 106 S.Ct.1172, 89 L.Ed.2d 291 (1986), the Seventh Circuit invalidated a city ordinance prohibiting pornography that portrayed women submissively or in a degrading manner. In *Hudnut,* an argument about the consequences of pornography was put forth to justify the Indianapolis ordinance. *See* 771 F.2d at 328. The defendants maintained that pornography influences attitudes, and that the ordinance was a way to alter the socialization of men and women rather than to vindicate community standards of offensiveness. *See id.* at 328–29. It was argued that the ordinance would play an important role "in reducing the tendency of men to view women as sexual objects, a tendency that leads to both unacceptable attitudes and discrimination in the workplace and violence away from it." The Court accepted the premise that "depictions of subordination tend to perpetuate subordination" which in turn leads to "affront and lower pay at work, insult and injury at home, and battery and rape on the streets." Even so, the *Hudnut* court reasoned that pornography's role, if any, in preserving systems of sexual oppression "simply demonstrate[d] the power of pornography as speech. . . . Pornography affects how people see the world, their fellows, and social relations."

As the Seventh Circuit noted, however, the unhappy effects of pornography depend on mental intermediation. *See id.* This is particularly so when the images are not of real human beings, but are representations of a loathsome mind reduced to virtual reality by the technology of graphic computer art. Further,

> Sexual responses often are unthinking responses, and the association of sexual arousal with the subordination of women therefore may have a substantial effect. But almost all cultural stimuli provoke unconscious responses. . . . If the fact that speech plays a role in a process of conditioning were enough to permit governmental regulation, that would be the end of freedom of speech.

> —*Id.* at 330.

By the same token, any victimization of children that may arise from pedophiles' sexual responses to pornography apparently depicting children engaging in explicit sexual activity is not a sufficiently compelling justification for CPPA's speech restrictions. This is so because to hold otherwise enables the criminalization of foul figments of creative technology that do not involve any human victim in their creation or in their presentation. *Cf. Jacobson v. United States,* 503 U.S. 540, 548–49, 112 S.Ct. 1535, 118 L.Ed.2d 174 (1992) (invalidating a federal child pornography conviction and holding that even the compelling interest in protecting children from sexual exploitation does not justify modifications in otherwise applicable rules of criminal procedure); *United States v. X-Citement Video, Inc.,* 513 U.S. 64, 78, 115 S.Ct. 464, 130 L.Ed.2d 372 (1994) (interpreting 18 U.S.C. § 2252 to require the prosecution to prove the defendant knew the material was produced with the use of a minor, in part because to find otherwise would be constitutionally problematic).

The critical ingredient of our analysis is the relationship between the dissemination of fabricated images of child pornography and additional acts of sexual abuse. Factual studies that establish the link between computer-generated child pornography and the subsequent sexual abuse of children apparently do not yet exist. *See* Ronald W. Adelman, *The Constitutionality of Congressional Efforts to Ban Computer-Generated Child Pornography: A First Amendment Assessment of S. 1237,* 14 J. Marshall J. Computer & Info. L. 483, 488, 490 (1996). The legislative justification for the proposition was based upon the Final Report of the Attorney General's Commission on Pornography, a report that predates the existing technology. *See id.* at 490. The Final Report emphasized the victimization of real children by adult distribution of the pornographic material. The report shows that the use of sexually explicit photos or films of actual children to lure other children played a small part in the overall problem involving harm to children. *See id.* (citing AG Report at 649–50). Thus, while such images are unquestionably morally repugnant, they do not involve real children nor is there a demonstrated basis to link computer-generated images with harm to real children. Absent this nexus, the law does not withstand constitutional scrutiny.

By criminalizing all visual depictions that "appear to be" or "convey the impression" of child pornography, even where no child is ever used or harmed in its production, Congress has outlawed the type of depictions explicitly protected by the Supreme Court's interpretation of the First Amendment. Because the 1996 Act attempts to criminalize disavowed impulses of the mind, manifested in illicit creative acts, we determine that censorship through the enactment of criminal laws intended to control an evil idea cannot satisfy the constitutional requirements of the First Amendment.

Our determination is not to suggest that anyone condones the implicit or explicit harmful secondary effects of child pornography. Rather it is a determination to measure the statute by First Amendment standards articulated by the Supreme Court. To accept the secondary effects argument as the gauge against which the statute must be measured requires a remarkable shift in the First Amendment paradigm. Such a transformation, how speech impacts the listener or viewer, would turn First Amendment jurisprudence on its head.

In short, we find the articulated compelling state interest cannot justify the criminal proscription when no actual children are involved in the illicit images either by production or depiction. Because we find that Congress has not provided a compelling interest, we do not address the "narrow tailoring" requirement.

3.

The district court found the CPPA is not unconstitutionally vague as it gives sufficient guidance to a person of reasonable intelligence as to what it prohibits. The *Hilton* court scrutinized the statute with a "skeptical eye" because the new law impinges on freedom of expression. See 167 F.3d at 75. In doing so, it concluded, as the district court did here, that the CPPA was not unconstitutionally vague. *See id.* at 76–77. In making its determination the First Circuit applied an objective standard to determine the meaning of the phrase, "appears to be a minor." *See id.* at 75.

A statute is void for vagueness if it fails to "define the criminal offense with sufficient definiteness that ordinary people can understand what conduct is prohibited and in a manner that does not encourage arbitrary or discriminatory enforcement." *Kolender v. Lawson,* 461 U.S. 352, 357, 103 S.Ct. 1855, 75 L.Ed.2d 903 (1983). The requirement involves an understanding by a putative actor about what conduct is prohibited. It is impermissible to define a criminal offense so vaguely that an ordinary person is left guessing about what is prohibited and what is not. Notice that does not provide a meaningful understanding of what conduct is prohibited is vague and unenforceable. Such is the case with the statutory language prohibiting material that "appears to be" or that "conveys the impression."

The CPPA's criminalizing of material that "appears to be a minor" and "convey[s] the impression" that the material is a minor engaged in explicit sexual activity, is void for vagueness. It does not "give the person of ordinary intelligence a reasonable opportunity to know what is prohibited," and it fails to provide explicit standards for those who must apply it, "with the attendant dangers of arbitrary and discriminatory application." *Grayned v. City of Rockford,* 408, U.S. 104, 108–09, 92 S.Ct. 2294, 33 L.Ed.2d 222 (1972).

The two phrases in question are highly subjective. There is no explicit standard as to what the phrases mean. The phrases provide no measure to guide an ordinarily intelligent person about prohibited conduct and any such person could not be reasonably certain about whose perspective defines the appearance of a minor, or whose impression that a minor is involved leads to criminal prosecution.

In the same light, the absence of definitions for these key phrases in the CPPA allows law enforcement officials to exercise their discretion, subjectively, about what "appears to be" or what "conveys the impression" of prohibited material. Thus, the vagueness of the statute's key phrases regarding computer images permits enforcement in an arbitrary and discriminatory fashion.

4.

The district court held that the CPPA is not overbroad because it prohibits only those works necessary to prevent the secondary pernicious effects of child pornography from reaching minors. *See The Free Speech Coalition,* 1997 WL 487758, at *6. In addition, the First Circuit reasoned that "a few possibly impermissible applications of the Act does not warrant its condemnation[,]" and found that "[w]hatever overbreadth may exist at the edges are more appropriately cured through a more precise case-by-case evaluation of the facts in a given case." *Hilton,* 167 F.3d at 74. We do not agree.

Although overbreadth must "be 'substantial' before the statute involved will be invalidated on its face[,]" *Ferber,* 458 U.S. at 769, 102 S.Ct. 3348, such overbreadth is present here. On its face, the CPPA prohibits material that has been accorded First Amendment protection. That is, non-obscene sexual expression that does not involve actual children is protected expression under the First Amendment. *See id.* at 764–65, 102 S.Ct. 3348. This rule abides even when the subject matter is distasteful.

Congress may serve its legitimate purpose in protecting children from abuse by prohibiting pornography actually involving minors. The Senate considered the constitutional impediment discussed here but disagreed with the assertion that it could not prohibit visual depictions that "appear to be" of minors engaging in sexually explicit conduct when the depictions were produced without using actual children. See S.Rep. No. 104-358, at 21 (1996). The Senate reasoned that advances in technology distinguished the *Ferber* Court's holding because in 1982 when *Ferber* was decided "the technology to produce visual depictions of child sexual activity indistinguishable from unretouched photographs of actual children engaging in 'live performances' did not exist." *Id.*

The danger with this analysis is that it suggests that the more realistic an imaginary creation is, the less protection it is entitled to under the First Amendment. This is not because of any harm caused in its creation, rather it is because of the consequences of its purported reality. Yet, the Supreme Court has restricted the regulation of pornographic material involving minors because of the harm caused by its creation, not necessarily because of the consequences of its creation. The government's interest in prohibiting computer-generated child pornographic depictions is not the same as its interest in prohibiting child pornography produced by using actual children. In the latter instance there may be direct and indirect harm to a child. In the former instance there is no harm, and there can be none, to an actual child, if no real human is used in the production of the images. What is left then is an inconsistent effort to regulate the evil consequences of abusing children to make such images, even though no children are used in its production.

As explained, the CPPA is insufficiently related to the interest in prohibiting pornography actually involving minors to justify its infringement of protected speech. *See Village of Schaumburg v. Citizens for a Better Env't*, 444 U.S. 620, 637-39, 100 S.Ct. 826, 63 L.Ed.2d 73 (1980) (village could serve its legitimate interest in preventing fraud by less intrusive measures than direct prohibition of solicitation; concluding that village ordinance was overbroad, as it had insufficient relationship with protection of public safety or residential privacy to justify interference with protected speech). The CPPA's inclusion of constitutionally protected activity as well as legitimately prohibited activity makes it overbroad. *See Broadrick v. Oklahoma,* 413 U.S. 601, 612, 93 S.Ct. 2908, 37 L.Ed.2d 830 (1973) (describing Supreme Court's findings of overbreadth in cases in which statutes burden protected speech and rights of association).

5.

The district court found that because the CPPA does not require advance approval for production or distribution of adult pornography that does not use minors and does not effect a complete ban on constitutionally protected material, it does not constitute an improper prior restraint on speech. We agree.

Prior restraint describes "administrative and judicial orders forbidding certain communications" before the communication occurs. *See Alexander v. United States,* 509 U.S. 544, 550, 113 S.Ct. 2766, 125 L.Ed.2d 441 (1993). The

CPPA only penalizes speech after it occurs. As such it is not a prior restraint of speech. The possibility of self-censorship and the contention that the CPPA has a chilling effect do not amount to a prior restraint. *See Fort Wayne Books, Inc. v. Indiana,* 489 U.S. 46, 60, 109 S.Ct. 916, 103 L.Ed.2d 34 (1989).

V.

We hold that the language of "appears to be a minor" set forth in 18 U.S.C. § 2256(8)(B) and the language "convey[s] the impression" set forth in 18 U.S.C. § 2256(8)(D) are unconstitutionally vague and overbroad. The statute is severable. The law is enforceable, except for these amendments to 18 U.S.C. § 2256, § 4 of Senate Bill 1237, through the free standing savings provisions of § 9, codified at 18 U.S.C. § 2256(9).

The judgment of the district court is AFFIRMED on the questions of standing and prior restraint. The judgment of the district court is REVERSED on the questions of the constitutionality of the statutory language "appears to be a minor" and "convey[s] the impression." . . .

The case is remanded to the district court with instructions to enter judgment on behalf of the plaintiffs consistent with this opinion.

Note

1. The dissent rhetorically asks "Why should virtual child pornography be treated differently than real child pornography?" and then suggests there is no "value" in any pornography involving children, whether it involves real persons or imaginary computer images. This is the critical fault in the secondary effects analysis because it shifts the argument focus from whether the questioned speech or images are constitutionally protected to a focus on how the speech or image affects those who hear it or see it.

Dissenting Opinion of Warren J. Ferguson

FERGUSON, Circuit Judge, Dissenting:

The majority holds that Congress cannot regulate virtual child pornography because it does not require the use of actual children in its production. Without the use of actual children, the majority believes that Congress is simply attempting to regulate "evil idea[s]." I disagree. Congress has provided compelling evidence that virtual child pornography causes real harm to real children. As a result, virtual child pornography should join the ranks of real child pornography as a class of speech outside the protection of the First Amendment. In addition, I do not believe that the statutory terms "appears to be" or "conveys the impression" are substantially overbroad or void for vagueness. Accordingly, I would find the Child Pornography Prevention Act of 1996 ("CPPA") constitutional.

I.

For more than two decades, Congress has been trying to eliminate the scourge of child pornography. Each time Congress passes a law, however, child pornographers find a way around the law's prohibitions. *See* S.Rep. No. 104–358, at 26 (statement of Sen. Grassley). This cycle recently repeated itself and prompted Congress to enact the CPPA.

Prior to the CPPA, federal law imposed penalties on individuals who produced, distributed, or possessed visual depictions of actual minors engaging in sexually explicit conduct. *See* 18 U.S.C.A. § 2252 (West Supp. 1999). Recent advances in computer-imaging technology, however, have made this law ineffective for two reasons. First, purveyors of child pornography can now produce visual depictions that appear to be actual children engaged in sexual conduct "without using children" at all, "thereby placing such depictions outside the scope of federal law." 141 Cong. Rec. S13542 (daily ed. Sept. 13, 1995) (remarks of Sen. Hatch). Second, even where actual children are used, computers can "alter sexually explicit photographs, films, and videos in such a way as to make it virtually impossible for prosecutors to identify individuals, or to prove that the offending material was produced using [actual] children." *Id.*

From *Free Speech Coalition v. Janet Reno,* 198 F.3d 1083 (9th Cir. 1999). Notes and case citations omitted.

In an effort to close the loopholes, Congress enacted the CPPA which, *inter alia,* bans visual depictions that "appear[ ] to be of a minor engaging in sexually explicit conduct" or that are "advertised, promoted, presented, described, or distributed in such a manner that conveys the impression that the material is or contains a visual depiction of a minor engaging in sexually explicit conduct." 18 U.S.C.A. § § 2256(8)(B), (D) (West Supp. 1999). Along with the CPPA, Congress included thirteen detailed legislative findings that explain why virtual child pornography needs to be prohibited.

Despite these detailed legislative findings, the majority rules that Congress failed to articulate a "compelling state interest" to justify criminalizing virtual child pornography. Majority Op. at 1905. The majority argues that Congress cannot constitutionally regulate virtual child pornography because it does not depict "actual children." Once "actual children" are eliminated from the equation, the majority believes that Congress is impermissibly trying to regulate "evil idea[s]." I disagree for the following reasons.

First. The majority improperly suggests that preventing harm to depicted children is the only legitimate justification for banning child pornography. Although this was the Supreme Court's focus in *New York v. Ferber,* 458 U.S. 747, 102 S.Ct. 3348, 73 L.Ed.2d 1113 (1982), the Court has subsequently indicated a willingness to consider additional factors. *See Osborne v. Ohio,* 495 U.S. 103, 110–11, 110 S.Ct. 1691, 109 L.Ed.2d 98 (1990). In *Osborne,* the Supreme Court addressed the issue of whether Ohio could ban the possession of child pornography. *Id.* at 108, 110 S.Ct. 1691. In finding it could, the Court relied not only on the harm caused to the children who were used in its production (i.e., *Ferber*), but also on the harm that children suffer when child pornography is used to seduce or coerce them into sexual activity. *Id.* at 111, 110 S.Ct. 1691. Thus, in *Osborne,* the Court indicated that protecting children who are not actually pictured in the pornographic image is a legitimate and compelling state interest. *See Id. See also United States v. Hilton,* 167 F.3d 61, 70 (1st Cir.) (recognizing the Supreme Court's "subtle, yet crucial, extension" of valid state interests to include protecting children not actually depicted).

Second. The majority ignores the fact that the Supreme Court has already endorsed many of the justifications Congress relied on when it passed the CPPA. As discussed above, the Court in *Osborne* recognized that states have a legitimate interest in preventing pedophiles from "us[ing] child pornography to seduce other children into sexual activity." *Osborne,* 495 U.S. at 111, 110 S.Ct. 1691. Relying on this justification, Congress enacted the CPPA after finding that "child pornography is often used as part of a method of seducing other children into sexual activity; a child who is reluctant to engage in sexual activity with an adult, or to pose for sexually explicit photographs, can sometimes be convinced by viewing depictions of other children 'having fun' participating in such activity." *Congressional Findings,* at 3. More importantly, Congress found that when child pornography is "used as a means of seducing or breaking down a child's inhibitions," the images are equally as effective regardless of whether they are real photographs or computer-generated pictures that are "virtually indistinguishable." *Congressional Findings,* at 8.

The Supreme Court has also recognized that states have a legitimate interest in destroying the child pornography market. *Osborne,* 495 U.S. at 110. Similarly, in enacting the CPPA, Congress declared that the statute would encourage people to destroy all forms of child pornography, thereby reducing the market for the material. *Congressional Findings,* at 12. At the hearing before the Senate Judiciary Committee, witnesses testified that persons who trade and sell images that are indistinguishable from those of actual children engaged in sexual activity "keep the market for child pornography thriving." *Senate Hearing,* at 91 (testimony of Bruce Taylor). This is because pictures that *look* like children engaged in sexual activities can be exchanged for pictures that *are* of actual children engaged in such activities. By limiting the production and distribution of images that appear to be of children having sex, the CPPA helps rid the market of all child pornography.

Third. Even though Congress presented some new justifications that the Supreme Court has not specifically endorsed, the majority still had an obligation to consider them, especially if they advance the general goal of protecting children. In both *Ferber* and *Osborne,* the Court stated that "[i]t is evident beyond the need for elaboration that a State's interest in 'safeguarding the physical and psychological well-being of a minor' is 'compelling.'" *Osborne,* 495 U.S. at 109, 110 S.Ct. 1691, quoting *Ferber,* 458 U.S. at 756–57, 102 S.Ct. 3348. "A democratic society rests, for its continuance, upon the healthy, well-rounded growth of young people into full maturity as citizens." *Ferber,* 458 U.S. at 757, 102 S.Ct. 3348. Thus, the Court will generally "sustain[ ] legislation aimed at protecting the physical and emotional well-being of children even when the laws . . . operate[ ] in sensitive areas." *Id.*

The lesson from *Ferber* and *Osborne* is that legislators should be given "greater leeway" when acting to protect the well-being of children. *See Id.* at 756, 102 S.Ct. 3348. The majority, however, ignores this principle and fails to consider any of the new justifications supporting the CPPA. For example, the majority fails to address Congress' concern that computer-imaging technology is making it increasingly difficult in criminal cases for the government "to meet its burden of proving that a pornographic image is of a real child." S.Rep. No. 104–358, at 20. At a hearing before the Senate Judiciary Committee, Deputy Assistant Attorney General Kevin Di Gregory told the committee that in one federal child pornography case, the defendant relied on advances in computer technology to argue that the government had failed to meet its "burden of proving that each item of the alleged child pornography did, in fact, depict an actual minor rather than an adult made to look like one." *Id.* at 17, citing *United States v. Kimbrough,* 69 F.3d 723, 733 (5th Cir. 1995), *cert. denied,* 517 U.S. 1157, 116 S.Ct. 1547, 134 L.Ed.2d 650 (1996). Although jurors in that case rejected this argument, Congress recognized that as computer imaging software progressed, similar arguments might undermine "the enforcement of existing laws" by raising "a built-in reasonable doubt argument in every child exploitation/pornography prosecution." S. Rep. No. 104–358, at 16–17. Congress believed that the CPPA was necessary to close this loophole, and therefore, the majority should have factored this concern into its evaluation of the case.

Fourth.   The majority ignores the fact that child pornography, real or virtual, has little or no social value. *See Ferber,* 458 U.S. at 762, 102 S.Ct. 3348 (stating that the value of child pornography is "exceedingly modest, if not de minimis"). It is well established that "[t]he protection given to speech and press was fashioned to assure unfettered interchange of ideas for bringing about the political and social changes desired by people." *Roth v. United States,* 354 U.S. 476, 484, 77 S.Ct. 1304, 1 L.Ed.2d 1498 (1957). "All ideas having even the slightest redeeming social importance—unorthodox ideas, controversial ideas, even ideas hateful to the prevailing climate of opinion—have... full protection..." *Id.* The First Amendment, however, does not protect certain limited categories of speech that are "utterly without redeeming social importance." *Id. See also R.A.V. v. City of St. Paul,* 505 U.S. 377, 382–83, 112 S.Ct. 2538, 120 L.Ed.2d 305 (1992) (stating that "[f]rom 1791 to present... our society, like other free but civilized societies, has permitted restrictions upon the content of speech in a few limited areas"). These categories include obscenity, *Roth,* 354 U.S. at 483, 77 S.Ct. 1304, libel, *Beauharnais v. Illinois,* 343 U.S. 250, 266, 72 S.Ct. 725, 96 L.Ed. 919 (1952), and "fighting words," *Chaplinsky v. New Hampshire,* 315 U.S. 568, 571–73, 62 S.Ct. 766, L.Ed. 1031 (1942). Child pornography is also one of these categories of speech. *Ferber,* 458 U.S. at 763–64, 102 S.Ct. 3348.

Why should virtual child pornography be treated differently than real child pornography? Is it more valued speech? I do not think so. Both real and virtual child pornography contain visual depictions of children engaging in sexually explicit activity. The only difference is that real child pornography uses actual children in its production, whereas virtual child pornography does not. While this distinction is noteworthy, it does not somehow transform virtual child pornography into meaningful speech. Virtual child pornography, like its counterpart real child pornography, is of "slight social value" and constitutes "no essential part of the exposition of ideas." *See Chaplinsky,* 315 U.S. at 572, 62 S.Ct. 766. Therefore, the majority is wrong to accord virtual child pornography the full protection of the First Amendment.

Fifth.   The majority improperly analyzes the CPPA under a strict scrutiny approach. In so doing, the majority misreads the Supreme Court's previous child pornography decisions. These decisions indicate that the proper mode of analysis is to weigh the state's interest in regulating child pornography against the material's limited social value. *See Ferber,* 458 U.S. at 756–64 102 S.Ct. 3348; *Osborne,* 495 U.S. at 108–111, 110 S.Ct. 1691. The Supreme Court used this test in *Ferber* and found that "the balance of competing interests [was] clearly struck and that it [was] permissible to consider these materials as without the protection of the First Amendment." *Id.* at 764, 102 S.Ct. 3348. *See also Osborne,* 495 U.S. at 111, 110 S.Ct. 1691 (finding that the "gravity of the State's interests" outweighed Osborne's limited First Amendment right to possess child pornography).

Virtual child pornography should be evaluated in a similar fashion. The majority should have weighed Congress' reasons for banning virtual child pornography against the limited value of such material. If the majority had, it would have realized that Congress' interests in destroying the child pornography market and in preventing the seduction of minors outweigh virtual child pornography's exceedingly modest social value. Since the balance of competing interests tips in favor of the government, virtual child pornography should join the ranks of real child pornography as a class of speech outside the protection of the First Amendment.

II.

The analysis does not end with a finding that virtual child pornography is without First Amendment protection. Statutes can be found unconstitutional if they are worded so broadly that they "criminalize an intolerable range of constitutionally protected conduct." *Osborne*, 495 U.S. at 112, 110 S.Ct. 1691. This case focuses on the CPPA's new definition of child pornography which prohibits visual depictions that "appear[ ] to be," or are promoted or distributed "in such a manner that conveys the impression," that they are "of a minor engaging in sexually explicit conduct." 18 U.S.C.A. § § 2256(8)(B), (D) (West Supp. 1999). The majority holds that this language is overbroad because it bans "material that has been accorded First Amendment protection." Majority Op. at 1095–96. I disagree.

As a general rule, statutes should not be invalidated as overbroad unless the overbreadth is "substantial ... in relation to the statute's plainly legitimate sweep." *Broadrick v. Oklahoma*, 413 U.S. 601, 615, 93 S.Ct. 2908, 37 L.Ed.2d 830 (1973). The Court has cautioned that the overbreadth doctrine is "strong medicine" that should be employed "sparingly and only as a last resort." *Id.* at 613, 93 S.Ct. 2908. Accordingly, a statute should not be invalidated as overbroad "when a limiting construction has been or could be placed on the challenged statute." *Id.*

Appellants suggest that the "appears to be" language is so broad that everyday artistic expressions like paintings, drawings, and sculptures that depict youthful looking subjects in a sexual manner will be criminalized under the CPPA. However, even a glancing look at the legislative history belies this assertion. Congress enacted the CPPA to address the problem of "computer-generated" child pornography. S.Rep. No. 104–358, at 7. In the findings filed with the CPPA, Congress repeatedly stated that the law is targeted at visual depictions that are "virtually indistinguishable to the unsuspecting viewer from unretouched photographic images of actual children engaging in sexually explicit conduct." *Congressional Findings*, at 5, 8, 13. The Senate Judiciary Committee explained that the "appears to be" language was necessary to cover the "same type of photographic images *already* prohibited, but which do[ ] not require the use of an actual minor." S.Rep. No. 104–358, at 21 (emphasis in original).

From reading the legislative history, it becomes clear that the CPPA merely extends the existing prohibitions on "real" child pornography to a narrow class of computer-generated pictures easily mistaken for real photographs of real children. *See Congressional Findings,* at 13. Therefore, I agree with the United States Court of Appeals for the First Circuit which found that "drawings, cartoons, sculptures, and paintings depicting youthful persons in sexually explicit poses plainly lie beyond the Act." *Hilton,* 167 F.3d at 72. "By definition, they would not be 'virtually indistinguishable' from an image of an actual minor." *Id.* "The CPPA therefore does not pose a threat to the vast majority of every day artistic expression, even to speech involving sexual themes." *Id.*

There has also been concern that the CPPA prohibits constitutionally protected photographic images of adults in sexually explicit poses. This contention, however, is also without merit. The CPPA explicitly states that "[i]t shall be an affirmative defense" to a charge of distributing, reproducing or selling child pornography that the pornography (1) "was produced using an actual person or persons," (2) each of whom "was an adult at the time the material was produced," and (3) "the defendant did not advertise, promote, present, describe, or distribute the material in such a manner as to convey the impression that it is or contains visual depictions of a minor engaging in sexually explicit conduct." 18 U.S.C.A. 2252A(c) (West Supp. 1999). The CPPA thus shields from prosecution sexually explicit visual depictions so long as they are produced using actual adults and "the material has not been pandered as child pornography." S.Rep. No. 104–358, at 10, 21. Persons—like the appellants in this case—who produce and distribute works depicting the sexual conduct of actual adults, and do not market the depictions as if they contain sexual images of children, are thus explicitly protected from culpability under the CPPA.

While there may be other potentially impermissible applications of the CPPA, I doubt that they would be "substantial... in relation to the statute's plainly legitimate sweep." *Broadrick,* 413 U.S. at 615, 93 S.Ct. 2908. Rather than invalidate part of the statute based on possible problems that may never occur, it is best to deal with those situations on a case-by-cases basis. *See Ferber,* 458 U.S. at 781, 102 S.Ct. 3348 (Stevens, J., concurring) (noting that "[h]ypothetical rulings are inherently treacherous and prone to lead us into unforeseen errors"). Accordingly, I would find that the CPPA is not substantially overbroad. *See Hilton,* 167 F.3d at 71–74 (finding that the CPPA is not unconstitutionally overbroad); *United States v. Acheson,* 195 F.3d 645, 650–52 (11th Cir. 1999) (same).

III.

I also disagree with the majority that the CPPA is unconstitutionally vague. It is well settled that a statute is not void for vagueness unless it fails to "define the criminal offense with sufficient definiteness that ordinary people can understand what conduct is prohibited." *Kolender v. Lawson,* 461 U.S. 352, 357, 103 S.Ct. 1855, 75 L.Ed.2d 903 (1983).

Here, the key phrases of the CPPA are clearly defined. The CPPA applies to visual depictions of a minor engaging in sexually explicit conduct. A minor is defined as "any person under the age of eighteen years." 18 U.S.C.A. § 2256(1) (West Supp. 1999). In addition, "sexually explicit conduct" is defined as actual or simulated "sexual intercourse... ; bestiality; masturbation; sadistic or masochistic abuse; or lascivious exhibition of the genitals or pubic area." 18 U.S.C.A. § 2256(2) (West Supp. 1999). Given the detailed definition of sexually explicit activity, it is unlikely that a person of ordinary intelligence would be unable to determine what activities are prohibited.

The majority nevertheless finds fault with the CPPA because it believes that the terms "appears to be" and "conveys the impression" are highly subjective and could be enforced "in an arbitrary and discriminatory fashion." Majority Op. at 1095. Once again, I disagree. With regard to the apparent age of the depicted individuals, the government can use the same type of objective evidence that it relied on before the CPPA went into effect. For example, in cases involving prepubescent individuals, the government can show the jury the pictures and the jury can determine for itself whether the virtual image "appears to be" of a minor. *See e.g. United States v. Arvin,* 900 F.2d 1385, 1390 n. 4 (9th Cir. 1990) (citing a jury instruction that requires the members of the jury to decide whether the prepubescent girls are "minors" based upon their own "observation of the pictures"), *cert. denied* 498 U.S. 1024, 111 S.Ct. 672, 112 L.Ed.2d 664 (1991). In cases in which the depicted children have reached puberty, the government can call expert witnesses to testify as to the physical development of the depicted person, and present testimony regarding the way the creator, distributor, or possessor labeled the disks, files, or videos. *See e.g. United States v. Robinson,* 137 F.3d 652, 653 (1st Cir. 1998) (noting that the pornographic photographs listed the ages of boys depicted). Based on these examples, I agree with the First Circuit which found that the standard for evaluating the key provisions of the CPPA "is an objective one." *Hilton,* 167 F.3d at 75. "A jury must decide, based on the totality of the circumstances, whether an unsuspecting viewer would consider the depiction to be an actual individual under the age of eighteen engaging in sexual activity." *Id.*

As an additional safeguard against arbitrary prosecutions, the government must satisfy the element of scienter before it can obtain a valid conviction under the CPPA. *See* 18 U.S.C.A. § 2252A (West Supp. 1999). In any CPPA prosecution, the government must prove beyond a reasonable doubt that the individual "knowingly" produced, distributed, or possessed sexually explicit material and that the material depicts a person who appeared to the pornographer to be under the age of eighteen. *See Id. See also United States v. X-Citement Video, Inc.,* 513 U.S. 64, 78, 115 S.Ct. 464, 130 L.Ed.2d 372 (1994) (holding that the scienter requirement "extends to both the sexually explicit nature of the material and to the age of the performers").

"Thus, a defendant who honestly believes that the individual depicted in the image appears to be 18 years old or older (and is believed by a jury), or who can show that he knew the image was created by having a youthful-looking adult pose for it, must be acquitted, so long as the image was not presented or marketed as if it contained a real minor." *Hilton,* 167 F.3d at 75–76. Based on these safeguards, the majority's concerns about arbitrary and discriminatory prosecutions are misplaced. *See Id.* at 74–77 (finding that the CPPA is not unconstitutionally vague); Acheson, 195 F.3d at 652-53 (same).

IV.

In sum, the CPPA is not, as the majority claims, an attempt to regulate "evil idea[s]." Instead, the CPPA is an important tool in the fight against child sexual abuse. The CPPA's definition of child pornography provides adequate notice of the type of images that are prohibited and does not substantially encroach on protected expression. Accordingly, I would find the CPPA constitutional.

POSTSCRIPT

Is Virtual Child Pornography Legal?

The First Amendment does not provide absolute protection to every word that is spoken or every image that is published. The most common example of unprotected speech is obscenity. Obscene publications have been deemed to contribute so little to society that the courts have held the First Amendment to be essentially irrelevant to obscene publications. Similarly, "fighting words," in which someone advocates illegal acts "where such advocacy is directed to inciting or producing imminent lawless action and is likely to incite or produce such action," can sometimes be punished. In general, however, constitutional theory holds that the solution to speech that someone does not like is more speech. According to the Supreme Court, a function of speech is to invite dispute. It may indeed best serve its high purpose when it induces a condition of unrest, creates dissatisfaction with conditions as they are, or even stirs people to anger. Speech is often provocative and challenging. It may strike at prejudices and preconceptions and have profound unsettling effects.

The existing legal model for regulating obscenity and pornography is often misunderstood. These terms are often used synonymously by laypeople, but the courts distinguish between them and, as a consequence, obscenity can be punished in any medium while pornographic communications involving adults, no matter how offensive they may be to some people, may not be barred. In *Miller v. California,* 413 U.S. 15 (1974), the Supreme Court defined obscenity as material that, when taken as a whole, meets three criteria: appeals to prurient interest; portrays sexual conduct in a patently offensive way; and lacks serious literary, artistic, political, or scientific value. Pornographic material may be highly offensive but cannot be banned unless it satisfies all three conditions.

Dial-a-porn was the subject of *Sable Communications, Inc. v. FCC,* 492 U.S. 115 (1989) and 492 U.S. 889 (1989). Indecent radio communication was considered in *FCC v. Pacifica Foundation,* 438 U.S. 726 (1978). The impact of computers and electronic communication on the First Amendment is discussed in Stuart Biegel, *Beyond Our Control: Confronting the Limits of Our Legal System in Cyberspace* (MIT Press, 2001); M. Ethan Katsh, *The Electronic Media and the Transformation of Law* (Oxford University Press, 1989) and *Law in a Digital World* (Oxford University Press, 1995); Symposium, "Emerging Media Technology and the First Amendment," 104 *Yale Law Journal* 1805 (1995); Donald Lively, "The Information Superhighway: A First Amendment Roadmap," 35 *Boston College Law Review* 1067 (1994); and Debra D. Burke, "Cybersmut and the First Amendment: A Call for a New Obscenity Standard," 9 *Harvard Journal of Law and Technology* 87 (1996). On the Internet itself, information about government regulation can be found at http://www.aclu.org, http://www.epic.org, http://www.eff.org, and http://www.cdt.org.

ISSUE 11

Is It Constitutional to Impose the Death Penalty on the Mentally Retarded?

YES: Sandra Day O'Connor, from Majority Opinion, *Penry v. Lynaugh*, U.S. Supreme Court (June 26, 1989)

NO: American Bar Association, from Brief Amicus Curiae of the American Bar Association in Support of Petitioner, *Ernest Paul McCarver v. State of North Carolina*, North Carolina Supreme Court (June 6, 2001)

ISSUE SUMMARY

YES: Supreme Court justice Sandra Day O'Connor holds that the Constitution does not preclude the execution of a mentally retarded person who is convicted of a capital offense.

NO: The American Bar Association, the principal voluntary national membership organization of the legal profession, argues that the Eighth Amendment should be held to exempt people with mental retardation from capital punishment.

I n *Ford v. Wainwright*, 477 U.S. 399 (1986), the U.S. Supreme Court ruled that the execution of insane criminals violated the Eighth Amendment protection against cruel and unusual punishment. Writing for the majority, Justice William J. Brennan, Jr., declared that "the natural abhorrence civilized societies feel at killing one who has no capacity to come to grips with his own conscience or deity is still vivid today. And the intuition that such an execution simply offends humanity is evidently shared across this Nation." But should this feeling extend to the mentally retarded or disabled as well?

According to the American Association on Mental Retardation (AAMR), "The death penalty is disproportionate to the level of culpability possible for people with mental retardation." The AAMR's official policy statement asserts that "mental retardation is a substantially disabling condition which may affect an individual's ability to appreciate and understand fully the consequences of actions, and which may impair the individual's ability to confirm his or her conduct to the requirements of the law. Thus mental retardation should always be considered to be a mitigating circumstance in selecting an appropriate punishment for a serious offense."

Human rights and legal groups have voiced similar opinions. In 1997 the American Bar Association (ABA), which claims to be neutral on the subject of capital punishment, passed a resolution against the execution of the mentally retarded in order to "ensure that death penalty cases are administered fairly and impartially, in accordance with due process, and minimize the risk that innocent persons may be executed." Both Amnesty International and Human Rights Watch have condemned the use of the death penalty against the mentally retarded, the latter calling it "barbaric" and "senseless cruelty." Even the United Nations has chimed in, with both its Committee on Crime Prevention and Control and its Economic and Social Council issuing recommendations and resolutions against the practice.

In the selection that follows, Justice Sandra Day O'Connor, in the 1989 case *Penry v. Lynaugh,* holds that the execution of the mentally retarded is not "cruel and unusual." In that case, O'Connor also ruled that mental retardation was a mitigating factor, which the jury should have been told it could take into account in deciding whether or not to impose the death penalty. Since the jury had not been properly instructed, the case was sent back to the lower court.

Penry was again sentenced to death. Again he appealed, and in June 2001 the Supreme Court again ruled that the execution of mentally retarded individuals is constitutional. Furthermore, the Court again found fault with the judge's instructions to the jury and sent the case back.

As you read O'Connor's opinion, you will see that there is no doubt that Penry committed a horrific crime. He also had the misfortune to commit the crime in Texas, the state where the death penalty has been employed most often. Of 683 executions since 1977, 239, or almost 35 percent, have taken place in Texas. Of the 85 executions in 2000, 40 took place in Texas. Penry, who has now been on death row for more than 20 years, may still, at some point, be executed.

 **YES**

Majority Opinion

Penry *v.* Lynaugh

JUSTICE O'CONNOR delivered the opinion of the Court, except as to Part IV-C.

In this case, we must decide whether petitioner, Johnny Paul Penry, was sentenced to death in violation of the Eighth Amendment because the jury was not instructed that it could consider and give effect to his mitigating evidence in imposing its sentence. We must also decide whether the Eighth Amendment categorically prohibits Penry's execution because he is mentally retarded.

I

On the morning of October 25, 1979, Pamela Carpenter was brutally raped, beaten, and stabbed with a pair of scissors in her home in Livingston, Texas. She died a few hours later in the course of emergency treatment. Before she died, she described her assailant. Her description led two local sheriff's deputies to suspect Penry, who had recently been released on parole after conviction on another rape charge. Penry subsequently gave two statements confessing to the crime and was charged with capital murder.

At a competency hearing held before trial, a clinical psychologist, Dr. Jerome Brown, testified that Penry was mentally retarded. As a child, Penry was diagnosed as having organic brain damage, which was probably caused by trauma to the brain at birth. Penry was tested over the years as having an IQ between 50 and 63, which indicates mild to moderate retardation. Dr. Brown's own testing before the trial indicated that Penry had an IQ of 54. Dr. Brown's evaluation also revealed that Penry, who was 22 years old at the time of the crime, had the mental age of a 6½-year-old, which means that "he has the ability to learn and the learning or the knowledge of the average 6½ year old kid." Penry's social maturity, or ability to function in the world, was that of a 9- or 10-year-old. Dr. Brown testified that "there's a point at which anyone with [Penry's] IQ is always incompetent, but, you know, this man is more in the borderline range."

The jury found Penry competent to stand trial. The guilt-innocence phase of the trial began on March 24, 1980. The trial court determined that Penry's

From *Penry v. Lynaugh*, 492 U.S. 302 (1989). Notes and some case citations omitted.

confessions were voluntary, and they were introduced into evidence. At trial, Penry raised an insanity defense and presented the testimony of a psychiatrist, Dr. Jose Garcia. Dr. Garcia testified that Penry suffered from organic brain damage and moderate retardation, which resulted in poor impulse control and an inability to learn from experience. Dr. Garcia indicated that Penry's brain damage was probably caused at birth, but may have been caused by beatings and multiple injuries to the brain at an early age. In Dr. Garcia's judgment, Penry was suffering from an organic brain disorder at the time of the offense which made it impossible for him to appreciate the wrongfulness of his conduct or to conform his conduct to the law.

Penry's mother testified at trial that Penry was unable to learn in school and never finished the first grade. Penry's sister testified that their mother had frequently beaten him over the head with a belt when he was a child. Penry was also routinely locked in his room without access to a toilet for long periods of time. As a youngster, Penry was in and out of a number of state schools and hospitals, until his father removed him from state schools altogether when he was 12. Penry's aunt subsequently struggled for over a year to teach Penry how to print his name.

The State introduced the testimony of two psychiatrists to rebut the testimony of Dr. Garcia. Dr. Kenneth Vogtsberger testified that although Penry was a person of limited mental ability, he was not suffering from any mental illness or defect at the time of the crime, and that he knew the difference between right and wrong and had the potential to honor the law. In his view, Penry had characteristics consistent with an antisocial personality, including an inability to learn from experience and a tendency to be impulsive and to violate society's norms. He testified further that Penry's low IQ scores underestimated his alertness and understanding of what went on around him.

Dr. Felix Peebles also testified for the State that Penry was legally sane at the time of the offense and had a "full-blown anti-social personality." In addition, Dr. Peebles testified that he personally diagnosed Penry as being mentally retarded in 1973 and again in 1977, and that Penry "had a very bad life generally, bringing up." In Dr. Peebles' view, Penry "had been socially and emotionally deprived and he had not learned to read and write adequately." Although they disagreed with the defense psychiatrist over the extent and cause of Penry's mental limitations, both psychiatrists for the State acknowledged that Penry was a person of extremely limited mental ability, and that he seemed unable to learn from his mistakes. The jury rejected Penry's insanity defense and found him guilty of capital murder. . . .

IV

Penry's second claim is that it would be cruel and unusual punishment, prohibited by the Eighth Amendment, to execute a mentally retarded person like himself with the reasoning capacity of a 7-year-old. He argues that because of their mental disabilities, mentally retarded people do not possess the level of moral culpability to justify imposing the death sentence. He also argues that there is an emerging national consensus against executing the mentally retarded. The State responds that there is insufficient evidence of a national consensus against executing the retarded, and that existing procedural safeguards adequately protect the interests of mentally retarded persons such as Penry....

B

The Eighth Amendment categorically prohibits the infliction of cruel and unusual punishments. At a minimum, the Eighth Amendment prohibits punishment considered cruel and unusual at the time the Bill of Rights was adopted. The prohibitions of the Eighth Amendment are not limited, however, to those practices condemned by the common law in 1789. The prohibition against cruel and unusual punishments also recognizes the "evolving standards of decency that mark the progress of a maturing society." In discerning those "evolving standards," we have looked to objective evidence of how our society views a particular punishment today. The clearest and most reliable objective evidence of contemporary values is the legislation enacted by the country's legislatures. We have also looked to data concerning the actions of sentencing juries.

It was well settled at common law that "idiots," together with "lunatics," were not subject to punishment for criminal acts committed under those incapacities. As Blackstone wrote:

> "The second case of a deficiency in will, which excuses from the guilt of crimes, arises also from a defective or vitiated understanding, viz. in an *idiot* or a *lunatic.* . . . [I]diots and lunatics are not chargeable for their own acts, if committed when under these incapacities: no, not even for treason itself. . . . [A] total idiocy, or absolute insanity, excuses from the guilt, and of course from the punishment, of any criminal action committed under such deprivation of the senses. . . ."

— 4 W. Blackstone, Commentaries *24 - *25 (emphasis in original)

See also 1 W. Hawkins, Pleas of the Crown 1–2 (7th ed. 1795) ("[T]hose who are under a natural disability of distinguishing between good and evil, as . . . ideots, and lunaticks are not punishable by any criminal prosecution whatsoever"). Idiocy was understood as "a defect of understanding from the moment of birth," in contrast to lunacy, which was "a partial derangement of the intellectual faculties, the senses returning at uncertain intervals." *Id.,* at 2, n. 2.

There was no one definition of idiocy at common law, but the term "idiot" was generally used to describe persons who had a total lack of reason or understanding, or an inability to distinguish between good and evil. Hale wrote that a person who is deaf and mute from birth "is in presumption of law an ideot . . . because he hath no possibility to understand what is forbidden by law to be done, or under what penalties: but if it can appear, that he hath the use of understanding, . . . then he may be tried, and suffer judgment and execution." M. Hale, Please of the Crown 34 (1736) (footnote omitted). See also *id.,* at 29 (citing A. Fitzherbert, 2 Natura Brevium 233 (7th ed. 1730)); Trial of Edward Arnold, 16 How. St. Tr. 695, 765 (Eng. 1724) ("[A] man that is totally deprived of his understanding and memory, and doth not know what he is doing, no more than an infant, than a brute, or a wild beast, such a one is never the object of punishment"); S. Glueck, Mental Disorder and the Criminal Law 128–144 (1925).

The common law prohibition against punishing "idiots" and "lunatics" for criminal acts was the precursor of the insanity defense, which today generally includes "mental defect" as well as "mental disease" as part of the legal definition of insanity. See, e.g., American Law Institute, Model Penal Code 4.01, p. 61 (1985) ("A person is not responsible for criminal conduct if at the time of such conduct as a result of mental disease or defect he lacks substantial capacity either to appreciate the criminality [wrongfulness] of his conduct or to conform his conduct to the requirements of law"); 18 U.S.C. 17 (1982 ed., Supp. V) (it is an affirmative defense to federal prosecution if "the defendant, as a result of a severe mental disease or defect, was unable to appreciate the nature and quality or the wrongfulness of his acts" at the time the offense was committed). See generally Ellis & Luckasson, Mentally Retarded Criminal Defendants, 53 Geo. Wash. L. Rev. 414, 432–444 (1985).

In its emphasis on a permanent, congenital mental deficiency, the old common law notion of "idiocy" bears some similarity to the modern definition of mental retardation. Ellis & Luckasson, *supra,* at 417. The common law prohibition against punishing "idiots" generally applied, however, to persons of such severe disability that they lacked the reasoning capacity to form criminal intent or to understand the difference between good and evil. In the 19th and early 20th centuries, the term "idiot" was used to describe the most retarded of persons, corresponding to what is called "profound" and "severe" retardation today. See AAMR, Classification in Mental Retardation 179 (H. Grossman ed. 1983); *id.,* at 9 ("idiots" generally had IQ of 25 or below).

The common law prohibition against punishing "idiots" for their crimes suggests that it may indeed be "cruel and unusual" punishment to execute persons who are profoundly or severely retarded and wholly lacking the capacity to appreciate the wrongfulness of their actions. Because of the protections afforded by the insanity defense today, such a person is not likely to be convicted or face the prospect of punishment. See ABA Standards for Criminal Justice 7-9.1, commentary, p. 460 (2d ed. 1980) (most retarded people who reach the point of sentencing are mildly retarded). Moreover, under *Ford v. Wainwright,* 477 U.S. 399 (1986), someone who is "unaware of the punishment they are about to suffer and why they are to suffer it" cannot be executed. *Id.,* at 422 (Powell, J., concurring in part and concurring in judgment).

Such a case is not before us today. Penry was found competent to stand trial. In other words, he was found to have the ability to consult with his lawyer with a reasonable degree of rational understanding, and was found to have a rational as well as factual understanding of the proceedings against him. In addition, the jury rejected his insanity defense, which reflected their conclusion that Penry knew that his conduct was wrong and was capable of conforming his conduct to the requirements of the law. Tex. Penal Code Ann. 8.01(a) (1974 and Supp. 1989).

Penry argues, however, that there is objective evidence today of an emerging national consensus against execution of the mentally retarded, reflecting the "evolving standards of decency that mark the progress of a maturing society." *Trop v. Dulles,* 356 U.S., at 101. Brief for Petitioner 37-39. The federal Anti-Drug Abuse Act of 1988, Pub. L. 100-690, 7001(1), 102 Stat. 4390, 21 U.S.C. 848(1) (1988 ed.), prohibits execution of a person who is mentally retarded. Only one State, however, currently bans execution of retarded persons who have been found guilty of a capital offense. Ga. Code Ann. 17-7-131(j) (Supp. 1988). Maryland has enacted a similar statute which will take effect on July 1, 1989. Md. Ann. Code, Art. 27, 412(f)(1) (1989).

In contrast, in *Ford v. Wainwright,* which held that the Eighth Amendment prohibits execution of the insane, considerably more evidence of a national consensus was available. No State permitted the execution of the insane, and 26 States had statutes explicitly requiring suspension of the execution of a capital defendant who became insane. Ford, 477 U.S., at 408, n. 2. Other States had adopted the common law prohibition against executing the insane. Moreover, in examining the objective evidence of contemporary standards of decency in *Thompson v. Oklahoma,* the plurality noted that 18 States expressly established a minimum age in their death penalty statutes, and all of them required that the defendant have attained at least the age of 16 at the time of the offense. In our view, the two state statutes prohibiting execution of the mentally retarded, even when added to the 14 States that have rejected capital punishment completely, do not provide sufficient evidence at present of a national consensus.

Penry does not offer any evidence of the general behavior of juries with respect to sentencing mentally retarded defendants, nor of decisions of prosecutors. He points instead to several public opinion surveys that indicate strong public opposition to execution of the retarded. For example, a poll taken in Texas found that 86% of those polled supported the death penalty, but 73% opposed its application to the mentally retarded. A Florida poll found 71% of those surveyed were opposed to the execution of mentally retarded capital defendants, while only 12% were in favor. A Georgia poll found 66% of those polled opposed to the death penalty for the retarded, 17% in favor, with 16% responding that it depends how retarded the person is. In addition, the AAMR, the country's oldest and largest organization of professionals working with the mentally retarded, opposes the execution of persons who are mentally retarded. The public sentiment expressed in these and other polls and resolutions may ultimately find expression in legislation, which is an objective indicator of contemporary values upon which we can rely. But at present, there is insufficient evidence of a national consensus against executing mentally retarded people convicted of capital offenses for us to conclude that it is categorically prohibited by the Eighth Amendment.

C

Relying largely on objective evidence such as the judgments of legislatures and juries, we have also considered whether application of the death penalty to particular categories of crimes or classes of offenders violates the Eighth Amendment because it "makes no measurable contribution to acceptable goals of punishment and hence is nothing more than the purposeless and needless imposition of pain and suffering" or because it is "grossly out of proportion to the severity of the crime." *Coker v. Georgia,* 433 U.S., at 592 (plurality opinion); *Thompson v. Oklahoma,* 487 U.S., at 833 (plurality opinion); *Tison v. Arizona,* 481 U.S. 137 (1987); *Enmund v. Florida,* 458 U.S., at 798-801. *Gregg* noted that "[t]he death penalty is said to serve two principal social purposes: retribution and deterrence of capital crimes by prospective offenders." *Gregg v. Georgia,* 428 U.S., at 183 (joint opinion of Stewart, Powell, and STEVENS, JJ.). "The heart of the retribution rationale is that a criminal sentence must be directly related to the personal culpability of the criminal offender." *Tison v. Arizona, supra,* at 149. See also Enmund, *supra,* at 825 (O'CONNOR, J., dissenting) (the Eighth Amendment concept of "proportionality requires a nexus between the punishment imposed and the defendant's blameworthiness").

Penry argues that execution of a mentally retarded person like himself with a reasoning capacity of approximately a 7-year-old would be cruel and unusual because it is disproportionate to his degree of personal culpability. Just as the plurality in *Thompson* reasoned that a juvenile is less culpable than an adult for the same crime, 487 U.S., at 835, Penry argues that mentally retarded people do not have the judgment, perspective, and self-control of a person of normal intelligence. In essence, Penry argues that because of his diminished ability to control his impulses, to think in long-range terms, and to learn from his mistakes, he "is not capable of acting with the degree of culpability that can justify the ultimate penalty."

The AAMR and other groups working with the mentally retarded agree with Penry. They argue as *amici* that all mentally retarded people, regardless of their degree of retardation, have substantial cognitive and behavioral disabilities that reduce their level of blameworthiness for a capital offense. *Amici* do not argue that people with mental retardation cannot be held responsible or punished for criminal acts they commit. Rather, they contend that because of "disability in the areas of cognitive impairment, moral reasoning, control of impulsivity, and the ability to understand basic relationships between cause and effect," mentally retarded people cannot act with the level of moral culpability that would justify imposition of the death sentence. Thus, in their view, execution of mentally retarded people convicted of capital offenses serves no valid retributive purpose.

It is clear that mental retardation has long been regarded as a factor that may diminish an individual's culpability for a criminal act. In its most severe forms, mental retardation may result in complete exculpation from criminal responsibility. Moreover, virtually all of the States with death penalty statutes that list statutory mitigating factors include as a mitigating circumstance evidence that "[t]he capacity of the defendant to appreciate the criminality of his conduct or to conform his conduct to the requirements of law was substantially impaired." A number of States explicitly mention "mental defect" in connection with such a mitigating circumstance. Indeed, ... the sentencing body must be allowed to consider mental retardation as a mitigating circumstance in making the individualized determination whether death is the appropriate punishment in a particular case.

On the record before the Court today, however, I cannot conclude that all mentally retarded people of Penry's ability—by virtue of their mental retardation alone, and apart from any individualized consideration of their personal responsibility—inevitably lack the cognitive, volitional, and moral capacity to act with the degree of culpability associated with the death penalty. Mentally retarded persons are individuals whose abilities and experiences can very greatly. As the AAMR's standard work, Classification in Mental Retardation, points out:

> "The term *mental retardation,* as commonly used today, embraces a heterogeneous population, ranging from totally dependent to nearly independent people. Although all individuals so designated share the common attributes of low intelligence and inadequacies in adaptive behavior, there are marked variations in the degree of deficit manifested and the presence or absence of associated physical handicaps, stigmata, and psychologically disordered states."

> — Classification in Mental Retardation, at 12.

In addition to the varying degrees of mental retardation, the consequences of a retarded person's mental impairment, including the deficits in his or her adaptive behavior, "may be ameliorated through education and habilitation." Although retarded persons generally have difficulty learning from experience, some are fully "capable of learning, working, and living in their communities." In light of the diverse capacities and life experiences of mentally retarded persons, it cannot be said on the record before us today that all mentally retarded people, by definition, can never act with the level of culpability associated with the death penalty. *Penry* urges us to rely on the concept of "mental age," and to hold that execution of any person with a mental age of seven or below would constitute cruel and unusual punishment. Mental age is "calculated as the chronological age of nonretarded children whose average IQ test performance is equivalent to that of the individual with mental retardation." Such a rule should not be adopted today. First, there was no finding below by the judge or jury concerning Penry's "mental age." One of Penry's expert witnesses, Dr. Brown, testified that he estimated Penry's "mental age" to be 6½. That same expert estimated that Penry's "social maturity" was that of a 9- or 10-year-old. As a more general matter, the "mental age" concept, irrespective of its intuitive appeal, is problematic in several respects. As the AAMR acknowledges, "[t]he equivalence between nonretarded children and retarded adults is, of course, imprecise." The "mental age" concept may underestimate the life experiences of retarded adults, while it may overestimate the ability of retarded adults to use logic and foresight to solve problems. The mental age concept has other limitations as well. Beyond the chronological age of 15 or 16, the mean scores on most intelligence tests cease to increase significantly with age. As a result, "[t]he average mental age of the average 20 year old is not 20 but 15 years." See also In re Ramon M., 22 Cal. 3d 419, 429, 584 P.2d 524, 531 (1978) ("[T]he 'mental age' of the average adult under present norms is approximately 16 years and 8 months").

Not surprisingly, courts have long been reluctant to rely on the concept of mental age as a basis for exculpating a defendant from criminal responsibility. Moreover, reliance on mental age to measure the capabilities of a retarded person for purposes of the Eighth Amendment could have a disempowering effect if applied in other areas of the law. Thus, on that premise, a mildly mentally retarded person could be denied the opportunity to enter into contracts or to marry by virtue of the fact that he had a "mental age" of a young child. In light of the inherent problems with the mental age concept, and in the absence of better evidence of a national consensus against execution of the retarded, mental age should not be adopted as a line-drawing principle in our Eighth Amendment jurisprudence.

In sum, mental retardation is a factor that may well lessen a defendant's culpability for a capital offense. But we cannot conclude today that the Eighth Amendment precludes the execution of any mentally retarded person of Penry's ability convicted of a capital offense simply by virtue of his or her mental retardation alone. So long as sentencers can consider and give effect to mitigating evidence of mental retardation in imposing sentence, an individualized determination whether "death is the appropriate punishment" can be made in each particular case. While a national consensus against execution of the mentally retarded may someday emerge reflecting the "evolving standards of decency that mark the progress of a maturing society," there is insufficient evidence of such a consensus today.

Accordingly, the judgment below is affirmed in part and reversed in part, and the case is remanded for further proceedings consistent with this opinion.

It is so ordered.

Brief Amicus Curiae of the American Bar Association in Support of Petitioner

Introduction and Summary of Argument

"Whatever you think about the death penalty, a system that will take life must first give justice." With these few words, former ABA [American Bar Association] President John J. Curtin Jr. summarized the ABA's view of the death penalty. The ABA takes no position on the constitutionality or appropriateness of the death penalty as a general matter, but maintains that sentencing individuals with mental retardation to death erodes the integrity of the criminal justice system.

Over the past 12 years—since this Court held, in *Penry v. Lynaugh,* 492 U.S. 302 (1989) (*"Penry I"*), that the Eighth Amendment does not bar the execution of defendants with mental retardation—the ABA has used its unique perspective to analyze the impact of these executions on the criminal justice system. That focus has reinforced the ABA's policy that allowing defendants with mental retardation to be sentenced to death undercuts efforts to ensure that the death penalty is implemented in a fair manner. The purpose of this brief is to highlight some of the numerous concerns that have led the ABA unequivocally to oppose the execution of individuals with mental retardation.

In particular, such defendants are far too likely to lack adequate representation, to be convicted and sentenced to death despite being innocent, and to be sentenced to death by fact-finders who do not or cannot give appropriate mitigating weight to the defendants' mental retardation. The criminal justice system is incapable of affording society sufficient assurance that defendants with mental retardation receive adequate representation, because their condition adversely affects the defense process. Similarly, individuals with mental retardation are at a significant risk of being convicted and sentenced to death for crimes they did not commit, again as the result of their condition and the myriad ways that condition decreases the likelihood of an effective defense. Furthermore, even after the Court's ruling in *Penry I* (492 U.S. at 328), it remains

From Brief Amicus Curiae of the American Bar Association in Support of Petitioner, *Ernest Paul McCarver v. State of North Carolina,* No. 00-8727 (June 6, 2001). Notes omitted.

uniquely difficult to present evidence of mental retardation at the penalty phase and to ensure that it will be considered by the sentencer and given mitigating effect. Only a prohibition against the imposition of the death penalty on individuals with mental retardation will protect the criminal justice system and also be consistent with "contemporary standards of decency" (1989 ABA Report, *supra;* App. A1), and the decreased culpability of mentally retarded defendants (*ibid.;* App. A5).

Argument

Drawing on its experience as an association of lawyers, many of whom confront the death-penalty system on a day-to-day basis as prosecutors and defense attorneys, the ABA adopted its policy opposing the execution of individuals with mental retardation. The unique disability of mental retardation warrants a complete exemption from capital punishment.

I. Allowing Defendants With Mental Retardation to Be Executed Subverts the Integrity of the Adversarial System

The ABA has long expressed concern about the prevalence of underfunded and unqualified lawyers in the capital context. These problems unfortunately are magnified many times over in cases involving defendants with mental retardation. See Richard J. Bonnie, The Competency of Defendants With Mental Retardation to Assist in Their Own Defense, in RONALD W. CONLEY ET AL., THE CRIMINAL JUSTICE SYSTEM AND MENTAL RETARDATION 97, 99-100 (1992). Even counsel whose performance would otherwise be competent may provide inadequate representation to a person with mental retardation. Defense counsel, prosecutors, and judges all need to recognize, as former Attorney General Richard Thornburgh explained, that "people with mental retardation cannot be 'processed' exactly like others who come into contact with our criminal justice system because, for them, it may be a system they do not understand or a system that does not understand them." Richard Thornburgh, Foreword, in CONLEY ET AL., *supra,* at xi, xvi. The reality is that counsel typically have little or no knowledge of mental retardation, and do not recognize the countless ways in which their clients are unable to comprehend, much less deal with, the justice system. The result of this failure can be catastrophic—innocent defendants sentenced to death; important mitigating evidence never presented to juries; and an erosion of confidence in the fairness of our criminal justice system. Nor would attempting to educate counsel solve these problems, for many are inherent in the interaction between the mentally retarded and all the participants in our criminal justice system—defense counsel, prosecutors, judges, and juries.

A. Imposition of the Death Penalty on Defendants With Mental Retardation Pervasively Undermines the Reliability of the Justice System

"The finality of the death penalty requires 'a greater degree of reliability' when it is imposed." *Murray v. Giarratano,* 492 U.S. 1, 8–9 (1989) (plurality op. of Rehnquist, C. J.) quoting *Lockett v. Ohio,* 438 U.S. 586, 604 (1978); see also, e.g., *Woodson v. North Carolina,* 428 U.S. 280, 305 (1976) (plurality op. of Stewart, J.) ("Because of [the] qualitative difference [between death and a sentence of imprisonment], there is a corresponding difference in the need for reliability in the determination that death is the appropriate punishment in a specific case."). But when individuals with mental retardation stand trial, we lack adequate certainty of guilt and moral culpability for death sentences to be acceptable under the parameters of the Eighth Amendment.

It is well documented that ineffective representation is commonplace in death penalty cases. For this among other reasons, recent studies have shown, two thirds or more of death sentences are eventually reversed on appeal or through post-conviction proceedings—and numerous other cases in which justice was denied slip by, never caught by the system. While neither the exact extent of this problem nor many of its underlying reasons are relevant for present purposes, it is plain that the prevalence of incompetent representation in capital cases is gravely exacerbated when defendants suffer from mental retardation. In cases involving defendants who suffer from mental retardation, there is such a decrease in reliability of conviction and sentence that the result is a criminal justice system in which no one can invest adequate confidence to warrant imposition of the death penalty.

1. All too frequently, counsel never realize their client is an individual with mental retardation. Many such defendants actively attempt to mask their disability behind a "cloak of competence" in an unfortunate, but often successful, effort to "pass" with the countless defense attorney, prosecutors, and judges who lack understanding of mental retardation. As an appellate attorney for mentally retarded capital defendant Limmie Arthur explained after Arthur's impairment was discovered post-trial, "retarded people who function at [his] level are good at one thing and one thing only and that is covering up their disability. . . . A lawyer or prosecutor or judge talking to him is not going to realize that he is talking to a retarded person." Joseph Frazier, Too Retarded to Die for Crimes? Laws Say No, L.A. TIMES, Apr. 17, 1988, at 22.

Counsel are also misled by their preconceived notions of mental retardation, which are biased toward the stereotypical Hollywood portrayals of pronounced, physically identifiable examples of this disorder. Thus, when faced with a more typical case, counsel generally do not comprehend that the behavior they are observing is symptomatic of mental retardation and highly significant. See Denis W. Keyes et al., Mitigating Mental Retardation in Capital Cases: Finding the "Invisible" Defendant, 22 MENTAL & PHYSICAL DISABILITIES L. REP. 529, 530 (1998). What lawyers "see" may not seem abnormal to them, because most defendants with mental retardation appear fairly "normal," lacking the "atypical facial features," "obviously different" dress, and other characteristics both "commonly found among people with severe retardation" and expected by untrained observers. *Id.* at 531. The outward manifestations of mental retardation are in most cases far more subtle than counsel and courts expect, and hence more difficult to detect and understand. But though the behavioral signs may be subtle, the impact of mental retardation on the defense of the client and the fairness of the judicial process is, as we discuss below, dramatic.

2. Equally well established is the fact that individuals with mental retardation will sometimes confess to crimes they never committed. Ten years ago, then-Attorney General Thornburgh described a hypothetical defendant with mental retardation: "the man who has confessed to something he did not do because he did not understand his Miranda rights and because he wanted to please those questioning him" (see Thornburgh, Foreword, *supra,* at xv). But such cases are far from hypothetical, and are a predictable outcome when individuals with mental retardation become enmeshed in our criminal justice system. Individuals with mental retardation often make a concerted effort to please authority figures. In their normal, day-to-day lives this behavior is a harmless or even beneficial coping mechanism. When, however, the authorities whom an individual with mental retardation seeks to please are interrogators set on obtaining a confession, the result can be a tragic miscarriage of justice. Standard 7-5.8 of the ABA's Criminal Justice Mental Health Standards therefore admonishes courts to question the reliability and voluntariness of confessions by individuals with mental retardation. Standard 7-5.9 stresses that when such individuals waive rights, such as the Miranda rights, such waivers might not be knowing, intelligent, and voluntary. But such warnings have proven to be of little effect when a confession is presented to a judge or jury considering a hideous crime, especially when no one has successfully diagnosed the existence or extent of the accused's mental retardation.

3. Mental retardation also frequently interferes with the development of a meaningful relationship between client and attorney, and with the ability of counsel to represent the client adequately. For example, "clients with mental retardation tend to act as though they understand their attorneys when they do not, and to bias with responses in favor of what they believe their attorneys want them to say or in the direction of concrete, though inaccurate, responses." Richard J. Bonnie, The Competence of Criminal Defendants With Mental Retardation to Participate in Their Own Defense, 81 J. CRIM. L. & CRIMINOLOGY 419, 423 [*12] (1990). The result is that attorneys may be misled by clients with mental retardation, believing responses that have little or nothing to do with the actual facts of the crime and everything to do with the defendant's mental retardation. Counsel also tend to "spend less time interviewing clients with mental retardation when more time is really needed" because of the ways the client's mental retardation affects his responses. *Ibid.*

Many individuals with mental retardation also find it difficult to recall information that might help an attorney, or have difficulty answering open-ended questions. See Ellis & Luckasson, *supra,* 53 GEO. WASH. L. REV. at 428–429. Similarly, where a client without this disability would be able to assist in his or her own defense, most defendants with mental retardation are hapless bystanders to a process they simply cannot comprehend, "in no position to monitor the attorney's performance even in a superficial way" (Bonnie, Competence of Criminal Defendants, *supra,* 81 J. CRIM. L. & CRIMINOLOGY at 423), and unable to provide even a rudimentary check on their attorney's defense strategy.

4. The courtroom demeanor of an individual with mental retardation can also become a prejudicial factor in his or her conviction and sentencing, despite being a direct result of mental retardation rather than demonstrative of a culpable mental state, guilt, or lack of remorse. Thus, the prosecutor in Herbert Welcome's trial "cited Herbert's smiles as evidence that he lacked remorse," even though they simply reflected an overly-well-learned reflex to smile in order to gain the approval of others. See ROBERT PERSKE, UNEQUAL JUSTICE 19 (1991). Johnny Penry "sat at the defense table and drew pictures" while the prosecutor summed up why Penry should be sentenced to die. *Id.* at 21–22. And mentally retarded defendant Anthony Porter, sentenced to death but later determined to be innocent (see page 14, *infra*), "walks into a room slowly, real cool, like some streetwise punk, a smirk on his face, eyes shifting back and forth, as if he's on to something or in on a big secret" (Eric Zorn, Questions Persist as Troubled Inmate Faces Execution, CHI. TRIB., Sept. 21, 1998, at 1 (quotation marks omitted))—clearly inappropriate behavior from someone accused of a heinous crime. Juries do not understand that this seemingly inculpatory behavior during a capital trial is not the result of callousness, consciousness of guilt or lack of remorse, but merely fairly common and predictable conduct for an individual with mental retardation *irrespective* of culpability or "death-worthiness."

The net result of these problems is inevitable: taken together, the behavioral patterns of mentally retarded defendants, the all-too-common deficient performance of defense counsel, and ignorance and misperceptions about mental retardation on the part of all participants in the criminal justice system produce miscarriages of justice. Innocent defendants are convicted and sentenced to die; juries reach death verdicts uninformed about the defendant's mental retardation; and, more generally, counsel are significantly less able to provide competent representation than when representing defendants who do not have this disability. See Bonnie, Competency of Defendants, *supra,* at 100.

B. Numerous Defendants With Mental Retardation Have Been Sentenced to Death Despite Their Innocence

The factors described above have caused numerous individuals with mental retardation to be convicted and sentenced to die for crimes they did not commit:

- Mentally retarded defendant Albert Ronnie Burrell spent 13 years on death row in Louisiana, convicted on the basis of evidence that unraveled after he was sentenced to death.

- Burrell's case was the subject of a recent three-part newspaper article, Christopher Baughman & Tom Guarisco, Justice for None, THE [BATON ROUGE] ADVOCATE, March 18–20, 2001.
- Mentally retarded defendant Alejandro Hernandez was freed in 1995, after spending 10 years in prison, some of them on death row, for a crime another person later confessed to committing.
- Mentally retarded defendant Anthony Porter, who at one point came within *two days* of execution, was later proven to be innocent by journalism students engaged in a class project. The discovery of Porter's innocence was a key factor in Illinois Governor George Ryan's decision to institute a state-wide moratorium on executions.

Moreover, Attorney General Thornburgh's hypothetical defendant "who has confessed to something he did not do" is prescient of real-life cases of individuals sentenced to die for crimes they did not commit. The case of mentally retarded defendant Earl Washington, Jr., is a particularly illuminating example of how a suspect's mental retardation can lead to miscarriages of justice. In 1983, Washington confessed to the brutal rape and murder of Rebecca Lynn Williams; based on that confession he was convicted and sentenced to death. In October 2000, DNA testing proved that Washington had not been involved in the crime, despite his confession. Thus, seventeen years after his conviction —almost ten of them spent on Virginia's death row—Washington was pardoned and released.

Indeed, it is not unusual for individuals with mental retardation to give false confessions. Other individuals with mental retardation have confessed to crimes they did not commit and thereafter have pleaded guilty in order to avoid a capital trial. For example, mentally retarded defendant Johnny Lee Wilson was charged with capital murder in Missouri after being coaxed into confessing to a crime by interrogators who fed him the answers that suggested his guilt. Because of that confession Wilson's attorneys pressed him to plead guilty, a plea that was accepted despite serious questions about whether Wilson understood what he was doing. A decade later, Missouri Governor Mel Carnahan pardoned Wilson because of conclusive evidence that another person had committed the crime, and declared "it is evident that the only facts this mentally retarded man knew about this hideous crime were the facts given to him by investigators who felt pressure to solve the case quickly." Similarly, mentally retarded defendant David Vasquez was charged with capital murder in Virginia after "confessing" to the crime as described to him by his interrogators. He pleaded guilty to second-degree murder to avoid the death penalty, and spent five years in prison before the actual perpetrator was discovered and Vasquez was pardoned.

Mental retardation is the common factor in these examples of justice denied. In each case, it was the defendant's mental retardation, combined with the serious ways in which such retardation undermined the legal process, that almost caused an innocent person to be executed. Without understanding or even knowing about a client's mental retardation, both prosecutors and defense counsel will presume that a confession is reliable. Police and prosecutors may therefore not investigate other leads, and, without the client's active and adequate assistance, defense counsel will have even less ability to discover evidence that might point to another as the guilty party or otherwise lead to a client's acquittal. And without evidence of mental retardation and a sophisticated grasp of its significance, counsel will be hard pressed to convince a jury that a defendant's confession might not be reliable or that his courtroom demeanor might reflect something other than culpability.

C. *Penry I* Does Not Ensure That Evidence of Mental Retardation Will Be Developed in Sentencing Proceedings or Treated as a Mitigating Factor

Central to this Court's holding in *Penry I* is that a defendant's mental retardation must receive serious consideration as a mitigating factor. Individuals with mental retardation have a diminished understanding of cause and effect, the law, and criminal processes; a lessened ability to control their impulses; and less developed moral reasoning. But all too frequently, evidence of the defendant's mental retardation is not presented to the judge and jury; and even when such evidence is presented, it is rarely given appropriate mitigating weight. This systemic problem is again the inevitable consequence of the very nature of mental retardation. The result is predictable and tragic: death sentences for, and executions of, individuals who should not have been sentenced to die.

There are numerous examples of cases in which *no* evidence of a defendant's mental retardation was ever provided at the penalty phase, even though subsequent investigation demonstrated that there was ample evidence that should have been introduced. Not infrequently, the failure to present such evidence is caused in one way or another by the defendant's disability. All instances in which evidence of mental retardation is not offered, regardless of cause, constitute grave injustices. Such cases necessarily are fundamentally unfair to individuals with mental retardation and inconsistent with this Court's expectation that a defendant's sentence be based on a "reasoned moral response to the defendant's background, character, and crime" (*Penry I*, 492 U.S. at 319 (emphasis in original) (quoting *California v. Brown*, 479 U.S. 538, 545 (1987)) (O'Connor, J., concurring)).

In at least two of the cases discussed above—where an innocent defendant with mental retardation was sentenced to death—the jury was never told of the defendant's mental disability. Anthony Porter's original trial lawyer did not realize that his client was mentally retarded, and so never offered it as a mitigating factor. Similarly, Ronnie Burrell's trial attorneys never raised his mental retardation at trial, even though he "cannot read or write and spent years in a school for the retarded."

Quite apart from cases of actual innocence, in numerous instances judges and juries are never even told of a capital defendant's mental retardation as a mitigating circumstance, let alone educated about that evidence's significance.

In these situations, the combination of inadequate defense counsel and the defendant's disability casts doubt on the fundamental fairness of the system:

- Jerome Bowden's execution in 1986 led Georgia to enact the first statute barring the death penalty for individuals with mental retardation. Despite the fact that Bowden was unable to read or count to ten, his trial lawyers presented no evidence of his mental retardation to the jury.
- The jury that sentenced Mario Marquez to death never heard about "his severe childhood abuse, mental retardation, and brain damage." Instead, they saw a handcuffed and visibly shackled defendant. He was executed in 1995.
- Horace Dunkins was sentenced to death in Alabama, without any evidence of his mental retardation ever being presented to the jury. Shortly before his execution, when facts about his mental retardation became public, a trial juror signed an affidavit stating that she would not have voted for his execution had she known of his mental disability. Dunkins was nonetheless executed in 1989.
- No testimony about Ramon Martinez-Villareal's mental retardation was presented at trial. "The sentencing judge in Martinez-Villareal's case has said he would have given him life in prison if he'd known the severity of his mental problems. In addition, Martinez-Villareal's original prosecutor also has come out against the execution, saying he was unaware of Martinez-Villareal's mental retardation." Martinez-Villareal remains on death row.
- Jerome Holloway signed a murder confession he could not read. After the Georgia Supreme Court vacated his conviction and death sentence because the lower court had not held a competency hearing, the prosecution agreed not to seek another death sentence—at least in part because of Holloway's mental retardation.
- Limmie Arthur was convicted and sentenced to die after a trial in which his mental disability went unrecognized, even by his own attorney. After his trial, Arthur "believed that he was sentenced to death because he couldn't read, [and] diligently tried to learn so he could earn his GED because he thought he would get a reprieve if he was successful." When his mental retardation became known, the South Carolina Supreme Court overturned his death sentence, ruling that he had not voluntarily waived his right to a jury trial. Prosecutors then agreed to accept a term of life imprisonment.

These cases highlight just some of the ways in which our system of capital punishment fails to safeguard against wrongful convictions, wrongful death sentences, and wrongful executions of the mentally retarded. First, the instances discussed above represent only that subset of cases in which, at some point in time, a defendant's mental retardation was discovered—not the countless other cases in which no such fortuitous revelation occurred. Second, many defendants with mental retardation are represented by incompetent defense counsel, who fail to perform even rudimentary tasks adequately. Third, in some number of cases under the current system even competent counsel may be choosing not to present evidence of mental retardation because of the tendency such evidence has to act as a two-edged sword (see *Penry I*, 492 U.S. at 324). Fourth, defendants with mental retardation may be actively trying to hide their mental disability, and thus even competent counsel may not realize that they represent such individuals. This veneer of normality regularly leads counsel not to present critical evidence of mental retardation *even where* that counsel otherwise is competent, attentive, and provided with adequate resources to undertake a capital defense.

A critical aspect of many of the cases discussed above is that once these individuals' mental retardation became known, many involved in their initial sentencing considered those sentences to be unjust. Holloway and Arthur have been removed from death row. While Martinez-Villareal remains on death row, the original prosecutor and judge have stated that they oppose his execution. Had Dunkins' mental retardation been mentioned at trial, at least one juror would not have voted for a death sentence. And the outcry over Bowden's execution was sufficient to lead the Georgia legislature to pass the first statutory bar to all such executions.

Thus, when evidence of mental retardation is found, even years later, it commonly alters the views of those involved in a defendant's sentencing. All too frequently, however, for the reasons discussed above, evidence of mental retardation is not presented at either phase of capital traits.

II. Only Prohibition of Capital Punishment for Individuals With Mental Retardation Will Protect Society's Interest in a Fair Criminal Justice System and Accord With Contemporary Standards of Decency

The ABA first pressed for a ban on the execution of individuals with mental retardation in 1989. Such executions violate "contemporary standards of decency" (1989 ABA Report; App. A1), and are inherently disproportionate to the culpability of such defendants (*ibid.;* App. A5). Furthermore, the criminal justice system simply cannot adequately "ensure the fairness of . . . death sentences [for mentally retarded defendants]." Death Without Justice, *supra.*

This brief has not attempted to address all or even many of the numerous reasons why the basic concerns of the Eighth Amendment cannot be satisfied without excluding persons with mental retardation, as a class, from capital punishment. Instead, in Part I, we have illustrated some of the miscarriages of justice that have occurred to mentally retarded defendants under the current system. And these disastrous outcomes will continue to occur unless the present scheme is changed.

As this Court has said, "the finality of the death penalty requires 'a greater degree of reliability' when it is imposed." *Murray,* 492 U.S. at 8–9 (plurality op. of Rehnquist, C.J.) (quoting *Lockett,* 438 U.S. at 604). The very nature of this mental disability is such, however, that greater reliability in the administration of justice cannot be achieved as long as individuals with mental retardation are subject to the death penalty. False confessions, uninvestigated leads, mitigating evidence never presented, the wrong individuals convicted, and individuals improperly sentenced to die are inevitable outcomes.

Given the examples discussed in this brief, it is unsurprising that more and more states have acted to bar the execution of mentally retarded defendants: Fourteen states and the federal government have now enacted legislation prohibiting the death penalty for such defendants. Similarly, at least 100 countries now bar, by treaty or legislation, the execution of persons with mental retardation. Of the remaining nations, all but three—Kyrgyzstan, Japan, and the United States—avoid such executions as a matter of practice. Thus there is an emerging consensus of nations as well to prohibit the execution of persons with mental retardation.

Even though many of the mentally retarded defendants discussed in this brief were never executed—some who were innocent have been released, and some have been removed from death row—the system as it presently functions fails to assure fundamental fairness. The defendants discussed here are merely those whose circumstances, through fortuity, were brought to light. Unfortunately the very nature of mental retardation makes other similar miscarriages of justice inevitable. Recognition that the Constitution bars the execution of the mentally retarded is the only means available to protect the defendants of whose plight we may otherwise never learn until it is too late.

Conclusion

For the foregoing reasons, the ABA respectfully submits that the Eighth Amendment should be held to prohibit the imposition or execution of a death sentence upon any individual with mental retardation, including Ernest McCarver.

Respectfully Submitted.

POSTSCRIPT

Is It Constitutional to Impose the Death Penalty on the Mentally Retarded?

In her opinion for the Court in the 1989 *Penry* case (*Penry I*), O'Connor stated that the execution of mentally retarded individuals is permissible for two reasons. First, although the Eighth Amendment prohibits punishments considered cruel and unusual at the time the Bill of Rights was adopted, the execution of a person of the accused's moderate degree of mental retardation was not categorically prohibited against punishing "idiots" or "lunatics" for their crimes. Second, although the Eighth Amendment categorically prohibits punishments considered cruel and unusual under evolving societal standards of decency, there was insufficient evidence of a national consensus against the execution of mentally retarded people convicted of capital cases.

While the first reason may still hold true, many recent polls have found that a majority of the population is against the execution of those with mental retardation. A February 2001 nationwide poll by the *Houston Chronicle* even found that only 16 percent of death penalty advocates support executing the mentally retarded. Almost 20 states now bar the execution of people with mental retardation. Congress has also prohibited application of the death penalty to federal defendants with mental retardation.

Although O'Connor has refused to find that capital punishment is cruel and unusual, she recently publicly questioned the fairness of the death penalty. "If statistics are any indication," she stated, "the system may well be allowing some innocent defendants to be executed." She noted that 6 death row inmates were exonerated and released in 2000, and 90 have been exonerated and set free since 1973. While DNA testing could be helpful, O'Connor also noted that most states with capital punishment have not passed laws addressing postconviction testing.

General information about pro and con positions on the death penalty can be found online at http://sun.soci.niu.edu/~critcrim/dp/pro/pro.html and http://www.ncadp.org. The Death Penalty Information Center, at http://www.deathpenaltyinfo.org, also provides comprehensive statistics about the use of capital punishment in the United States and has set up http://www.deathpenaltyinfo.org/dpicmr.html specifically to address the topic of the mentally disabled and the death penalty. Human Rights Watch recently published a report criticizing the United States for continuing to use capital punishment against the mentally disabled. The report, entitled "Beyond Reason: The Death Penalty and Offenders With Mental Retardation," is available online at http://www.hrw.org/reports/2001/ustat/. Finally, the friends and family of Pamela Moseley Carpenter, whom Penry raped and murdered, set up an online memorial for her at http://www.murdervictims.com/Voices/pamela_carpenter.htm.

ISSUE 12

Is It Constitutionally Permissible to Detain "Sexually Dangerous" Individuals After They Have Served Their Prison Sentences?

YES: Clarence Thomas, from Majority Opinion, *Kansas v. Hendricks*, U.S. Supreme Court (June 23, 1997)

NO: Stephen G. Breyer, from Dissenting Opinion, *Kansas v. Hendricks*, U.S. Supreme Court (June 23, 1997)

ISSUE SUMMARY

YES: Supreme Court justice Clarence Thomas finds that a Kansas law that allows civil commitment of "mentally abnormal" persons is constitutional and does not violate the Constitution's double jeopardy prohibition or its ban on ex post facto lawmaking.

NO: Supreme Court justice Stephen G. Breyer finds that the Kansas law was an effort to inflict further punishment upon Leroy Hendricks and that the ex post facto clause should apply since Hendricks committed his crimes prior to its enactment.

Recent FBI statistics suggest that major metropolitan areas are witnessing a decrease in the commission of violent crimes. Yet many Americans feel more concerned for their safety and, in particular, for the safety and well-being of their children than ever before. This is partly because people have been inundated by media coverage of horrible crimes committed against the most vulnerable segment of the population. States and local communities have struggled with the legal and public policy questions of how to protect citizens from the most dangerous and predatory members of society. Certainly, longer prison terms for those convicted of such crimes has been one response, as has the diminished availability (or outright elimination) of parole.

Ultimately, however, most of those who have been convicted of even the most serious of crimes serve their time and are released back into the community. For those who have been rehabilitated, or who have found the means to provide for themselves and lead a productive life within society's legal framework, so much the better. But what about those who persist in or are unable to control deviant behavior? How should society protect itself from the risks posed by these dangerous individuals? The readings that follow concern just such an issue. They are drawn from the majority and dissenting opinions of the U.S. Supreme Court in which *Kansas v. Hendricks* was decided in 1997.

Kansas v. Hendricks concerns the constitutionality of the Sexually Violent Predator Act, a 1994 Kansas law that permitted the indefinite and involuntary *civil* commitment of "sexually violent predators." This class of individuals was defined as those who have been "convicted of or charged with a sexually violent offense" and who suffer from a "mental abnormality or personality disorder" that renders them "likely to engage in predatory acts of sexual violence." Prior to the enactment of the Kansas law, Leroy Hendricks had been convicted of various sexual offenses against children. Hendricks repeatedly insisted that he was unable to control his pedophilic impulses. As he neared the end of a 5- to 20-year prison sentence imposed for his most recent offenses against small children, the state of Kansas filed a petition under the 1994 statute that served to classify Hendricks as a "sexually violent predator" and paved the way to his civil commitment upon release from prison.

After civil commitment in a specified Kansas state facility, Hendricks challenged the statute, arguing that it was violative of a broad range of constitutionally protected rights. A sharply divided Kansas Supreme Court agreed with one of Hendricks's claims and struck down the statute because it violated the Fourteenth Amendment's guarantee of due process. However, the majority opinion did not support Hendricks's other constitutional claims: that the statute violated constitutional prohibitions against double jeopardy and ex post facto laws. Consequently, both the state of Kansas and Hendricks requested that the U.S. Supreme Court hear their constitutional claims. The Supreme Court did in fact grant certiorari on both the state's petition challenging the Kansas Supreme Court's analysis of the due process issues and on Hendricks's cross-petition, which argued that the Kansas law, although ostensibly civil in nature, was in fact *criminal*.

In the following selections, Justice Clarence Thomas delivers the majority opinion rejecting all of Hendricks's constitutional claims and thereby reversing the decision of the Kansas Supreme Court. Justice Stephen G. Breyer dissents from the majority's treatment of the double jeopardy and ex post facto claims.

Clarence Thomas  **YES**

Majority Opinion

Kansas *v.* Hendricks

B

We granted Hendricks' cross-petition to determine whether the Act violates the Constitution's double jeopardy prohibition or its ban on *ex post facto* law-making. The thrust of Hendricks' argument is that the Act establishes criminal proceedings; hence confinement under it necessarily constitutes punishment. He contends that where, as here, newly enacted "punishment" is predicated upon past conduct for which he has already been convicted and forced to serve a prison sentence, the Constitution's Double Jeopardy and *Ex Post Facto* Clauses are violated. We are unpersuaded by Hendricks' argument that Kansas has established criminal proceedings. . . .

As a threshold matter, commitment under the Act does not implicate either of the two primary objectives of criminal punishment: retribution or deterrence. The Act's purpose is not retributive because it does not affix culpability for prior criminal conduct. Instead, such conduct is used solely for evidentiary purposes, either to demonstrate that a "mental abnormality" exists or to support a finding of future dangerousness. We have previously concluded that an Illinois statute was nonpunitive even though it was triggered by the commission of a sexual assault, explaining that evidence of the prior criminal conduct was "received not to punish past misdeeds, but primarily to show the accused's mental condition and to predict future behavior." . . .

Moreover, unlike a criminal statute, no finding of scienter is required to commit an individual who is found to be a sexually violent predator; instead, the commitment determination is made based on a "mental abnormality" or "personality disorder" rather than on one's criminal intent. The existence of a scienter requirement is customarily an important element in distinguishing criminal from civil statutes. See *Kennedy v. Mendoza-Martinez,* 372 U.S. 144, 168, 83 S.Ct. 554, 567–568, 9 L.Ed.2d 644 (1963). The absence of such a requirement here is evidence that confinement under the statute is not intended to be retributive.

From *Kansas v. Hendricks,* 117 S. Ct. 2072 (1997).

Nor can it be said that the legislature intended the Act to function as a deterrent. Those persons committed under the Act are, by definition, suffering from a "mental abnormality" or a "personality disorder" that prevents them from exercising adequate control over their behavior. Such persons are therefore unlikely to be deterred by the threat of confinement. And the conditions surrounding that confinement do not suggest a punitive purpose on the State's part. The State has represented that an individual confined under the Act is not subject to the more restrictive conditions placed on state prisoners, but instead experiences essentially the same conditions as any involuntarily committed patient in the state mental institution. App. 50–56, 59–60. Because none of the parties argues that people institutionalized under the Kansas general civil commitment statute are subject to punitive conditions, even though they may be involuntarily confined, it is difficult to conclude that persons confined under this Act are being "punished."

Although the civil commitment scheme at issue here does involve an affirmative restraint, "the mere fact that a person is detained does not inexorably lead to the conclusion that the government has imposed punishment." *United States v. Salerno,* 481 U.S. 739, 746, 107 S.Ct. 2095, 2101, 95 L.Ed.2d 697 (1987). The State may take measures to restrict the freedom of the dangerously mentally ill. This is a legitimate non-punitive governmental objective and has been historically so regarded. Cf. *id.,* at 747, 107 S.Ct., at 2101–2102. The Court has, in fact, cited the confinement of "mentally unstable individuals who present a danger to the public" as one classic example of nonpunitive detention. *Id.,* at 748–749, 107 S.Ct., at 2102–2103. If detention for the purpose of protecting the community from harm *necessarily* constituted punishment, then all involuntary civil commitments would have to be considered punishment. But we have never so held.

Hendricks focuses on his confinement's potentially indefinite duration as evidence of the State's punitive intent. That focus, however, is misplaced. Far from any punitive objective, the confinement's duration is instead linked to the stated purposes of the commitment, namely, to hold the person until his mental abnormality no longer causes him to be a threat to others. Cf. *Jones,* 463 U.S., at 368, 103 S.Ct., at 3051–3052 (noting with approval that "because it is impossible to predict how long it will take for any given individual to recover [from insanity]—or indeed whether he will ever recover—Congress has chosen . . . to leave the length of commitment indeterminate, subject to periodic review of the patient's suitability for release"). If, at any time, the confined person is adjudged "safe to be at large," he is statutorily entitled to immediate release. Kan. Stat. Ann. § 59–29a07 (1994).

Furthermore, commitment under the Act is only *potentially* indefinite. The maximum amount of time an individual can be incapacitated pursuant to a single judicial proceeding is one year. § 59–29a08. If Kansas seeks to continue the detention beyond that year, a court must once again determine beyond a reasonable doubt that the detainee satisfies the same standards as required for the initial confinement. *Ibid.* This requirement again demonstrates that Kansas does not intend an individual committed pursuant to the Act to remain confined any longer than he suffers from a mental abnormality rendering him unable to control his dangerousness....

Finally, Hendricks argues that the Act is necessarily punitive because it fails to offer any legitimate "treatment." Without such treatment, Hendricks asserts, confinement under the Act amounts to little more than disguised punishment. Hendricks' argument assumes that treatment for his condition is available, but that the State has failed (or refused) to provide it. The Kansas Supreme Court, however, apparently rejected this assumption, explaining:

> "It is clear that the overriding concern of the legislature is to continue the segregation of sexually violent offenders from the public. Treatment with the goal of reintegrating them into society is incidental, at best. The record reflects that treatment for sexually violent predators is all but nonexistent. The legislature concedes that sexually violent predators are not amenable to treatment under [the existing Kansas involuntary commitment statute]. If there is nothing to treat under [that statute], then there is no mental illness. In that light, the provisions of the Act for treatment appear somewhat disingenuous." 259 Kan., at 258, 912 P.2d, at 136.

It is possible to read this passage as a determination that Hendricks' condition was *untreatable* under the existing Kansas civil commitment statute, and thus the Act's sole purpose was incapacitation. Absent a treatable mental illness, the Kansas court concluded, Hendricks could not be detained against his will.

Accepting the Kansas court's apparent determination that treatment is not possible for this category of individuals does not obligate us to adopt its legal conclusions. We have already observed that, under the appropriate circumstances and when accompanied by proper procedures, incapacitation may be a legitimate end of the civil law. See *Allen, supra,* at 373, 106 S.Ct., at 2994; *Salerno,* 481 U.S., at 748–749, 107 S.Ct., at 2102–2103. Accordingly, the Kansas court's determination that the Act's "overriding concern" was the continued "segregation of sexually violent offenders" is consistent with our conclusion that the Act establishes civil proceedings, 259 Kan., at 258, 912 P.2d, at 136, especially when the concern is coupled with the State's ancillary goal of providing treatment to those offenders, if such is possible. While we have upheld state civil commitment statutes that aim both to incapacitate and to treat, see *Allen, supra,* we have never held that the Constitution prevents a State from civilly detaining those for whom no treatment is available, but who nevertheless pose a danger to others. A State could hardly be seen as furthering a "punitive" purpose by involuntarily confining persons afflicted with an untreatable, highly contagious disease. Accord *Compagnie Francaise de Navigation a Vapeur v. Louisiana Bd. of Health,* 186 U.S. 380, 22 S.Ct. 811, 46 L.Ed. 1209 (1902) (permitting involuntary quarantine of persons suffering from communicable diseases). Similarly, it would be of little value to require treatment as a precondition for civil confinement of the dangerously insane when no acceptable treatment existed. To conclude otherwise would obligate a State to release certain confined individuals who were both mentally ill and dangerous simply because they could not be successfully treated for their afflictions....

Where the State has "disavowed any punitive intent"; limited confinement to a small segment of particularly dangerous individuals; provided strict procedural safeguards; directed that confined persons be segregated from the general prison population and afforded the same status as others who have been civilly committed; recommended treatment if such is possible; and permitted immediate release upon a showing that the individual is no longer dangerous or mentally impaired, we cannot say that it acted with punitive intent. We therefore hold that the Act does not establish criminal proceedings and that involuntary confinement pursuant to the Act is not punitive. Our conclusion that the Act is nonpunitive thus removes an essential prerequisite for both Hendricks' double jeopardy and *ex post facto* claims.

1

The Double Jeopardy Clause provides: "[N]or shall any person be subject for the same offence to be twice put in jeopardy of life or limb." Although generally understood to preclude a second prosecution for the same offense, the Court has also interpreted this prohibition to prevent the State from "punishing twice, or attempting a second time to punish criminally, for the same offense." *Witte v. United States,* 515 U.S. 389, 396, 115 S.Ct. 2199, 2204, 132 L.Ed.2d 351 (1995) (emphasis and internal quotation marks omitted). Hendricks argues that, as applied to him, the Act violates double jeopardy principles because his confinement under the Act, imposed after a conviction and a term of incarceration, amounted to both a second prosecution and a second punishment for the same offense. We disagree.

Because we have determined that the Kansas Act is civil in nature, initiation of its commitment proceedings does not constitute a second prosecution. Cf. *Jones v. United States,* 463 U.S. 354, 103 S.Ct. 3043, 77 L.Ed.2d 694 (1983) (permitting involuntary civil commitment after verdict of not guilty by reason of insanity). Moreover, as commitment under the Act is not tantamount to "punishment," Hendricks' involuntary detention does not violate the Double Jeopardy Clause, even though that confinement may follow a prison term. Indeed, in *Baxstrom v. Herold,* 383 U.S. 107, 86 S.Ct. 760, 15 L.Ed.2d 620 (1966), we expressly recognized that civil commitment could follow the expiration of a prison term without offending double jeopardy principles. We reasoned that "there is no conceivable basis for distinguishing the commitment of a person who is nearing the end of a penal term from all other civil commitments." *Id.,* at 111–112, 86 S.Ct., at 763. If an individual otherwise meets the requirements for involuntary civil commitment, the State is under no obligation to release that individual simply because the detention would follow a period of incarceration.

Hendricks also argues that even if the Act survives the "multiple punishments" test, it nevertheless fails the "same elements" test of *Blockburger v. United States,* 284 U.S. 299, 52 S.Ct. 180, 76 L.Ed. 306 (1932). Under *Blockburger,* "where the same act or transaction constitutes a violation of two distinct statutory provisions, the test to be applied to determine whether there are two offenses or only one, is whether each provision requires proof of a fact which the other does not." *Id.,* at 304, 52 S.Ct., at 182. The *Blockburger* test, however, simply does not apply outside of the successive prosecution context. A proceeding under the Act does not define an "offense," the elements of which can be compared to the elements of an offense for which the person may previously have been convicted. Nor does the Act make the commission of a specified "offense" the basis for invoking the commitment proceedings. Instead, it uses a prior conviction (or previously charged conduct) for evidentiary purposes to determine whether a person suffers from a "mental abnormality" or "personality disorder" and also poses a threat to the public. Accordingly, we are unpersuaded by Hendricks' novel application of the *Blockburger* test and conclude that the Act does not violate the Double Jeopardy Clause.

2

Hendricks' *ex post facto* claim is similarly flawed. The *Ex Post Facto* Clause, which " 'forbids the application of any new punitive measure to a crime already consummated,' " has been interpreted to pertain exclusively to penal statutes. *California Dept. of Corrections v. Morales,* 514 U.S. 499, 505, 115 S.Ct. 1597, 1601, 131, L.Ed.2d 588 (1995) (quoting *Lindsey v. Washington,* 301 U.S. 397, 401, 57 S.Ct. 797, 799, 81 L.Ed. 1182 (1937)). As we have previously determined, the Act does not impose punishment; thus, its application does not raise *ex post facto* concerns. Moreover, the Act clearly does not have retroactive effect. Rather, the Act permits involuntary confinement based upon a determination that the person *currently* both suffers from a "mental abnormality" or "personality disorder" and is likely to pose a future danger to the public. To the extent that past behavior is taken into account, it is used, as noted above, solely for evidentiary purposes. Because the Act does not criminalize conduct legal before its enactment, nor deprive Hendricks of any defense that was available to him at the time of his crimes, the Act does not violate the *Ex Post Facto* Clause.

III

We hold that the Kansas Sexually Violent Predator Act comports with due process requirements and neither runs afoul of double jeopardy principles nor constitutes an exercise in impermissible *ex post facto* lawmaking. Accordingly, the judgment of the Kansas Supreme Court is reversed.

It is so ordered.

NO ✒

Stephen G. Breyer

Dissenting Opinion of Stephen G. Breyer

II

Kansas' 1994 Act violates the Federal Constitution's prohibition of "any... *ex post facto* Law" if it "inflicts" upon Hendricks "a greater punishment" than did the law "annexed to" his "crime[s]" when he "committed" those crimes in 1984. *Calder v. Bull*, 3 Dall. 386, 390, 1 L.Ed. 648 (1798) (opinion of Chase, J.); U.S. Const., Art. I, § 10. The majority agrees that the Clause " 'forbids the application of any *new punitive measure* to a crime already consummated.' " *California Dept. of Corrections v. Morales*, 514 U.S. 499, 505, 115 S.Ct. 1597, 1601, 131 L.Ed.2d 588 (1995) (citation omitted; emphasis added). *Ante*, at 2086. But it finds the Act is not "punitive." With respect to that basic question, I disagree with the majority.

Certain resemblances between the Act's "civil commitment" and traditional criminal punishments are obvious. Like criminal imprisonment, the Act's civil commitment amounts to "secure" confinement, Kan. Stat. Ann. § 59–29a07(a) (1994), and "incarceration against one's will." *In re Gault*, 387 U.S. 1, 50, 87 S.Ct. 1428, 1455, 18 L.Ed.2d 527 (1967). See Testimony of Terry Davis, SRS Director of Quality Assurance (App. 52–54, 78–81) (confinement takes place in the psychiatric wing of a prison hospital where those whom the Act confines and ordinary prisoners are treated alike). Cf. *Browning-Ferris Industries of Vt., Inc. v. Kelco Disposal, Inc.* 492 U.S. 257, 298, 109 S.Ct. 2909, 2932, 106 L.Ed.2d 219 (1989) (O'CONNOR, J., concurring in part and dissenting in part). In addition, a basic objective of the Act is incapacitation, which, as Blackstone said in describing an objective of criminal law, is to "depriv[e] the party injuring of the power to do future mischief." 4 W. Blackstone, Commentaries *11–*12 (incapacitation is one important purpose of criminal punishment); see also *Foucha*, 504 U.S., at 99, 112 S.Ct., at 1795 (KENNEDY, J., dissenting) ("Incapacitation for the protection of society is not an unusual ground for incarceration"); *United States v. Brown*, 381 U.S. 437, 458, 85 S.Ct. 1707, 1720, 14 L.Ed.2d 484 (1965) (punishment's "purposes: retributive, rehabilitative, deterrent—and preventative. One of the reasons society imprisons those convicted of crimes is to keep them from inflicting future harm, but that does not make imprisonment any the less punishment"); 1 W. LaFave & A. Scott, Substantive Criminal Law § 1.5, p. 32 (1986);

From *Kansas v. Hendricks*, 117 S. Ct. 2072 (1997). Some case citations omitted.

18 U.S.C. § 3553(a); United States Sentencing Guidelines, Guidelines Manual, ch. 1, pt. A (Nov. 1995).

Moreover, the Act, like criminal punishment, imposes its confinement (or sanction) only upon an individual who has previously committed a criminal offense. Kan. Stat. Ann. §§ 59–29a02(a), 59–29a03(a) (1994). Cf. *Department of Revenue of Mont. v. Kurth Ranch,* 511 U.S. 767, 781, 114 S.Ct. 1937, 1947, 128 L.Ed.2d 767 (1994) (fact that a tax on marijuana was "conditioned on the commission of a crime" is " 'significant of [its] penal and prohibitory intent' ") (citation omitted); *Lipke v. Lederer,* 259 U.S. 557, 561–562, 42 S.Ct. 549, 550–551, 66 L.Ed. 1061 (1922). And the Act imposes that confinement through the use of persons (county prosecutors), procedural guarantees (trial by jury, assistance of counsel, psychiatric evaluations), and standards ("beyond a reasonable doubt") traditionally associated with the criminal law. Kan. Stat. Ann. §§ 59–29a06, 59–29a07 (1994).

These obvious resemblances by themselves, however, are not legally sufficient to transform what the Act calls "civil commitment" into a criminal punishment. Civil commitment of dangerous, mentally ill individuals by its very nature involves confinement and incapacitation. Yet "civil commitment," from a constitutional perspective, nonetheless remains civil. *Allen v. Illinois,* 478 U.S. 364, 369–370, 106 S.Ct. 2988, 2992–2993, 92 L.Ed.2d 296 (1986). Nor does the fact that criminal behavior triggers the Act make the critical difference. The Act's insistence upon a prior crime, by screening out those whose past behavior does not concretely demonstrate the existence of a mental problem or potential future danger, may serve an important noncriminal evidentiary purpose. Neither is the presence of criminal law-type procedures determinative. Those procedures can serve an important purpose that in this context one might consider noncriminal, namely helping to prevent judgmental mistakes that would wrongly deprive a person of important liberty. *Id.,* at 371–372, 106 S.Ct., at 2993–2994.

If these obvious similarities cannot by themselves prove that Kansas' "civil commitment" statute is criminal, neither can the word "civil" written into the statute, § 59–29a01, by itself prove the contrary. This Court has said that only the "clearest proof" could establish that a law the legislature called "civil," was, in reality a "punitive" measure. *United States v. Ward,* 448 U.S. 242, 248–249, 100 S.Ct. 2636, 2641, 65 L.Ed.2d 742 (1980). But the Court has also reiterated that a "civil label is not always dispositive," *Allen v. Illinois, supra,* at 369, 106 S. Ct., at 2992; it has said that in close cases the label is " 'not of paramount importance,' " *Kurth Ranch, supra,* at 777, 114 S.Ct., at 1944–1945 (citation omitted); and it has looked behind a "civil" label fairly often. *E.g., United States v. Halper,* 490 U.S. 435, 447, 109 S.Ct. 1892, 1901, 104 L.Ed.2d 487 (1989).

In this circumstance, with important features of the Act pointing in opposite directions, I would place particular importance upon those features that would likely distinguish between a basically punitive and a basically nonpunitive purpose. *United States v. Ursery,* 518 U.S. ——, ——, ——, 116 S.Ct. 2135, 2142, 135 L.Ed.2d 549 (1996) (asking whether a statutory scheme was so punitive " 'either in purpose or effect' " to negate the legislature's " 'intention to establish a civil remedial mechanism' ") (citations omitted). And I note that the

Court, in an earlier civil commitment case, *Allen v. Illinois,* 478 U.S., at 369, 106 S.Ct., at 2992, looked primarily to the law's concern for treatment as an important distinguishing feature. I do not believe that *Allen* means that a particular law's lack of concern for treatment, by itself, is enough to make an incapacitative law punitive. But, for reasons I will point out, when a State believes that treatment does exist, and then couples that admission with a legislatively required delay of such treatment until a person is at the end of his jail term (so that further incapacitation is therefore necessary), such a legislative scheme begins to look punitive....

The *Allen* Court's focus upon treatment, as a kind of touchstone helping to distinguish civil from punitive purposes, is not surprising, for one would expect a nonpunitive statutory scheme to confine, not simply in order to protect, but also in order to cure. That is to say, one would expect a nonpunitively motivated legislature that confines *because of* a dangerous mental abnormality to seek to help the individual himself overcome that abnormality (at least insofar as professional treatment for the abnormality exists and is potentially helpful, as Kansas, supported by some groups of mental health professionals, argues is the case here, see *supra,* at 2090). Conversely, a statutory scheme that provides confinement that does not reasonably fit a practically available, medically oriented treatment objective, more likely reflects a primarily punitive legislative purpose.

Several important treatment-related factors—factors of a kind that led the five-member *Allen* majority to conclude that the Illinois' legislature's purpose was primarily civil, not punitive—in this case suggest precisely the opposite. First, the State Supreme Court here, unlike the state court in *Allen,* has held that treatment is not a significant objective of the Act. The Kansas court wrote that the Act's purpose is "segregation of sexually violent offenders," with "treatment" a matter that was "incidental at best." 259 Kan., at 258, 912 P.2d, at 136. By way of contrast, in *Allen* the Illinois court had written that " 'treatment, not punishment' " was "the aim of the statute." *Allen, supra,* at 367, 106 S.Ct., at 2991 (quoting *People v. Allen,* 107 Ill.2d, at 99–101, 89 Ill. Dec. at 851–852, 481 N.E.2d, at 694–695)....

The record provides support for the Kansas court's conclusion. The court found that, as of the time of Hendricks' commitment, the State had not funded treatment, it had not entered into treatment contracts, and it had little, if any, qualified treatment staff. See *Hendricks,* 912 P.2d, at 131, 136; Testimony of Dr. Charles Befort, App. 255 (acknowledging that he has no specialized training); Testimony of John House, SRS Attorney, *id.,* at 367 (no contract has been signed by bidders); Testimony of John House, SRS Attorney, *id.,* at 369 (no one hired to operate SVP program or to serve as clinical director, psychiatrist, or psychologist). Indeed, were we to follow the majority's invitation to look beyond the record in this case,... it would reveal that Hendricks, according to the commitment program's own director, was receiving "essentially no treatment." Dr. Charles Befort in State Habeas Corpus Proceeding, App. 393; 259 Kan., at 249, 258, 912 P.2d, at 131, 136. See also App. 421 ("the treatment that is prescribed by statute" is "still not available"); *id.,* at 420–421 (the "needed treatment" "hasn't been delivered yet" and "Hendricks has wasted ten months" in "terms of treatment effects"); *id.,* at 391–392 (Dr. Befort admitting that he is not qualified to be SVP program director).

It is therefore not surprising that some of the Act's official supporters had seen in it an opportunity permanently to confine dangerous sex offenders....

Second, the Kansas statute insofar as it applies to previously convicted offenders, such as Hendricks, commits, confines, and treats those offenders *after* they have served virtually their entire criminal sentence. That time-related circumstance seems deliberate. The Act explicitly defers diagnosis, evaluation, and commitment proceedings until a few weeks prior to the "anticipated release" of a previously convicted offender from prison. Kan. Stat. Ann. § 59–29a03(a)(1) (1994). But why, one might ask, does the Act not commit and require treatment of sex offenders sooner, say soon after they begin to serve their sentences?

An Act that simply seeks confinement, of course, would not need to begin civil commitment proceedings sooner. Such an Act would have to begin proceedings only when an offender's prison term ends, threatening his release from the confinement that imprisonment assures. But it is difficult to see why rational legislators who seek treatment would write the Act in this way —providing treatment years after the criminal act that indicated its necessity. And it is particularly difficult to see why legislators who specifically wrote into the statute a finding that "prognosis for rehabilitating... in a prison setting is poor" would leave an offender in that setting for months or years before beginning treatment. This is to say, the timing provisions of the statute confirm the Kansas Supreme Court's view that treatment was not a particularly important legislative objective.

I recognize one possible counterargument. A State, wanting both to punish Hendricks (say, for deterrence purposes) and also to treat him, might argue that it should be permitted to postpone treatment until after punishment in order to make certain that the punishment in fact occurs. But any such reasoning is out of place here. Much of the treatment that Kansas offered here (called "ward milieu" and "group therapy") can be given at the same time as, and in the same place where, Hendricks serves his punishment.... Hence, assuming arguendo that it would be otherwise permissible, Kansas need not postpone treatment in order to make certain that sex offenders serve their full terms of imprisonment, *i.e.,* to make certain that they receive the entire punishment that Kansas criminal law provides. To the contrary, the statement in the Act itself, that the Act aims to respond to special "long term" "treatment needs," suggests that treatment should begin during imprisonment. It also suggests that, were those long-term treatment needs (rather than further punishment) Kansas' primary aim, the State would require that treatment begin soon after conviction, not 10 or more years later.

Third, the statute, at least as of the time Kansas applied it to Hendricks, did not require the committing authority to consider the possibility of using less restrictive alternatives, such as postrelease supervision, halfway houses, or other methods that *amici* supporting Kansas here have mentioned....

This Court has said that a failure to consider, or to use, "alternative and less harsh methods" to achieve a nonpunitive objective can help to show that legislature's "purpose... was to punish." *Bell v. Wolfish,* 441 U.S. 520, 539, n.

20, 99 S.Ct. 1861, 1874, n. 20, 60 L.Ed.2d 447 (1979). And one can draw a similar conclusion here. Legislation that seeks to help the individual offender as well as to protect the public would avoid significantly greater restriction of an individual's liberty than public safety requires. See Keilitz, Conn, & Gianpetro, Least Restrictive Treatment of Involuntary Patients: Translating Concepts into Practice, 29 St. Louis U.L.J. 691, 693 (1985) (describing "least restrictive alternativ[e]" provisions in the ordinary civil commitment laws of almost all States); Lyon, Levine, & Zusman, Patients' Bill of Rights: a Survey of State Statutes, 6 Mental Disability L. Rep. 178, 181–183 (1982) (same). Legislation that seeks almost exclusively to incapacitate the individual through confinement, however, would not necessarily concern itself with potentially less restrictive forms of incapacitation. I would reemphasize that this is not a case in which the State claims there is no treatment potentially available. Rather, Kansas, and supporting *amici,* argue that pedophilia is treatable. See *supra,* at 2090....

III

To find that the confinement the Act imposes upon Hendricks is "punishment" is to find a violation of the *Ex Post Facto* Clause. Kansas does not deny that the 1994 Act changed the legal consequences that attached to Hendricks earlier crimes, and in a way that significantly "disadvantage[d] the offender," *Weaver v. Graham,* 450 U.S. 24, 29, 101 S.Ct. 960, 964, 67 L.Ed.2d 17 (1981). See Brief for Respondent State of Kansas 37–39.

To find a violation of that Clause here, however, is not to hold that the Clause prevents Kansas, or other States, from enacting dangerous sexual offender statutes. A statute that operates prospectively, for example, does not offend the *Ex Post Facto* Clause. *Weaver,* 450 U.S., supra, at 29, 101 S.Ct., at 964–965. Neither does it offend the *Ex Post Facto* Clause for a State to sentence offenders to the fully authorized sentence, to seek consecutive, rather than concurrent, sentences, or to invoke recidivism statutes to lengthen imprisonment. Moreover, a statute that operates retroactively, like Kansas' statute, nonetheless does not offend the Clause *if the confinement that it imposes is not punishment—* if, that is to say, the legislature does not simply add a later criminal punishment to an earlier one. *Ibid.*

The statutory provisions before us do amount to punishment primarily because, as I have said, the legislature did not tailor the statute to fit the nonpunitive civil aim of treatment, which it concedes exists in Hendricks' case. The Clause in these circumstances does not stand as an obstacle to achieving important protections for the public's safety; rather it provides an assurance that, where so significant a restriction of an individual's basic freedoms is at issue, a State cannot cut corners. Rather, the legislature must hew to the Constitution's liberty-protecting line. See The Federalist, No. 78, p. 466 (C. Rossiter ed. 1961) (A. Hamilton).

I therefore would affirm the judgment.

POSTSCRIPT

Is It Constitutionally Permissible to Detain "Sexually Dangerous" Individuals After They Have Served Their Prison Sentences?

*K*ansas v. *Hendricks* concerns the definition of *punishment.* That is, what form of state proceedings constitute "punishment" for the purposes of the double jeopardy and ex post facto clauses of the U.S. Constitution? Is it the case, as Leroy Hendricks framed the issue, that the Kansas statute, even though labeled "civil" in nature, was really so punitive that it required the courts to characterize it as "criminal"? As the Thomas and Breyer opinions indicate, this is not simply a matter of drawing facile legalistic distinctions. Rather, important procedural differences attach to the distinction between civil and criminal cases in American law.

For example, the Constitution requires a long list of procedural and evidentiary protections for criminal defendants but not for civil litigants. Should such constitutional safeguards be lowered simply because a proceeding has been identified as a civil proceeding? Do such legal distinctions have meaning when the effect in either case is the loss of personal liberty and the stigma of state sanction?

For some helpful, general discussions of the nature of punishment and social control, see Stanley Cohen, *Visions of Social Control: Crime, Punishment, and Classification* (Blackwell, 1985) and David Garland, *Punishment and Modern Society: A Study in Social Theory* (University of Chicago Press, 1990). For a provocative treatment of the concept of "dangerousness" and the mutual influence of civil and criminal categories of legal analysis, see Michel Foucault's essay "The Dangerous Individual," in his book *Politics, Philosophy, Culture: Interviews and Other Writings, 1977–1984* (Routledge, 1990). The issues in this case are also covered in Stephen R. McAllister, "Kansas v. Hendricks Package: 'Punishing' Sex Offenders," 46 *University of Kansas Law Review* 27 (1997) and Ross E. Cheit and Erica B. Goldschmidt, "Child Molesters in the Criminal Justice System: A Comprehensive Case-Flow Analysis of the Rhode Island Docket (1985–1993)," 23 *New England Journal on Criminal and Civil Confinement* 2 (1997). Information on the Internet about corrections and criminal justice can be found at http://www.vera.org and http://www.cji-inc.com.

ISSUE 13

Should Drug Use Be Legalized?

YES: Steven B. Duke, from "Drug Prohibition: An Unnatural Disaster," *Connecticut Law Review* (Winter 1995)

NO: Gregory A. Loken, from "The Importance of Being More Than Earnest: Why the Case for Drug Legalization Remains Unproven," *Connecticut Law Review* (Winter 1995)

ISSUE SUMMARY

YES: Steven B. Duke, a professor of law of science and technology, contends that the war on drugs has led to an increase in criminal behavior, including robberies, assaults with guns, and police corruption, and that the financial, health, and civil rights costs of drug prohibition are enormous. Therefore, he recommends decriminalization and government regulation of drugs.

NO: Professor of law Gregory A. Loken, directly responding to Duke, asserts that the war on drugs has successfully reduced crime and that legalization would have devastating consequences, particularly for children.

O ne can hardly miss the impact of illegal drugs on the fabric of American life. There is a continuing link between drugs and violent crime in urban neighborhoods, with most of the victims of violence being young. The lure of the "get very rich quick" lifestyle of drug dealers has tempted many poor teenagers into a life of violence, even against their own families. It is hard to believe that a child would turn the family apartment into a "shooting gallery" or sell all the family possessions for money to purchase drugs, but it happens.

The drug problem invades every institution in society. It touches some children even before they are born. In one urban hospital, it was estimated that one-fifth of the 3,000 babies that are born each year are born to addicted mothers. That is a staggering figure, particularly because these children will be among hundreds of other similarly afflicted children born in other urban hospitals across the nation.

The drug problem touches everyone. One poll indicated that Americans are far more worried about the impact of drugs on their lives than about problems of international peace or terrorism abroad. And so they should be because the drug problem is not just the problem of the poor teenager in Detroit or Philadelphia. In Massachusetts a mother was tried for leaving her two small children alone in an apartment, which they set fire to and in which they died. Her defense was astonishing—she asked for leniency because she was a drug addict and had to leave her home to get a fix.

What is the solution to this situation, which is ripping apart American society? Should we legalize drugs, or should we continue with the traditional approach of criminalizing drug use? In the following selections, Steven B. Duke argues that there is only an illusion of prohibition in the United States and that only through legalization of drugs can we get a grip on the situation. He contends that present approaches, relying heavily on the police and court systems, are not putting much of a dent in either the rate of use or the supply of drugs. Furthermore, the present system is draining the government coffers of billions of dollars while urban street crime increases.

Gregory A. Loken is skeptical of Duke's arguments. He takes issue with Duke's conclusions about links between drug use and crime, points out several areas where Duke's conclusions may be unwarranted, and argues that Duke minimizes the worst harms that drugs pose for children.

The question of whether or not illicit drugs should be legalized is an extremely difficult one that will continue to confront us. Current public opinion surveys find that the "legalizing" option has insignificant public support. But another few years of drug-related violence and complaints by judges and court administrators that drug cases are clogging the courts could bring about a shift in public attitudes.

Steven B. Duke  **YES**

Drug Prohibition: An Unnatural Disaster

The idea that government should determine for its people which psychoactive drugs they are free to consume and jail them for using others is a fairly recent arrival in the United States. Except for an occasional fling with prohibition at the state level, Americans were free until 1914 to consume any drugs they chose and to buy from anyone who chose to sell them. Those rights were widely exercised. In addition to alcohol, tobacco, and caffeine, tens of millions of Americans consumed cocaine and opiates in the nineteenth century. Cocaine was even an ingredient in Coca Cola until 1905, and opium was included in nostrums fed to colicky babies. Heroin was originally sold as a cough suppressant. Although dependence on these drugs was not uncommon, it was never as serious a problem as alcoholism. Indeed, although the proportions of the population using these drugs in the late nineteenth century was probably higher than it is now, the problems associated with their use were less serious than they are today.

In 1914, Congress enacted the Harrison Act, which was designed to medicalize cocaine and heroin by confining their distribution to health professionals. In 1919, on the eve of alcohol prohibition and doubtless influenced by prohibitionist fervor, the Supreme Court converted the Harrison Act into a ban on the distribution of such drugs, holding that prescribing drugs to addicts was not the practice of medicine and was therefore criminal. Drug and alcohol prohibition then proceeded to wreck the country. Crime, corruption, and disrespect for law grew at unprecedented rates. Because of alcohol prohibition, many Americans replaced their appetite for beer with a newly discovered preference for the cocktail, containing distilled spirits, which poisoned thousands.

Thirteen years of alcohol prohibition was enough. It was repealed in 1933 by the Twenty-first Amendment, which left alcohol regulation to the states. The repeal of alcohol prohibition coincided with the depth of the depression, when unemployment reached record levels and millions of Americans were without food, shelter, welfare, or hope. Despite this widespread misery and despair, crime rates dropped precipitously after the repeal, as did alcohol poisoning and contempt for law. Hardly anyone considers the repeal of alcohol prohibition to have been a mistake. Why, then, did we not repeal the Harrison Act at the same time? Why don't we repeal its modern sequelae? We are addicted to

From Steven B. Duke, "Drug Prohibition: An Unnatural Disaster," *Connecticut Law Review,* vol. 27, no. 2 (Winter 1995). Copyright © 1995 by The Connecticut Law Review Association. Reprinted by permission. Notes omitted.

drug prohibition. A manifestation of that addiction is "denial" of the harms we are inflicting upon ourselves by prohibition.

A sober analysis of prohibition requires us to acknowledge that the use of psychoactive drugs, be they tobacco, alcohol, heroin, cocaine, or any of hundreds of others, has adverse effects on the physical or mental health of *some* users. The nature and seriousness of adverse effects vary greatly among both drugs and drug users. Many people can consume almost any popular drug, legal or illegal, without adverse physical or psychological effects, while others become horribly addicted to almost any drug they use. Because of the terrible consequences of drug abuse to some users, it is hard to make a positive case for the increased consumption of any pleasure drug. One who believes that we should repeal prohibition so that more people will enjoy a wider variety of drugs does not speak for me nor would such a person have a sympathetic audience among a large segment of the American population. Rather, I assume *arguendo* that the consumption of psychoactive drugs for other than medical reasons is, on the whole, undesirable.

We must also acknowledge, however, that most Americans use psychoactive drugs on a daily basis, as did their ancestors for thousands of years, and that they will continue to do so, no matter what the state of the law. Most Americans insist, often at great personal cost, on the right to consume substances that they desire. Many of those same Americans are just as insistent that others be denied their own drug of choice. That is why tobacco, alcohol, and caffeine are permitted while only much less popular drugs are banned. The appetite for chemical intoxication is innate in humans (and most other animals as well) and indulging it has been a part of most cultures since the dawn of history. In addition to general notions of individual autonomy, a hunch that it could be dangerous to tamper with urges so "natural" may explain why we stayed out of the prohibition business for so long.

Reconsidering the problem compels us to compare the costs of drug prohibition as presently pursued with the costs of drug consumption in a hypothetical system in which prohibition has been repealed or in which enforcement is much less intense than is the case today. Most of the evils of drug prohibition would be drastically reduced if we simply took an attitude of benign neglect toward illicit drug consumption and distribution, which is largely what occurred until the early 1970s. The drug war is an indefensible disaster that harms almost everyone....

Some Costs of "Drug War" Prohibition

The Criminogenics of Drug Prohibition

Contrary to what our government told us when it imposed drug prohibition, most illegal recreational drugs have no pharmacological properties that produce violence or other criminal behavior. Heroin and marijuana diminish rather than increase aggressive behavior. Cocaine—or cocaine withdrawal— occasionally triggers violence but usually does not. Very little crime is generated by the mere use of these drugs, especially in comparison to alcohol, which is causally related to thousands of homicides and hundreds of thousands of assaults annually. The major linkages between illegal drugs and crime must be found elsewhere—in prohibition.

Prohibition Creates Motivation to Steal and Rob

One of the main strategic goals of the drug war is to increase the costs of producing and distributing, and hence of buying, illicit drugs. As the price to the consumer is increased, demand can hopefully be curtailed and the number of users or the quantities of illicit drugs used can be reduced. The tactics for increasing producer and distributor costs include impeding production or distribution of the raw materials used in making drugs, attempting to interdict the products before they reach the consumer (with border searches, busts of stash houses, and the like), and putting smugglers and distributors of the illicit products in prison. Until recently, the strategy had considerable "success" in that prices for marijuana, heroin, cocaine, and other illicit drugs were quite high. A heroin addict would commonly need $200 or more per day to support a habit, and a cocaine user, before the era of cheap "crack," might need even more than that. Many cocaine users spent a thousand dollars a week on powder cocaine.

There is little evidence that demand is greatly reduced by jacking up the free market price of these drugs by a factor of 100 or more, but there is strong evidence that the consumers of these products increase their participation in acquisitive crimes in order to feed their habits. In a recent survey of persons in prison for robbery or burglary, one out of three said that they committed their crimes in order to get money to buy drugs. Those who commit crimes for drug money also seem to commit them at a much greater rate than less strongly motivated robbers, burglars, and thieves.

In a study of 356 heroin users in Miami, James Inciardi found that they admitted to committing nearly 120,000 crimes (an average of 332 per person) during a single year. In another study of 573 heroin users, Inciardi found them responsible for about 215,000 offenses during the previous year. Included were 25,000 shopliftings, 45,000 thefts and frauds, 6,000 robberies and assaults, and 6,700 burglaries. In another study of 459 nonnarcotic drug users (chiefly cocaine), Inciardi found them to have admitted to an average of 320 crimes apiece during the previous year. In a survey of callers to a cocaine hotline, 45% of the callers said they had stolen to buy cocaine. In a survey of adolescents, the 1.3% who admitted using cocaine accounted for 40% of the admitted crimes. In several studies of drug use by persons imprisoned, 65% to 80% have admitted regular or lifetime illicit drug use. All this data suggests that about 75% of our robberies, thefts, burglaries, and related assaults are committed by drug abusers. Some of the crimes committed by drug abusers—perhaps one-third—would be committed in any event, but numerous studies show that drug users commit far fewer crimes when undergoing outpatient treatment or even when the prices of drugs go down. Half of America's property crime, robberies, and burglaries are probably the result of the high costs of drug acquisition created by the drug war.

Systemic Causes

Creating an incentive to steal in order to buy drugs is only one of many criminogenic effects of drug prohibition. The illegal drug market is itself a cauldron of criminality. Murder is employed to protect or acquire drug-selling turf, to settle disputes among drug merchants and their customers, to enforce contracts, to remediate fraud, and to steal drugs and drug money from dealers. In many cities, such as New Haven, Connecticut, at least half of the killings are drug-business related. Nationwide, between 5,000 and 10,000 murders per year are systemic to the drug business. Thus, more people are killed by the prohibition of drugs than by the drugs themselves.

Drug money is also the lifeblood of criminal gangs, members of whom kill members of rival gangs, and innocent bystanders, for almost any reason, including showing off.

Victimogenics

Another way in which drug prohibition causes crime is by making victims vulnerable to predators. Many drug customers have to enter crime-infested territory to get their supplies. Since they are criminals themselves, obviously in the neighborhood to "score," they have strong disincentives to complain to the police about having been robbed or assaulted. As such, they are prime targets.

Proliferation of Deadly Weapons

Drug prohibition also accounts for much of the recent proliferation of handguns and assault rifles (which are doubling every twenty years). Guns are essential to carrying on the drug trade, since drug dealers must enforce their own contracts and provide their own protection from predators. Even "mules" who deliver drugs or money need weapons. Due in part to its association with the glamorous drug trade, packing a gun, like fancy clothing or costly jewelry, has become a status symbol among many adolescents. In such an atmosphere, other youngsters carry guns in the hope they will provide them with some protection. As a result, disputes that used to be settled with fists are now settled with guns. A decade ago only 15% of teenagers who got into serious trouble in New York City were carrying guns. Now the rate is 60% to 65%.

The more guns there are in the hands of drug dealers and others, the more the rest of the population feels the need to have guns for self-defense. So, partly as a result of the huge black-market drug business that creates a voracious appetite for guns, many ordinary citizens are arming themselves with guns. The more people who have guns, the more people get killed. Hence, many deaths by guns—intentional killings, accidental killings, even suicides—are causally linked to the drug trade in the sense that the guns would not be there but for the drug business. There is little that gun control laws can do about this problem. Unless we can greatly shrink the black-market drug business, we can do little about the proliferation of guns in this country.

Corruption Costs

Drug prohibition also fosters crime by producing police corruption. The news media are full of accounts of cops caught stealing money or drugs from drug dealers and reselling the drugs, simply taking money from drug dealers in exchange for looking the other way, or providing tips about police raids or other plans. The recently released report of New York City's Mollen Commission provides chilling accounts of drug-prohibition-related corruption in that city. Such corruption denigrates and demoralizes all police. It spreads like cancer into all phases of police work.

Distraction of Law Enforcement

The distractive effects of the drug war on the police are also indirectly but profoundly criminogenic. In many cities, half or more of the arrests are for drugs or other crimes related to drug trafficking. The energy expended by the police on drug criminals is not available to be focused on domestic violence, rape, and other nondrug offenses. As a consequence, criminals who are not directly involved in drug trafficking have a much better chance of escaping detection and punishment than they would have otherwise.

If, as the just enacted Violent Crime Control and Law Enforcement Act correctly presumes, the number of police available to detect and prosecute crimes has a strong effect on the number of crimes committed, then wasting half of our available police resources on drug and drug-related crimes—effectively cutting our police forces in half—clearly causes crime. Repeal of drug prohibition would in effect add 400,000 police officers—at no cost. On that account alone, it would surely eliminate one-fourth or more of our violent and property crimes.

Paralyzing Our Courts

Our court system is on the verge of collapse, mainly because of drug-related cases. Criminal cases are not decided on their merits. In many cities, most people who are indicted end up having their cases dismissed. Only a fraction of the people charged with felonies are ever convicted of those felonies. There are simply too many cases for the system to handle, and at least half of them, in many courts, are drug cases or drug-prohibition-caused cases.

Dilution of Incarceration Resources

The drug war deeply undercuts the role of imprisonment in dealing with nondrug related crimes, such as child molesting, rape, and homicide. We now jail or imprison 1.3 million Americans, the second highest rate of incarceration in the world. Our prisons are filled beyond capacity even as our rates of incarceration are increasing faster than ever before. Forty states are under court orders for overcrowding. Funds are not available to build prisons fast enough to provide the needed space. Child molesters and kidnappers are being paroled early or having their sentences cut to make prison space for drug users and drug dealers. Many dangerous criminals don't even make it to prison because there is no room for them. Because many drug users and dealers—most of them nonviolent—have mandatory sentences, they have priority for prison space. Repeal of drug prohibition would open up about 500,000 jail and prison spaces. The beneficial effects on crime rates can hardly be exaggerated....

Prohibition Wastes at Least $100 Billion Per Year

The federal, state, and local governments spend about $75 billion a year on law enforcement and criminal justice programs. About $20 billion of that is directly related to drug law enforcement. Roughly another $15 billion is related to crimes committed to obtain drug money or is systemically related in some way to drug commerce. Hence, about $35 billion per year spent on law enforcement can be saved by repeal of drug prohibition.

As Gore Vidal put it, "[F]ighting drugs is nearly as big a business as pushing them." Drug legalization threatens the jobs and careers of police officers and politician-drug warriors. Defense attorneys and prosecutors, who make their living on drug cases, will also lose from drug legalization. Former Drug Enforcement Administration (DEA) officer Michael Levine exaggerated when he told CBS News: "The whole drug war is a political grab bag, in that everybody has got their arm in looking for that political jackpot that will either win them an election, win them a lucrative position as a consultant or you name it." But serious de-escalation of the drug war does threaten tens of thousands of careers that the taxpayers would no longer need to support. That is a major impediment to repeal. Nonetheless, many law-enforcement officers are well ahead of politicians in recognizing the futility and economic wastefulness of the drug war. As Robert Stutman, previously a high-ranking DEA official, stated: "Those of us who carry a badge learned a long time ago we're not going to solve the problem, and yet an awful lot of policy makers continue to depend on us, and we keep telling them we can't do it."

Ralph Salerno, a famous organized crime expert and long-time drug warrior himself, goes further. He asserts not only that the drug war "will never work" but that police on the front line, risking their lives and their physical, psychological, and moral health, "are being lied to, just as I was lied to 20 years ago." . . .

Adding the money squandered on the ineffective drug-suppression activities of state and federal governments to the money we all lose as a result of the unnaturally high price of drugs, the total would come to well over $100 billion per year.

Urban Blight

Drug prohibition is a major contributor to the destruction of our inner-cities. In America's most disadvantaged neighborhoods, open-air drug markets and gang violence related to drug-turf battles make life miserable. Residents of neighborhoods where drug trade is concentrated also suffer disproportionately from the crimes generated by drug prohibition, such as crimes to get drug money. When the drug business leaves the cities, our homes, streets, and schools will become much safer. It may even become possible to educate children in urban public schools. . . .

Public Health Costs

Drug prohibition makes the inevitable use of psychotropic drugs far more dangerous than would be the case under regulation. Most overdoses and drug poisonings are attributable to the operation of the illicit market. Drug analyst James Ostrowski concludes that 80% of drug-use-deaths are caused by prohibition, only 20% by the inherent qualities of the drugs. That estimate does not include the fact that needle sharing by intravenous drug users now does as much or more to spread HIV, hepatitis, and other deadly diseases as do unsafe sexual practices. Our drug war mentality has widely blocked the implementation of clean-needle programs that clearly reduce the spread of AIDS and other deadly diseases. Drug prohibition also deters drug users from seeking treatment for a myriad of other medical conditions, many of which are communicable. Ironically, the criminal status of drugs even deters drug abusers from seeking treatment for drug addiction.

The "war" approach to drugs also makes health professionals afraid to prescribe legally controlled drugs, which are capable of curbing and controlling mental illness and making bearable much intractable pain. They fear that they will be suspected of "addicting" their patients or even of being drug dealers with a medical license. Physicians are also prohibited by law from prescribing marijuana, even though it is of unique medical utility in treatment of glaucoma, nausea resulting from chemotherapy, loss of appetite due to AIDS, and other serious medical conditions....

Relegalizing heroin, cocaine, and marijuana would probably produce a net reduction in the use of tobacco and alcohol, saving thousands of lives every year, perhaps tens of thousands. This reduction would come from several sources. Our present demonization of illicit drugs permits us to avoid confronting the realities of alcohol and tobacco—that they are our two deadliest popular drugs. Prohibition of some drugs encourages consumption of permitted drugs. As prohibitionists commonly argue, relegalizing the illegal drugs would convey the "wrong" message—that the legal and illegal drugs are in the same socio-cultural-medical-moral family. Some of the billions of dollars that the government, and the tobacco and alcohol industries, have spent trying to convince us that illegal drugs are immoral, suicidal, treasonous, dumb, and so forth will be symbolically transferred to previously legal drugs, therefore, deterring some potential drinkers or smokers from using or abusing those drugs. Alcohol is nearly nine times as popular as all illegal drugs combined and tobacco is four times as popular. A significant decrement in favorable public perceptions of these two legal drugs can therefore have enormous health benefits. Any change in law that blurs distinctions in attitudes toward alcohol and tobacco on the one hand and illicit drugs on the other is likely to have positive effects on Americans' health. This would be true even if consumption of presently illicit drugs were to increase by several multiples—and even if the safety of those drugs were not to improve at all.

Wholly apart from how relegalization would affect attitudes toward alcohol and tobacco, increased availability (i.e. reductions in cost) of illicit drugs will, if it increases consumption of those drugs, almost certainly reduce consumption of alcohol, especially among alcohol abusers, with significant benefits to their health. Many of the illegal drugs are substitutes for alcohol, and vice versa. Studies demonstrate that when access to alcohol is restricted—as when the drinking age was raised from 18 to 21—there is a substantial corresponding increase in the consumption of marijuana, not otherwise explainable. This supports the reverse inference that increased consumption of marijuana would reduce alcohol consumption. Thus, if repeal of prohibition produced more consumption of marijuana, an offsetting benefit would be reduced consumption of alcohol—our second deadliest popular drug.

When heroin addicts are deprived of heroin, they become alcoholics. When drinkers are deprived of alcohol, they turn to opiates. If repeal were to cause more consumption of heroin (by no means certain), some of the increase would probably represent a substitution for alcohol. To the extent heavy alcohol drinkers were to substitute opiates for alcohol, that would create significant health benefits (opiates cause virtually no physical damage to the body). Despite common misconceptions about the relative health costs of using legal and illegal drugs, health benefits could even accrue if consumers were to switch from alcohol or tobacco to cocaine or heroin. . . .

Drug Prohibition Destroys Civil Liberties

Each year, as some supposed "loophole" used by drug dealers is closed, we all lose important civil liberties. Many Americans are persuaded we must sacrifice any constitutional safeguard in order to keep drug felons from escaping on "technicalities." However, the "technicalities" are the substance of our liberty, which took a revolution to establish.

Under the pressure of drug war necessity, the Fourth, Fifth, Sixth, and Eighth Amendments of the Bill of Rights have been subverted and have lost much of their meaning. We permit police to enter and search our houses, cars, and effects on the flimsiest of suspicion. We allow them to arrest and search minorities in reliance on racist stereotypes, euphemistically called "profiles." We let them terrorize us in our homes and even kill our children without recourse. We have all but destroyed the right of property with expansive notions of forfeiture. We have become so inured to daily excesses that the drug war disease is spreading to other areas. Based on drug forfeiture precedents, we are now willing to confiscate the cars of persons who cruise for prostitutes or drive under the influence. As a result of drug war forfeiture precedents, we are now positioned in principle to take the homes and offices of anyone who commits, or permits others to commit, *any* crime on the premises, including tax evasion or neglect of pets. George Orwell would be astonished. Such is the effect of drug war morbidity. It is as destructive to the Constitution as AIDS is lethal to the body.

Drug Prosecutions Destroy the Lives of Otherwise Productive Citizens

Most users of presently illegal drugs, like most users of tobacco and alcohol, are productive and generally law abiding people. But treating their drug consumption as a serious crime makes it harder for them to be so and makes it impossible for some to be so—those who are socially and economically marginal to begin with. Legalizing drugs would greatly increase the capacity of the users of presently illicit drugs to be productive citizens.

I estimate that about 500,000 of our 1.3 million jail and prison inmates are there for illegal drug or drug-related offenses, and as many as 300,000 would not be there if drug prohibition were repealed because they would not be criminals. They would be available to their families and would have an opportunity to be useful members of society rather than embittered criminals enraged over their unjust punishment. No one who gets a prison term of any duration for using drugs or selling drugs to a willing adult buyer is likely to be persuaded that his punishment was deserved. Hundreds of thousands of Americans who might otherwise be integrated into the mainstream of society have that possibility virtually eliminated by a combination of embitterment and stigma, rendering their acceptance of and by the mainstream unlikely. This appalling waste of human lives, which itself far exceeds any plausible cost of illegal drug use, would be eliminated by repeal.

Prohibition Creates and Sustains Racial Mistrust and Hostility

The greatest social problem plaguing the United States near the end of the twentieth century is the same one that has plagued the continent for five centuries: racial mistrust and hostility. The drug war did not cause that problem; however, the drug war widens the hostility and deepens the mistrust between the races. By almost any measure, blacks suffer disproportionately from drug prohibition. They are not only more drug-dependent than whites, they are more likely to get AIDS, syphilis, hepatitis, and other diseases in the course of taking drugs or interacting with infected drug abusers. They are far more often the victims of drug-systemic violence than whites....

A *New York Times/WCBS-TV* poll in late 1990 revealed that "[a] quarter of the blacks polled said that the government deliberately makes sure that drugs are easily available in poor black neighborhoods in order to harm black people." Another third of those surveyed believed that the availability of drugs might be the result of deliberate government activity.

Support for conspiracy theories, as they apply to drugs, seems to lie in the fact that racial minorities suffer from drugs and drug prohibition vastly out of proportion to their representation in the population, while drug dealing openly occurs on the streets of their neighborhoods, seemingly tolerated by the police....

African-Americans are incarcerated at a rate six times that of whites. There are twice as many black males in New York's prisons as there are in its colleges. Nationwide, one out of four black males in his twenties is in prison or under some form of court supervision, such as probation or parole. (Of black males aged 18–35, the court-enmeshed figure is 42% in Washington, D.C. and a mind-boggling 56% in Baltimore.) Fewer than one in sixteen white males of the same age is caught up in the criminal justice system.

As many as 70% of black men in Washington, D.C. are arrested by the time they turn 35. Although about 77% of current illegal drug users are white and less than 17% are black, of 13,000 drug arrests in Baltimore in 1991, 11,000, about 85%, were of blacks. Nationwide, about 45% of drug arrests are of African-Americans."...

Approaching Repeal

Eliminating or greatly reducing almost any one of the costs associated with prohibition discussed above itself warrants a declaration of drug peace. When the benefits of reducing or ridding ourselves of all of them are combined, the case for repeal becomes overwhelming. If legalization is too large a leap, courageous governors and a courageous president could give us some of the benefits of repeal simply by deescalating the war. Cut the drug law enforcement budgets by two-thirds (as President Clinton cut the personnel of the "drug czar"), stop civil forfeitures, grant executive clemency to most of the nonviolent drug violators stuffing our prisons, and much of the evil of prohibition will disappear. When the benefits of de-escalation are experienced, the nation will then be ready for *de jure* reform.

The meekest among us must admit that the case for relegalizing marijuana is unanswerable. Jimmy Carter was right when he proposed decriminalization of marijuana during his presidency. All Americans would be better off if he had succeeded. Marijuana poses some health risks, but far fewer than any other pleasure drug, with the possible exception of caffeine, and it substitutes for and, therefore, competes with all psychoactive drugs. Pending the legalization of marijuana, our nation's chief executives and law enforcement officers should end all prosecution for marijuana possession or trafficking and open the prison doors for all who are there solely for such offenses. Even an ardent prohibitionist ought to join in this proposal. Everyone agrees that cocaine and heroin are worse drugs, by any standards, than marijuana. If marijuana is legalized, drug warriors can then focus their resources on the war against "hard" drugs.

Should we retain the prohibition of hard drugs but reduce the penalties for distributing them, treating drug trafficking as just another vice, like prostitution or illegal gambling? That would be a great improvement over our drug war approach, but I don't think it is the answer. The slight benefits we might get from such a parsimonious retention of prohibition—deterring those whose consumption patterns are highly responsive to legal norms—would not be worth what we would give up—regulation of the distribution of drugs and control over the content of the product, the packaging, the distributors, and the informational flow about them. What we gain in a safer, less addictive product would greatly exceed the minor deterrent value of a largely symbolic prohibition. Moreover, if we were to roll back drug prohibition to something defensible, ignorant or unprincipled politicians would soon seize the opportunity to escalate the drug war all over again. Drugs are too convenient a scapegoat for demagogues to resist.

Drug prohibition has clearly eclipsed alcohol prohibition as the nation's costliest, most catastrophic social program. It has been such a colossal failure that even to question it has become political heresy. Too much has been spent, too much crime created, and too many lives destroyed by it to allow us to consider its merits. We have fried our brains not with drugs but with their prohibition.

Gregory A. Loken

 **NO**

The Importance of Being More Than Earnest: Why the Case for Drug Legalization Remains Unproven

Drugs and Crime

Reducing crime, for most Americans, is a matter of the highest priority. [Professor Steven] Duke's case for legalization shrewdly presents itself as a response to that concern with a series of empirical assertions that all carry at least a scent of plausibility: (1) that crime has "nearly doubled" since Richard Nixon declared the war on drugs in 1973; (2) that "simultaneous ascents in drug war budgets and crime rates are not coincidental," because the "drug war causes crime"; (3) that because drugs are illegal, they cost more to buy, and the "motivation to steal and rob" leads to a vast increase in theft and other "acquisitive crimes" in order to "feed [drug consumers'] habits"; and (4) that "Systemic Violence" and "Proliferation of Deadly Weapons" are also caused, not cured, by our prohibition regime. Furthermore, Duke declares the fear that ingestion of heroin, marijuana, or cocaine causes crime to be greatly exaggerated, with "[v]ery little crime . . . generated by the mere use of these drugs"—though Duke does acknowledge that cocaine "occasionally triggers violence." He argues that none of these illicit drugs are as criminogenic as alcohol and that the prohibition of the former leads to increased consumption of the latter, thus generating, on balance, more crime. Above all, he urges that we should have learned our lesson about the inevitable increase in crime and violence resulting from criminal anti-drug strategies from the "unprecedented" increase in crime that marked our experiment with alcohol prohibition from 1920 to the end of 1933.

Before assessing any of these arguments, of course, it is important to acknowledge, as Duke appears only somewhat grudgingly to do, that assertions about causation of crime are notoriously difficult: for example, the debate over heredity versus environment as the primary "cause" of crime remains highly inconclusive. Likewise, human aggression has been blamed on gender, racism, erotica, drugs, and violent programming on television, while crime rates in general are hostage to simple fluctuations in the percentage of adolescents in the

From Gregory A. Loken, "The Importance of Being More Than Earnest: Why the Case for Drug Legalization Remains Unproven," *Connecticut Law Review,* vol. 27, no. 2 (Winter 1995). Copyright © 1995 by The Connecticut Law Review Association. Reprinted by permission. Notes omitted.

population along with unemployment and breakdowns in family life. In asserting that drug prohibition caused the crime which followed it, Duke risks, although pardonably, falling into a classic *post hoc propter hoc* ["after this, (therefore) on account of it"] fallacy. Occasionally it will be worth returning to the problem of rival causal factors, but for the sake of argument it is certainly worth examining our experience with prohibition of alcohol and other drugs to see whether it supports Duke's assertions.

Alcohol Prohibition and the Lessons of the 1920s

Central to Duke's historical account of drug prohibition is his characterization of the 1920s as a decade racked with violence and social disintegration, with the adoption of the Twenty-First Amendment bringing substantial benefits. Even more importantly, he uses the failure of the prohibition "experiment" as support for his analysis of the effects of prohibition of marijuana, heroin, and cocaine.

Yet the evidence of a crime epidemic fairly attributable to Prohibition is far weaker than Duke would have us suppose. It rests heavily on the assertion of James Ostrowski that "[t]he murder rate rose with the start of Prohibition, . . . then declined for eleven consecutive years when Prohibition ended." Yet that statement, while literally true, tells, as Ostrowski himself glancingly acknowledges, only a highly misleading part of the story of murder rates during this century. A careful look at the same historical statistics used by Ostrowski suggests a remarkably different historical account of Prohibition's effects.

. . . As Ostrowski claims, the rate of both murders and assaults by firearm climbed during the period of Prohibition (from 1920 to 1933), with a 35 percent increase in the murder rate from the level of 1919. Yet compare those figures to the same ones for the decade immediately prior: in 1919 the murder rate stood 56 percent above the murder rate in 1910 and 500 percent higher than the rate in 1900. If Ostrowski and Duke wish to infer anything from these trends in homicide rates, then they should conclude that Prohibition dramatically *slowed* a radically increasing homicide rate in the early part of the century. Indeed, other scholars of the era have concluded simply that "[t]here is no convincing evidence that Prohibition brought on a crime wave."

Duke's analysis is all the more unpersuasive because of its failure to take into account two enormously important historical events that could easily explain changing crime rates. First, he neglects to mention that more than half of the increase in crime between 1919 and 1933 occurred in the years 1930 through 1933, during the deepest depths of the Great Depression. Perhaps even more important—because more relevant to crime rates throughout the entire first half of the century—he fails to consider the impact of the adoption of America's first highly restrictive laws on immigration in the early 1920s, and their final effectiveness in the 1930s. Thus the immigration rates (per 1000 residents) were 10.4 for the decade from 1901 to 1910, 5.7 from 1911 to 1920, 3.5 from 1921 to 1930, and only 0.4 for 1931 to 1940. This slowing rate of immigration coincides far better with changes in homicide rates than does adoption of Prohibition. Additionally, this suggests the danger of ignoring rival causal factors. It could be that changing crime rates in the first four decades of this century were attributable to enormous social changes—in particular, tumultuous economic fluctuations combined with record numbers of often destitute immigrants.

Even if we concede, however, that Prohibition "caused" an increase in crime, what exactly would it prove? Perhaps, as Duke implies, it shows that *all* government prohibition of *any* recreational drug is doomed. Or perhaps it suggests, as the Panel on Alternative Policies Affecting the Prevention of Alcohol Abuse and Alcoholism concluded in its 1981 report, that "[d]rinking customs in the United States are strongly held and resistant to frontal assault." If that is true, our nation's negative experience with alcohol control points to two possible conclusions very different from Duke's. First, even if history shows alcohol to be, as Duke repeatedly asserts, the worst of the popular recreational drugs, it has such a unique place in our national history and psyche that our experience with it provides little guide to current policymaking on other drugs. Alternatively, alcohol's stubborn presence may simply suggest that we must, if at all possible, avoid having the use of any other recreational drugs become so customary that direct controls on their distribution and abuse will become impossible.

The "War on Drugs" and Crime

If Duke's account of Prohibition as a "cause" of crime is unpersuasive for the 1920s, his argument becomes wholly insupportable in our own era. For once we have accepted his view that "benign neglect" of illicit drug use prevailed until 1973, when the war on drugs began in earnest, the kind of empirical evidence on which he relies points overwhelmingly in a direction he would likely find quite surprising—toward, if anything, the conclusion that the war on drugs has *suppressed* crime.

For example, the homicide-rate trends that Duke favors for judging the 1920s suggest a rather favorable view of recent drug policy. From 1960 to 1972, the last years prior to the drug war, murder and non-negligent manslaughter rates climbed 76 percent, including a 55 percent increase for the years 1965 to 1970 alone. By contrast, from 1972 to 1980, homicide rates rose only 13 percent and from 1980 to 1992, they declined 9 percent, to a level equivalent to that of 1972. Far from suggesting that the war on drugs was responsible for greater violence in our society, these rates whisper that such violence is a legacy of the "benign neglect" of drugs that occurred in the late 1960s.

Moreover, Duke's thesis does not appear to fare well when glancing at the evidence that he presents. Duke's assertion that "violent crime rates have nearly doubled" in the period since President Nixon declared the "war on drugs" in 1973 relies wholly on F.B.I. data that reports "offenses *known to police*"—data which, of course, is subject to a variety of confounding variables, in particular the willingness of the public to report crimes, which may in turn be a function of the number of police and other criminal justice system employees available to take their reports. Worse, his evidence neglects the fact that this data shows a 150 percent increase in violent crime for the ten year period from 1963 to 1973. Duke never bothers to explain how such crime could increase more during the last ten years of "benign neglect" than it did in the twenty years thereafter. Finally, the F.B.I.'s "Total Crime Index" has actually shown a significant decrease since 1980, which, as I will shortly argue, is a better year for dating the beginning of the war on drugs.

Since 1973, happily, a better tool than the reported-to-police figures has been available: the annual National Crime Victimization Survey conducted by the Department of Justice. These annual surveys can hardly be considered definitive measures of crime; nevertheless, they do not suffer from the same reporting and resource limitations as the previously available statistics. A quick glance at the trends they reflect reveals how far Duke and other proponents of legalization must travel before their more-crime—because-of-drug-prohibition contentions can be supportable.

Again, it is important to recognize the extreme difficulty of correctly inferring anything about crime "causation" from broad statistical measures, but given Duke's reliance on those measures, it seems fair to examine them for whatever they might reveal about his thesis.

... [C]rime victimization has *decreased* across the board since the late 1970s. During the same period, the rate of removal of cocaine and heroin by law enforcement from the domestic market ... indicates that the beginning of a "war" on illicit drugs only began in earnest in the early 1980s, at about the same time victimization rates began to fall rapidly. Most significantly, victimization of Americans by theft—the crime most commonly related (because of drug consumers' obvious need for cash under the prohibition regime) to the drug "war" —declined more than 35 percent from 1979 to 1992. Victimization by violent crime fell nearly 7 percent during this same period—paralleling the fall in homicide rates. Overall, the risk of being victimized by any kind of personal crime fell nearly 28 percent from 1979 to 1992....

The Special Problem of Cocaine

Duke consistently rejects or minimizes evidence showing links between illicit drug use and violent behavior, except insofar as that violence is connected to the need for obtaining drug money. His treatment of cocaine is particularly disturbing in this respect, especially since it is currently the second most widely used illegal drug—far behind marijuana, but far ahead of other rivals such as heroin. In slighting the growing weight of scholarship linking the use of cocaine to aggression and crime, Duke seriously damages the credibility of his advocacy for legalization. He [does] concede, almost as an aside, that the drug "sometimes leads to violence against others," but declare[s] (with extraordinarily thin supporting authority) that it is "unclear" and "doubtful" that cocaine increases by any "substantial" amount the risk that a consumer will commit a crime. Yet a significant number of careful experiments have shown that regular administration of cocaine to normal human volunteers can produce otherwise unexplainable paranoid psychotic behavior, while others, including one in 1993 by researchers at the University of Virginia, have demonstrated a causal connection between ingestion of high doses of cocaine and increased aggression. Moreover, the clinical evidence is in accord: as one recent, comprehensive review concluded, there "are several lines of evidence that support a psychopharmacologic basis for cocaine-induced violent behavior in humans." The American Psychiatric Association now recognizes Cocaine-Induced Psychotic Disorder (with either delusions or hallucinations) as a well-defined reality of clinical practice. So much a reality, in fact, that one recent study advised: "Given ... [cocaine's] profound association with extreme anger, irritability, agitation, and aggressive behavior, cocaine intoxication must be suspected for any patient who comes for treatment with such symptoms." Indeed, of homicide victims testing positive for recent cocaine use, a study by the Los Angeles County Medical Examiner found that "20% ... were found to have been acting violently themselves at the time of death," and a similar study in New York found that cocaine-using "[h]omicide victims may have provoked violence through irritability, paranoid thinking, or verbal or physical aggression, which are known to be pharmacologic effects of cocaine." In failing to confront fully and fairly the evidence of cocaine use and the danger it poses in the event of legalization, Duke does the debate over drug prohibition a disservice.

Furthermore, Duke does not grapple fully with the other highly dangerous feature of cocaine that links it intimately with the commission of crime: its addictive properties. Duke cites studies from the early 1980s, a period when cocaine was characterized by many as a "safe, nonaddicting euphoriant agent," for the propositions that there is little or no development of tolerance for cocaine, and no clear evidence of withdrawal symptoms. Oddly, those assertions are in direct conflict with the settled views both of the American Psychiatric Association and of academic physicians. Worse, according to Dr. Herbert Kleber, a national authority on substance abuse, "[c]ocaine is a much more addictive drug than alcohol," and its legalization might lead to a nine-fold increase in the number of compulsive cocaine users.

That Duke downplays the evidence of cocaine's aggression-producing and addictive properties is not wholly surprising, for they seriously compromise the ability of legalization proponents to promise benefits from the end of prohibition. How do we balance a promised reduction in drug-distribution-related violence against the potential for substantial increases in aggressive behavior by legions of new compulsive cocaine users? What difference in drug-related theft will reducing the price for cocaine make if cocaine addicts will spend *whatever* money they have for the drug, even to the neglect of food and shelter? Duke refreshingly declares that "[a]ny analysis of drug consumption that disregards the differences between [various drugs], and treats all drug consumption as equivalent, makes no sense outside the realm of theology," but in the case of cocaine he and other advocates of legalization seem to substitute faith for hard analysis.

Drug Law Enforcement and Racism

One problem Duke does attack with *some* success is the disparate impact of enforcement of drug laws on racial minorities. He argues that minority youths are at special risk of extraordinarily severe penalties for becoming involved in a drug culture that is an all too attractive alternative to the dreariness and squalor of urban ghettos. Surely it is plausible, as he asserts, that the presence of drug-enforcement efforts in the inner city will subject minorities to disproportionately higher rates of arrest and incarceration than those suffered by whites.

Nevertheless, Duke's assertion is not true. If Duke's thesis were correct, we would expect that from 1973 to 1992 (using his dates for the drug war), the overall arrest rate for blacks would have grown at a rate wholly disproportionate to that of whites, thereby causing the ratio of black arrest rates to white arrest rates to climb substantially. In fact, that ratio actually decreased significantly both for adults and juveniles. In 1973, blacks over the age of 18 were, relative to population, arrested at a ratio of 5.69 times that of whites and by 1992, that ratio had declined to 4.96. The comparable black-white arrest ratio for persons under 18 was 2.93 in 1973; by 1992, it had fallen to 2.34....

Drug Legalization and Children

... In a 1990 article focusing on cocaine, Dr. James Kennedy and I addressed the problems faced by one particular group of victims, children and adolescents, and reached three conclusions: (1) that cocaine abuse causes devastating harm to the young, whether through perinatal exposure, parental neglect, or direct, addictive consumption as adolescents; (2) that greater availability of hard drugs following legalization would lead to substantially greater exposure of the young to those drugs; and (3) that no adequate strategy has been developed to prevent that exposure upon legalization. Ultimately we proposed that discussion of drug legalization for *adults* be tabled until both proponents and opponents of legalization commit themselves to developing a strategy which would radically reduce cigarette and alcohol use by the young. Such a strategy could be used as a case study for possible drug legalization.

While not directly addressing our analysis or commenting on our proposal, Duke does make a brief effort to confront the problem that drug legalization poses to children. With respect to the harms that hard drugs could cause to children, he does acknowledge that "distribution of drugs to children [is] ... child abuse," thereby appearing to concede to our first point. However, Duke's discussion minimizes, or barely acknowledges, many of the worst harms that drugs threaten to inflict on children. As for the danger of increased drug use and exposure among the young after legalization, and the difficulty of devising legal barriers to such exposure, Duke is dismissive. Indeed, he advances the remarkable claim that we could be "far more successful" in protecting our children from drug use if drugs were legal for adults. The result is a blind alley, but one worth strolling down briefly.

Dangers to Children Resulting From Legalization

Whether or not children obtain easier access to drugs after the repeal of prohibition, many children will suffer the consequences of substance abuse through their parents' increased drug use. For example, it is well documented that drug use during pregnancy substantially increases the risk that a child will be born with a low birthweight and a small head circumference, which, along with other factors, increases the infant mortality risk by a factor of three. Although some of the suffering endured by drug-exposed newborns may, as Duke notes, be attributed to their mothers' lifestyle, as opposed to the chemical effects of the drugs, much of it cannot. Duke's analysis neglects to mention, for example, that children born of mothers regularly using heroin must go through a full "abstinence syndrome" (i.e. withdrawal), which encompasses the certainty of enormous pain and the potential for death. Without even advocating a full-scale research effort to rule out heroin, cocaine, and marijuana use as major risks for children in utero, Duke simply proposes legalization followed by an unspecified "comprehensive policy" for "dealing with" substance-abusing pregnant women.

Beyond the womb, sadly, Duke does not appear to recognize any further risks to children from their parents' use of now-illicit drugs. He ignores substantial evidence that prenatal and postnatal drug exposure causes enormous damage to children for years after birth. In the words of one recent journal article, prenatal and postnatal exposure leaves children vulnerable to "a variety of physical, cognitive, emotional, motor, and social developmental difficulties." Perhaps more tellingly—because this extends to drug abuse by adults outside the context of pregnancy—Duke and other proponents of drug legalization consistently fail to reckon the consequences of drug dependence for the quality of parenting that children receive. As Dr. Judy Howard, professor of pediatrics at U.C.L.A. and a clinician who works with children in drug-abusing households, recently put it: "When a parent is chemically dependent, ... the pediatrician cannot be confident that parenting functions are not compromised." Chronic drug use can so "impair and distort a parent's thoughts and perceptions" that she will have "difficulty remembering [her] own children's birthdates;" worse, the child faces a substantially elevated risk of abuse and neglect.

Most damaging of all, though, is the failure of legalization proponents to face up to the dangers of greater drug abuse *by* children. Duke ignores altogether the strong association between substance abuse and homelessness among adolescents, which leads thousands of kids every year into a desperately destructive life "on the street." Likewise, drug use has been shown to be strongly related to suicidal behaviors among high school students, as well as HIV-related sexual behaviors—facts not explicitly counted in Duke's cost-benefit analysis.

The most surprising omission from Duke's analysis, considering how heavily it focuses on the nexus between drugs and crime, is any discussion of the literature exploring the links between drugs and delinquency—in particular, evidence that substance abuse leads to delinquency. Indeed, the most substantial longitudinal study of at-risk youths ever conducted recently presented strong evidence that, "if substance use [by the adolescents studied] increased in seriousness this was accompanied by an increase in delinquency seriousness," but that increases in delinquency did not much affect substance abuse. This pattern tends to contradict the picture presented by Duke of youths becoming involved in the violent drug culture because it offers the chance for high illicit earnings under prohibition. Moreover, the drug that currently leads youths most directly toward delinquency is alcohol, which of course offers no black market reward for traffickers. If other now-illicit drugs became legal, and as readily available to teenagers as alcohol is, we should expect crime rates for that age group to rise, not fall, along with all the suffering that increased drug use can cause youths.

Preventing Youth Access

Why worry about harm to children when, as Duke declares, we can "treat the distribution of drugs to children like the child abuse that it is and put flagrant violators in prison for it," and when "adults who encourage children to engage in such 'adult' activities can[] be condemned"? At first these words seem strong, but then doubts creep in. Do the quotation marks around "adult" betray a recognition that it is adolescence, not comfortable middle age, when the urge to experiment with drugs is at its peak? And does that adjective "flagrant" inadvertently reveal just how little a post-prohibition state is likely to invest in nabbing casual, non-"flagrant" distributors of hard drugs who now give kids alcohol? . . .

How do we persuade young people to avoid substances that we adults embrace? And how do we expect the same drug traffickers who survive the war on drugs to neglect the only black market remaining to them once drugs are legal for adults?

Duke's answer, incredibly, appears to be that we can protect the young from drugs in the same way we have "severely condemned" sex between adults and children. No doubt sexual abuse is universally condemned, but it is nevertheless epidemic. The recent National Health and Social Life Survey, which comprehensively studied the sex life of Americans, found that 17 percent of women reported having been sexually touched before the age of 14, usually involving genital contact by men over the age of 18. And at least one study has found an association between drug abuse by a parent and sexual abuse of a child: the authors of the study conclude that this "suggests that . . . [the parents'] chemical dependence rendered them inadequate protectors of their daughters." What kind of child protectors will we be if we adopt legalization?

Drug Substitution

Even if no effective barriers can be raised to prevent juvenile access to drugs, Duke has one last line of defense for drug legalization. He asserts that any increase in juvenile use of marijuana, heroin, or cocaine might well be matched by a corresponding decrease in the use of alcohol, cigarettes, or inhalants, all of which he believes to be more dangerous. The assumption that cocaine, in particular, is a more benign substance than any of these drugs is highly questionable—especially given the limited knowledge we have regarding successful cocaine treatment. Nevertheless, it is worth lingering briefly to consider the claimed negative relationship between licit and illicit drug use.

On its face, this claim seems improbable and careful inspection does not improve its plausibility. For example, cigarettes are highly addictive, and as one recent longitudinal study found, "students who smoke are increasingly unlikely to quit as they get older." Even adolescents enrolled in model drug-prevention programs cannot be easily weaned from tobacco. So why would we expect kids to *substitute* cocaine and heroin for cigarettes, as opposed simply to adding them? As for inhalants, Duke is wrong to paint them either as "popular" or as an increasing threat to kids. Less than three percent of twelfth graders use inhalants regularly, and from 1976 to 1992 fluctuations in this rate have been statistically insignificant. And again, what, other than speculation, supports Duke's view that adolescents would be better off smoking crack than sniffing glue, or indeed would not do both *together* if given the chance.

Alcohol presents a more intriguing problem, for it is used more than any other drug by adolescents; at the same time, the percentage of young people who use it has tended to vary more than other "licit" drugs. As a result, it is possible to put Duke's substitution theory to a rough test. For if adolescents who use marijuana or cocaine do so instead of using alcohol, we would expect that in years with a higher percentage of students using those illicit drugs we would find a lower percentage of alcohol users. However, ... there is a strong *positive* correlation between rates of marijuana and cocaine use and rates of alcohol use. That is, in years when more kids use marijuana or cocaine, we can expect that more kids will also be using alcohol. Such correlations do not show that one kind of substance abuse causes another, but it does indicate the improbability of Duke's theory. Furthermore, these correlations must cause a small shiver of fear that drug legalization would make under-age abuse of alcohol even worse....

Benefits, Costs, and Irreducible Values

Because Duke and other proponents of drug legalization fail to take seriously the extremely knotty problem of protecting children from parental substance abuse and personal addiction, they cannot present us with a realistic estimate of the costs of legalization. And because their promise of less crime upon repeal of prohibition seems unlikely, the principle benefit they hold out is questionable. But one final aspect of their case against prohibition—the offense to fundamental notions of personal autonomy—is not lightly dismissed. Although this aspect of the debate is not the focus of Duke's commentary here, it merits at least brief consideration in conclusion.

Placed in a "rights" framework, the legalization debate can become uncomfortable for those defending prohibition. How is it, exactly, that a person wishing simply to enhance her private feelings in her own home can be punished by the state for doing so in the absence of a demonstrated harm to another? Why, as Duke asks, should we not ban swimming, motorcycles, and obesity, all of which put our lives and health at risk? Is not drug prohibition, as he calls it, a " 'gross usurpation' of [John Stuart] Mill's concept of liberty"?

Those of us who remain skeptical of legalization must, of course, quickly take refuge in Mill's famous proviso that "[a]cts injurious to others require a totally different treatment." We can return to the vulnerabilities of children and the problems this poses for drug legalization. We can point out how incapable the young are of defending themselves against the ravages of a drug culture or of making rational choices about drug use. We can argue that widespread drug use will increase the risks everyone faces while driving their cars or out in public. We can maintain that simply because we tolerate some risks, and some risky behavior (such as alcohol consumption), we do not have to tolerate all risks and any behavior. And even if the attack on prohibition has answers for these arguments, we still may view the legalization alternative, when dressed in the garb of "rights," as fundamentally incoherent, proving too little and too much all at once.

The case for legalization proves too little in failing to give clear shape to its agenda. Thus, Duke is wholly unwilling to follow a "rights" perspective to its logical conclusion and propose the elimination of *all* controls on drugs—he would retain prohibition against highly dangerous *and unpopular drugs*. While certainly an understandable qualification, this seemingly minor reservation is a gaping hole in the "liberty" rationale for legalization. Are only *unpopular* rights the ones to be suppressed? If so, what is the point, in a democracy anyway, of having "rights" at all? Likewise, what is the moral basis in "liberty" for Duke's generous, but undeveloped, dictum that "[w]e should make treatment available at no cost to any abuser who wants it"?

That last question perhaps points most properly to a sense in which the libertarian underpinnings of the case for legalization prove too much. For why should taxpayers, and not the person who has exercised her privacy right to choose drug abuse, pay for any necessary treatment? Fear of just this kind of question caused advocates for the homeless to suppress for years any suggestion that many of their clients might be chemically dependent. Indeed, why should the government ever intervene against any personal choice, whether it is to buy uninspected meat, spoiled cheese, or unsafe medicines? Specifically, how is it that Duke wants the Food and Drug Administration to continue to exist and yet have no authority over recreational drugs?

More insidiously, though, the case for legalization, in seeking to rehabilitate "popular" illicit drugs through a narrow libertarianism yoked to a myopic cost-benefit analysis, seems to be "proving" a new corollary to Mill's harm principle. It will now read: I cannot exercise my liberty in a way that will cause you serious harm, *unless* I do so with so determinedly malevolent an intent and so viciously efficient a means that I make life cheap, neighborhoods ugly, children expendable, and law enforcement all but impossible. *Then* you will see that your "costs" of denying my "right" are simply too high and the "benefits" of generous surrender will be great, indeed. But this generosity—slavish to miscreants, blind to victims, just, ultimately, only to the unjust—is generosity misplaced.

POSTSCRIPT

Should Drug Use Be Legalized?

It should be emphasized that one choice is not necessarily the easy one and the other the hard one. The "legalizers" are occasionally depicted as advocates of a free market of drugs, of letting individuals make decisions about personal use of drugs, and of letting the market regulate the price of a product that now has an artificially elevated price. But most "legalizers" are, in fact, asking that government involvement in dealing with the drug problem continue. To suggest a noncriminal approach to drugs is not to advocate a hands-off approach. Treatment and education are needed. It is not all that clear that this would be cheaper than the current approach.

It would also not necessarily be easier. Other than complete legalization, where drugs might be as readily available as aspirin, most approaches call for some regulation by the state. Choices would have to be made among alternatives ranging from outlawing sales to minors to requiring medical prescriptions for some drugs to establishing clinics that would distribute the drugs. Each of these alternatives would raise questions about free access and about effects on the black market for drugs.

Recent writings on the legalization question include Steven B. Duke and Albert C. Gross, *America's Longest War: Rethinking Our Tragic Crusade Against Drugs* (Putnam's Sons, 1993); Ronald Bayer and Gerald M. Oppenheimer, eds., *Confronting Drug Policy: Illicit Drugs in a Free Society* (Cambridge University Press, 1993); Arnold S. Trebach and James A. Inciardi, *Legalize It? Debating American Drug Policy* (American University Press, 1993); Mark H. Moore, "Drugs: Getting a Fix on the Problem and the Solution," 8 *Yale Law and Policy Review* 8 (1990); and James Q. Wilson, "Against the Legalization of Drugs," *Commentary* (February 1990). A. Morgan Cloud, in "Cocaine, Demand, and the Addiction: A Study of the Possible Convergence of Rational Theory and National Policy," 42 *Vanderbilt Law Review* 725 (1989), discusses the legislative history of prevention and treatment programs. Herbert L. Packer, in *The Limits of the Criminal Sanction* (Stanford University Press, 1968), analyzes problems associated with legal enforcement of moral norms. The myths and realities of the Prohibition era are examined in Norman H. Clark, *Deliver Us From Evil* (W. W. Norton, 1976) and David E. Kyvig, ed., *Law, Alcohol, and Order: Perspectives on National Prohibition* (Greenwood Press, 1985).

Online Ombuds Office

If cyberspace is a place where communities are formed, then it will also be a place where disputes need to be solved. The Online Ombuds Office was one of the first projects in online dispute resolution.

```
http://www.ombuds.org/center/ombuds.html
```

Organized Crime: A Crime Statistics Site

This is one of the best sites for finding out about crime statistics, where they come from, and how reliable they are.

```
http://www.crime.org
```

Politics1.com

This site links to organizations—representing the Left, the Right, and the middle—that are working on many controversial legal issues.

```
http://www.politics1.com/issues.htm
```

Law.com

At Law.com you can read about recent cases as well as current legal issues in the news.

```
http://www.lawnewsnetwork.com
```

PART 3

Law and the Community

*W*hile we are all citizens of a state, we are also participants in various communities whose members generally hold shared values and hope
to satisfy shared goals. The challenge of finding appropriate relationships between the individual, the state, and the community is examined
in this section.

- Should Law Enforcement Officials Notify the Community When
  a Convicted Sex Offender Moves In?

- Does the First Amendment Protect an Informational Web Site
  That May Encourage Violent Acts?

- Should Same-Sex Marriages Be Lawful?

- Are Public School Officials Liable for Damages in Cases of
  Student-on-Student Sexual Harassment?

- Should Children With Disabilities Be Provided With
  Extraordinary Care in Order to Attend Regular Classes
  in Public Schools?

- Do Affirmative Action Programs in Public School Admissions
  Policies Violate the Fourteenth Amendment?

ISSUE 14

Should Law Enforcement Officials Notify the Community When a Convicted Sex Offender Moves In?

YES: Simeon Schopf, from " 'Megan's Law': Community Notification and the Constitution," *Columbia Journal of Law and Social Problems* (vol. 29, 1995)

NO: Bonnie Steinbock, from "Megan's Law: A Policy Perspective," *Criminal Justice Ethics* (Summer/Fall 1995)

ISSUE SUMMARY

YES: Simeon Schopf, a writing and research editor for the *Columbia Journal of Law and Social Problems*, looks at various constitutional objections to Megan's Law and concludes that, in the balance of interests, such laws are constitutional.

NO: Bonnie Steinbock, a legal philosopher, focuses on the moral issues posed by the notification statutes and argues that Megan's Law fails to serve its ultimate goal—protecting children.

O n July 29, 1994, seven-year-old Megan Kanka was sexually assaulted and murdered a short distance from her home in Hamilton Township, New Jersey. Her neighbor Jesse Timmendequas was arrested and ultimately convicted of this crime. Timmendequas, who enticed Megan to come into his house with the promise of a puppy waiting inside for her, was a twice-convicted sexual offender who had previously served time for fondling and then attempting to strangle another seven-year-old girl. Timmendequas shared the house across the street from the Kankas with two other convicted sexual offenders, men he had served time with at Avenal, the New Jersey facility for sex offenders. Neither the Kankas nor their neighbors were aware of the prior criminal record of Timmendequas and his housemates.

Spurred on by the grief and outrage of many of its citizens, the New Jersey legislature acted quickly, and by the end of October 1994 it had enacted a comprehensive statutory scheme to meet the perceived threat to society posed by sexual offenders. Legislation was passed that allowed for the civil commitment of convicted sexual offenders who had finished their prison sentences but, according to psychiatric professionals, still posed a serious danger to society. What has come to be known as "Megan's Law" was part of this larger statutory scheme and dealt specifically with the registration of released sexual offenders and notification to communities when such individuals relocated within their jurisdiction. The law called for a three-tier classification of released sexual offenders based on a calculus of perceived risk. County prosecutors were assigned the duty of actually making the risk assessment, which ranged from low- to high-risk individuals. Low-risk offenders required notification only to law enforcement agencies within the community in which the offender was released; moderate-risk assessments called for notification to school and community organizations as well; and high-risk offenders called for notice by means of public postings and mailings to the entire community, in addition to the means of notification utilized for low- and moderate-risk offenders.

As was to be expected, Megan's Law was quickly subjected to various constitutional challenges: Some argued that it ran afoul of the Fifth Amendment's double jeopardy clause or that it violated the Eighth Amendment's proscription against "cruel and unusual punishment." Others contended that it violated the Fourteenth Amendment's due process clause. Many critics of the law have argued that even convicted sex offenders have privacy interests that are worthy of constitutional protection; simply put, once released from prison, they have a right to be left alone. Finally, some have argued that Megan's Law and similar pieces of legislation risk bringing more violence to the community in the form of vigilante attacks on the identified (or worse, *mis*identified) offender. Defenders of Megan's Law counter that any rights such individuals have must be balanced against the right of communities to defend themselves against the dangers posed by sex offenders living within the general population.

In the readings that follow, two perspectives are offered on this controversial issue. Simeon Schopf defends Megan's Law from a legalistic point of view. He concludes that, in the balance of interests, such laws are constitutional. Bonnie Steinbock turns away from the constitutional questions involved to focus on the moral issues posed by the notification statutes. From this perspective, argues Steinbock, Megan's Law fails to serve its ultimate goal—protecting children.

Simeon Schopf

 **YES**

"Megan's Law": Community Notification and the Constitution

Introduction

In late July 1994 seven-year-old Megan Kanka was raped and strangled to death. What separates this act of violence from those that litter the newspapers every day is that Megan's alleged killer lived across the street. The three men who lived in the house across the street from the Kankas in Hamilton Township, New Jersey had served time together in Avenel, the facility for sex offenders in New Jersey. Of course, the Kankas and their neighbors were unaware of the presence of this club. Megan's parents and neighbors learned of Jesse Timmendequas's history only after he was arrested and had confessed to the murder. They discovered that Timmendequas, like his roommates, was a convicted pedophile, who had served time for fondling a seven-year-old girl and almost strangling her. The police say that Timmendequas enticed Megan to come into his house by promising to show her his puppy, and then he raped her and strangled her to death.

Unfortunately, incidents like this one are not limited to the quiet streets of Hamilton Township. Megan's murder brought national attention to yet another issue in the raging war on violent crime: how to deal with released sex offenders. The public outrage led to a push for new legislation which culminated in the inclusion of special provisions in the Federal Violent Crime Control and Law Enforcement Act of 1994 (the "Act") to protect children from sex offenders. The Act, signed into law by President Clinton on September 13, 1994, requires states to set up programs to protect against violent sex offenders. The Act requires released sex offenders and those who commit crimes against children to register with the local police and notify the authorities of any change of address. Moreover, in response to the public concern spurred by Megan Kanka's brutal murder, the Act goes even further:

> (d) RELEASE OF INFORMATION. The information collected under a State registration program shall be treated as private data except that—

From Simeon Schopf, " 'Megan's Law': Community Notification and the Constitution," *Columbia Journal of Law and Social Problems*, vol. 29 (1995). Copyright © 1995 by Columbia Journal of Law and Social Problems, Inc. Reprinted by permission. Notes omitted.

1. such information may be disclosed to law enforcement agencies for law enforcement purposes;
2. such information may be disclosed to government agencies conducting confidential background checks; and
3. the designated State law enforcement and any local law enforcement agency authorized by the State agency may release relevant information that is necessary to protect the public concerning a specific person required to register under this section, except that the identity of a victim of an offense that requires registration under this section shall not be released.

This community notification provision has been the subject of considerable controversy. "Megan's Law," as the provision is sometimes called, has been challenged by civil libertarians as a violation of sex offenders' constitutional rights. As this article will demonstrate, "Megan's Law" survives these challenges and is constitutional....

State Legislation

Before the enactment of "Megan's Law," most states permitted disclosure of information about sex offenders only to police and school officials. However, even then, a number of states seriously considered allowing broader disclosure to promote public safety. Since 1990, twenty-nine states have passed community notification or offender registration laws, many in response to violent crimes like the one that took Megan Kanka's life. Washington's Community Protection Act of 1990 allows the community access to information regarding sex offenders registered there. Offenders required to register must do so with the sheriff in the county where they will reside. According to this law, the police determine what information is to be released and who is entitled to it....

Cruel and Unusual Punishment and Ex Post Facto

[A] potential obstacle facing advocates of "Megan's Law" is the claim that the provision violates the Eighth Amendment as cruel and unusual punishment. Released offenders could argue that they have paid their debt to society and have done all that the penal system requires of them. Therefore, any additional sanctions must be considered cruel and unusual punishment and be invalidated.

While the question of the Eighth Amendment's applicability to "Megan's Law" is a new one, the issue of cruel and unusual punishment has been considered in the context of registration laws. Many states have laws requiring that certain released convicts register with the local law enforcement authorities. Often the question of whether a violation of the Eighth Amendment has occurred hinges on whether the registration requirement can be considered "punishment." Courts have used a variety of tests to determine whether a registration requirement is a punishment. In *Kennedy v. Mendoza-Martinez,* the U.S.

Supreme Court said that when it is unclear whether the legislature intended the requirement to be penal or regulatory, the court must ask:

> Whether the sanction involves an affirmative disability or restraint, whether it has historically been regarded as a punishment, whether it comes into play only on a finding of *scienter,* whether its operation will promote the traditional aims of punishment—retribution and deterrence, whether the behavior to which it applies is already a crime, whether an alternative purpose to which it may rationally be connected is assignable for it, and whether it appears excessive in relation to the alternative purpose assigned. . . .

In *In re Reed,* the California Supreme Court applied the *Kennedy* test in holding that California's Sex Offender Registration Act did punish those required to register.

In *People v. Adams,* the Illinois Supreme Court refused to apply the *Kennedy* test and instead relied on the standard set by the Supreme Court in *Trop v. Dulles:*

> In deciding whether or not a law is penal, this Court has generally based its determination upon the purpose of the statute. If the statute imposes a disability for the purposes of punishment—that is, to reprimand the wrongdoer, to deter others, etc.—it has been considered penal. But a statute has been considered nonpenal if it imposes a disability, not to punish, but to accomplish some other legitimate governmental purpose.

The Supreme Court added that, along with the general purpose of the statute, the severity of the disability it imposed is relevant in determining the nature of the law. In *Adams,* the defendant argued that the Act was cruel and unusual punishment and thus violated the federal and state constitutions. The court concluded that the registration duty placed on sex offenders did not constitute a punishment and thus was not within the scope of the Eighth Amendment. Applying the principles stated in *Trop,* the Illinois court found that the requirement of registration "is an innocuous duty compared to the potential alternative of spending an extended period of years in prison." Moreover, the purpose of the Registration Act, in the court's view, was clearly to give an advantage to the law enforcement officials in protecting the children, rather than to burden the offender with additional punishment.

This analysis can be applied to "Megan's Law." Community notification, after all, begins with the offender's duty to register. The fact that law enforcement officials are instructed in certain instances to notify the community of the presence of the offender does not, in itself, create any additional punitive burden on the offender. All that is required of the released offender is registration; the other obligations imposed by the Act are directed at law enforcement officials. It is possible that some courts may view notification as more intrusive than mere registration. However, as was true in the case of the Illinois Registration Act, the purpose of "Megan's Law" is to facilitate the protection of the community and its children. The language of the community notification provision is unambiguous. "The designated State law enforcement agency authorized by the State agency may release relevant information that is necessary to protect the public concerning a specific person required to register under this section." The goal of the law is not to make life miserable for the released offender, but to protect the vulnerable from those most likely to commit violent crimes. Given the standard established by the Supreme Court in *Trop v. Dulles*, "Megan's Law" would not be considered penal in its nature. Community notification was enacted, "not to punish, but to accomplish some other legitimate governmental purpose." The possibility exists that a court might apply the *Kennedy* test to "Megan's Law." However, the bulk of recent case law suggests that such an application would be inappropriate.

Even assuming that a court found the community notification provision to be a punishment, it would not violate the Eighth Amendment unless it were deemed "cruel and unusual." In *Solem v. Helm* the Supreme Court developed a three-prong test for determining whether a punishment is proportional to the crime and therefore not an Eighth Amendment violation. The court should question "the gravity of the offense and the harshness of the penalty[,] . . . the sentences imposed on other criminals in the same jurisdiction . . . and the sentences imposed for commission of the same crime in other jurisdictions."

It could be argued that the stigma associated with public notification places it in the category of excessive punishment. However, the Supreme Court's decision in *Harmelin v. Michigan* suggests that this argument is not likely to succeed.

> The Harmelin plurality recognized that reviewing courts should grant substantial deference to the authority of legislatures to determine the proper types and limits of punishments for crimes. Furthermore, the Court noted that the Eighth Amendment does not mandate strict proportionality between crime and sentence but rather "forbids extreme sentences that are grossly disproportionate to the crime." A statute providing for the release of information regarding only the most dangerous criminals promotes the important purpose of notifying the public of their presence while still protecting the privacy of those willing to undergo treatment.

The Ex Post Facto Clause of the U.S. Constitution forbids the enactment of any law that imposes punishment for an act that was not punishable when it was committed, or any law that increases the penalty applicable to the crime when it was committed. In *Beazell v. Ohio,* the Supreme Court interpreted the Ex Post Facto Clause as follows:

> It is settled, by decisions of this Court so well known that their citation may be dispensed with, that any statute which punishes as a crime an act previously committed, which was innocent when done; which makes more burdensome the punishment for a crime, after its commission, or which deprives one charged with crime of any defense available according to law at the time when the act was committed, is prohibited as ex post facto.

The basic message of the Ex Post Facto Clause is that "[l]egislatures may not retroactively alter the definition of crimes or increase the punishment for criminal acts." Released offenders suddenly subject to community notification laws may claim that at the time of their incarceration no law existed requiring them, as a result of their crime, to register and face the sanction of community notification. Therefore, their argument might be that "Megan's Law' is invalid as a violation of the Ex Post Facto Clause.

Long ago the Supreme Court established that the prohibition on ex post facto laws applies to penal statutes which disadvantage the individual subject to them. In *Collins v. Youngblood,* the Supreme Court rejected a broad reading of the Ex Post Facto Clause and limited application of the ex post facto prohibition to the *Calder* categories. "After *Collins,* the proper inquiry is not whether the law is a burden, or 'disadvantageous' to the defendant, but whether it makes more burdensome the *punishment* for the crime."

The Ex Post Facto Clause only applies to laws imposing criminal punishment. Therefore the question of the applicability of the ex post facto prohibition to "Megan's Law" necessarily comes down, as it did in the analysis of cruel and unusual punishment, to a determination of whether its provisions are penal in their nature. Again relying on *Trop v. Dulles,* we must look to the legislative purpose in creating the community notification provision. As was shown above, the very language of "Megan's Law" indicates that its purpose is other than penal.

Here, as with the discussion of cruel and unusual punishment, comparison of "Megan's Law" and state registration laws can be enlightening. In *State v. Ward,* Washington's sex offender registration statute was challenged on, among other things, ex post facto grounds. The court dismissed the challenge saying that

> appellants are not "disadvantaged" by the statute because it does not *alter the standard of punishment* which existed under prior law. While the requirement to register as a sex offender may indeed be burdensome, the focus of the inquiry is whether registration constitutes punishment. We conclude that it does not.

The appellants argued that the act did amount to a punishment because it allowed law enforcement agencies to release information regarding the offenders to the public. The court, however, rejected this claim, holding that "because the Legislature has limited the disclosure of registration information to the public, the statutory registration scheme does not impose additional punishment on registrants." The limits placed by the Washington State legislature on disclosure in this case are remarkably similar to the conditions enumerated in "Megan's Law." "The statute regulating disclosure, RCW 4.24.550, provides that '[p]ublic agencies are authorized to release relevant and necessary information regarding sex offenders to the public when the release of the information is necessary for public protection.'" The language of "Megan's Law" provides that "the designated State law enforcement agency and any local law enforcement agency authorized by the State agency may release relevant information that is necessary to protect the public...." It seems then from the virtually identical language of the two statutes that the Washington court would conclude that "Megan's Law" also features an allowance only for limited disclosure. In concluding that the Ex Post Facto Clause is not violated by the registration act's disclosure provision, the court explained that "[a]ny publicity or other burdens which may result from disclosure arise from the offender's future dangerousness, and not as punishment for past crimes. We conclude, therefore, that registration and limited public disclosure does not alter the standard of punishment which existed under prior law." ...

Judicial reaction to community notification and the ex post facto question will depend largely on how each state decides to draft its legislation. However, as the New Jersey Supreme Court points out, as long as the legislation has as its clear purpose the protection of society, the sanctions imposed are unlikely to be deemed punishment by the reviewing courts and the community notification provision should not face serious ex post facto challenge.

Due Process and Privacy Rights

The final constitutional issue that will be discussed is the sex offender's privacy rights under the Fifth Amendment's Due Process Clause.... [T]he Constitution does not explicitly grant a right to privacy. Nevertheless, a privacy right protected by the Due Process Clause has been identified and adopted by the Supreme Court. The Court in *Griswold v. Connecticut* explained that:

> specific guarantees in the Bill of Rights have penumbras, formed by emanations from those guarantees that help give them life and substance. Various guarantees create zones of privacy. The right of association contained in the penumbra of the First Amendment is one, as we have seen. The Third Amendment in its prohibition against the quartering of soldiers "in any house" in time of peace without the consent of the owner is another facet of that privacy. The Fourth Amendment explicitly affirms the "right of the people to be secure in their persons, houses, papers, and effects, against unreasonable searches and seizures." The Fifth Amendment in its Self-Incrimination Clause enables the citizen to create a zone of privacy which government many not force him to surrender to his detriment.

These several guarantees in the Bill of Rights combine to protect the individual's "privacy interest" by creating a "zone of privacy," and adding privacy to the list of fundamental rights protected by the Due Process Clause.

... Critics have referred to "Megan's Law" as "scarlet letter" law, arguing that those subject to its provisions are branded and precluded from living private lives. However, ... the right to privacy is not unlimited.

> The right of privacy is not absolute, however, and in almost every case, the court must resolve a conflict between the rights of the individual on one hand, and the interests of society ... on the other. The public has an interest in the free dissemination of news and information, and the press has a duty to publish such news qualified only by propriety, the law of libel, and the right of the individual to have his private life protected.

... It is very difficult to know objectively what is necessary to achieve the goal of public safety. However, if the standard is to take into account the sentiment of the public to be protected, the need for community notification is persuasive....

The national outcry after Megan Kanka's murder suggests that the nation fears for the safety of its children and feels particularly vulnerable with regard to released sex offenders. As long as sex offenders are allowed to return to the community, community notification may be the only way for their neighbors to feel that they have any control over the protection of the neighborhood's children. Indeed, it is hard to imagine how the community could be adequately protected, or freed from its vulnerability, if sex offenders continue to be allowed to live anonymously among their neighbors.

Whenever individual privacy rights are at issue, a delicate balance must be struck. In the case of "Megan's Law," society's right to be protected is compelling, and could not easily be limited by the sex offender's right to live anonymously. Community notification should pass even the strictest scrutiny and survive any challenge on privacy grounds.

Additional Challenges

Constitutional challenges are not the only obstacles that "Megan's Law" faces. Since the law's enactment in September of 1994, critics have questioned the effect that the law would have on the rehabilitation of sex offenders. Some argue that

> branding sexual offenders might actually do more harm than good. They say the crime bill's community notification provision—known as "Megan's law" —and similar state measures could drive sexual predators away from getting help and irretrievably harm released offenders who have served their time and truly are controlling their dangerous urges.

James Pedigo, chief psychiatrist at the Joseph J. Peters Institute in Philadelphia, adds this concern: "If it prevented them from getting a job ... it could strongly affect their self-esteem, which would effect recidivism." Mental health professionals say that rehabilitation of sex offenders is possible. Assuming that rehabilitation is the best way to limit repeat offenses, the argument is that anything that could hinder the rehabilitation process would be counterproductive. On the other hand, Pedigo himself admits that community notification "would help people in the neighborhood to be on the alert." The question of the effect of community notification on rehabilitation, and the likelihood of successful rehabilitation of sex offenders, complicates the issue of the appropriateness of "Megan's Law."

A related concern raised by critics of community notification is that the law will not actually remedy the problem of violent sexual crime but rather will simply move it someplace else. Therapists wonder: "Would a notification law merely prompt an offender intent on assault to shift the hunt to a neighborhood where the pedophile is not known?" New Jersey Governor Christine Todd Whitman cautioned that "[t]here is a concern here for doing something that is really going to make a difference and not just creating a class of people who are moving from community to community."

Perhaps the most serious non-constitutional challenge to "Megan's Law" is that it has led, and will continue to lead, to vigilantism. In Lynwood, Washington in 1993, the sheriffs handed out fliers to warn local residents that a child molester was soon to be released and was moving into their neighborhood. The day the rapist was to move in, his house was torched. More recently, after the community notification law passed in New Jersey, two men broke into a home in Phillipsburg and attacked a man they mistook for a sex offender who was staying at the same address. The prospect of angry citizens taking the law into their own hands may complicate the job that local law enforcement officials have ahead of them in the new community notification scheme.

Conclusion

... The future of "Megan's Law" depends in large part on the way states draft their respective laws. If the states draft plans that make no provision for distinguishing between different offenders, ... they may face serious constitutional and practical obstacles. If, however, states are careful to draft legislation limiting community notification to those instances where it is truly necessary to protect the public, their plans should be well received by both the public and the courts.

Bonnie Steinbock

A Policy Perspective

O n July 29, 1994, Jesse Timmendequas invited seven-year-old Megan Kanka into his home to see his puppy. Once inside, Timmendequas forced Megan into his room, strangled her with a belt, and sexually assaulted her. She died from asphyxiation. Only after Megan's death did authorities reveal that Timmendequas had two previous convictions for child sexual abuse. Timmendequas had been sentenced to ten years at the Adult Diagnostic and Treatment Center, known as Avenel. With time off for good behavior, Timmendequas was released after serving only six years. At the time of Megan's murder, Timmendequas lived across the street from the Kankas with two other convicted sex offenders whom he had met at Avenel.

The outrage of community members that convicted sex offenders could live anonymously in their communities led to the passage of "Megan's Law" in New Jersey. In 1990, Washington State enacted its Community Protection Act after a seven-year-old Tacoma boy was lured into a wooded area by a recently released sex offender who orally and anally raped the boy and then cut off his penis. The man had a twenty-four-year record of assaults on young people, including the kidnapping and assault of two teenage girls and involvement in the murder of a fifteen-year-old schoolmate.

Registration of sex offenders with police is relatively unproblematic. It is community notification that has sparked the greatest controversy. In arguments before New Jersey's Supreme Court, lawyers opposed to Megan's Law criticized the law as stigmatizing and humiliating for offenders. They also said it was punitive, increasing the punishment to which offenders had originally been sentenced, and was therefore unconstitutional. In addition, they said that the law was an invasive measure that infringed the privacy and liberties of convicted sex offenders who had supposedly paid their debt to society. Other commentators point out that the stigma attached to sex offenders by society, and reinforced by notification laws, interferes with their ability to find jobs and places to live and to resume a normal life.

Whatever the merit of these objections as a matter of law—an issue I leave to those with legal backgrounds—they do not have much moral force. As Megan's mother, Maureen Kanka, expressed it, "I have a dead little girl. How can they sit there and worry about if it's punishment? What about our kids?

From Bonnie Steinbock, "Megan's Law: A Policy Perspective," *Criminal Justice Ethics,* vol. 14, no. 2 (Summer/Fall 1995). Copyright © 1995 by *Criminal Justice Ethics.* Reprinted by permission of The Institute for Criminal Justice Ethics, 555 West 57th Street, Suite 601, New York, NY 10019-1029. Notes omitted.

That's ultimately what it comes down to. Our kids have rights and it's time someone started addressing them." It seems to me that Mrs. Kanka has framed the issue correctly. When a little boy has been raped and had his penis cut off, or when a little girl has been raped and murdered, worry about humiliating the people who committed these crimes seems a little overly sensitive.

I start then with the assumption that the paramount issue is the protection of children, that their rights to be safe from violent sexual assault certainly outweigh the rights of sexual predators not to be stigmatized. The trouble is that notification laws will not protect children. They are at best ineffective and at worse create a false sense of security that may actually expose children to risk. In addition, there is the danger of vigilantism that risks harming innocent bystanders and is contrary to the rule of law even when directed at the guilty.

First, Megan's Law focuses on a tiny percentage of those who commit sexual crimes against children, namely, dangerous strangers. Between seventy-five and eighty-nine percent of child sexual abuse is committed by relatives and friends. Yet Megan's Law explicitly targets for community notification sexual predators whose "sexual preference is for minor children *outside his or her immediate family.*" Thus, it fails to protect children from the most common kind of sexual abuse, that inflicted by friends and relatives. Indeed, such laws may "promote a false sense of security, lulling parents and kids into the big-bad-man mindset when many molesters are in fact trusted authority figures or family members."

It might be objected that it is not unreasonable to focus on the dangerous stranger even though this accounts for a very small percentage of child sexual abusers, simply because the dangerous stranger is likely to inflict greater harm on the child than a relative or family friend. Although all sexual abuse of children is undesirable, there is a much greater need to protect children from violent sexual predators than from pedophiles who fondle children or expose themselves.

However, this raises the question whether it is possible to determine who are the truly dangerous sex offenders. At first glance, this might seem simple. Columnist Suzanne Fields notes that Jesse Timmendequas had served just six years after two convictions for sexually assaulting two young girls and asks rhetorically, "Was there any doubt that he would strike again?" Yet while it may seem obvious, with 20-20 hindsight, that Timmendequas would commit more crimes if released, in fact it is not easy to predict either dangerousness or the propensity to reoffend. Studies indicate that predictions of an offender's dangerousness or propensity to reoffend average only a one-third accuracy rate. Thus, it is relatively arbitrary which offenders are placed into tier three and subject to community notification. This is the second reason why Megan's Law is not a good bet for protecting children. Inevitably, some sex offenders who would not have committed future crimes will be placed erroneously in the third tier, and unfairly stigmatized, while others who will go on to harm other children will escape community notification.

Nevertheless, perhaps some offenders are so clearly sociopaths that professionals can tell with a high degree of certainty that they are dangerous, violent, and likely to repeat their crimes. Then the question has to be, why on earth do we release such people? Worse, why do we release them *without supervision*? Under current law, once sex offenders complete their sentences at Avenel, they do not have to attend outpatient therapy or report to any authorities. In a psychiatric evaluation in February 1988, shortly before he was released, Timmendequas himself said that he needed more therapy and expressed fears about adjusting to life outside of the center. His therapist also urged that he remain institutionalized, or at least undergo "intensive psychotherapy in the community following release," but this was not done since Timmendequas had completed his sentence. "[W]e have no legal jurisdiction over anyone who has completed a jail sentence," says Grace Rogers, acting superintendent of the Avenel prison. "There's absolutely nothing we can do." Why has there not been community outrage and a "Megan's Law" about this absurd flaw in the law?

Aside from the epistemological problem of correctly identifying recidivists, some dangerous sex offenders escape notification because they have not been convicted of a crime. Some just were never caught, but there are other ways to escape notification. For example, the suspect arrested in the Polly Klaas kidnapping case, Richard Allen Davis, had spent more than fifteen years in prison since 1973 for sex convictions, but because he had avoided sex offense charges through plea bargains, he was exempt from registration and notification.

A third reason why Megan's Law will not protect children is that notifying community members of the presence of convicted sex offenders will not prevent offenders from reoffending. "Released sex offenders ... who experience a compulsion to offend, will find a victim regardless of whether the victim resides in a notified or unnotified community." In some jurisdictions, neighbors within a three-block radius must be notified of the presence of a paroled sex offender. What's to stop an energetic pedophile from walking four or five blocks to find a victim? One demonstrated effect of community notification laws is that sex offenders tend to flee the notified community. Thus, even if notification provides some measure of protection to one community, it may be at the expense of another. Offenders are likely to relocate in areas that either do not have notification laws or that do not enforce them. "In particular, sex offenders find large cities and inner city areas attractive because law enforcement agencies in these areas usually lack the time and resources to enforce community notification laws." Community notification simply transfers the problem of dangerous sex offenders from middle and upper-class communities to poor inner-city neighborhoods.

Fourth, the success of Megan's Law depends on the cooperation of convicted sex offenders. Although they are required by law to register with the police, not all do. Some register under a phony address. Many move frequently. Police lack the resources to track down those who fail to comply, in part because New Jersey legislators passed Megan's Law without appropriating any funds for its enforcement. The inevitable conclusion is that the legislators were not really serious about protecting children, but did what was likely to be politically popular.

However, even if there is little reason to think that Megan's Law will protect children, is there any harm from such laws, which are, after all, wanted by many voters? Quite aside from the problem of promoting false security, the greatest harm posed by notification laws is vigilantism. In Washington, notification laws have prompted several incidents of vigilantism. The family home of Joseph Gallardo, a convicted child rapist, was burned down by angry neighbors who had heard he was about to be released from prison. Not only the convicted offenders, but their relatives have been subjected to death threats, eggs thrown at their homes, and eviction. Worse, in Warren County, New Jersey, a father and son broke into a house, looking for a convicted child molester whose address was made public, and beat an innocent man who happened to be staying there. Thus, Megan's Law is not harmless pandering to voter preference, but is itself a threat to innocent people and a law-abiding society.

Some commentators oppose notification because it does not address the root problems of child abuse. One writes:

> [N]otifying community members of released sex offenders neither confronts the causes of child sexual abuse nor looks to help offenders control their deviant behavior. Thus, Megan's Law represents a short-term solution that will not deter convicted sex offenders from reoffending.

But can sex offenders be taught to control their behavior? This is extremely controversial. A 1989 article in the journal *Psychological Bulletin,* reviewing studies of treatment for sex offenders before 1985, concluded that there was no successful treatment. Andrew Vachss, a lawyer who represents children, characterizes sexual predators as crafty sociopaths who "laugh behind their masks at our attempts to understand and rehabilitate them." He calls rehabilitation for chronic sexual predators "a joke":

> A 1992 study of 767 rapists and child molesters in Minnesota found those who completed psychiatric treatment were arrested more often for new sex crimes than those who had not been treated at all. A Canadian survey that tracked released child molesters for 20 years revealed a 43 percent recidivism rate regardless of the therapy.

However, a new generation of more sophisticated therapies is challenging the conventional wisdom that sex offenders cannot be rehabilitated. "The new view is that, as with alcoholism, there is no complete 'cure' for sex offenders, but that with help they can manage their sexual impulses without committing new crimes." The new treatment, called "relapse prevention," focuses on helping sex offenders control the cycle of troubling emotions, distorted thinking, and deviant sex fantasies that lead to their sex crimes, whether rape, child molesting, exhibitionism, or voyeurism. A first step is helping the men develop empathy for their victims by reading accounts and watching videotapes from the victims' perspective. Proponents claim that the recidivism rate of those who complete programs in relapse prevention is about half that of offenders who receive no treatment.

There is probably truth in the claims of both sides. Therapy is probably helpful for some sex offenders, but unlikely to rehabilitate sexual sociopaths who are incapable of empathy. Psychologists agree that sex offenders must be highly motivated for the therapy to work, and some offenders have no interest in changing their behavior. In any event, relatively few convicted sex offenders (about twenty-five percent) receive any treatment at all. Consider what has occurred at Avenel, once a model treatment center. When it opened in 1976, it provided inmates with individual and small group therapy, sometimes on a daily basis, and was headed by a superintendent with an expertise in mental health. However, its budget was reduced, staff was cut, the quality of therapy declined, and the inmate population, designed to be 594, grew to 681. By 1989, Avenel had changed from a treatment center into a maximum-security prison. "What passes for treatment is one and one-half hours of group therapy per week. There are no bilingual counselors and no one-to-one therapy."

It is beyond the scope of this essay to attempt to determine whether it is worthwhile to put resources into treatment programs for sex offenders. The evidence of success in Vermont and California suggests that further research and experimentation should be tried. Nevertheless, it seems likely that some sex offenders—the hard-core, violent sexual predators—cannot be rehabilitated. They should get longer sentences and be released, if at all, only under strict supervision.

The remaining avenues for protecting children are supervision and education. Indeed, notification is supported by some partly because they think it will motivate parents to educate their children about sex crimes. However, this is a weak argument for notification, in light of all its problems. Parents will be motivated to educate their children simply by understanding that this is the best way to protect them. But what should be the content of the education? I dissent from the view that we should be educating young children about sex crimes. It seems to me that this is more likely to frighten them than to protect them. Nor will pointing out individuals the children should avoid provide adequate protection. Mrs. Kanka said, "If I had known that three sex perverts were living across the street from me, Megan would be alive today." Perhaps so, but notification would not prevent another Megan in another neighborhood from becoming a victim. Nor would notification protect Megan from a sex pervert who was not registered or who had escaped tier-three classification. A better way to protect children is by giving them sensible safety rules, for example, that they are not to go with strangers: not into their houses, in their cars, or into the woods. Parents should role-play various situations with children, such as, "What if a stranger says that I'm hurt, and I've asked him to come get you? Would you get into a car with him then?" or "What if he says he has candy or a toy or a puppy for you to play with? Would you go into his house then?" Parents can teach these safety rules to children in a non-frightening way, without scaring them with the details of rape and sexual mutilation. Such rules can protect children not only from tier-three offenders, but from those in tiers one and two as well as those who have not yet committed or been convicted of a sexual offense.

Children also need to be protected from the vastly more common form of sexual abuse, that committed by friends and relatives. Children must feel that they can tell their parents, or other trusted adults, about anything that is bothering them, that they will not be dismissed or ridiculed. It is often shame or the fear of being disbelieved that makes children reluctant to reveal sexual abuse. They need to know that they will not be blamed or punished if they tell, but will be protected.

Education is only part of the story. As parents, we are responsible for supervising our children. How closely a child needs to be supervised depends on several factors, such as the child's age and maturity, and the kind of community in which one lives. Parents in New York City cannot safely let six-year-olds out of their sight; parents in suburbs and small towns can let children play by themselves with only periodic checks so long as they do not leave the yard or block. There are no hard and fast rules, and it is often a matter of judgment as to what is safe.

The difficulty that parents face is to strike a balance between teaching our children to be prudent and cautious while not making them excessively dependent or timid. After all, neighborliness is also an important virtue we want our children to learn. My children are in and out of the houses of their playmates on our street; their friends frequently visit in our house. We permit this even though it is possible that, unbeknownst to us, their friends' parents are sexual predators. That risk is too minute to worry about, any more than I would keep my children indoors to protect them from lightning (though I would call them inside if there was a thunder storm in the area) or refuse to let them ride bicycles (though they must wear helmets). Instead, we tell them that we need to know where they are, and so they must tell us before they go to play with their friends.

It may be that Megan thought of Jesse Timmendequas as a friend. Apparently, he was considered a gentle man, and the neighborhood children often played with his puppy. We do not know if Megan asked permission from her parents before going inside Timmendequas's house, but probably it never occurred to her to do so. It may not have occurred to her parents to teach her to do so. Unfortunately, in today's world, parents must be a little more suspicious than was necessary in the past. We need to have our antennae up. A childless adult who makes friends with children may be perfectly harmless, but it does not hurt to tell children that they are not allowed to go inside a grown-up's house without first getting permission. Had Megan been taught this rule, she would probably be alive today.

Supporters of community notification ask, "But wouldn't you want to know if there was a dangerous sex offender in your neighborhood?" This is not the right basis for making law or policy. Some people would want to know the HIV-status of their doctor or dentist even though the risk to patients from HIV-infected doctors is miniscule and the dangers of such notification very great indeed. We should not ask, then, what people are likely to want to know, but rather, what are the effects of community notification? If, as I have argued, it does not increase safety but rather promotes a false sense of security and furthermore is likely to lead to vigilantism, then we need to find more effective, less dangerous ways of achieving the paramount goal of protecting children.

POSTSCRIPT

Should Law Enforcement Officials Notify the Community When a Convicted Sex Offender Moves In?

The shock and outrage over Megan Kanka's murder was not limited to New Jersey. Megan's death brought to national attention the issues discussed by Schopf and Steinbock. How shall we ease the difficult tension between protecting an individual's constitutional rights and respecting a community's desire to protect its most vulnerable members?

The public's anger over Megan's death led to a push at the federal level for new laws to deal with the situation. As a consequence, special provisions were included in the Federal Violent Crime Control and Law Enforcement Act of 1994 to protect children from violent sex offenders. The act was signed into law by President Bill Clinton on September 13, 1994. It requires states to establish programs to protect communities from dangerous sex offenders through registration and notification provisions.

All 50 U.S. states have a version of Megan's Law, although the Pennsylvania Supreme Court recently declared that it is "constitutionally repugnant" (to the Pennsylvania Constitution) to put the burden of proof on the criminal to demonstrate that he is not a "violent sexual predator" when America's system of justice presumes innocence. Also, in 1998 the U.S. Supreme Court refused to review a lower court ruling upholding the constitutionality of Megan's Law.

For a discussion of the issues involved in this complex area of public policy, you may wish to consult the exchange between Bruce Fein and Edward Martone in the March 1995 issue of the *ABA Journal*. In addition, a symposium held at the New York Law School provides a useful range of perspectives on this approach to criminal justice policy. See "Critical Perspectives of Megan's Law: Protection Versus Privacy," *New York Law School Journal of Human Rights*. See also "Symposium on Megan's Law," 6 *Boston University Public Interest Law Journal* 29 (1996).

ISSUE 15

Does the First Amendment Protect an Informational Web Site That May Encourage Violent Acts?

YES: Alex Kozinski, from Majority Opinion, *Planned Parenthood of the Columbia/Willamette Inc. v. American Coalition of Life Activists*, U.S. Court of Appeals for the Ninth Circuit (September 15, 2000)

NO: O. Lee Reed, from "The State Is Strong but I Am Weak: Why the 'Imminent Lawless Action' Standard Should Not Apply to Targeted Speech That Threatens Individuals With Violence," *American Business Law Journal* (vol. 38, no. 1, 2000)

ISSUE SUMMARY

YES: U.S. Circuit Court judge Alex Kozinski rules that Web sites that contain intimidating but not explicitly threatening content are protected by the First Amendment.

NO: O. Lee Reed, a professor of legal studies, contends that intimidating speech directed at individuals—even speech that does not threaten imminent violence—is significantly harmful and should not be considered protected speech.

The following selections concern a lawsuit brought by Planned Parenthood against the sponsors of an antiabortion Internet site called "The Nuremberg Files." The site contained a picture of a group of abortion providers labeled the "Deadly Dozen." They were also called "baby butchers," "murderers," and "criminals." In addition, the site provided information about where the doctors lived and worked, their automobile license plates, and even the names of their children and spouses. There were no explicit threats against the doctors, but the names were grayed out if they had been injured by antiabortionists and blacked out if they had been killed.

A reward of up to $5,000 was offered for further information about the doctors and their spouses, children, homes, and friends. In addition, language on the Internet site asked, "Won't you help us arrest the evil?" and there were links to other sites that justified killing abortionists. On one of these sites a person told of his "joy" in murdering an abortion provider.

The case was brought under the Freedom of Access to Clinic Entrances Act (FACE), 18 U.S.C., Section 248(c) (1998), which prohibited the "threat of force" in order to "intimidate or interfere with any person... obtaining or providing reproductive health services." The defendants argued that there was no "threat" here, simply information, and that their activities are protected by the First Amendment. The plaintiffs argued that threats could exist even when there is no explicit threatening language and even when the violent act that might result could be weeks, months, or years away.

How should speakers, writers, and publishers whose words might lead to criminal acts be treated? Those who actually commit a criminal act are guilty of a crime. And those who clearly threaten someone are also guilty of a crime. But how should those who fall in between, whose words can be traced to a crime but cannot be clearly and directly linked, be treated?

Such cases are difficult, but Nuremberg was not the first such case. In *Brandenburg v. Ohio*, 395 U.S. 444 (1969), Brandenburg, the leader of a Ku Klux Klan group, invited news reporters to a Klan rally. At the rally, 12 hooded figures burned a cross as Brandenburg told the crowd,

> We're not a revengent organization, but if our President, our Congress, our Supreme Court, continues to suppress the white, Caucasian race, it's possible that there might have to be some revengeance taken. We are marching on Congress July the Fourth, four hundred thousand strong. From there we are dividing into two groups, one group to march on St. Augustine, Florida, the other group to march into Mississippi. Thank you.

The Supreme Court held that it was unconstitutional "to punish mere advocacy and to forbid, on pain of criminal punishment, assembly with others merely to advocate the described type of action." But does the publication of doctors' names and addresses and the blackening of the names of doctors who had been killed move "The Nuremberg Files" beyond mere advocacy? Even if it does, is there likely to be "imminent lawless action," and is what is presented on the Internet site likely to "incite or produce such action"?

The Nuremberg case was tried in the federal district court, and a jury awarded the plaintiffs $108 million. In the following selection, the Court of Appeals overturns the verdict. Judge Alex Kozinski presents the majority opinion. In the second selection, O. Lee Reed argues that the "imminent lawless action" standard should not be used in this case and that the First Amendment should not be interpreted to protect such speech. At this point it is unclear whether or not a further appeal will be made to the Supreme Court. What is clear is that the Internet will continue to challenge us to clarify standards for expression that is protected by the First Amendment.

Alex Kozinski  **YES**

Majority Opinion

Planned Parenthood *v.* American Coalition of Life Activists

Anti-abortion activists intimidated abortion providers by publishing their names and addresses. A jury awarded more than $100 million in actual and punitive damages against the activists, and the district court enjoined their speech. We consider whether such speech is protected by the First Amendment.

I

During a 1995 meeting called to mark the anniversary of *Roe v. Wade,* 410 U.S. 113, 93 S.Ct. 705, L.Ed.2d 147 (1973), the American Coalition of Life Activists (ACLA) unveiled a poster listing the names and addresses of the "Deadly Dozen," a group of doctors who perform abortions. In large print, the poster declared them guilty of "crimes against humanity" and offered $5,000 for information leading to the "arrest, conviction and revocation of license to practice medicine." The poster was later published in an affiliated magazine, *Life Advocate,* and distributed at ACLA events.

Later that year, in front of the St. Louis federal courthouse, ACLA presented a second poster, this time targeting Dr. Robert Crist. The poster accused Crist of crimes against humanity and various acts of medical malpractice, including a botched abortion that caused the death of a woman. Like the Deadly Dozen List, the poster included Crist's home and work addresses, and in addition, featured his photograph. The poster offered $500 to "any ACLA organization that successfully persuades Crist to turn from his child killing through activities within ACLA guidelines" (which prohibit violence).

In January 1996, at its next *Roe* anniversary event, ACLA unveiled a series of dossiers it had compiled on doctors, clinic employees, politicians, judges and other abortion rights supporters. ACLA dubbed these the "Nuremberg Files," and announced that it had collected the pictures, addresses and other information in the files so that Nuremberg-like war crimes trials could be conducted in "perfectly legal courts once the tide of this nation's opinion turns against the wanton slaughter of God's children." ACLA sent hard copies of the files to Neal

From *Planned Parenthood of the Columbia/Willamette Inc. v. American Coalition of Life Activists,* 244 F.3d 1007 (9th Cir. 2001). Some notes omitted.

Horsley, an anti-abortion activist, who posted the information on a website. The website listed the names of doctors and others who provide or support abortion and called on visitors to supply additional names. The website marked the names of those already victimized by anti-abortion terrorists, striking through the names of those who had been murdered and graying out the names of the wounded. Although ACLA's name originally appeared on the website, Horsley removed it after the initiation of this lawsuit.

Neither the posters nor the website contained any explicit threats against the doctors. But the doctors knew that similar posters prepared by others had preceded clinic violence in the past. By publishing the names and addresses, ACLA robbed the doctors of their anonymity and gave violent anti-abortion activists the information to find them. The doctors responded to this unwelcome attention by donning bulletproof vests, drawing the curtains on the windows of their homes and accepting the protection of U.S. Marshals.

Some of the doctors went on the offensive. Along with two Portland-based health centers, the doctors sued ACLA, twelve activists and an affiliated organization, alleging that their threatening statements violated state and federal law, including the Freedom of Access to Clinic Entrances Act of 1994 (FACE), 18 U.S.C. § 248. Because the doctors claimed they were harmed by defendants' speech, the district court instructed the jury that defendants could only be liable if their statements were "true threats" and therefore unprotected by the First Amendment. In a special verdict, the jury found that all the statements were true threats and awarded the doctors $107 million in actual and punitive damages. The district court then issued an injunction barring defendants from making or distributing the posters, the webpage or anything similar. ACLA and the other defendants appeal, claiming that their statements are protected by the First Amendment.

II

A. Extreme rhetoric and violent action have marked many political movements in American history. Patriots intimidated loyalists in both word and deed as they gathered support for American independence. John Brown and other abolitionists, convinced that God was on their side, committed murder in pursuit of their cause. In more modern times, the labor, antiwar, animal rights and environmental movements all have had their violent fringes. As a result, much of what was said even by nonviolent participants in these movements acquired a tinge of menace.

The Supreme Court confronted this problem in *NAACP v. Claiborne Hardware Co.,* 458 U.S. 886, 102 S.Ct. 3409, 73 L.Ed.2d 1215 (1982). There, a group of white-owned businesses sued the NAACP and others who organized a civil rights boycott against the stores. To give the boycott teeth, activists wearing black hats stood outside the stores and wrote down the names of black patrons. After these names were read aloud at meetings and published in a newspaper, sporadic acts of violence were committed against the persons and property of those on the list. At one public rally, Charles Evers, a boycott organizer, threatened that boycott breakers would be "disciplined" and warned that the sheriff could not protect them at night. *See id.* at 902, 102 S.Ct. 3409. At another rally, Evers stated, "If we catch any of you going in any of them racist stores, we're gonna break your damn neck." *See id.* The Mississippi courts held the boycott organizers liable based on Evers's statements and the activities of the black-hatted activists.

The Supreme Court acknowledged that Evers's statements could be interpreted as inviting violent retaliation, "or at least as *intending to create a fear of violence* whether or not improper discipline was specifically intended." *Id.* at 927, 102 S.Ct. 3409 (emphasis added). Nevertheless, it held that the statements were protected because there was insufficient evidence that Evers had "authorized, ratified, or directly threatened acts of violence." *Id.* at 929, 102 S.Ct. 3409. Nor was publication of the boycott violators' names a sufficient basis for liability, even though collecting and publishing the names contributed to the atmosphere of intimidation that had harmed plaintiffs. *See id.* at 925–26, 102 S.Ct. 3409. While Charles Evers and the defendants in our case pursued very different political goals, the two cases have one key thing in common: Political activists used words in an effort to bend opponents to their will.

The First Amendment protects ACLA's statements no less than the statements of the NAACP. Defendants can only be held liable if they "authorized, ratified, or directly threatened" violence. If defendants threatened to commit violent acts, by working alone or with others, then their statements could properly support the verdict. But if their statements merely encouraged unrelated terrorists, then their words are protected by the First Amendment.

Political speech may not be punished just because it makes it more likely that someone will be harmed at some unknown time in the future by an unrelated third party. In *Brandenburg v. Ohio,* 395 U.S. 444, 89 S.Ct. 1827, 23 L.Ed.2d 430 (1969) (per curiam), the Supreme Court held that the First Amendment protects speech that encourages others to commit violence, unless the speech is capable of "producing imminent lawless action. "*Id.* at 447 89 S.Ct. 1827. It doesn't matter if the speech makes future violence more likely; advocating "illegal action at some indefinite future time" is protected. *Hess v. Indiana,* 414 U.S. 105, 108, 94 S.Ct. 326, 38 L.Ed.2d 303 (1973) (per curiam). If the First Amendment protects speech advocating violence, then it must also protect speech that does not advocate violence but still makes it more likely. Unless ACLA threatened that its members would themselves assault the doctors, the First Amendment protects its speech.[1]

B.   ACLA's speech no doubt frightened the doctors, but the constitutional question turns on the source of their fear.[2] The doctors might have understood the statements as veiled threats that ACLA's members (or others working with ACLA) would inflict bodily harm on the doctors unless they stopped performing abortions. So interpreted, the statements are unprotected by the First Amendment, regardless of whether the activists had the means or intent to carry out the threats. *See United States v. Orozco-Santillan,* 903 F.2d 1262, 1265 n3. (9th Cir. 1990). So long as they should have foreseen that the doctors would take the threats seriously, the speech is unlawful. *See id.* at 1265.[3]

But the statements might also have scared the doctors in another way. By singling out the plaintiffs from among the thousands across the country who are involved in delivering abortion services, ACLA called them to the unfriendly attention of violent anti-abortion activists. And by publishing the doctors' addresses, ACLA made it easier for any would-be terrorists to carry out their gruesome mission.[4] From the doctors' point of view, such speech may be just as frightening as a direct threat, but it remains protected under *Claiborne Hardware.*

The jury would be entitled to hold defendants liable if it understood the statements as expressing their intention to assault the doctors but not if it understood the statements as merely encouraging or making it more likely that others would do so. But the jury instruction was ambiguous on this critical point. The instruction provided that "[a] statement is a 'true threat' when a reasonable person making the statement would foresee that the statement would be interpreted by those to whom it is communicated as a serious expression of an intent to bodily harm or assault." Jury Instruction No. 10, at 14. This instruction was consistent with our previous threat cases. See *Lovell* v. *Poway Unified Sch. Dist.,* 90 F.3d 367, 372 (9th Cir. 1996). But in those previous cases, there was no need to emphasize that threats must be direct because the speakers themselves made it perfectly clear that they would be the ones to carry out the threats.[5] Under the instruction in this case, the jury could have found the anti-abortion activists liable based on the fact that, by publishing the doctors' names, the activists made it more likely that the doctors would be harmed by third parties.

This is not a fanciful possibility. The record contains much evidence that the doctors were frightened, at least in part, because they anticipated that their unwelcome notoriety could expose them to physical attacks from third parties unrelated to defendants. For example, plaintiff Dr. Elizabeth Newhall testified, "I feel like my risk comes from being identified as a target. And . . . all the John Salvis in the world know who I am, and that's my concern."[6] Testimony of Elizabeth Newhall, *Planned Parenthood of the Columbia/Willamette, Inc. v. American Coalition of Life Activists,* No. CV 95–01671–JO, at 302 (D.Or. Jan. 8, 1999); *see also id.* at 290 ("[U]p until January of '95, I felt relatively diluted by the—you know, in the pool of providers of abortion services. I didn't feel particularly visible to the people who were—you know, to the John Salvis of the world, you know. I sort of felt one of a big, big group."). Likewise, Dr. Warren Martin Hern, another plaintiff, testified that when he heard he was on the list, "I was terrified. . . . [I]t's hard to describe the feeling that—that you are on a list of people to—who have been brought to public attention in this way. I felt that this was a—a list of doctors to be killed." Testimony of Warren Martin Hern, *Planned Parenthood,* No. CV 95–01671–JO, at 625 (Jan. 11, 1999).

Were the instruction taken literally, the jury could have concluded that ACLA's statements contained "a serious expression of intent to harm," not because they authorized or directly threatened violence, but because they put the doctors in harm's way. However, the First Amendment does not permit the imposition of liability on that basis.

C.   Although the jury instruction was ambiguous, we need not decide whether the ambiguity was so great as to require us to set aside the verdict. Even if the jury drew only the permissible inference, we must evaluate the record for ourselves to ensure that the judgment did not trespass on the defendants' First Amendment rights. Specifically, we must determine whether ACLA's statements could reasonably be construed as saying that ACLA (or its agents) would physically harm doctors who did not stop performing abortions. Because the district court rejected the First Amendment claim, we conduct a *de novo* review of both the law and the relevant facts. *See Lovell,* 90 F.3d at 370. The question therefore is not whether the facts found below are supported by the record but whether we, looking at the record with fresh eyes, make the same findings. If we disagree with the district court, our findings prevail. *See Eastwood v. National Enquirer, Inc.,* 123 F.3d 1249, 1252 (9th Cir. 1997).

We start by noting that none of the statements ACLA is accused of making mention violence at all. While pungent, even highly offensive, ACLA's statements carefully avoid threatening the doctors with harm "in the sense that there are no 'quotable quotes' calling for violence against the targeted providers." *Planned Parenthood of the Columbia/Willamette, Inc. v. American Coalition of Life Activists,* 23 F.Supp.2d 1182, 1186 (D.Or. 1998). Instead, ACLA offers rewards to those who take nonviolent measures against the doctors, such as seeking the revocation of their medical licenses and protesting their activities. One poster talks about persuading Crist to "turn from his child killing," but stops short of suggesting any violence or other criminal conduct against him. The website seeks to gather information about abortion supporters and encourages others to do the same. ACLA also speaks of future "perfectly legal" Nuremberg-like trials, to be held at a time when public opinion has turned in its favor.

We recognize that the words actually used are not dispositive, because a threat may be inferred from the context in which the statements are made.[7] However, there are at least two kinds of ambiguity that context can resolve. The first deals with statements that call for violence on their face, but are unclear as to *who* is to commit the violent acts—the speaker or a third party. All cases of which we are aware fall into this category: They hold that, where the speaker expressly mentions future violence, context can make it clear that it is the speaker himself who means to carry out the threat. *See* note 13 supra.

A more difficult problem arises when the statements, like the ones here, not only fail to threaten violence by the defendants, but fail to mention future violence at all.[8] Can context supply the violent message that language alone leaves out? While no case answers this question, we note important theoretical objections to stretching context so far. Context, after all, is often not of the speaker's making. For example, the district court in this case admitted evidence of numerous acts of violence surrounding the abortion controversy, almost none of them committed by the defendants or anyone connected with them.[9] In the jury's eyes, then, defendants' statements were infused with a violent meaning, at least in part, because of the actions of others. If this were a permissible inference, it could have a highly chilling effect on public debate on any cause where somebody, somewhere has committed a violent act in connection with that cause. A party who does not intend to threaten harm, nor say anything at all suggesting violence, would risk liability by speaking out in the midst of a highly charged environment.

In considering whether context could import a violent meaning to ACLA's non-violent statements, we deem it highly significant that all the statements were made in the context of public discourse, not in direct personal communications. Although the First Amendment does not protect all forms of public speech, such as statements inciting violence or an imminent panic, the public nature of the speech bears heavily upon whether it could be interpreted as a threat.[10] As we held in *McCalden v. California Library Ass'n,* 955 F.2d 1214 (9th Cir. 1992), "public speeches advocating violence" are given substantially more leeway under the First Amendment than "privately communicated threats." *Id.* at 1222; *see also Orozco-Santillan,* 903 F.2d at 1265 ("Although a threat must be 'distinguished from what is constitutionally protected speech,' this is not a case involving statements with a political message." (quoting *Watts v. United States,* 394 U.S. 705, 707, 89 S.Ct. 1399, 226 EdL.2 664 (1969) (per curiam)).

There are two reasons for this distinction: First, what may be hyperbole in a public speech may be understood (and intended) as a threat if communicated directly to the person threatened, whether face-to-face, by telephone or by letter. In targeting the recipient personally, the speaker leaves no doubt that he is sending the recipient a message of some sort. In contrast, typical political statements at rallies or through the media are far more diffuse in their focus because they are generally intended, at least in part, to shore up political support for the speaker's position.

Second, and more importantly, speech made through the normal channels of group communication, and concerning matters of public policy, is given the maximum level of protection by the Free Speech Clause because it lies at the core of the First Amendment. *See Claiborne Hardware,* 458 U.S. at 926–27, 102 S.Ct. 3409 ("Since respondents would impose liability on the basis of a public address—which predominantly contained highly charged political rhetoric lying at the core of the First Amendment—we approach this suggested basis of liability with extreme care."). With respect to such speech, we must defer to the well-recognized principle that political statements are inherently prone to exaggeration and hyperbole. *See Watts,* 394 U.S. at 708, 89 S.Ct. 1399 ("The language of the political arena... is often vituperative, abusive, and inexact." (citation omitted)). If political discourse is to rally public opinion and challenge conventional thinking, it cannot be subdued. Nor may we saddle political speakers with implications their words do not literally convey but are later "discovered" by judges and juries with the benefit of hindsight and by reference to facts over which the speaker has no control.

Our guiding light, once again, is *Claiborne Hardware.* There, Charles Evers expressly threatened violence when he warned the boycott violators that "we're gonna break your damn neck[s]," and that the sheriff could not protect them from retribution. *See* 458 U.S. at 902, 104 S.Ct. 3409. Evers made these statements at a time when there had already been violence against the boycott breakers. Evers did not himself identify specific individuals to be disciplined, but his associates had gathered and published the names, and there's no doubt that the black community in the small Mississippi county where the boycott was taking place knew whom Evers was talking about. The Supreme Court held that, despite his express call for violence, and the context of actual violence, Evers's statements were protected, because they were quintessentially political statements made at a public rally, rather than directly to his targets. *See id.* at 928–29, 102 S.Ct. 3409.

If Charles Evers's speech was protected by the First Amendment, then ACLA's speech is also protected.[11] Like Evers, ACLA did not communicate privately with its targets; the statements were made in public fora. And, while ACLA named its targets, it said nothing about planning to harm them; indeed, it did not even call on others to do so. This stands in contrast to the words of Charles Evers, who explicitly warned his targets that they would suffer broken necks and other physical harm. Under the standard of *Claiborne Hardware,* the jury's verdict cannot stand.

VACATED and REMANDED with instructions that the district court dissolve the injunction and enter judgment for the defendants on all counts.

Notes

1. If such statements were unprotected threats, newspapers might face liability for publishing stories that increased the likelihood that readers would harm particular persons, for example by disclosing the identity of mobsters in hiding or convicted child molesters. This would permit the imposition of liability for the mere publication of news, dramatically undercutting the freedom constitutionally accorded to the press. *Cf. New York Times Co. v. Sullivan,* 376 U.S. 254, 270, 84 S.Ct. 710, 11 L.Ed.2d 686 (1964) (recognizing the need to protect our "profound national commitment to the principle that debate on public issues should be uninhibited, robust, and wide-open").

2. It is not unlawful to say things that frighten other people. A doctor who discloses an adverse prognosis often instills fear in the patient and his family; predicting a future event—"That bus is about to hit your child!"—can cause the listener intense apprehension. Yet such statements are not (and cannot be made) unlawful. Nor does it matter that the speaker makes the statement for the very purpose of causing fear. Let's say your malicious neighbor sees your house is burning. He calls you at work and announces: "Your house is on fire!" This may scare you—it may have no other purpose—yet it is lawful because it is speech and does not fall within one of the narrow categories the Supreme Court has held is unprotected under the First Amendment.

    The matter is more complicated where the speech is intended to intimidate the listener into changing his conduct. Blackmail and extortion—the threat that the speaker will say or do something unpleasant unless you take, or refrain from taking, certain actions—are not constitutionally protected. *See, e.g., Watts,* 394 U.S. 705, 89 S.Ct. 1399, 22 L.Ed.2d 664. On the other hand, the statement, "If you smoke cigarettes you will die of lung cancer," is protected, even though its purpose is to scare you into quitting smoking. So is, "If you mess around with Tom's girlfriend, he'll break your legs," unless the speaker is sent by Tom. The difference is this: In the case of blackmail and extortion, you are given to understand that, unless you do what's asked of you, the speaker himself (or someone acting on his behalf) will bring about that which you abhor; in the other examples, the speaker has no control over the adverse consequences and merely predicts what is likely to happen if you act (or refrain from acting) in a particular way.

3. Our case law has not been entirely consistent as to whether a speaker may be penalized for negligently uttering a threat or whether he must have specifically

intended to threaten. *Compare Orozco-Santillan,* 903 F.2d at 1265 ("Whether a particular statement may properly be considered to be a threat is governed by an objective standard—whether a reasonable person would foresee that the statement would be interpreted by those to whom the maker communicates the statement as a serious expression of intent to harm or assault."), *with United States v. Gilbert (Gilbert I),* 813 F.2d 1523, 1529 (9th Cir.1987) ("[Gilbert] correctly identifies the element of intent specified in section 3631 as the determinative factor separating protected expression from unprotected criminal behavior.... [T]he statute's requirement of intent to intimidate serves to insulate the statute from unconstitutional application to protected speech. "(citation omitted)). While we believe that *Gilbert I* states the correct rule, the result here is the same under either standard. We therefore presume that the less speech-protective standard of *Orozco-Santillan* applies.

4. We need not decide here whether the First Amendment would protect defendants from a suit for invasion of privacy, because plaintiffs do not claim damages based solely on the publication of private facts, namely their addresses and telephone numbers. *Cf. Anderson v. Fisher Broadcasting Cos.,* 300 Or. 452, 712 P.2d 803. 807 (1986) (recognizing a tort for invasion of privacy when the tortfeasor has the specific intent to cause plaintiff severe mental or emotional distress and such conduct exceeds "the farthest reach of socially tolerable behavior").

5. *See, e.g. Lovell,* 90 F.3d at 369 (student told administrator, "I'm going to shoot you"). *Melugin v. Hames,* 38 F.3d 1478, 1481 (9th Cir.1994) (civil defendant sent letter to judge threatening to kill him); *Orozco-Santillan,* 903 F.2d at 1264 (arrestee threatened INS agent at his arrest and during subsequent phone calls); *United States v. Gilbert (Gilbert II),* 884 F.2d 454, 455–56 (9th Cir.1989) (white supremacist mailed a letter to the head of an inter-racial adoption agency, condemning her occupation and enclosing posters suggesting he would commit violence against inter-racial couples and ethnic minorities). *United States v. Mitchell,* 812 F.2d 1250, 1252 (9th Cir.1987) (defendant told Secret Service agents he was going to kill them and the President); *Roy v. United States,* 416 F.2d 874, 875 (9th Cir.1969) (marine called the White House and said he was going to kill the President). The instruction continues to be good law in cases where the source of the threatened violence is not an issue.

6. In December 1994, John Salvi killed two clinic workers and wounded five others in attacks on two clinics in Brookline, Massachusetts; Salvi later fired shots at a clinic in Norfolk, Virginia before he was apprehended. Salvi is not a defendant in this case.

7. *See, e.g., Orozco-Santillan,* 903 F.2d at 1265 ("Alleged theats should be considered in light of their entire factual context, including the surrounding events and reaction of the listeners."); *Gilbert II,* 884 F.2d at 457 ("The fact that a threat is subtle does not make it less of a threat."). Other courts have also recognized that ambiguous language may still constitute a threat. *See United States v. Dinwiddie,* 76 F.3d 913, 925 (8th Cir. 1996) (holding that an anti-abortion activist, who had previously used force against clinic personnel, threatened Dr. Crist when she screamed at him on numerous occasions that he could be killed if he kept on committing abortions); *United States v. Malik,* 16 F.3d 45, 49 (2d Cir.1994) (finding a threat where defendant sent letters to a federal appellate judge suggesting he would use force against the panel unless it reversed its decision); *United States v. Khorrami,* 895 F.2d 1186, 1193 (7th Cir.1990) (holding that defendant made a threat by repeatedly making anti-Semitic phone calls to a Jewish organization and sending it letters calling for the deaths of Israeli leaders).

8. The defendants come closest to suggesting violence on the webpage, where the names of the murdered doctors are stricken and the wounded ones are grayed. We read the striketype and graying as the equivalent of marking "killed" or

"wounded" next to the names. This clearly reports past violent acts and may connote approval. But it cannot fairly be read as calling for future violence against the several hundred other doctors, politicians, judges and celebrities on the list; otherwise any statement approving past violence could automatically be construed as calling for future violence.

9. Defendants objected to admission of much of this evidence and press their objections on appeal. Given our ruling on the merits, we need not pass on this issue. Nothing we say, therefore, should be construed as approving the district court's evidentiary rulings.

10. The doctors do not claim that ACLA's speech amounted to incitement. To rise to incitement, the speech must be capable of "producing imminent lawless action." *Brandenburg*, 395 U.S. at 447, 89 S.Ct. 1827. Here, the statements were made at public rallies, far away from the doctors, and before an audience that included members of the press. ACLA offered rewards to those who stopped the doctors at "some indefinite future time," *Hess*, 414 U.S. at 108, 94 S.Ct. 326, and the ambiguous message was hardly what one would say to incite others to immediately break the law. Finally, the statements were not in fact followed by acts of violence. *See Claiborne Hardware*, 458 U.S. at 928, 102 S.Ct. 3409 ("[H]ad [the speech] been followed by acts of violence, a substantial question would be presented" as to incitement but "[w]hen such appeals do not incite lawless action, they must be regarded as protected speech.").

11. We cannot distinguish this case from *Clairborne Hardware* on the ground that the speech is aimed at impeding abortions, which are constitutionally protected against government interference. The speech in *Claiborne Hardware* likewise sought to prevent lawful conduct—black citizens' patronage of white stores—that the government could not ban without violating the Equal Protection Clause. The Constitution protects rights against government interference; it doesn't justify the suppression of private speech that tries to deter people from exercising those rights.

NO ↩

O. Lee Reed

The State Is Strong but I Am Weak

Speech is the jewel in the crown of human achievement, the achievement upon which most of other human accomplishments are based. The genius of the First Amendment is that it frees speech to do its work—to facilitate thought, communication, and choice not only in politics but also in economic, social, and religious arenas as well. Free speech fosters creativity and dynamism in what Justice Holmes called "the competition of the market" and Justice Brennan later termed "the marketplace of ideas."

Speech also harms. Speech can deceive, defraud, defame, discriminate, harass, intimidate, misrepresent, threaten, and terrorize. Professor [Kent] Greenawalt lists twenty-one different types of crimes that derive from speech, and two of the Ten Commandments specifically prohibit types of speech. Going far beyond merely conveying ideas, speech can actually *do* things like make a contract. Considering the many speech harms, Justice Frankfurter admonished that it would be better if there were no freedom of speech at all than for the populace to believe that the First Amendment protects every form of speech.

In the twentieth century, the freedom of speech became a Rorschach figure into which numerous, often politically polarized, groups read their images of a free society. Anarchists and advertisers, libertarians and communists, labor and management, pornographers and Jehovah's Witnesses, the Ku Klux Klan and the NAACP [National Association for the Advancement of Colored People] each sought constitutional protection under the First Amendment to express themselves and their ideas, to encourage others to their views, and to participate in the democratic life of the nation. If in its early application freedom of speech protected mostly liberal and radical expression, today many scholars believe it is increasingly asserted to protect conservative and reactionary expression. A tension always exists, however, between the interpretation of free speech guaranteed by the First Amendment and the maintenance of what J. S. Mill asserted was the primary purpose of government: to protect citizens from "harm." If freedom of speech is not absolute, where do the parameters of free speech lie in an increasingly uncivil society when parsed against the claims of

From O. Lee Reed, "The State Is Strong but I Am Weak: Why the 'Imminent Lawless Action' Standard Should Not Apply to Targeted Speech That Threatens Individuals With Violence," *American Business Law Journal*, vol. 38, no. 1 (2000). Copyright © 2000 by O. Lee Reed. Reprinted by permission. Notes omitted.

speech harm? What is certain is that as we enter the twenty-first century, new issues involving freedom of speech will continue to arise, that existing First Amendment doctrine may not be adequate to evaluate these new claims, and that new claims may require fresh doctrine.

... The "imminent lawless action" standard (hereinafter the ILA standard) is the current version of clear and present danger, which Justices Holmes and Brandeis asserted in the 1920s as a test for speech not protected by the First Amendment.

... The Supreme Court developed both the clear and present danger and the ILA standard in cases evaluating when the government could criminalize advocacy and incitement against general state interests in legal obedience, public policy, public order, and judicial administration. Because the state is strong and its democratic framework not easily threatened, but individuals are weak and easily threatened and intimidated, the ILA standard should not apply to speech targeted to threaten individuals with violence unless it applies in a presumptive way, i.e., through a presumption that violent threats to individuals constitute imminent lawless action. ILA is inappropriate both as a general categorical standard for determining when speech lies outside First Amendment protection, and as a specific categorical test covering all threats or intimidating incitement....

NAACP v. Claiborne Hardware Co.

One Supreme Court case potentially stands in the way of understanding incitements and threats against the state and incitements and threats targeted to individuals as separate categories of prohibitable speech. *National Association for the Advancement of Colored People v. Claiborne Hardware Co.* arguably applied the ILA standard to an instance of threats made against individuals. However, consideration of that case shows that it is really the plaintiffs' failure to prove that they had been harmed by the defendant's speeches, rather than their failure to show imminent lawless action, that determined the outcome of the case.

In *Claiborne* seventeen white merchants in Hinds County Mississippi filed suit against the NAACP, its field secretary Charles Evers, and several other individuals for the common law tort of malicious interference with the merchants' businesses. On the basis of damages sustained by the businesses during a seven-year boycott organized by the defendants, the Mississippi Supreme Court upheld a lower court's imposition of damage, concluding that defendants maintained the boycott through "[i]ntimidation, threats, social ostracism, vilification, and traduction...". "Unquestionably, the evidence shows that the volition of many black persons was overcome out of sheer fear, and they were forced and compelled against their personal wills to withhold their trade and business intercourse from the complainants." The opinion cited statements by Charles Evers that blacks who violated the boycott by patronizing the stores would have their "necks broken," that they had "better not be caught on these streets shopping in these stores" and that "we are going to discipline them (boycott violators) the way we want to." In the context of a speech to his supporters, he warned potential boycott violators that the sheriff would not be able to "sleep with them," i.e., protect them, at night. The names of boycott violators were read to NAACP supporters and listed in a newsletter.

In an opinion by Justice Stevens, the U.S. Supreme Court reversed the state courts. The opinion acknowledged that the speech statements might have been understood as intending to create a fear of violence, but that in context the First Amendment protected them. It cited *Brandenburg* and stated that *Brandenburg* depended on "the principle that the constitutional guarantees of free speech and free press do not permit a State to forbid or proscribe advocacy of the use of force or of law violation except where such advocacy is directed to inciting or producing imminent lawless action and is likely to incite or produce such action." The opinion then asserted: "The emotionally charged rhetoric of Charles Evers' speeches did not transcend the bounds of protected speech set forth in *Brandenburg.*"

From these words it may appear that Justice Stevens relied on *Brandenburg* and thus on the ILA standard for the result in *Claiborne.* Certainly, several scholars and journalists writing in the media on the Nuremberg Files case [Planned Parenthood of the Columbia/Willamette, Inc. *v.* American Coalition of Life Activists, in which the jury awarded plaintiffs $107 million in damages as a result of violence perpretrated against abortion providers and clinics] have believed as much, but an examination of *Claiborne* does not substantially support this view. At best the doctrinal connection between *Claiborne* and *Brandenburg* is tenuous and unfortunate.

Positioned near the end of the lengthy opinion in two short paragraphs, *Claiborne's* mention of *Brandenburg* did not discuss the ILA standard, especially how the word *imminent* would apply to a case where individuals are targeted by threatening speech. Throughout the opinion, Justice Stevens' focus was on the *likelihood* of a forbidden effect, on whether adequate evidence supported the interpretation that the threats made any identifiable contribution to the boycott's overall effectiveness and adequately induced a fear in the black population that overcame their will, intimidating them to support the boycott. He emphasized that support for the boycott against the merchants was largely voluntary and that the defendants could not be held liable for all of the defendants' business losses when those losses were due largely to voluntary participation in the boycott. In an approach based more on threat to individuals than on the ILA standard, he asserted that "[u]nquestionably" the defendants could be held responsible for injuries caused by "violence or *threats of violence,*" whereas Evers' " 'threats' of vilification or social ostracism" were "constitutionally protected and beyond the reach of a damages award. "Justice Stevens seemed to discount the importance of imminence to his constitutional evaluation of threat when he stated that "a finding that his (Evers') public speeches were likely to incite lawless action could justify holding him liable for unlawful conduct that in fact followed *within a reasonable period.*" The opinion emphasized the necessary evidentiary connection between incitement and violence within a reasonable time, a connection lacking in this case, but avoided discussing why the state could impose civil liability for threats of violence toward individuals only if the threats encouraged *imminent* lawless action.

If anything, *Claiborne* surprises in how little it relies on *Brandenburg,* containing as it does a mere recitation of the ILA standard and the unadorned statement that Evers' speeches did not "transcend the bounds of protected speech set forth in *Brandenburg."* Perhaps, Justice Stevens, who has criticized the results of categorical balancing, was aware of the difference between threats against the state and the alleged threats by Evers against individuals. In any event, *Claiborne* differs from the Nuremberg Files case because in the former there was no evidence of fear and intimidation actually inspired by Evers' incitement, whereas in the latter abundant testimony indicated that the defendants' incitement terrorized the plaintiffs. *Claiborne* is a case about the substantiality of evidence required to prove speech harm rather than about what categorical standard applies to harmful speech targeted to individuals. Seen in this light, Justice Stevens' statement that "Evers' speeches did not transcend the bounds of protected speech set forth in *Brandenburg"* constitutes a comment about the lack of evidence that the threats harmed the merchant plaintiffs rather than application of a constitutional requirement of imminent lawless action in cases where threats reasonably terrorize individuals.

Claiborne's mention of the ILA standard does not significantly contradict the force of the fact that the Court has not applied the ILA standard nor clear and present danger in an instance when targeted speech actually intimidates individuals through threats or directed harassment. It leaves open the possibility that the Court may specifically establish a categorical standard for harmful speech aimed at individuals and, perhaps, already has suggested a standard in various dicta asserting that threats are not constitutionally protected speech.

The Reasonable Person Standard

Recognizing that individuals are more sensitive to harmful speech than is the state severely undermines the argument that the government cannot constitutionally limit individually targeted speech unless it advocates imminent lawless action. Targeted incitements or direct threats by even one person against another can inspire fear that intimidates, debilitates, and overcomes the will of the victim even when the speaker does not state a date for action, leaves open the date, indicates a future date, or specifies that the timeframe is contingent on the target's response. Once the speech harm has been categorized, however, the standard by which the law measures when threat has occurred must be articulated. This step requires acknowledgement that targeted speech such as threats or incitement to violence against individuals can be spoken "rhetorically, emotionally, or insincerely" and also depends upon the intended listeners' reactions to such speech. Historically, the general legal standard for measuring the reactions of individuals to speech is the reasonable person standard. When someone alleges that co-workers have said things severe and pervasive in nature that constitute hostile environment discrimination, the Supreme Court measures the harm by the reaction of a reasonable person in that situation. Establishment of obscenity requires evaluation based on an "average person" or "community" determination that is similar to the reasonable person standard. In *Chaplinsky* fighting words are measured against the reactions of an "average person," and potential reliance on the deceptive misrepresentations that *Virginia Board of Pharmacy* categorizes outside constitutional protection must be "reasonable." Even clear and present danger and the ILA standard arguably require a determination of reasonableness. In *Whitney v. California* Justice Brandeis wrote in his concurrence: "To justify suppression of free speech there must be *reasonable* ground to fear that serious evil will result if free speech is practiced. There must be *reasonable* ground to believe that the danger apprehended is imminent." In *Shafer v. United States* Brandeis specifically referred to the clear and present danger doctrine as setting a "rule of reason." Although Brandeis' use of reasonableness does not equate precisely with the reasonable person standard as applied to an individual's reaction to speech, it does help explain why the judge's reasonable person instruction to the Nuremberg Files jury was correct, and why it is the appropriate contextual standard for evaluating listener response to targeted threatening language.

Those commentators who have expressed concern about application of the reasonable person standard in the Nuremberg Files case confuse whether certain harms should be prohibitable with the standard for determining whether a victim of speech has appropriately responded to the words. They conflate the issue of what types of speech harm properly fall outside First Amendment protection with the issue of how courts and juries should evaluate listener reaction to potentially harmful speech when listener reaction is evidence of what makes the speech constitutionally harmful. As to the former issue, the type of speech directed against the state that the Court categorizes as prohibitable is advocacy of "imminent lawless action," whereas the types of prohibitable speech targeted at individuals that the Court recognizes include "threats," "defamation," "fighting words," and "deception and misrepresentation" in commercial speech. As to the latter issue involving when listener reaction properly indicates that the harm exists, the Court has generally and appropriately invoked a standard of reasonableness whether the type of speech has been advocacy of imminent lawless action against the state or fighting words, fraud, or threats targeted to individuals.

The commentators' concern is fueled by their belief that any time the courts (or juries) consider listener reaction to speech they give audiences a veto over a speaker's expression and thus the reasonable person standard facilitates the exercise of this veto. However, speech meaning always derives from the community, and evaluation of not only what a speaker intends but also how individuals reasonably respond to speech is inevitable if harmful speech targeted to individuals is ever subject to control. As Justice Brandeis explained, even clear and present danger is subject to a reasonableness standard of interpretation. Ultimately, in evaluating the state's response to an instance of speech regulated under clear and present danger, courts must determine the reasonableness of the state's assessment of clear and present danger. The same reasonableness standard also applies to assessing imminent lawless action, determining fighting words, evaluating obscenity, and identifying fraudulent commercial speech.

The proper focus in the Nuremberg Files case and in other cases involving speech that substantially harms individuals is not whether the reasonable person standard should apply in determining listener reaction to potentially prohibitable speech. It is whether speech threatening or advocating illegal action that targets individuals and speech that threatens or incites against the state should comprise one or two categories, whether the government can under FACE [Freedom of Access to Clinic Entrances Act] proscribe intimidating threats when these threats do not advocate imminent violence. I maintain that the strength of the state and the relative weakness of individuals, who are reasonably fearful for their physical safety and the security of their loved ones even when threats and incitements do not portend imminent harm, argue for two categories. But whatever the outcome of the debate, the reasonable person standard applies specifically to the facts of the Nuremberg Files case and generally to other harmful speech whether aimed at individuals or the state, especially as listener reaction by the very nature of speech is a significant determinant of the harm.

Conclusion

In *Watts v. United States* the Supreme Court emphasized that "what is a threat must be distinguished from what is constitutionally protected speech." It is likewise true that threats against the state or the general institutions of society like the industrial system should be distinguished from threats or incitements against named or targeted individuals. Case law requiring the likelihood of speech producing "imminent lawless action" before it can be proscribed does not contradict this conclusion, and the Court's frequent designation of individually harmful speech as "conduct" merely underscores the distinction.

Ultimately, freedom of speech exists to prevent the state and its democratic majority from censoring the beliefs, opinions, and expressions of the minority. It constitutes a primary form of liberty that both allows the minority self-expression and ensures the mechanism by which new ideas can be tested against the old. In the marketplace of ideas metaphor, freedom of speech maximizes the efficient dissemination of human knowledge for effective decision making in the social, political, and economic arenas. As its place in the Bill of Rights suggests, freedom of speech is properly first among our liberties.

Nothing in First Amendment values and very little in Supreme Court cases indicates, however, that free speech doctrine permits targeted speech that threatens individuals with violence or causes other substantial harm to individuals. Concerns about censorship of speech directed against the government and its general policies do not apply to speech that falsely and recklessly defames, deceives and defrauds consumers, causes reasonable fear to individuals through threat or intimidation, or targets employees for discriminatory harassment. Such speech harms targeted individuals, and the Supreme Court appropriately should categorize it under different standards than the Court does speech against the state and measure listener reaction to it according to the reasonable person standard.

In the final analysis, the issue of substantial harm dominates when the government can constitutionally limit freedom of speech, and how this harm is defined becomes the critical determinant. The ILA standard is ill-suited as a general category defining harm both in the context of incitement or threat against the state and in the context of incitement, threat, intimidation, or harassment against individuals. It should not apply to targeted speech that threatens or substantially harms individuals.

POSTSCRIPT

Does the First Amendment Protect an Informational Web Site That May Encourage Violent Acts?

One of the most well known cases involving speech and violence is *Chaplinsky v. New Hampshire,* 315 U.S. 568 (1942). In that case, a Jehovah's Witness was convicted of breach of the peace for calling the town constable "a God damned racketeer" and "a damned Fascist." The Court upheld the conviction and declared that "fighting words" were unprotected by the First Amendment, noting:

> There are certain well-defined and narrowly limited classes of speech, the prevention and punishment of which have never been thought to raise any Constitutional problem. These include the lewd and obscene, the profane, the libelous, and the insulting or "fighting" words—those which by their very utterance inflict injury or tend to incite an immediate breach of the peace. It has been well observed that such utterances are no essential part of any exposition of ideas, and are of such slight social value as a step to truth that any benefit that may be derived from them is clearly outweighed by the social interest in order and morality.

Kozinski and Reed do not suggest that the legal standards for defining a threat should be changed because of the Internet, but it is possible that the number of cases involving alleged threats may increase because of the Internet. One of the first criminal cases involving online behavior concerned a person known as Jake Baker. See *United States v. Abraham Jacob Alkhabaz,* 104 F.3d (1942). Baker was a University of Michigan student who wrote lurid, gruesome, and violent stories and circulated them via a news group. The victim in the stories was a person with the same name as one of Baker's classmates. Baker was charged with violating Title 18, Section 875(c), of the United States Code, which states:

> Whoever transmits in interstate or foreign commerce any communication containing any threat to kidnap any person or any threat to injure the person of another, shall be fined under this title or imprisoned not more than five years, or both.

The Court of Appeals quoted the following lines from Shakespeare and found that what Baker did was not a violation of the statute:

> His acts did not o'ertake his bad intent;
> And must be buried but as an intent
> That perish'd by the way: thoughts are no subjects,
> Intents but merely thoughts.

On the other hand, in a non-Internet case, a federal appeals court held that the publisher of a murder manual entitled *Hit Man: A Technical Manual for Independent Contractors* could be held liable. See *Rice v. Paladin Enters., Inc.*, 128 F.3d 233, 267 (4th Cir. 1997), cert. denied, 573 U.S. 1074 (1998). The murder manual was originally published in 1983, but the murders at issue did not take place until 1993. The alleged murderer apparently purchased the murder manual in 1992, several months before the killings.

The Court found that:

> In soliciting, preparing for, and committing these murders, Perry meticulously followed countless of *Hit Man's* 130 pages of detailed factual instructions on how to murder and to become a professional killer. Perry, for example, followed many of the book's instructions on soliciting a client and arranging for a contract murder in his solicitation of and negotiation with Lawrence Horn.

Cases of relevance to this issue are *Hess v. Indiana,* 414 U.S. 105 (1973) (Vietnam protest); *NAACP v. Claiborne Hardware Co.,* 458 U.S. 886 (1982) (civil rights boycott); *Cohen v. California,* 403 U.S. 15 (1971) (vulgar antidraft message); and *Texas v. Johnson,* 491 U.S. 397 (1989) (flag burning to protest Republican Party policies). An excellent analysis of the underlying issues in this case can be found in Rodney A. Smolla, "Should the *Brandenburg v. Ohio* Incitement Test Apply in Media Violence Tort Cases?" 27 *Northern Kentucky University Law Review* 1 (2000).

ISSUE 16

Should Same-Sex Marriages Be Lawful?

YES: Andrew Sullivan, from *Virtually Normal* (Alfred A. Knopf, 1995)

NO: James Q. Wilson, from "Against Homosexual Marriage," *Commentary* (March 1996)

ISSUE SUMMARY

YES: Andrew Sullivan, a journalist and magazine editor, seeks to transcend the traditional liberal and conservative terms of the debate over same-sex marriages and argues that all public discrimination against homosexuals should be ended.

NO: James Q. Wilson, an emeritus professor of management and public policy, finds unpersuasive the various arguments that Sullivan puts forward.

In late November 1990 Craig Dean and Patrick Gill filed a civil suit in the Superior Court of the District of Columbia. The complaint alleged that the district's marriage ordinance should be construed so as to allow for same-sex marriages. Dean and Gill argued that failure to allow for same-sex marriages constituted a violation of the district's Human Rights Act, which banned discrimination in public services, in part, on the basis of gender and sexual orientation. However, the superior court rejected the couple's argument, finding that the district's marriage laws must be understood within the larger context of Western civilization; that is, the historic meaning of marriage is a union between a man and a woman (see *Dean v. District of Columbia*, 653 A.2d 307, 1995). Consequently, the trial court held that the District of Columbia's Human Rights Act did not require the legal recognition of same-sex marriages. The District of Columbia Court of Appeals agreed with the reasoning of the lower court and upheld its decision.

Although the plaintiffs' claim was rejected in the District of Columbia courts, the moral and political questions raised by the litigation have remained within the public consciousness. Indeed, for the past several years the issue of same-sex marriage has been prominent in public policy discussions. And although the legal questions involved in same-sex marriages have been before various state courts since the early 1970s, it was not until 1993 that the question of whether or not same-sex marriages should be legally recognized emerged at the center of national political debate.

In the same year that Dean and Gill brought suit in the District of Columbia, the foundation for similar legal action was being put in place in the state of Hawaii. In December 1990 Nina Baehr and Genora Dancel, along with two other same-sex couples, applied for marriage licenses. When their requests were denied, they took legal action against the state. Their claims were initially unsuccessful, but in 1993 the state supreme court overturned a lower court decision and held that the denial of marriage licenses to same-sex couples constituted a violation of the equal protection clause of the Hawaii Constitution (see *Baehr v. Lewin*, 852 P.2d 44, 1993).

In a groundbreaking decision, the Hawaii Supreme Court held that the state constitution could be interpreted to compel the state government to issue marriage licenses to same-sex couples. The court rejected the plaintiffs' argument that they had a *fundamental right* to marry that was protected by a constitutional right to privacy. However, the court did conclude that by restricting the right to marry to opposite-sex couples only, the state had created a sex-based classification that, absent narrow tailoring to achieve a compelling state interest, was forbidden by the Hawaii Constitution. The action was then remanded to the circuit court for a trial on the merits of the case. Although Baehr and her coplaintiffs did not receive an immediate trial date, political and cultural forces on both sides of the issue were immediately engaged.

In Hawaii, the state legislature, although reluctant to overrule the supreme court by constitutional amendment, did act promptly to amend the state's marriage law in order to clarify the point that legal recognition of marriage should be granted only to opposite-sex couples. Beyond Hawaii, however, more than 30 state legislatures moved to legally define *marriage*, seeking to exclude same-sex couples as contrary to public policy. The expressed fear was that if such marriages were legally recognized in Hawaii, then under the full faith and credit clause of the U.S. Constitution (art. 4, sec. 1) all other states would be required to recognize the legality of same-sex marriages performed in Hawaii. Although only 16 states ultimately passed legislation in direct response to the Hawaii situation, Congress acted to minimize the states' concerns. With the Defense of Marriage Act of 1996, Congress sought to relieve the states of any obligation under the U.S. Constitution to recognize same-sex marriages from other states. Congress took this unique step by introducing into the United States Code, for the first time, a federal definition of marriage. The law had overwhelming support in both houses of Congress and was promptly signed into law by President Bill Clinton.

The following readings should help to focus some of the issues under debate here. Andrew Sullivan, who identifies himself as gay and conservative, seeks to transcend the traditional liberal and conservative terms of the debate and forge a defense of gay marriage on the basis of a claim to "formal public equality." James Q. Wilson, a more traditional conservative thinker, rejects Sullivan's argument and reprises a number of familiar positions in opposing the legal recognition of gay marriage.

Andrew Sullivan

 **YES**

Virtually Normal

[The question of] equal access to civil marriage . . . is a question of formal public discrimination, since only the state can grant and recognize marriage. [This question] deals with the heart of what it means to be a citizen [because] it affects everyone. Marriage is not simply a private contract; it is a social and public recognition of a private commitment. As such, it is the highest public recognition of personal integrity. Denying it to homosexuals is the most public affront possible to their public equality.

This point may be the hardest for many heterosexuals to accept. Even those tolerant of homosexuals may find this institution so wedded to the notion of heterosexual commitment that to extend it would be to undo its very essence. And there may be religious reasons for resisting this that, within certain traditions, are unanswerable. But I am not here discussing what churches do in their private affairs. I am discussing what the allegedly neutral liberal state should do in public matters. For liberals, the case for homosexual marriage is overwhelming. As a classic public institution, it should be available to any two citizens.

Some might argue that marriage is by definition between a man and a woman; and it is difficult to argue with a definition. But if marriage is articulated beyond this circular fiat, then the argument for its exclusivity to one man and one woman disappears. The center of the public contract is an emotional, financial, and psychological bond between two people; in this respect, heterosexuals and homosexuals are identical. The heterosexuality of marriage is intrinsic only if it is understood to be intrinsically procreative; but that definition has long been abandoned in Western society. No civil marriage license is granted on the condition that the couple bear children; and the marriage is no less legal and no less defensible if it remains childless. In the contemporary West, marriage has become a way in which the state recognizes an emotional commitment by two people to each other for life. And within that definition, there is no public way, if one believes in equal rights under the law, in which it should legally be denied homosexuals.

Of course, no public sanctioning of a contract should be given to people who cannot actually fulfill it. The state rightly, for example, withholds marriage from minors, or from one adult and a minor, since at least one party is unable to understand or live up to the contract. And the state has also rightly barred

From Andrew Sullivan, *Virtually Normal* (Alfred A. Knopf, 1995). Copyright © 1995 by Andrew Sullivan. Reprinted by permission of Alfred A. Knopf, a division of Random House, Inc.

close family relatives from marriage because familial emotional ties are too strong and powerful to enable a marriage contract to be entered into freely by two autonomous, independent individuals; and because incest poses a uniquely dangerous threat to the trust and responsibility that the family needs to survive. But do homosexuals fall into a similar category? History and experience strongly suggest they don't. Of course, marriage is characterized by a kind of commitment that is rare—and perhaps declining—even among heterosexuals. But it isn't necessary to prove that homosexuals or lesbians are less—or more —able to form long-term relationships than straights for it to be clear that at least *some* are. Moreover, giving these people an equal right to affirm their commitment doesn't reduce the incentive for heterosexuals to do the same.

... Few people deny that many homosexuals are capable of the sacrifice, the commitment, and the responsibilities of marriage. And indeed, for many homosexuals and lesbians, these responsibilities are already enjoined—as they have been enjoined for centuries. The issue is whether these identical relationships should be denied equal legal standing, not by virtue of anything to do with the relationships themselves but by virtue of the internal, involuntary nature of the homosexuals involved. Clearly, for liberals, the answer to this is clear. Such a denial is a classic case of unequal protection of the laws.

But perhaps surprisingly,... one of the strongest arguments for gay marriage is a conservative one. It's perhaps best illustrated by a comparison with the alternative often offered by liberals and liberationists to legal gay marriage, the concept of "domestic partnership." Several cities in the United States have domestic partnership laws, which allow relationships that do not fit into the category of heterosexual marriage to be registered with the city and qualify for benefits that had previously been reserved for heterosexual married couples. In these cities, a variety of interpersonal arrangements qualify for health insurance, bereavement leave, insurance, annuity and pension rights, housing rights (such as rent-control apartments), adoption and inheritance rights. Eventually, the aim is to include federal income tax and veterans' benefits as well. Homosexuals are not the only beneficiaries; heterosexual "live-togethers" also qualify.

The conservative's worries start with the ease of the relationship. To be sure, potential domestic partners have to prove financial interdependence, shared living arrangements, and a commitment to mutual caring. But they don't need to have a sexual relationship or even closely mirror old style marriage. In principle, an elderly woman and her live-in nurse could qualify, or a pair of frat buddies. Left as it is, the concept of domestic partnership could open a Pandora's box of litigation and subjective judicial decision making about who qualifies. You either are or you're not married; it's not a complex question. Whether you are in a domestic partnership is not so clear.

More important for conservatives, the concept of domestic partnership chips away at the prestige of traditional relationships and undermines the priority we give them. Society, after all, has good reasons to extend legal advantages to heterosexuals who choose the formal sanction of marriage over simply living together. They make a deeper commitment to one another and to society; in exchange, society extends certain benefits to them. Marriage provides an anchor, if an arbitrary and often weak one, in the maelstrom of sex and relationships to which we are all prone. It provides a mechanism for emotional stability and economic security. We rig the law in its favor not because we disparage all forms of relationship other than the nuclear family, but because we recognize that not to promote marriage would be to ask too much of human virtue.

For conservatives, these are vital concerns. There are virtually no conservative arguments either for preferring no social incentives for gay relationships or for preferring a second-class relationship, such as domestic partnership, which really does provide an incentive for the decline of traditional marriage. Nor, if conservatives are concerned by the collapse of stable family life, should they be dismayed by the possibility of gay parents. There is no evidence that shows any deleterious impact on a child brought up by two homosexual parents; and considerable evidence that such a parental structure is clearly preferable to single parents (gay or straight) or no effective parents at all, which, alas, is the choice many children now face. Conservatives should not balk at the apparent radicalism of the change involved, either. The introduction of gay marriage would not be some sort of leap in the dark, a massive societal risk. Homosexual marriages have always existed, in a variety of forms; they have just been euphemized. Increasingly they exist in every sense but the legal one. As it has become more acceptable for homosexuals to acknowledge their loves and commitments publicly, more and more have committed themselves to one another for life in full view of their families and friends. A law institutionalizing gay marriage would merely reinforce a healthy trend. Burkean conservatives should warm to the idea.

It would also be an unqualified social good for homosexuals. It provides role models for young gay people, who, after the exhilaration of coming out, can easily lapse into short-term relationships and insecurity with no tangible goal in sight. My own guess is that most homosexuals would embrace such a goal with as much (if not more) commitment as heterosexuals. Even in our society as it is, many lesbian and gay male relationships are virtual textbooks of monogamous commitment; and for many, "in sickness and in health" has become a vocation rather than a vow. Legal gay marriage could also help bridge the gulf often found between homosexuals and their parents. It could bring the essence of gay life—a gay couple—into the heart of the traditional family in a way the family can most understand and the gay offspring can most easily acknowledge. It could do more to heal the gay-straight rift than any amount of gay rights legislation.

More important, perhaps, as gay marriage sank into the subtle background consciousness of a culture, its influence would be felt quietly but deeply among gay children. For them, at last, there would be some kind of future; some older faces to apply to their unfolding lives, some language in which their identity could be properly discussed, some rubric by which it could be explained—not in terms of sex, or sexual practices, or bars, or subterranean activity, but in terms of their future life stories, their potential loves, their eventual chance at some kind of constructive happiness. They would be able to feel by the intimation of a myriad examples that in this respect their emotional orientation was not merely about pleasure, or sin, or shame, or otherness (although it might always be involved in many of those things), but about the ability to love and be loved as complete, imperfect human beings. Until gay marriage is legalized, this fundamental element of personal dignity will be denied a whole segment of humanity. No other change can achieve it.

Any heterosexual man who takes a few moments to consider what his life would be like if he were never allowed a formal institution to cement his relationships will see the truth of what I am saying. Imagine life without a recognized family; imagine dating without even the possibility of marriage. Any heterosexual woman who can imagine being told at a young age that her attraction to men was wrong, that her loves and crushes were illicit, that her destiny was single-hood and shame, will also appreciate the point. Gay marriage is not a radical step; it is a profoundly humanizing, traditionalizing step. It is the first step in any resolution of the homosexual question—more important than any other institution, since it is the most central institution to the nature of the problem, which is to say, the emotional and sexual bond between one human being and another. If nothing else were done at all, and gay marriage were legalized, ninety percent of the political work necessary to achieve gay and lesbian equality would have been achieved. It is ultimately the only reform that truly matters.

So long as conservatives recognize, as they do, that homosexuals exist and that they have equivalent emotional needs and temptations as heterosexuals, then there is no conservative reason to oppose homosexual marriage and many conservative reasons to support it. So long as liberals recognize, as they do, that citizens deserve equal treatment under the law, then there is no liberal reason to oppose it and many liberal reasons to be in favor of it. So long as intelligent people understand that homosexuals are emotionally and sexually attracted to the same sex as heterosexuals are to the other sex, then there is no human reason on earth why it should be granted to one group and not the other.

[Providing for the legal recognition of homosexual marriage is] simple, direct, and require[s] no change in heterosexual behavior and no sacrifice from heterosexuals. [It] represent[s] a politics that tackles the heart of prejudice against homosexuals while leaving bigots their freedom. This politics marries the clarity of liberalism with the intuition of conservatism. It allows homosexuals to define their own future and their own identity and does not place it in the hands of the other. It makes a clear, public statement of equality while leaving all the inequalities of emotion and passion to the private sphere, where they belong. It does not legislate private tolerance; it declares public equality. It banishes the paradigm of victimology and replaces it with one of integrity.

It requires for its completion one further step, which is to say the continuing effort for honesty on the part of homosexuals themselves. This is not easily summed up in the crude phrase "coming out"; but it finds expression in the many ways in which gay men and lesbians talk, engage, explain, confront and seek out the other. Politics cannot substitute for this; heterosexuals cannot provide it. And while it is not in some sense fair that homosexuals have to initiate the dialogue, it is a fact of life. Silence, if it does not equal death, equals the living equivalent.

It is, of course, not the least of the ironies of this politics—and of this predominantly political argument—that, in the last resort, its objectives are in some sense not political at all. The family is prior to the liberal state; the military is coincident with it. Heterosexuals would not conceive of such rights as things to be won, but as things that predate modern political discussion. But it says something about the unique status of homosexuals in our society that we now have to be political in order to be prepolitical. Our battle, after all, is not for political victory but for personal integrity. In the same way that many of us had to leave our families in order to join them again, so now as citizens, we have to embrace politics if only ultimately to be free of it. Our lives may have begun in simplicity, but they have not ended there. Our dream, perhaps, is that they might.

NO ⬅

James Q. Wilson

Against Homosexual Marriage

O ur courts, which have mishandled abortion, may be on the verge of mis-handling homosexuality. As a consequence of two pending decisions, we may be about to accept homosexual marriage....

Contemporaneous with these events, an important book has appeared under the title *Virtually Normal* [Knopf, 209 pp., $22.00]. In it, Andrew Sul-livan... makes a strong case for a new policy toward homosexuals. He argues that "all *public* (as opposed to private) discrimination against homosexuals be ended.... *And that is all."* The two key areas where this change is necessary are the military and marriage law. Lifting bans in those areas, while also disallowing anti-sodomy laws and providing information about homosexuality in publicly supported schools, would put an end to the harm that gays have endured. Be-yond these changes, Sullivan writes, American society would need no "cures [of homophobia] or reeducations, no wrenching private litigation, no political imposition of tolerance."

It is hard to imagine how Sullivan's proposals would, in fact, end efforts to change private behavior toward homosexuals, or why the next, inevitable, step would not involve attempts to accomplish just that purpose by using cures and reeducations, private litigation, and the political imposition of tolerance.... In her review of it in *First Things* (January 1996), Elizabeth Kristol asks us to try to answer the following question: what would life be like if we were not allowed to marry? To most of us, the thought is unimaginable; to Sullivan, it is the daily existence of declared homosexuals. His response is to let homosexual couples marry.

⁕

Sullivan recounts three main arguments concerning homosexual marriage, two against and one for. He labels them prohibitionist, conservative, and liberal.... I think it is easier to grasp the origins of the three main arguments by referring to the principles on which they are based.

The prohibitionist argument is in fact a biblical one; the heart of it was stated by Dennis Prager in an essay in the *Public Interest* ("Homosexuality, the Bible, and Us," Summer 1993). When the first books of the Bible were written,

From James Q. Wilson, "Against Homosexual Marriage," *Commentary,* vol. 101, no. 3 (March 1996). Copyright © 1996 by *Commentary.* Reprinted by permission.

and for a long time thereafter, heterosexual love is what seemed at risk. In many cultures—not only in Egypt or among the Canaanite tribes surrounding ancient Israel but later in Greece, Rome, and the Arab world, to say nothing of large parts of China, Japan, and elsewhere—homosexual practices were common and widely tolerated or even exalted. The Torah reversed this, making the family the central unit of life, the obligation to marry one of the first responsibilities of man, and the linkage of sex to procreation the highest standard by which to judge sexual relations. Leviticus puts the matter sharply and apparently beyond quibble:

> Thou shalt not live with mankind as with womankind; it is an abomination.... If a man also lie with mankind, as he lieth with a woman, both of them have committed an abomination; they shall surely be put to death; their blood shall be upon them.

Sullivan acknowledges the power of Leviticus but deals with it by placing it in a relative context. What is the nature of this "abomination"? Is it like killing your mother or stealing a neighbor's bread, or is it more like refusing to eat shellfish or having sex during menstruation? Sullivan suggests that all of these injunctions were written on the same moral level and hence can be accepted or ignored *as a whole.* He does not fully sustain this view, and in fact a refutation of it can be found in Prager's essay. In Prager's opinion and mine, people at the time of Moses, and for centuries before him, understood that there was a fundamental difference between whom you killed and what you ate, and in all likelihood people then and for centuries earlier linked whom you could marry closer to the principles that defined life than they did to the rules that defined diets.

The New Testament contains an equally vigorous attack on homosexuality by St. Paul. Sullivan partially deflects it by noting Paul's conviction that the earth was about to end and the Second Coming was near; under these conditions, all forms of sex were suspect. But Sullivan cannot deny that Paul singled out homosexuality as deserving of special criticism. He seems to pass over this obstacle without effective retort.

Instead, he takes up a different theme, namely, that on grounds of consistency many heterosexual practices—adultery, sodomy, premarital sex, and divorce, among others—should be outlawed equally with homosexual acts of the same character. The difficulty with this is that it mistakes the distinction alive in most people's minds between marriage as an institution and marriage as a practice. As an institution, it deserves unqualified support; as a practice, we recognize that married people are as imperfect as anyone else. Sullivan's understanding of the prohibitionist argument suffers from his unwillingness to acknowledge this distinction.

⋘◉⋙

The second argument against homosexual marriage—Sullivan's conservative category—is based on natural law as originally set forth by Aristotle and Thomas Aquinas.... How it is phrased varies a bit, but in general its advocates support a position like the following: man cannot live without the care and support of other people; natural law is the distillation of what thoughtful people have learned about the conditions of that care. The first thing they have learned is the supreme importance of marriage, for without it the newborn infant is unlikely to survive or, if he survives, to prosper. The necessary conditions of a decent family life are the acknowledgment by its members that a man will not sleep with his daughter or a woman with her son and that neither will openly choose sex outside marriage.

Now, some of these conditions are violated, but there is a penalty in each case that is supported by the moral convictions of almost all who witness the violation. On simple utilitarian grounds it may be hard to object to incest or adultery; if both parties to such an act welcome it and if it is secret, what differences does it make? But very few people, and then only ones among the overeducated, seem to care much about mounting a utilitarian assault on the family. To this assault, natural-law theorists respond much as would the average citizen—never mind "utility," what counts is what is right. In particular, homosexual uses of the reproductive organs violate the condition that sex serve solely as the basis of heterosexual marriage.

To Sullivan, what is defective about the natural-law thesis is that it assumes different purposes in heterosexual and homosexual love: moral consummation in the first case and pure utility or pleasure alone in the second. But in fact, Sullivan suggests, homosexual love can be as consummatory as heterosexual. He notes that as the Roman Catholic Church has deepened its understanding of the involuntary—that is, in some sense genetic—basis of homosexuality, it has attempted to keep homosexuals in the church as objects of affection and nurture, while banning homosexual acts as perverse.

But this, though better than nothing, will not work, Sullivan writes. To show why, he adduces an analogy to a sterile person. Such a person is permitted to serve in the military or enter an unproductive marriage; why not homosexuals? If homosexuals marry without procreation, they are no different (he suggests) from a sterile man or woman who marries without hope of procreation. Yet people, I think, want the form observed even when the practice varies; a sterile marriage, whether from choice or necessity, remains a marriage of a man and a woman. To this Sullivan offers essentially an aesthetic response. Just as albinos remind us of the brilliance of color and genius teaches us about moderation, homosexuals are a "natural foil" to the heterosexual union, "a variation that does not eclipse the theme." Moreover, the threat posed by the foil to the theme is slight as compared to the threats posed by adultery, divorce, and prostitution. To be consistent, Sullivan once again reminds us, society would have to ban adulterers from the military as it now bans confessed homosexuals.

But again this misses the point. It would make more sense to ask why an alternative to marriage should be invented and praised when we are having enough trouble maintaining the institution at all. Suppose that gay or lesbian marriage were authorized; rather than producing a "natural foil" that would "not eclipse the theme," I suspect such a move would call even more seriously into question the role of marriage at a time when the threats to it, ranging from single-parent families to common divorces, have hit record highs. Kenneth Minogue recently wrote of Sullivan's book that support for homosexual marriage would strike most people as "mere parody," one that could further weaken an already strained institution.

To me, the chief limitation of Sullivan's view is that it presupposes that marriage would have the same, domesticating, effect on homosexual members as it has on heterosexuals, while leaving the latter largely unaffected. Those are very large assumptions that no modern society has ever tested.

Nor does it seem plausible to me that a modern society resists homosexual marriages entirely out of irrational prejudice. Marriage is a union, sacred to most, that unites a man and woman together for life. It is a sacrament of the Catholic Church and central to every other faith. Is it out of misinformation that every modern society has embraced this view and rejected the alternative? Societies differ greatly in their attitude toward the income people may have, the relations among their various races, and the distribution of political power. But they differ scarcely at all over the distinctions between heterosexual and homosexual couples. The former are overwhelmingly preferred over the latter. The reason, I believe, is that these distinctions involve the nature of marriage and thus the very meaning—even more, the very possibility—of society.

The final argument over homosexual marriage is the liberal one, based on civil rights.

... [T]he Hawaiian Supreme Court ruled that any state-imposed sexual distinction would have to meet the test of strict scrutiny, a term used by the U.S. Supreme Court only for racial and similar classifications. In doing this, the Hawaiian court distanced itself from every other state court decision—there are several—in this area so far.* A variant of the suspect-class argument, though, has been suggested by some scholars who contend that denying access to a marriage license by two people of the same sex is no different from denying access to two people of different sexes but also different races. The Hawaiian Supreme Court embraced this argument as well, explicitly comparing its decision to that of the U.S. Supreme Court when it overturned state laws banning marriages involving miscegenation.

But the comparison with black-white marriages is itself suspect. Beginning around 1964, and no doubt powerfully affected by the passage of the Civil Rights Act of that year, public attitudes toward race began to change dramatically. Even allowing for exaggerated statements to pollsters, there is little doubt that people in fact acquired a new view of blacks. Not so with homosexuals. Though the campaign to aid them has been going on vigorously for about a

---

* [Minnesota refused a claim for a marriage license by two gay men even though the relevant state statute does not mention sex; the federal Ninth Circuit rejected a claim that Congress, in defining a spouse in the Immigration and Naturalization Act of 1982, meant to include same-sex spouses. In Pennsylvania a court refused to allow a same-sex couple to contract a common-law marriage. A Kentucky court did the same in the case of two lesbians applying for a marriage license, as did a Washington court in the case of two gay men. The District of Columbia Court of Appeals acted similarly (by a divided vote) in 1995.]

quarter of a century, it has produced few, if any, gains in public acceptance, and the greatest resistance, I think, has been with respect to homosexual marriages.

Consider the difference. What has been at issue in race relations is not marriage among blacks (for over a century, that right has been universally granted) or even miscegenation (long before the civil-rights movement, many Southern states had repealed such laws). Rather, it has been the routine contact between the races in schools, jobs, and neighborhoods. Our own history, in other words, has long made it clear that marriage is a different issue from the issue of social integration.

There is another way, too, in which the comparison with race is less than helpful, as Sullivan himself points out. Thanks to the changes in public attitudes I mentioned a moment ago, gradually race was held to be not central to decisions about hiring, firing, promoting, and schooling, and blacks began to make extraordinary advances in society. But then, in an effort to enforce this new view, liberals came to embrace affirmative action, a policy that said that race *was* central to just such issues, in order to ensure that *real* mixing occurred. This move created a crisis, for liberalism had always been based on the proposition that a liberal political system should encourage, as John Stuart Mill put it, "experiments in living" free of religious or political direction. To contemporary liberals, however, being neutral about race was tantamount to being neutral about a set of human preferences that in such matters as neighborhood and schooling left groups largely (but not entirely) separate.

Sullivan, who wisely sees that hardly anybody is really prepared to ignore a political opportunity to change lives, is not disposed to have much of this either in the area of race or in that of sex. And he points out with great clarity that popular attitudes toward sexuality are anyway quite different from those about race, as is evident from the fact that wherever sexual orientation is subject to local regulations, such regulations are rarely invoked. Why? Because homosexuals can "pass" or not, as they wish; they can and do accumulate education and wealth; they exercise political power. The two things a homosexual cannot do are join the military as an avowed homosexual or marry another homosexual.

The result, Sullivan asserts, is a wrenching paradox. On the one hand, society has historically tolerated the brutalization inflicted on people because of the color of their skin, but freely allowed them to marry; on the other hand, it has given equal opportunity to homosexuals, while denying them the right to marry. This, indeed, is where Sullivan draws the line. A black or Hispanic child, if heterosexual, has many friends, he writes, but a gay child "generally has no one." And that is why the social stigma attached to homosexuality is different from that attached to race or ethnicity—"because it attacks the very heart of what makes a human being human: the ability to love and be loved." Here is the essence of Sullivan's case. It is a powerful one, even if (as I suspect) his pro-marriage sentiments are not shared by all homosexuals.

❧

Let us assume for the moment that a chance to live openly and legally with another homosexual is desirable. To believe that, we must set aside biblical injunctions, a difficult matter in a profoundly religious nation. But suppose we manage the diversion, perhaps on the grounds that if most Americans skip church, they can as readily avoid other errors of (possibly) equal magnitude. Then we must ask on what terms the union shall be arranged. There are two alternatives—marriage or domestic partnership.

Sullivan acknowledges the choice, but disparages the domestic-partnership laws that have evolved in some foreign countries and in some American localities. His reasons, essentially conservative ones, are that domestic partnerships are too easily formed and too easily broken. Only real marriages matter. But—aside from the fact that marriage is in serious decline, and that only slightly more than half of all marriages performed in the United States this year will be between never-before-married heterosexuals—what is distinctive about marriage is that it is an institution created to sustain child-rearing. Whatever losses it has suffered in *this* respect, its function remains what it has always been.

The role of raising children is entrusted in principle to married heterosexual couples because after much experimentation—several thousand years, more or less—we have found nothing else that works as well. Neither a gay nor a lesbian couple can of its own resources produce a child; another party must be involved. What do we call this third party? A friend? A sperm or egg bank? An anonymous donor? There is no settled language for even describing, much less approving of, such persons.

Suppose we allowed homosexual couples to raise children who were created out of a prior heterosexual union or adopted from someone else's heterosexual contact. What would we think of this? There is very little research on the matter. Charlotte Patterson's famous essay, "Children of Gay and Lesbian Parents" (*Journal of Child Development,* 1992), begins by conceding that the existing studies focus on children born into a heterosexual union that ended in divorce or that was transformed when the mother or father "came out" as a homosexual. Hardly any research has been done on children acquired at the outset by a homosexual couple. We therefore have no way of knowing how they would behave. And even if we had such studies, they might tell us rather little unless they were conducted over a very long period of time.

But it is one thing to be born into an apparently heterosexual family and then many years later to learn that one of your parents is homosexual. It is quite another to be acquired as an infant from an adoption agency or a parent-for-hire and learn from the first years of life that you are, because of your family's position, radically different from almost all other children you will meet. No one can now say how grievous this would be. We know that young children tease one another unmercifully; adding this dimension does not seem to be a step in the right direction.

Of course, homosexual "families," with or without children, might be rather few in number. Just how few, it is hard to say. Perhaps Sullivan himself would marry, but, given the great tendency of homosexual males to be promiscuous, many more like him would not, or if they did, would not marry with as much seriousness.

That is problematic in itself. At one point, Sullivan suggests that most homosexuals would enter a marriage "with as much (if not more) commitment as heterosexuals." Toward the end of his book, however, he seems to withdraw from so optimistic a view. He admits that the label "virtually" in the title of his book is deliberately ambiguous, because homosexuals as a group are *not* "normal." At another point, he writes that the "openness of the contract" between two homosexual males means that such a union will in fact be more durable than a heterosexual marriage because the contract contains an *"understanding of the need for extramarital outlets"* (emphasis added). But no such "understanding" exists in heterosexual marriage; to suggest that it might in homosexual ones is tantamount to saying that we are now referring to two different kinds of arrangements. To justify this difference, perhaps, Sullivan adds that the very "lack of children" will give "gay couples greater freedom." Freedom for what? Freedom, I think, to do more of those things that heterosexual couples do less of because they might hurt the children.

⋅⊙⋅

The courts in Hawaii and in the nation's capital must struggle with all these issues under the added encumbrance of a contemporary outlook that makes law the search for rights, and responsibility the recognition of rights. Indeed, thinking of laws about marriage as documents that confer or withhold rights is itself an error of fundamental importance—one that the highest court in Hawaii has already committed. "Marriage," it wrote, "is a state-conferred legal-partnership status, the existence of which gives rise to a multiplicity of rights and benefits. . . ." A state-conferred legal partnership? To lawyers, perhaps; to mankind, I think not. The Hawaiian court has thus set itself on the same course of action as the misguided Supreme Court in 1973 when it thought that laws about abortion were merely an assertion of the rights of a living mother and an unborn fetus.

I have few favorable things to say about the political systems of other modern nations, but on these fundamental matters—abortion, marriage, military service—they often do better by allowing legislatures to operate than we do by deferring to courts. Our challenge is to find a way of formulating a policy with respect to homosexual unions that is not the result of a reflexive act of judicial rights-conferring, but is instead a considered expression of the moral convictions of a people.

POSTSCRIPT

Should Same-Sex Marriages Be Lawful?

After repeated postponements *Baehr v. Lewin* finally went to trial on September 10, 1996, the same day the Defense of Marriage Act was passed in the Senate. Judge Kevin Chang, of the Hawaii Circuit Court, ruled in favor of Nina Baehr and held that the state had failed to meet the constitutional burden imposed on it in order to justify its exclusion of same-sex couples from the institution of marriage (see *Baehr v. Miike*, 1996). As was to be expected, responses were immediate and highly partisan. For a full discussion of the moral, political, and legal questions involved in this issue, read William Eskridge's *The Case for Same-Sex Marriage: From Sexual Liberty to Civilized Commitment* (Free Press, 1996). Professor Eskridge, of the Georgetown University Law Center, writes from a position of deep involvement in the debate: he served as counsel to the plaintiffs in *Dean v. District of Columbia*. Also helpful is Mark Strasser's *Legally Wed: Same-Sex Marriage and the Constitution* (Cornell University Press, 1997). Finally, for an overview of the arguments on both sides of the debate, consult Andrew Sullivan, ed., *Same-Sex Marriage, Pro and Con: A Reader* (Vintage Books, 1997). Internet sites that provide information on same-sex marriage include http://www.courttv.com/legalcafe/family/dom_partners/; http://www.buddybuddy.com/toc.html; and http://www.ngltf.org.

ISSUE 17

Are Public School Officials Liable for Damages in Cases of Student-on-Student Sexual Harassment?

YES: Sandra Day O'Connor, from Majority Opinion, *Davis v. Monroe County Board of Education et al.*, U.S. Supreme Court (May 24, 1999)

NO: Anthony Kennedy, from Dissenting Opinion, *Davis v. Monroe County Board of Education et al.*, U.S. Supreme Court (May 24, 1999)

ISSUE SUMMARY

YES: Supreme Court justice Sandra Day O'Connor holds that under Title IX of the Education Amendments of 1972, actions for private damages may be brought against school board officials in cases of student-on-student sexual harassment.

NO: Supreme Court justice Anthony Kennedy argues that Title IX cannot be read to provide such a cause of action and that to do so opens the gate for the federal government to intrude into state and local educational decision making.

Writing for a unanimous court in the landmark decision of *Brown v. Board of Education*, 347 U.S. 483 (1954), Chief Justice Earl Warren underscored the importance of education both to the individual and, by implication, to the vitality of the American nation. There he observed,

> Today, education is perhaps the most important function of state and local governments.... It is the very foundation of good citizenship. Today it is a principal instrument in awakening the child to cultural value, in preparing him for later professional training, and in helping him to adjust normally to his environment. In these days, it is doubtful that any child may reasonably be expected to succeed in life if he is denied the opportunity of an education. 347 U.S. at 493.

The context for Warren's remarks was the racial integration of public schools. Yet his comments suggest as well why U.S. public schools are, for many, an important arena in which to engage in debate over fundamental questions of public policy.

Recently, parents, educators, school administrators, and legislators have made America's educational institutions the latest arena in the fight to end sexual harassment. Certainly, "teasing" has always been a part of life in primary and secondary schools—it is perhaps simply one form that human interaction takes. Yet many school authorities indicate that an issue does now exist. As a society, Americans have become more aware of the problem of sexual harassment in the workplace. Therefore, the public may now be more sensitive to similar forms of behavior in the classroom. Whether there has been an actual increase in sexual harassment or people are now more aware of the problem, school administrators must nonetheless find ways to respond.

Unfortunately, some schools have had difficulty in drawing the line between innocent behavior and more serious forms of harassment. For example, in the fall of 1996, radio talk shows filled a good deal of air time with the case of Jonathan Prevette, a six-year-old school boy from North Carolina. After Jonathan kissed a classmate on the cheek, school officials separated him from the rest of his class for violating the school's behavior code, which prohibited unwanted touching. But, as many were quick to point out, Jonathan's real punishment was missing a class ice cream party held during the required separation. This was all innocent enough—indeed, Jonathan was often portrayed as something of a victim at the "politically correct" hands of overzealous school administrators. Yet there are many other stories that fail to make the nightly news but that reveal far more disturbing behavior. The case of LaShonda Davis is one of these. Because the facts are important in a case such as this, they are set forth in some detail in Justice Sandra Day O'Connor's opinion for the U.S. Supreme Court, which is excerpted in the following selection. A harsh dissent is presented by Justice Anthony Kennedy in the second selection.

Sandra Day O'Connor  **YES**

Majority Opinion

Davis *v.* Monroe County Board of Education et al.

Petitioner brought suit against the Monroe County Board of Education and other defendants, alleging that her fifth-grade daughter had been the victim of sexual harassment by another student in her class. Among petitioner's claims was a claim for monetary and injunctive relief under Title IX of the Education Amendments of 1972 (Title IX), 86 [**9] Stat. 373, as amended, 20 U.S.C. § 1681 *et seq.* The District Court dismissed petitioner's Title IX claim on the ground that "student-on-student," or peer, harassment provides no ground for a private cause of action under the statute. The Court of Appeals for the Eleventh Circuit, sitting en banc, affirmed. We consider here whether a private damages action may lie against the school board in cases of student-on-student harassment. We conclude that it may, but only where the funding recipient acts with deliberate indifference to known acts of harassment in its programs or activities. More-over, we conclude that such an action will lie only for harassment that is so severe, pervasive, and objectively offensive that it effectively bars the victim's access to an educational opportunity or benefit....

I

Petitioner's minor daughter, LaShonda, was allegedly the victim of a prolonged pattern of sexual harassment by one of her fifth-grade classmates at Hubbard Elementary School, a public school in Monroe County, Georgia. According to petitioner's complaint, the harassment began in December 1992, when the classmate, G. F., attempted to touch LaShonda's breasts and genital area and made vulgar statements such as "I want to get in bed with you" and "I want to feel your boobs." Similar conduct allegedly occurred on or about January 4 and January 20, 1993. LaShonda reported each of these incidents to her mother and to her classroom teacher, Diane Fort. Petitioner, in turn, also contacted Fort, who allegedly assured petitioner that the school principal, Bill Querry, had been informed of the incidents. Petitioner contends that, notwithstanding these reports, no disciplinary action was taken against G. F.

From *Davis v. Monroe County Board of Education et al.*, 120 F.3d 1390 (1999).

G. F.'s conduct allegedly continued for many months. In early February, G. F. purportedly placed a door stop in his pants and proceeded to act in a sexually suggestive manner toward LaShonda during physical education class. LaShonda reported G. F.'s behavior to her physical education teacher, Whit Maples. Approximately one week later, G. F. again allegedly engaged in harassing behavior, this time while under the supervision of another classroom teacher, Joyce Pippin. Again, LaShonda allegedly reported the incident to the teacher, and again petitioner contacted the teacher to follow up.

Petitioner alleges that G. F. once more directed sexually harassing conduct toward LaShonda in physical education class in early March, and that LaShonda reported the incident to both Maples and Pippen. In mid-April 1993, G. F. allegedly rubbed his body against LaShonda in the school hallway in what LaShonda considered a sexually suggestive manner, and LaShonda again reported the matter to Fort.

The string of incidents finally ended in mid-May, when G. F. was charged with, and pleaded guilty to, sexual battery for his misconduct. The complaint alleges that LaShonda had suffered during the months of harassment, however; specifically, her previously high grades allegedly dropped as she became unable to concentrate on her studies, and, in April 1993, her father discovered that she had written a suicide note. The complaint further alleges that, at one point, LaShonda told petitioner that she "didn't know how much longer she could keep [G. F.] off her."

Nor was LaShonda G. F.'s only victim; it is alleged that other girls in the class fell prey to G. F.'s conduct. At one point, in fact, a group composed of LaShonda and other female students tried to speak with Principal Querry about G. F.'s behavior. According to the complaint, however, a teacher denied the students' request with the statement, "If [Querry] wants you, he'll call you."

Petitioner alleges that no disciplinary action was taken in response to G. F.'s behavior toward LaShonda. In addition to her conversations with Fort and Pippen, petitioner alleges that she spoke with Principal Querry in mid-May 1993. When petitioner inquired as to what action the school intended to take against G. F., Querry simply stated, "I guess I'll have to threaten him a little bit harder." Yet, petitioner alleges, at no point during the many months of his reported misconduct was G. F. disciplined for harassment. Indeed, Querry allegedly asked petitioner why LaShonda "was the only one complaining."

Nor, according to the complaint, was any effort made to separate G. F. and LaShonda. On the contrary, notwithstanding LaShonda's frequent complaints, only after more than three months of reported harassment was she even permitted to change her classroom seat so that she was no longer seated next to G. F. Moreover, petitioner alleges that, at the time of the events in question, the Monroe County Board of Education (Board) had not instructed its personnel on how to respond to peer sexual harassment and had not established a policy on the issue.

We granted *certiorari*, in order to resolve a conflict in the Circuits over whether, and under what circumstances, a recipient of federal educational funds can be liable in a private damages action arising from student-on-student sexual harassment.... We now reverse.

II

Title IX provides, with certain exceptions not at issue here, that

> "no person in the United States shall, on the basis of sex, be excluded from participation in, be denied the benefits of, or be subjected to discrimination under any education program or activity receiving Federal financial assistance." 20 U.S.C. § 1681(a).

... There is no dispute here that the Board is a recipient of federal education funding for Title IX purposes. Nor do respondents support an argument that student-on-student harassment cannot rise to the level of "discrimination" for purposes of Title IX. Rather, at issue here is the question whether a recipient of federal education funding may be liable for damages under Title IX under any circumstances for discrimination in the form of student-on-student sexual harassment.

A

Petitioner urges that Title IX's plain language compels the conclusion that the statute is intended to bar recipients of federal funding from permitting this form of discrimination in their programs or activities. She emphasizes that the statute prohibits a student from being *"subjected to discrimination* under any education program or activity receiving Federal financial assistance." 20 U.S.C. § 1681 (emphasis supplied). It is Title IX's "unmistakable focus on the benefited class," *Cannon v. University of Chicago,* 441 U.S. 677, 691, (1979), rather than the perpetrator, that, in petitioner's view, compels the conclusion that the statute works to protect students from the discriminatory misconduct of their peers.

Here, however, we are asked to do more than define the scope of the behavior that Title IX proscribes. We must determine whether a district's failure to respond to student-on-student harassment in its schools can support a private suit for money damages.... This Court has indeed recognized an implied private right of action under Title IX, see *Cannon v. University of Chicago, supra,* and we have held that money damages are available in such suits, *Franklin v. Gwinnett County Public Schools,* 503 U.S. 60, (1992). Because we have repeatedly treated Title IX as legislation enacted pursuant to Congress' authority under the Spending Clause, however... private damages actions are available only where recipients of federal funding had adequate notice that they could be liable for the conduct at issue. When Congress acts pursuant to its spending power, it generates legislation "much in the nature of a contract: in return for federal funds, the States agree to comply with federally imposed conditions." *Pennhurst State School and Hospital v. Halderman,* 451 U.S. 1, 17 (1981). In interpreting language in spending legislation, we thus "insist that Congress speak with a clear voice," recognizing that "there can, of course, be no knowing acceptance [of the terms of the putative contract] if a State is unaware of the conditions [imposed by the legislation] or is unable to ascertain what is expected of it." *Ibid.*; see also 451 U.S. at 24–25.

Invoking *Pennhurst,* respondents urge that Title IX provides no notice that recipients of federal educational funds could be liable in damages for harm arising from student-on-student harassment. Respondents contend, specifically, that the statute only proscribes misconduct by grant recipients, not third parties. Respondents argue, moreover, that it would be contrary to the very purpose of Spending Clause legislation to impose liability on a funding recipient for the misconduct of third parties, over whom recipients exercise little control.

We agree with respondents that a recipient of federal funds may be liable in damages under Title IX only for its own misconduct. The recipient itself must "exclude [persons] from participation in, . . . deny [persons] the benefits of, or . . . subject [persons] to discrimination under" its "programs or activities" in order to be liable under Title IX. The Government's enforcement power may only be exercised against the funding recipient, see § 1682, and we have not extended damages liability under Title IX to parties outside the scope of this power. . . .

We disagree with respondents' assertion, however, that petitioner seeks to hold the Board liable for G. F.'s actions instead of its own. Here, petitioner attempts to hold the Board liable for its own decision to remain idle in the face of known student-on-student harassment in its schools. In *Gebser v. Lago Vista Independent School Dist.*, we concluded that a recipient of federal education funds may be liable in damages under Title IX where it is deliberately indifferent to known acts of sexual harassment by a teacher. In that case, a teacher had entered into a sexual relationship with an eighth grade student, and the student sought damages under Title IX for the teacher's misconduct. We recognized that the scope of liability in private damages actions under Title IX is circumscribed by *Pennhurst*'s requirement that funding recipients have notice of their potential liability. 524 U.S. at 287–288. Invoking *Pennhurst, Guardians Assn. v. Civil Serv. Comm'n of New York City,* and *Franklin,* in *Gebser* we once again required "that 'the receiving entity of federal funds [have] notice that it will be liable for a monetary award' " before subjecting it to damages liability. *Id.*, at 287. We also recognized, however, that this limitation on private damages actions is not a bar to liability where a funding recipient intentionally violates the statute. 503 U.S. at 74–75. In particular, we concluded that *Pennhurst* does not bar a private damages action under Title IX where the funding recipient engages in intentional conduct that violates the clear terms of the statute.

Accordingly, we rejected the use of agency principles to impute liability to the district for the misconduct of its teachers. 524 U.S. at 283. Likewise, we declined the invitation to impose liability under what amounted to a negligence standard—holding the district liable for its failure to react to teacher-student harassment of which it knew or should have known. *Ibid.* Rather, we concluded that the district could be liable for damages only where the district itself intentionally acted in clear violation of Title IX by remaining deliberately indifferent to acts of teacher-student harassment of which it had actual knowledge. *Id.*, at 290. Contrary to the dissent's suggestion, the misconduct of the teacher in *Gebser* was not "treated as the grant recipient's actions." Liability arose, rather, from "an official decision by the recipient not to remedy the violation." *Gebser v. Lago Vista Independent School Dist.*, supra, at 290. By employing the "deliberate indifference" theory already used to establish municipal liability under Rev. Stat. § 1979, 42 U.S.C. § 1983 . . . we concluded in *Gebser* that recipients could be liable in damages only where their own deliberate indifference effectively "caused" the discrimination, 524 U.S. at 291.... The high standard imposed in *Gebser* sought to eliminate any "risk that the recipient would be liable in damages not for its own official decision but instead for its employees' independent actions." 524 U.S. at 290–291.

Gebser thus established that a recipient intentionally violates Title IX, and is subject to a private damages action, where the recipient is deliberately indifferent to known acts of teacher-student discrimination....

We consider here whether the misconduct identified in *Gebser*—deliberate indifference to known acts of harassment—amounts to an intentional violation of Title IX, capable of supporting a private damages action, when the harasser is a student rather than a teacher. We conclude that, in certain limited circumstances, it does....

The common law, too, has put schools on notice that they may be held responsible under state law for their failure to protect students from the tortious acts of third parties. See Restatement (Second) of Torts § 320, and Comment *a* (1965). In fact, state courts routinely uphold claims alleging that schools have been negligent in failing to protect their students from the torts of their peers....

This is not to say that the identity of the harasser is irrelevant. On the contrary, both the "deliberate indifference" standard and the language of Title IX narrowly circumscribe the set of parties whose known acts of sexual harassment can trigger some duty to respond on the part of funding recipients. Deliberate indifference makes sense as a theory of direct liability under Title IX only where the funding recipient has some control over the alleged harassment. A recipient cannot be directly liable for its indifference where it lacks the authority to take remedial action.

The language of Title IX itself—particularly when viewed in conjunction with the requirement that the recipient have notice of Title IX's prohibitions to be liable for damages—also cabins the range of misconduct that the statute proscribes. The statute's plain language confines the scope of prohibited conduct based on the recipient's degree of control over the harasser and the environment in which the harassment occurs. If a funding recipient does not engage in harassment directly, it may not be liable for damages unless its deliberate indifference "subjects" its students to harassment. That is, the deliberate indifference must, at a minimum, "cause [students] to undergo" harassment or "make them liable or vulnerable" to it. Random House Dictionary of the English Language 1415 (1966)....

These factors combine to limit a recipient's damages liability to circumstances wherein the recipient exercises substantial control over both the harasser and the context in which the known harassment occurs. Only then can the recipient be said to "expose" its students to harassment or "cause" them to undergo it "under" the recipient's programs....

Where, as here, the misconduct occurs during school hours and on school grounds—the bulk of G. F.'s misconduct, in fact, took place in the classroom—the misconduct is taking place "under" an "operation" of the funding recipient.... In these circumstances, the recipient retains substantial control over the context in which the harassment occurs. More importantly, however, in this setting the Board exercises significant control over the harasser.... We thus conclude that recipients of federal funding may be liable for "subjecting" their students to discrimination where the recipient is deliberately indifferent to known acts of student-on-student sexual harassment and the harasser is under the school's disciplinary authority....

B

The requirement that recipients receive adequate notice of Title IX's proscriptions also bears on the proper definition of "discrimination" in the context of a private damages action.... Students are not only protected from discrimination, but also specifically shielded from being "excluded from participation in" or "denied the benefits of" any "education program or activity receiving Federal financial assistance." § 1681(a). The statute makes clear that, whatever else it prohibits, students must not be denied access to educational benefits and opportunities on the basis of gender. We thus conclude that funding recipients are properly held liable in damages only where they are deliberately indifferent to sexual harassment, of which they have actual knowledge, that is so severe, pervasive, and objectively offensive that it can be said to deprive the victims of access to the educational opportunities or benefits provided by the school.

The most obvious example of student-on-student sexual harassment capable of triggering a damages claim would thus involve the overt, physical deprivation of access to school resources. Consider, for example, a case in which male students physically threaten their female peers every day, successfully preventing the female students from using a particular school resource—an athletic field or a computer lab, for instance. District administrators are well aware of the daily ritual, yet they deliberately ignore requests for aid from the female students wishing to use the resource. The district's knowing refusal to take any action in response to such behavior would fly in the face of Title IX's core principles, and such deliberate indifference may appropriately be subject to claims for monetary damages. It is not necessary, however, to show physical exclusion to demonstrate that students have been deprived by the actions of another student or students of an educational opportunity on the basis of sex. Rather, a plaintiff must establish sexual harassment of students that is so severe, pervasive, and objectively offensive, and that so undermines and detracts from the victims' educational experience, that the victim-students are effectively denied equal access to an institution's resources and opportunities. Cf. *Meritor Savings Bank, FSB v. Vinson,* 477 U.S. at 67....

C

Applying this standard to the facts at issue here, we conclude that the Eleventh Circuit erred in dismissing petitioner's complaint. Petitioner alleges that her daughter was the victim of repeated acts of sexual harassment by G. F. over a 5-month period, and there are allegations in support of the conclusion that

G. F.'s misconduct was severe, pervasive, and objectively offensive. The harassment was not only verbal; it included numerous acts of objectively offensive touching, and, indeed, G. F. ultimately pleaded guilty to criminal sexual misconduct. Moreover, the complaint alleges that there were multiple victims who were sufficiently disturbed by G. F.'s misconduct to seek an audience with the school principal. Further, petitioner contends that the harassment had a concrete, negative effect on her daughter's ability to receive an education. The complaint also suggests that petitioner may be able to show both actual knowledge and deliberate indifference on the part of the Board, which made no effort whatsoever either to investigate or to put an end to the harassment.

On this complaint, we cannot say "beyond doubt that [petitioner] can prove no set of facts in support of [her] claim which would entitle [her] to relief." ... Accordingly, the judgment of the United States Court of Appeals for the Eleventh Circuit is reversed, and the case is remanded for further proceedings consistent with this opinion.

It is so ordered.

NO ↩

Anthony Kennedy

Dissenting Opinion of Anthony Kennedy

Today the Court fails to heed, or even to acknowledge, [previously recognized] limitations on its authority. The remedial scheme the majority creates today is neither sensible nor faithful to Spending Clause principles. In order to make its case for school liability for peer sexual harassment, the majority must establish that Congress gave grant recipients clear and unambiguous notice that they would be liable in money damages for failure to remedy discriminatory acts of their students. The majority must also demonstrate that the statute gives schools clear notice that one child's harassment of another constitutes "discrimination" on the basis of sex within the meaning of Title IX, and that—as applied to individual cases—the standard for liability will enable the grant recipient to distinguish inappropriate childish behavior from actionable gender discrimination. The majority does not carry these burdens.

Instead, the majority finds statutory clarity where there is none and discovers indicia of congressional notice to the States in the most unusual of places. It treats the issue as one of routine statutory construction alone, and it errs even in this regard. In the end, the majority not only imposes on States liability that was unexpected and unknown, but the contours of which are, as yet, unknowable. The majority's opinion purports to be narrow, but the limiting principles it proposes are illusory. The fence the Court has built is made of little sticks, and it cannot contain the avalanche of liability now set in motion. The potential costs to our schools of today's decision are difficult to estimate, but they are so great that it is most unlikely Congress intended to inflict them.

The only certainty flowing from the majority's decision is that scarce resources will be diverted from educating our children and that many school districts, desperate to avoid Title IX peer harassment suits, will adopt whatever federal code of student conduct and discipline the Department of Education sees fit to impose upon them. The Nation's schoolchildren will learn their first lessons about federalism in classrooms where the federal government is the ever-present regulator. The federal government will have insinuated itself not only into one of the most traditional areas of state concern but also into one of the most sensitive areas of human affairs. This federal control of the discipline of our Nation's schoolchildren is contrary to our traditions and inconsistent with the sensible administration of our schools. Because Title IX did not give

From *Davis v. Monroe County Board of Education et al.*, 120 F.3d 1390 (1999).

States unambiguous notice that accepting federal funds meant ceding to the federal government power over the day-to-day disciplinary decisions of schools, I dissent.

I

I turn to the first difficulty with the majority's decision. Schools cannot be held liable for peer sexual harassment because Title IX does not give them clear and unambiguous notice that they are liable in damages for failure to remedy discrimination by their students. As the majority acknowledges, Title IX prohibits only misconduct by grant recipients, not misconduct by third parties.... The majority argues, nevertheless, that a school "subjects" its students to discrimination when it knows of peer harassment and fails to respond appropriately.

The mere word "subjected" cannot bear the weight of the majority's argument.... The majority does not even attempt to argue that the school's failure to respond to discriminatory acts by students is discrimination by the school itself.

A

In any event, a plaintiff cannot establish a Title IX violation merely by showing that she has been "subjected to discrimination." Rather, a violation of Title IX occurs only if she is "subjected to discrimination under any education program or activity," 20 U.S.C. § 1681(a), where "program or activity" is defined as "all of the operations of" a grant recipient, § 1687.

Under the most natural reading of this provision, discrimination violates Title IX only if it is authorized by, or in accordance with, the actions, activities, or policies of the grant recipient....

It is not enough, then, that the alleged discrimination occur in a "context subject to the school district's control." The discrimination must actually be "controlled by"—that is, be authorized by, pursuant to, or in accordance with, school policy or actions....

Teacher sexual harassment of students is "under" the school's program or activity in certain circumstances, but student harassment is not. Our decision in *Gebser v. Lago Vista Independent School Dist.* recognizes that a grant recipient acts through its agents and thus, under certain limited circumstances, even tortious acts by teachers may be attributable to the school....

Contrary to the majority's assertion, *ante,* at 12, however, we did not abandon agency principles altogether. Rather, we sought in *Gebser* to identify those employee actions which could fairly be attributed to the grant recipient by superimposing additional Spending Clause notice requirements on traditional agency principles. *Gebser,* 524 U.S. 274 at 288. We concluded that, because of the Spending Clause overlay, a teacher's discrimination is attributable to the school only when the school has actual notice of that harassment and is "deliberately indifferent." The agency relation between the school and the teacher is thus a necessary, but not sufficient, condition of school liability. Where the heightened requirements for attribution are met, the teacher's actions are treated as the grant recipient's actions. In those circumstances, then, the teacher sexual harassment is "under" the operations of the school.

I am aware of no basis in law or fact, however, for attributing the acts of a student to a school and, indeed, the majority does not argue that the school acts through its students.... Discrimination by one student against another therefore cannot be "under" the school's program or activity as required by Title IX. The majority's imposition of liability for peer sexual harassment thus conflicts with the most natural interpretation of Title IX's "under a program or activity" limitation on school liability. At the very least, my reading undermines the majority's implicit claim that Title IX imposes an unambiguous duty on schools to remedy peer sexual harassment.

B
1

Quite aside from its disregard for the "under the program" limitation of Title IX, the majority's reading is flawed in other respects. The majority contends that a school's deliberate indifference to known student harassment "subjects" students to harassment—that is, "causes [students] to undergo" harassment. The majority recognizes, however, that there must be some limitation on the third-party conduct that the school can fairly be said to cause. In search of a principle, the majority asserts, without much elaboration, that one causes discrimination when one has some "degree of control" over the discrimination and fails to remedy it.

To state the majority's test is to understand that it is little more than an exercise in arbitrary line-drawing. The majority does not explain how we are to determine what degree of control is sufficient—or, more to the point, how the States were on clear notice that the Court would draw the line to encompass students....

2

The majority nonetheless appears to see no need to justify drawing the "enough control" line to encompass students. In truth, however, a school's control over its students is much more complicated and limited than the majority acknowledges. A public school does not control its students in the way it controls its teachers or those with whom it contracts. Most public schools do not screen or select students, and their power to discipline students is far from unfettered.

Public schools are generally obligated by law to educate all students who live within defined geographic boundaries. Indeed, the Constitution of almost every State in the country guarantees the State's students a free primary and secondary public education....

In addition, federal law imposes constraints on school disciplinary actions.... The practical obstacles schools encounter in ensuring that thousands of immature students conform their conduct to acceptable norms may be even more significant than the legal obstacles. School districts cannot exercise the same measure of control over thousands of students that they do over a few hundred adult employees. The limited resources of our schools must be conserved for basic educational services. Some schools lack the resources even to deal with serious problems of violence and are already overwhelmed with disciplinary problems of all kinds. . . .

II

. . . The only real clue the majority gives schools about the dividing line between actionable harassment that denies a victim equal access to education and mere inappropriate teasing is a profoundly unsettling one: On the facts of this case, petitioner has stated a claim because she alleged, in the majority's words, "that the harassment had a concrete, negative effect on her daughter's ability to receive an education." In petitioner's words, the effects that might have been visible to the school were that her daughter's grades "dropped" and her "ability to concentrate on her school work [was] affected." Almost all adolescents experience these problems at one time or another as they mature.

III

The majority's inability to provide any workable definition of actionable peer harassment simply underscores the myriad ways in which an opinion that purports to be narrow is, in fact, so broad that it will support untold numbers of lawyers who will prove adept at presenting cases that will withstand the defendant school districts' pretrial motions. Each of the barriers to run-away litigation the majority offers us crumbles under the weight of even casual scrutiny.

For example, the majority establishes what sounds like a relatively high threshold for liability—"denial of equal access" to education—and, almost in the same breath, makes clear that alleging a decline in grades is enough to survive 12(b)(6) and, it follows, to state a winning claim. The majority seems oblivious to the fact that almost every child, at some point, has trouble in school because he or she is being teased by his or her peers. The girl who wants to skip recess because she is teased by the boys is no different from the overweight child who skips gym class because the other children tease her about her size in the locker room; or the child who risks flunking out because he refuses to wear glasses to avoid the taunts of "four-eyes"; or the child who refuses to go to school because the school bully calls him a "scaredy-cat" at recess. Most children respond to teasing in ways that detract from their ability to learn. The majority's test for actionable harassment will, as a result, sweep in almost all of the more innocuous conduct it acknowledges as a ubiquitous part of school life. . . .

The majority's limitations on peer sexual harassment suits cannot hope to contain the flood of liability the Court today begins. The elements of the Title IX claim created by the majority will be easy not only to allege but also to prove. A female plaintiff who pleads only that a boy called her offensive names, that she told a teacher, that the teacher's response was unreasonable, and that her school performance suffered as a result, appears to state a successful claim.

There will be no shortage of plaintiffs to bring such complaints. Our schools are charged each day with educating millions of children. Of those millions of students, a large percentage will, at some point during their school careers, experience something they consider sexual harassment.... The number of potential lawsuits against our schools is staggering.

The cost of defending against peer sexual harassment suits alone could overwhelm many school districts, particularly since the majority's liability standards will allow almost any plaintiff to get to summary judgment, if not to a jury. In addition, there are no damages caps on the judicially implied private cause of action under Title IX. As a result, school liability in one peer sexual harassment suit could approach, or even exceed, the total federal funding of many school districts. Petitioner, for example, seeks damages of $500,000 in this case. Respondent school district received approximately $679,000 in federal aid in 1992–1993. The school district sued in *Gebser* received only $120,000 in federal funds a year. 524 U.S. 289–290. Indeed, the entire 1992–1993 budget of that district was only $1.6 million....

The prospect of unlimited Title IX liability will, in all likelihood, breed a climate of fear that encourages school administrators to label even the most innocuous of childish conduct sexual harassment....

A school faced with a peer sexual harassment complaint in the wake of the majority's decision may well be beset with litigation from every side. One student's demand for a quick response to her harassment complaint will conflict with the alleged harasser's demand for due process. Another student's demand for a harassment-free classroom will conflict with the alleged harasser's claim to a mainstream placement under the Individuals with Disabilities Education Act or with his state constitutional right to a continuing, free public education. On college campuses, and even in secondary schools, a student's claim that the school should remedy a sexually hostile environment will conflict with the alleged harasser's claim that his speech, even if offensive, is protected by the First Amendment. In each of these situations, the school faces the risk of suit, and maybe even multiple suits, regardless of its response....

The majority's holding in this case appears to be driven by the image of the school administration sitting idle every day while male students commandeer a school's athletic field or computer lab and prevent female students from using it through physical threats. Title IX might provide a remedy in such a situation, however, without resort to the majority's unprecedented theory of school liability for student harassment. If the school usually disciplines students for threatening each other and prevents them from blocking others' access to school facilities, then the school's failure to enforce its rules when the boys target the girls on a widespread level, day after day, may support an inference that the school's decision not to respond is itself based on gender. That pattern of discriminatory response could form the basis of a Title IX action....

In the final analysis, this case is about federalism. Yet the majority's decision today says not one word about the federal balance. Preserving our federal system is a legitimate end in itself. It is, too, the means to other ends. It ensures that essential choices can be made by a government more proximate to the people than the vast apparatus of federal power. Defining the appropriate role of schools in teaching and supervising children who are beginning to explore their own sexuality and learning how to express it to others is one of the most complex and sensitive issues our schools face. Such decisions are best made by parents and by the teachers and school administrators who can counsel with them. The delicacy and immense significance of teaching children about sexuality should cause the Court to act with great restraint before it displaces state and local governments. . . .

Perhaps the most grave, and surely the most lasting, disservice of today's decision is that it ensures the Court's own disregard for the federal balance soon will be imparted to our youngest citizens. The Court clears the way for the federal government to claim center stage in America's classrooms. Today's decision mandates to teachers instructing and supervising their students the dubious assistance of federal court plaintiffs and their lawyers and makes the federal courts the final arbiters of school policy and of almost every disagreement between students. Enforcement of the federal right recognized by the majority means that federal influence will permeate everything from curriculum decisions to day-to-day classroom logistics and interactions. After today, Johnny will find that the routine problems of adolescence are to be resolved by invoking a federal right to demand assignment to a desk two rows away.

As its holding makes painfully clear, the majority's watered-down version of the Spending Clause clear-statement rule is no substitute for the real protections of state and local autonomy that our constitutional system requires. If there be any doubt of the futility of the Court's attempt to hedge its holding about with words of limitation for future cases, the result in this case provides the answer. The complaint of this fifth grader survives and the school will be compelled to answer in federal court. We can be assured that like suits will follow—suits, which in cost and number, will impose serious financial burdens on local school districts, the taxpayers who support them, and the children they serve. Federalism and our struggling school systems deserve better from this Court. I dissent.

POSTSCRIPT

Are Public School Officials Liable for Damages in Cases of Student-on-Student Sexual Harassment?

In a case against the Petaluma City School District in California, the plaintiff introduced into evidence the statistic that at least 85 percent of schoolgirls report that they have been exposed to some form of sexually harassing behavior in school. See *Doe v. Petaluma City School District,* 949 F.Supp. 1415, 1426 (N.D. Cal. 1996). Such a figure, if true, cries out for meaningful action on the part of some individual or some institution. Yet prior to the Supreme Court's decision in *Davis,* the question was who. Who is responsible for monitoring and preventing sexual harassment between students? Sexual harassment in the workplace has attracted widespread judicial and legislative attention over the past quarter century, and it is now clear that employers are legally responsible for sexual harassment among their employees. But the legal responsibilities of school officials for sexual harassment between students was not clear. Justice O'Connor's majority opinion in *Davis* settled disagreements among the various judicial circuits that had addressed this issue, and it establishes the standard for liability of school districts under Title IX of the Education Amendments of 1972 for peer sexual harassment. We need go no further than Justice Kennedy's dissent in *Davis,* however, to find a whole new realm of uncertainty. There Kennedy raises a traditional bogeyman of legal rhetoric—the "slippery slope." Specifically, Kennedy argues that the *Davis* opinion renders local school districts vulnerable to legal attack for all but the most innocuous behavior.

For further reading in this area, begin with Catharine MacKinnon's controversial yet influential study *The Sexual Harassment of Working Women: A Case of Sex Discrimination* (Yale University Press, 1979). Although it deals with workplace sexual harassment, MacKinnon's text provides a provocative introduction to arguments and a discourse that have shaped our understanding of such behavior in other contexts. For studies dealing more specifically with the issues addressed in *Davis,* see Nan Stein, Nancy L. Marshall, and Linda R. Tropp, *Secrets in Public: Sexual Harassment in Our Schools* (Center for Research on Women, Wellesley College, 1993); Edward S. Cheng, "Boys Being Boys and Girls Being Girls: Student-to-Student Sexual Harassment From the Courtroom to the Classroom," 7 *UCLA Women's Law Journal* 263 (1997); and Diane Welsh, "Limiting Liability Through Education: Do School Districts Have a Responsibility to Teach Students About Peer Sexual Harassment?" 6 *American University Journal of Gender and the Law* 165 (1997). Finally, there are several Web sites that provide information on this topic. A variety of sites are listed at http://www.igc.org/women/activist/harass.htn.

ISSUE 18

Should Children With Disabilities Be Provided With Extraordinary Care in Order to Attend Regular Classes in Public Schools?

YES: John Paul Stevens, from Majority Opinion, *Cedar Rapids Community School District v. Garret F.*, U.S. Supreme Court (March 3, 1999)

NO: Clarence Thomas, from Dissenting Opinion, *Cedar Rapids Community School District v. Garret F.*, U.S. Supreme Court (March 3, 1999)

ISSUE SUMMARY

YES: Supreme Court justice John Paul Stevens interprets the Individuals with Disabilities Education Act as requiring public school districts to provide students who have severe physical disabilities with individualized and continuous nursing services during school hours.

NO: Supreme Court justice Clarence Thomas argues that such an interpretation will impose serious and unanticipated financial obligations on the states.

More and more children with "special needs" are now enrolled in public schools and attend classes with nondisabled students. This is due in large part to the recognition that such students are perfectly capable of pursuing and achieving the same educational goals as their nondisabled counterparts if they are provided with the required medical care. Federal legislation such as the Americans with Disabilities Act (ADA) and the Individuals with Disabilities Education Act (IDEA) have played a large role in establishing regulatory guidelines as well as educating the general public on this matter. Accordingly, school districts have been required to hire school nurses and other educational support personnel to dispense or administer a variety of medications, to help with the insertion of catheters or breathing tubes, and to assist in a variety of other tasks.

Although the IDEA provides federal money to states that agree to "provide disabled children with special education and related services," cash-strapped local school districts have been concerned about the level of support they might receive and the scope of their responsibilities to the targeted student population. Potentially, the financial burden some school districts face is significant. Indeed, these are the issues raised in the readings that follow—the majority and dissenting opinions in *Cedar Rapids Community School District v. Garret F.,* a 1999 decision that has clarified the scope of coverage of "related services" under the IDEA. According to the language of the statute, the legislation was passed "to assure that all children with disabilities have available to them ... a free appropriate public education which emphasizes special education and related services designed to meet their unique needs." 20 U.S.C. sec. 1400(c). By the terms of the statute, the phrase "related services" means

> transportation, and such developmental, corrective, and other supportive services (including speech pathology and audiology, psychological services, physical and occupational therapy, recreation, including therapeutic recreation, social work services, counseling services, including rehabilitation counseling, and medical services, except that such medical services shall be for diagnostic and evaluation purposes only) as may be required to assist a child with a disability to benefit from special education, and includes the early identification and assessment of disabling conditions in children. 20 U.S.C. sec. 1401(a)(17).

The relevant facts of the case are set forth in Justice John Paul Stevens's opinion for the Court. Justice Clarence Thomas was joined in his dissent by Justice Anthony Kennedy.

Majority Opinion

Cedar Rapids Community School District *v.* Garret F.

The question presented in this case is whether the definition of "related services" in § 1401(a)(17) requires a public school district in a participating State to provide a ventilator-dependent student with certain nursing services during school hours.

I

Respondent Garret F. is a friendly, creative, and intelligent young man. When Garret was four years old, his spinal column was severed in a motorcycle accident. Though paralyzed from the neck down, his mental capacities were unaffected. He is able to speak, to control his motorized wheelchair through use of a puff and suck straw, and to operate a computer with a device that responds to head movements. Garret is currently a student in the Cedar Rapids Community School District (District), he attends regular classes in a typical school program, and his academic performance has been a success. Garret is, however, ventilator dependent, and therefore requires a responsible individual nearby to attend to certain physical needs while he is in school.

During Garret's early years at school his family provided for his physical care during the school day. When he was in kindergarten, his 18-year-old aunt attended him; in the next four years, his family used settlement proceeds they received after the accident, their insurance, and other resources to employ a licensed practical nurse. In 1993, Garret's mother requested the District to accept financial responsibility for the health care services that Garret requires during the school day. The District denied the request, believing that it was not legally obligated to provide continuous one-on-one nursing services.

Relying on both the IDEA and Iowa law, Garret's mother requested a hearing before the Iowa Department of Education. An Administrative Law Judge (ALJ) received extensive evidence concerning Garret's special needs, the District's treatment of other disabled students, and the assistance provided to other ventilator-dependent children in other parts of the country. In his 47-page

From *Cedar Rapids Community School District v. Garret F.*, 119 S. Ct. 992 (1999). Notes omitted.

report, the ALJ found that the District has about 17,500 students, of whom approximately 2,200 need some form of special education or special services. Although Garret is the only ventilator-dependent student in the District, most of the health care services that he needs are already provided for some other students. "The primary difference between Garret's situation and that of other students is his dependency on his ventilator for life support." The ALJ noted that the parties disagreed over the training or licensure required for the care and supervision of such students, and that those providing such care in other parts of the country ranged from nonlicensed personnel to registered nurses. However, the District did not contend that only a licensed physician could provide the services in question.

The ALJ explained that federal law requires that children with a variety of health impairments be provided with "special education and related services" when their disabilities adversely affect their academic performance, and that such children should be educated to the maximum extent appropriate with children who are not disabled. In addition, the ALJ explained that applicable federal regulations distinguish between "school health services," which are provided by a "qualified school nurse or other qualified person," and "medical services," which are provided by a licensed physician. See 34 CFR §§ 300.16(a), (b)(4), (b)(11) (1998). The District must provide the former, but need not provide the latter (except, of course, those "medical services" that are for diagnostic or evaluation purposes, § 1401(a)(17)). According to the ALJ, the distinction in the regulations does not just depend on "the title of the person providing the service"; instead, the "medical services" exclusion is limited to services that are "in the special training, knowledge, and judgment of a physician to carry out." The ALJ thus concluded that the IDEA required the District to bear financial responsibility for all of the services in dispute, including continuous nursing services.

The District challenged the ALJ's decision in Federal District Court, but that Court approved the ALJ's IDEA ruling and granted summary judgment against the District. The Court of Appeals affirmed. It noted that, as a recipient of federal funds under the IDEA, Iowa has a statutory duty to provide all disabled children a "free appropriate public education," which includes "related services." The Court of Appeals read our opinion in *Irving Independent School Dist. v. Tatro,* 468 U.S. 883 (1984), to provide a two-step analysis of the "related services" definition in § 1401(a)(17)—asking first, whether the requested services are included within the phrase "supportive services"; and second, whether the services are excluded as "medical services." The Court of Appeals succinctly answered both questions in Garret's favor. The Court found the first step plainly satisfied, since Garret cannot attend school unless the requested services are available during the school day. As to the second step, the Court reasoned that *Tatro* "established a bright-line test: the services of a physician (other than for diagnostic and evaluation purposes) are subject to the medical services exclusion, but services that can be provided in the school setting by a nurse or qualified layperson are not."

In its petition for certiorari, the District challenged only the second step of the Court of Appeals' analysis. The District pointed out that some federal courts have not asked whether the requested health services must be delivered by a physician, but instead have applied a multi-factor test that considers, generally speaking, the nature and extent of the services at issue. . . .

II

The District contends that § 1401(a)(17) does not require it to provide Garret with "continuous one-on-one nursing services" during the school day, even though Garret cannot remain in school without such care. However, the IDEA's definition of "related services," our decision in *Irving Independent School Dist. v. Tatro,* 468 U.S. 883 (1984), and the overall statutory scheme all support the decision of the Court of Appeals.

The text of the "related services" definition broadly encompasses those supportive services that "may be required to assist a child with a disability to benefit from special education." As we have already noted, the District does not challenge the Court of Appeals' conclusion that the in-school services at issue are within the covered category of "supportive services." As a general matter, services that enable a disabled child to remain in school during the day provide the student with "the meaningful access to education that Congress envisioned." *Tatro,* 468 U.S. at 891.

This general definition of "related services" is illuminated by a parenthetical phrase listing examples of particular services that are included within the statute's coverage. § 1401(a)(17). "Medical services" are enumerated in this list, but such services are limited to those that are "for diagnostic and evaluation purposes." *Ibid.* The statute does not contain a more specific definition of the "medical services" that are excepted from the coverage of § 1401(a)(17).

The scope of the "medical services" exclusion is not a matter of first impression in this Court. In *Tatro* we concluded that the Secretary of Education had reasonably determined that the term "medical services" referred only to services that must be performed by a physician, and not to school health services. 468 U.S. at 892–894. Accordingly, we held that a specific form of health care (clean intermittent catheterization) that is often, though not always, performed by a nurse is not an excluded medical service. We referenced the likely cost of the services and the competence of school staff as justifications for drawing a line between physician and other services, but our endorsement of that line was unmistakable. It is thus settled that the phrase "medical services" in § 1401(a)(17) does not embrace all forms of care that might loosely be described as "medical" in other contexts, such as a claim for an income tax deduction. See 26 U.S.C. § 213(d)(1) (1994 ed. and Supp. II) (defining "medical care").

The District does not ask us to define the term so broadly. Indeed, the District does not argue that any of the items of care that Garret needs, considered individually, could be excluded from the scope of § 1401(a)(17). It could not make such an argument, considering that one of the services Garret needs (catheterization) was at issue in *Tatro,* and the others may be provided competently by a school nurse or other trained personnel. As the ALJ concluded, most of the requested services are already provided by the District to other students, and the in-school care necessitated by Garret's ventilator dependency does not demand the training, knowledge, and judgment of a licensed physician. While more extensive, the in-school services Garret needs are no more "medical" than was the care sought in *Tatro*.

Instead, the District points to the combined and continuous character of the required care, and proposes a test under which the outcome in any particular case would "depend upon a series of factors, such as [1] whether the care is continuous or intermittent, [2] whether existing school health personnel can provide the service, [3] the cost of the service, and [4] the potential consequences if the service is not properly performed." The District's multifactor test is not supported by any recognized source of legal authority. The proposed factors can be found in neither the text of the statute nor the regulations that we upheld in *Tatro*. Moreover, the District offers no explanation why these characteristics make one service any more "medical" than another. The continuous character of certain services associated with Garret's ventilator dependency has no apparent relationship to "medical" services, much less a relationship of equivalence. Continuous services may be more costly and may require additional school personnel, but they are not thereby more "medical." Whatever its imperfections, a rule that limits the medical services exemption to physician services is unquestionably a reasonable and generally workable interpretation of the statute. Absent an elaboration of the statutory terms plainly more convincing than that which we reviewed in *Tatro*, there is no good reason to depart from settled law.

Finally, the District raises broader concerns about the financial burden that it must bear to provide the services that Garret needs to stay in school. The problem for the District in providing these services is not that its staff cannot be trained to deliver them; the problem, the District contends, is that the existing school health staff cannot meet all of their responsibilities and provide for Garret at the same time. Through its multi-factor test, the District seeks to establish a kind of undue-burden exemption primarily based on the cost of the requested services. The first two factors can be seen as examples of cost-based distinctions: intermittent care is often less expensive than continuous care, and the use of existing personnel is cheaper than hiring additional employees. The third factor—the cost of the service—would then encompass the first two. The relevance of the fourth factor is likewise related to cost because extra care may be necessary if potential consequences are especially serious.

The District may have legitimate financial concerns, but our role in this dispute is to interpret existing law. Defining "related services" in a manner that accommodates the cost concerns Congress may have had, cf. *Tatro*, 468 U.S. at 892, is altogether different from using cost itself as the definition. Given that § 1401(a)(17) does not employ cost in its definition of "related services" or excluded "medical services," accepting the District's cost-based standard as the sole test for determining the scope of the provision would require us to engage in judicial lawmaking without any guidance from Congress. It would also create some tension with the purposes of the IDEA. The statute may not require public schools to maximize the potential of disabled students commensurate with the opportunities provided to other children, see *[Board of Education of the Hendrick Hudson Central School District v.] Rowley*, 458 U.S. at 200; and the potential financial burdens imposed on participating States may be relevant to arriving at a sensible construction of the IDEA, see *Tatro,* 468 U.S. at 892. But Congress intended "to open the door of public education" to all qualified children and "required participating States to educate handicapped children with nonhandicapped children whenever possible."

This case is about whether meaningful access to the public schools will be assured, not the level of education that a school must finance once access is attained. It is undisputed that the services at issue must be provided if Garret is to remain in school. Under the statute, our precedent, and the purposes of the IDEA, the District must fund such "related services" in order to help guarantee that students like Garret are integrated into the public schools.

The judgment of the Court of Appeals is accordingly Affirmed.

Dissenting Opinion of Clarence Thomas

T he majority, relying heavily on our decision in *Irving Independent School Dist. v. Tatro,* 468 U.S. 883 (1984), concludes that the Individuals with Disabilities Education Act (IDEA), 20 U.S.C. § 1400 *et seq.*, requires a public school district to fund continuous, one-on-one nursing care for disabled children. Because *Tatro* cannot be squared with the text of IDEA, the Court should not adhere to it in this case. Even assuming that *Tatro* was correct in the first instance, the majority's extension of it is unwarranted and ignores the constitutionally mandated rules of construction applicable to legislation enacted pursuant to Congress' spending power.

I

As the majority recounts, IDEA authorizes the provision of federal financial assistance to States that agree to provide, inter alia, "special education and related services" for disabled children. § 1401(a)(18). In *Tatro, supra,* we held that this provision of IDEA required a school district to provide clean intermittent catheterization to a disabled child several times a day. In so holding, we relied on Department of Education regulations, which we concluded had reasonably interpreted IDEA's definition of "related services" to require school districts in participating States to provide "school nursing services" (of which we assumed catheterization was a subcategory) but not "services of a physician." This holding is contrary to the plain text of IDEA and its reliance on the Department of Education's regulations was misplaced.

A

Before we consider whether deference to an agency regulation is appropriate, "we first ask whether Congress has 'directly spoken to the precise question at issue. If the intent of Congress is clear, that is the end of the matter; for the court, as well as the agency, must give effect to the unambiguously expressed intent of Congress.'"

Unfortunately, the Court in *Tatro* failed to consider this necessary antecedent question before turning to the Department of Education's regulations

From *Cedar Rapids Community School District v. Garret F.*, 119 S. Ct. 992 (1999). Notes omitted.

implementing IDEA's related services provision. The Court instead began "with the regulations of the Department of Education, which," it said, "are entitled to deference." The Court need not have looked beyond the text of IDEA, which expressly indicates that school districts are not required to provide medical services, except for diagnostic and evaluation purposes. 20 U.S.C. § 1401(a)(17). The majority asserts that *Tatro* precludes reading the term "medical services" to include "all forms of care that might loosely be described as 'medical.'" The majority does not explain, however, why "services" that are "medical" in nature are not "medical services." Not only is the definition that the majority rejects consistent with other uses of the term in federal law, it also avoids the anomalous result of holding that the services at issue in *Tatro* (as well as in this case), while not "medical services," would nonetheless qualify as medical care for federal income tax purposes.

The primary problem with *Tatro,* and the majority's reliance on it today, is that the Court focused on the provider of the services rather than the services themselves. We do not typically think that automotive services are limited to those provided by a mechanic, for example. Rather, anything done to repair or service a car, no matter who does the work, is thought to fall into that category. Similarly, the term "food service" is not generally thought to be limited to work performed by a chef. The term "medical" similarly does not support *Tatro's* provider-specific approach, but encompasses services that are "of, *relating to, or concerned with* physicians *or* the practice of medicine." See Webster's Third New International Dictionary 1402 (1986) (emphasis added)....

IDEA's structure and purpose reinforce this textual interpretation. Congress enacted IDEA to increase the educational opportunities available to disabled children, not to provide medical care for them.... As such, where Congress decided to require a supportive service—including speech pathology, occupational therapy, and audiology—that appears "medical" in nature, it took care to do so explicitly. See § 1401(a)(17). Congress specified these services precisely because it recognized that they would otherwise fall under the broad "medical services" exclusion. Indeed, when it crafted the definition of related services, Congress could have, but chose not to, include "nursing services" in this list.

B

Tatro was wrongly decided even if the phrase "medical services" was subject to multiple constructions, and therefore, deference to any reasonable Department of Education regulation was appropriate. The Department of Education has never promulgated regulations defining the scope of IDEA's "medical services" exclusion. One year before *Tatro* was decided, the Secretary of Education issued proposed regulations that defined excluded medical services as "services relating to the practice of medicine." 47 Fed. Reg. 33838 (1982). These regulations, which represent the Department's only attempt to define the disputed term, were never adopted. Instead, "the regulations actually define only those 'medical services' that *are* owed to handicapped children," ... not those that *are not.* Now, as when *Tatro* was decided, the regulations require districts to provide services performed "by a licensed physician to determine a child's medically related handicapping condition which results in the child's need for special education and related services."

Extrapolating from this regulation, the *Tatro* Court presumed that this meant "that 'medical services' not owed under the statute are those 'services by a licensed physician' that serve other purposes." The Court, therefore, did not defer to the regulation itself, but rather relied on an inference drawn from it to speculate about how a regulation might read if the Department of Education promulgated one. Deference in those circumstances is impermissible. We cannot defer to a regulation that does not exist.

II

Assuming that *Tatro* was correctly decided in the first instance, it does not control the outcome of this case. Because IDEA was enacted pursuant to Congress' spending power, our analysis of the statute in this case is governed by special rules of construction. We have repeatedly emphasized that, when Congress places conditions on the receipt of federal funds, "it must do so unambiguously." *Pennhurst State School and Hospital v. Halderman,* 451 U.S. 1, 17 (1981). This is because a law that "conditions an offer of federal funding on a promise by the recipient... amounts essentially to a contract between the Government and the recipient of funds." *Gebser v. Lago Vista Independent School Dist.,* 524 U.S. 274, 276 (1998). As such, "the legitimacy of Congress' power to legislate under the spending power... rests on whether the State voluntarily and knowingly accepts the terms of the 'contract.' There can, of course, be no knowing acceptance if a State is unaware of the conditions or is unable to ascertain what is expected of it." It follows that we must interpret Spending Clause legislation narrowly, in order to avoid saddling the States with obligations that they did not anticipate.

The majority's approach in this case turns this Spending Clause presumption on its head. We have held that, in enacting IDEA, Congress wished to require "States to educate handicapped children with nonhandicapped children whenever possible," Congress, however, also took steps to limit the fiscal burdens that States must bear in attempting to achieve this laudable goal. These steps include requiring States to provide an education that is only "appropriate" rather than requiring them to maximize the potential of disabled students, see 20 U.S.C. § 1400(c); recognizing that integration into the public school environment is not always possible, see § 1412(5), and clarifying that, with a few exceptions, public schools need not provide "medical services" for disabled students, §§ 1401(a)(17) and (18).

For this reason, we have previously recognized that Congress did not intend to "impose upon the States a burden of unspecified proportions and weight" in enacting IDEA. These federalism concerns require us to interpret IDEA's related services provision, consistent with *Tatro,* as follows: Department of Education regulations require districts to provide disabled children with health-related services that school nurses can perform as part of their normal duties. This reading of *Tatro,* although less broad than the majority's, is equally plausible and certainly more consistent with our obligation to interpret Spending Clause legislation narrowly. Before concluding that the district was required to provide clean intermittent catheterization for Amber Tatro, we observed that school nurses in the district were authorized to perform services that were "difficult to distinguish from the provision of [clean intermittent catheterization] to the handicapped." We concluded that "it would be strange indeed if Congress, in attempting to extend special services to handicapped children, were unwilling to guarantee them services of a kind that are routinely provided to the nonhandicapped."

Unlike clean intermittent catheterization, however, a school nurse cannot provide the services that respondent requires, and continue to perform her normal duties. To the contrary, because respondent requires continuous, one-on-one care throughout the entire school day, all agree that the district must hire an additional employee to attend solely to respondent. This will cost a minimum of $18,000 per year. Although the majority recognizes this fact, it nonetheless concludes that the "more extensive" nature of the services that respondent needs is irrelevant to the question whether those services fall under the medical services exclusion. This approach disregards the constitutionally mandated principles of construction applicable to Spending Clause legislation and blindsides unwary States with fiscal obligations that they could not have anticipated.

For the foregoing reasons, I respectfully dissent.

POSTSCRIPT

Should Children With Disabilities Be Provided With Extraordinary Care in Order to Attend Regular Classes in Public Schools?

Like many cases decided by the Rehnquist court, this case ultimately comes down to an issue of federalism. Justice Thomas, joined in dissent by Justice Kennedy, is concerned about the financial burdens that local school districts will face under the weight of federal mandates. Indeed, Thomas suggests that Justice Stevens willfully ignores such concerns. Nonetheless, Stevens was able to carry six other votes in this decision.

For some background information on this issue, consult Stephen B. Thomas's *Health Related Legal Issues in Education* (Education Law Association, 1987) for a general treatment of the subject. In addition, see Rex R. Schultze, "Reading, Writing and Ritalin: The Responsibility of Public School Districts to Administer Medications to Students," 32 *Creighton Law Review* 793 (1999) for coverage of a different but related question. To fully comprehend the discussion in *Garret F.*, read the Court's earlier decision in this area, *Irving Independent School District v. Tatro,* 468 U.S. 883 (1984). Finally, there are several Web sites that contain pertinent information. See, for example, the Council for Disability Rights site at http://www.disabilityrights.org and the Disability Rights Education and Defense Fund site at http://www.dredf.org.

ISSUE 19

Do Affirmative Action Programs in Public School Admissions Policies Violate the Fourteenth Amendment?

YES: Bruce Seyla, from Majority Opinion, *Wessmann v. Gittens,* U.S. Court of Appeals for the First Circuit (November 19, 1998)

NO: Kermit Lipez, from Dissenting Opinion, *Wessmann v. Gittens,* U.S. Court of Appeals for the First Circuit (November 19, 1998)

ISSUE SUMMARY

YES: U.S. Circuit Court judge Bruce Seyla holds that the admissions policy of the Boston Latin School, which makes race a determining factor in the admission of a specified segment of each year's incoming class, violates the Constitution's guarantee of equal protection.

NO: U.S. Circuit Court judge Kermit Lipez finds that the Boston Latin School's admissions policy serves the state's compelling interest in remedying the continuing effects of past discriminatory practices in the Boston public school system.

Affirmative action continues to be one of the most hotly debated issues in America. Proponents justify the use of affirmative action policies by arguing that government should utilize race-conscious programs both to redress the continuing effects of past discrimination and to achieve more racially diverse educational and workplace environments. Opponents of affirmative action view it as unnecessary and unfair, arguing that it is, in essence, nothing more than "reverse discrimination." Opponents also assert that affirmative action policies stigmatize the beneficiaries of such programs, marking them as unable to succeed on their own merit. These opponents have been challenging the continued existence of affirmative action, bringing their case before federal and state legislatures. As with the original civil rights movement, however, this battle has been fought most intensely and successfully in the nation's courtrooms. For example, the Fifth Circuit Court of Appeals, in the highly publicized case *Hopwood v. Texas,* 78 F.3d 932 (C.A. 5, 1996), severely restricted the ability of institutions of higher education to consider race as a relevant factor in their admissions decisions. The *Hopwood* litigation was brought by an applicant who was denied admission to the prestigious University of Texas Law School at the Austin campus. Cheryl Hopwood, who is white, alleged that she was the victim of the unconstitutional use of racial preferences in the application process. Since the *Hopwood* decision, similar litigation has been threatened elsewhere. Although the Fifth Circuit's decision is not binding precedent in the other federal circuits, many colleges and universities have modified or ended the use of race-conscious admissions programs. And, as the following selections indicate, this constitutional struggle has moved from the arena of higher education to public elementary and secondary schools.

The selections that follow present arguments on both sides of the affirmative action issue from two judges of the First Circuit Court of Appeals. In *Wessmann v. Gittens,* charges that race-conscious admissions programs are unconstitutional were directed at one of Boston's prestigious "examination schools"—Boston Latin School (BLS). BLS had 90 available seats for its 1997 ninth-grade class. Sarah Wessmann, through her father Henry Wessmann, sued the Boston School Committee and its chairperson, Robert Gittens, when she was denied admission. Based on a complex admissions formula, Sarah's composite score ranked her as 91st in the applicant pool. Two of the students ranked above Sarah declined BLS's offer of admission in order to attend one of the city's other examination schools. Consequently, her composite score would have been sufficient for admission if the selection process were based solely on composite score rankings. They were not, however. Instead, with the assistance of a paid consultant, BLS had devised a race-conscious admissions policy that sought to remedy the effects of past racial discrimination in the Boston public school system and to promote racial and ethnic diversity within the present school-age population. This formula had the practical effect of denying admission to Sarah Wessmann. Suit was brought in the U.S. District Court where, after a 13-day bench trial, Chief Judge Joseph L. Tauro held that the committee's goals of achieving diversity and overcoming the vestiges of past discrimination were sufficiently compelling and that the admissions policy was tailored narrowly enough to pass constitutional review. On appeal, the U.S. Court of Appeals for the First Circuit held that the committee's admissions policy was an unconstitutional racial classification, reversed the lower court ruling, and ordered Sarah Wessmann's admission to BLS.

Bruce Seyla

 **YES**

Majority Opinion

Wessman *v.* Gittens

The Supreme Court consistently employs sweeping language to identify the species of racial classifications that require strict scrutiny, see *Adarand Constructors, Inc. v. Pena,* 515 U.S. 200 (1995).... We conclude, therefore, that strict scrutiny is the proper standard for evaluating the Policy. Hence, the Policy must be both justified by a compelling governmental interest and narrowly tailored to serve that interest in order to stand.

The School Committee's rejoinder—that the Policy is not a quota—is a non sequitur. We agree that the Policy does not constitute a quota—at least not in the literal sense of an unchanging set-aside—but that fact gains the School Committee little ground. At a certain point in its application process—specifically, during the selection of the second half of each incoming class—the Policy relies on race and ethnicity, and nothing else, to select a subset of entrants. Thus, whether the Policy is truly a quota or whether it is best described otherwise is entirely irrelevant for the purpose of equal protection analysis. Attractive labeling cannot alter the fact that any program which induces schools to grant preferences based on race and ethnicity is constitutionally suspect. See *Regents of Univ. of Cal. v. Bakke,* 438 U.S. 265, 289, 57 L. Ed. 2d 750, 98 S. Ct. 2733 (1978) (opinion of Powell, J.)....

The School Committee also asserts an entitlement to more lenient review because the Policy neither benefits nor burdens any particular group. Under the flexible guidelines, the argument goes, the racial/ethnic distribution of the entering classes will change yearly, and thus, there is no real preference for any single group.

This assertion leads nowhere, for the manner in which the Policy functions is fundamentally at odds with the equal protection guarantee that citizens will be treated "as individuals, not as simply components of a racial, religious, sexual or national class." *Miller v. Johnson,* 515 U.S. 900, 911, (1995). Even though we may not know before the fact which individuals from which racial/ethnic groups will be affected, we do know that someone from some group will be benefitted and a different someone from a different group will be burdened. Because a court's obligation to review race-conscious programs

From *Wessmann v. Gittens,* 160 F.3d 790 (1st Cir. 1998).

and policies cannot be made to depend "on the race of those burdened or benefitted by a particular classification," *City of Richmond v. J. A. Croson Co.,* 488 U.S. 469, 494 (1989), no more is exigible to bring strict scrutiny into play. . . .

The question of precisely what interests government may legitimately invoke to justify race-based classifications is largely unsettled. Of course, we know that such state action is acceptable upon a showing, *inter alia,* that it is needed to undo the continuing legacy of an institution's past discrimination. See *Miller,* 515 U.S. at 920. We also know that the Court has rejected the "role model" theory as a compelling interest. See *Croson,* 488 U.S. at 497–98. Beyond these examples, the case law offers relatively little guidance.

A few cases suggest (albeit in dictum) that remedying past discrimination is the only permissible justification for race-conscious action by the government. See, e.g., *id.* at 493. But in certain milieus, some courts have accepted race-based taxonomies that are not linked to remedying past discrimination, particularly in settings such as law enforcement and corrections. . . .

In considering whether other governmental interests, beyond the need to heal the vestiges of past discrimination, may be sufficiently compelling to justify race-based initiatives, courts occasionally mention "diversity." At first blush, it appears that a negative consensus may be emerging on this point. . . .

We think that any such consensus is more apparent than real. In the education context, *Hopwood* is the only appellate court to have rejected diversity as a compelling interest, and it did so only in the face of vigorous dissent from a substantial minority of the active judges in the Fifth Circuit. See *Hopwood v. State of Texas,* 84 F.3d 720, 721 (5th Cir. 1996). The question that divided the Fifth Circuit centered on the precedential value of Justice Powell's controlling opinion in *Bakke.* The panel in *Hopwood* pronounced that opinion dead. The dissenting judges countered that the reports of *Bakke's* demise were premature.

It may be that the *Hopwood* panel is correct and that, were the Court to address the question today, it would hold that diversity is not a sufficiently compelling interest to justify a race-based classification. It has not done so yet, however, and we are not prepared to make such a declaration in the absence of a clear signal that we should. This seems especially prudent because the Court and various individual Justices from time to time have written approvingly of ethnic diversity in comparable settings. . . .

As matters turn out, we need not definitively resolve this conundrum today. Instead, we assume *arguendo*—but we do not decide—that *Bakke* remains good law and that some iterations of "diversity" might be sufficiently compelling, in specific circumstances, to justify race-conscious actions. It is against this chiaroscuro backdrop that we address the School Committee's asserted "diversity" justification for the Policy. Thereafter, we turn to its alternate justification: that the Policy is an appropriate means of remediating the vestiges of past discrimination. . . .

The word "diversity," like any other abstract concept, does not admit of permanent, concrete definition. Its meaning depends not only on time and place, but also upon the person uttering it. . . . It would be cause for consternation were a court, without more, free to accept a term as malleable as "diversity" in satisfaction of the compelling interest needed to justify governmentally-sponsored racial distinctions.

The School Committee demurs. Citing to *Swann v. Charlotte-Mecklenburg Bd. of Educ.*, 402 U.S. 1 (1971), it labors to persuade us that we would be warranted in deferring to its judgment because school officials necessarily enjoy substantial discretion in making education policy. We are not convinced.

The *Swann* song upon which the School Committee relies cannot be wrested from the score.... *Swann* was decided when dual educational systems were a reality and efforts to dismantle them were being frustrated by school officials who demonstrated little ardor for implementing the mandates of desegregation. Chary that the exigencies of the need for change might precipitate a rush to judgment, the Justices confirmed that federal courts must put the horse before the cart, that is, they must diagnose some constitutional malady before beginning to dispense remedies. Thus, the *Swann* dictum, properly construed, recognizes that a low percentage of minority students in a particular school does not necessarily betoken unconstitutional conduct, but may result from innocent causes (say, the population distribution of a given district), and warns that, unless a skewed enrollment pattern is caused by unconstitutional student assignment practices, federal courts must defer to school officials' discretion and refrain from imposing remedies.

This well-accepted principle does not help the School Committee. The *Swann* Court had no occasion to consider the question, central to this appeal, of whether and to what extent the Constitution circumscribes school officials' discretion to formulate and implement an admissions policy that embraces a particular brand of pluralism.... In the end, then, the School Committee's reference to *Swann* only begs the question: *Swann* reiterated that federal courts must grant remedies where there are constitutional violations, and the question here is whether the School Committee itself has violated the Constitution. It follows that, in order to persuade us that diversity may serve as a justification for the use of a particular racial classification, the School Committee must do more than ask us blindly to accept its judgment. It must give substance to the word.

The School Committee endeavors to meet this challenge primarily by lauding benefits that it ascribes to diversity. Drawing on the testimony of various witnesses (school administrators, experts, and alumni), the Committee asserts that, because our society is racially and ethnically heterogeneous, future leaders must learn to converse with and persuade those who do not share their outlook or experience. This imperative becomes even more urgent because technology, now more than ever, forces heretofore estranged nations and cultures to communicate and cooperate. For these reasons, the School Committee exhorts us to find that diversity is essential to the modern learning experience.

Stated at this level of abstraction, few would gainsay the attractiveness of diversity. Encounters between students of varied backgrounds facilitate a vigorous exchange of ideas that not only nourishes the intellect, but also furthers mutual understanding and respect, thereby eroding prejudice and acting as a catalyst for social harmony. Indeed, Justice Powell's opinion in *Bakke* acknowledges that these very attributes may render an educational institution's interest in promoting diversity compelling. In the last analysis, however, the School Committee's reliance on generalizations undercuts its construct. If one is to limit consideration to generalities, any proponent of any notion of diversity could recite a similar litany of virtues. Hence, an inquiring court cannot content itself with abstractions. Just as Justice Powell probed whether the racial classification at issue in *Bakke* in fact promoted the institution's stated goals, we must look beyond the School Committee's recital of the theoretical benefits of diversity and inquire whether the concrete workings of the Policy merit constitutional sanction. Only by such particularized attention can we ascertain whether the Policy bears any necessary relation to the noble ends it espouses. In short, the devil is in the details.

By its terms, the Policy focuses exclusively on racial and ethnic diversity. Its scope is narrowed further in that it takes into account only five groups—blacks, whites, Hispanics, Asians, and Native Americans—without recognizing that none is monolithic. No more is needed to demonstrate that the School Committee already has run afoul of the guidance provided by the principal authority on which it relies: "The diversity that furthers a compelling state interest encompasses a far broader array of qualifications and characteristics of which racial or ethnic origin is but a single though important element." A single-minded focus on ethnic diversity "hinders rather than furthers attainment of genuine diversity." Nor is the Policy saved because the student assignments that it dictates are proportional to the composition of the RQAP.

When we articulated this concern at oral argument, the School Committee's able counsel responded that it is unnecessary for the Policy to consider other indicia of diversity because BLS [Boston Latin School] historically has been diverse with respect to everything but race and ethnicity. For empirical confirmation of this assertion, the School Committee points to Bain's handiwork. Having analyzed various admissions options, Bain suggested that all the options would result in substantial gender, neighborhood, and socioeconomic diversity, but that, unless race and ethnicity were explicitly factored into the admissions calculus, attainment of racial and ethnic diversity might be jeopardized. This attempted confirmation does not pass constitutional muster.

If, as we are told, diversity has been attained in all areas other than race and ethnicity, then the School Committee's argument implodes. Statistics compiled for the last ten years show that under a strict merit-selection approach, black and Hispanic students together would comprise between 15% and 20% of each entering class, and minorities, *in toto,* would comprise a substantially greater percentage. Even on the assumption that the need for racial and ethnic diversity alone might sometimes constitute a compelling interest sufficient to warrant some type of corrective governmental action, it is perfectly clear that the need would have to be acute—much more acute than the relatively modest deviations that attend the instant case. In short, the School Committee's flexible racial/ethnic guidelines appear to be less a means of attaining diversity in any constitutionally relevant sense and more a means for racial balancing. The Policy's reliance on a scheme of proportional representation buttresses this appearance and indicates that the School Committee intended mainly to achieve a racial/ethnic "mix" that it considered desirable. Indeed, Bain's Option N50 was chosen and incorporated into the Policy because it held out the promise of increasing minority representation over the roughly 18% that Bain anticipated would result on a strict merit-selection basis.

We do not question the School Committee's good intentions. The record depicts a body that is struggling valiantly to come to terms with intractable social and educational issues. Here, however, the potential for harmful consequences prevents us from succumbing to good intentions. The Policy is, at bottom, a mechanism for racial balancing—and placing our imprimatur on racial balancing risks setting a precedent that is both dangerous to our democratic ideals and almost always constitutionally forbidden. Nor does the School Committee's reliance on alleviating underrepresentation advance its cause. Underrepresentation is merely racial balancing in disguise—another way of suggesting that there may be optimal proportions for the representation of races and ethnic groups in institutions.

It cannot be said that racial balancing is either a legitimate or necessary means of advancing the lofty principles recited in the Policy. The closest the School Committee comes to linking racial balancing to these ideals is by introducing the concept of "racial isolation." The idea is that unless there is a certain representation of any given racial or ethnic group in a particular institution, members of that racial or ethnic group will find it difficult, if not impossible, to express themselves. Thus, the School Committee says, some minimum number of black and Hispanic students—precisely how many, we do not know—is required to prevent racial isolation.

Fundamental problems beset this approach. In the first place, the "racial isolation" justification is extremely suspect because it assumes that students cannot function or express themselves unless they are surrounded by a sufficient number of persons of like race or ethnicity. Insofar as the Policy promotes groups over individuals, it is starkly at variance with Justice Powell's understanding of the proper manner in which a diverse student body may be gathered. Furthermore, if justified in terms of group identity, the Policy suggests that race or ethnic background determines how individuals think or behave—although the School Committee resists this conclusion by arguing that the greater the number of a particular group, the more others will realize that the group is not monolithic. Either way, the School Committee tells us that a minimum number of persons of a given race (or ethnic background) is essential to facilitate individual expression. This very position concedes that the Policy's racial/ethnic guidelines treat "individuals as the product of their race," a practice that the Court consistently has denounced as impermissible stereotyping.

In the second place, the School Committee has failed to give us a plausible reason why we should believe that racial balancing of any type is necessary to promote the expression of ideas or any of the other ideals referenced in the Policy. We assume for argument's sake—albeit with considerable skepticism—that there may be circumstances under which a form of racial balancing could be justified by concerns for attaining the goals articulated by the Policy. To justify something so antithetical to our constitutional jurisprudence, however, a particularly strong showing of necessity would be required. The

School Committee has provided absolutely no competent evidence that the proportional representation promoted by the Policy is in any way tied to the vigorous exchange of ideas, let alone that, in such respects, it differs significantly in consequence from, say, a strict merit-selection process. Nor has the School Committee concretely demonstrated that the differences in the percentages of students resulting from the Policy and other, constitutionally acceptable alternatives are significant in any other way, such as students' capacity and willingness to learn. To the contrary, the School Committee relies only on broad generalizations by a few witnesses, which, in the absence of solid and compelling evidence, constitute no more than rank speculation. Given both the Constitution's general prohibition against racial balancing and the potential dangers of stereotyping, we cannot allow generalities emanating from the subjective judgments of local officials to dictate whether a particular percentage of a particular racial or ethnic group is sufficient or insufficient for individual students to avoid isolation and express ideas.

This brings us full circle. Although Justice Powell endorsed diversity as potentially comprising a compelling interest, he warned that a proper admissions policy would be such that if an applicant "loses out" to another candidate, he will "not have been foreclosed from all consideration for that seat simply because he was not the right color or had the wrong surname." *Bakke,* 438 U.S. at 318. The Policy does precisely what Justice Powell deemed anathematic: at a certain point, it effectively forecloses some candidates from all consideration for a seat at an examination school simply because of the racial or ethnic category in which they fall. That happened to Sarah Wessmann. It violated the Equal Protection Clause....

The School Committee endeavors, in the alternative, to uphold the Policy as a means of redressing the vestiges of past discrimination. The court below accepted this explanation. We do not.

Governmental bodies have a significant interest in adopting programs and policies designed to eradicate the effects of past discrimination. Before embarking on such projects, however, government actors must be able to muster a "strong basis in evidence" showing that a current social ill in fact has been caused by such conduct. See *Croson,* 488 U.S. at 500....

The threshold problem that we confront in this instance is that the School Committee disclaims the necessity for such evidence. Its disclaimer rests on the premise that a decree issued in the quarter-century-old desegregation litigation mandates local authorities to remedy any racial imbalance occurring in the school system and thereby obviates the need for an independent showing of causation. This premise lacks force.

The decree in question was entered in 1994 by Judge Garrity, pursuant to our instructions in *Morgan v. Nucci,* 831 F.2d 313 (1st Cir. 1987). The particular provision to which the School Committee refers is entitled "Permanent Injunction." It enjoins the School Committee "from discriminating on the basis of race in the operation of the public schools of the City of Boston and from creating, promoting or maintaining racial segregation in any school or other facility in the Boston public school system." Nothing in the plain language of this provision requires school officials to undertake any affirmative action.... As long as school officials do not engage in discrimination against minorities—and there is no evidence that such conduct persists at BLS—they have not violated the injunction....

That ends this aspect of the matter. We concluded over ten years ago that Boston had restored the unitariness of student assignments, see *Nucci,* 831 F.2d at 319–26, and there is no contention here that any municipal actor has attempted intentionally to subvert the demographic composition of BLS (or any other school, for that matter). Under such circumstances, neither the Constitution nor the 1994 decree impose a duty on Boston's school officials to ensure the maintenance of certain percentages of any racial or ethnic group in any particular school.

Because the 1994 decree turns out to be a blind alley, the School Committee must identify a vestige of bygone discrimination and provide convincing evidence that ties this vestige to the de jure segregation of the benighted past. To meet this challenge, the School Committee cites an "achievement gap" between black and Hispanic students, on the one hand, and white and Asian students, on the other, and claims that this gap's roots can be traced to the discriminatory regime of the 1970s and before....

The scope of what social phenomena the law considers vestiges of past discrimination presents an open question.... In sum, whether past discrimination necessitates current action is a fact-sensitive inquiry, and courts must pay careful attention to competing explanations for current realities....

Beyond history, the School Committee offers statistical and anecdotal evidence to satisfy its burden of demonstrating a strong evidentiary basis for the inauguration of remedial policies.... The centerpiece of the School Committee's showing consists of statistical evidence addressed to a persistent achievement gap at the primary school level between white and Asian students, on the one hand, and black and Hispanic students, on the other. One way to measure the achievement gap is in terms of relative performance on standardized tests. Over the years, whites and Asians have scored significantly higher, on average, than blacks and Hispanics. The School Committee theorizes that, because of this achievement gap, BLS receives fewer African-American and Hispanic applicants than otherwise might be the case, and even in comparison to this modest universe, an abnormally small number of black and Hispanic students qualify for admission. Accordingly, the Committee concludes that the statistics documenting the achievement gap, on their own, satisfy the "strong basis in evidence" requirement....

We do not propose that the achievement gap bears no relation to some form of prior discrimination. We posit only that it is fallacious to maintain that an endless gaze at any set of raw numbers permits a court to arrive at a valid etiology of complex social phenomena. Even strong statistical correlation between variables does not automatically establish causation....

The School Committee attempts to compensate for this shortcoming by pointing to certain alleged phenomena that it claims constitute substantial causes of the achievement gap. Chief among these is "low teacher expectations" vis-à-vis African-American and Hispanic students, a condition which the School Committee argues is an attitudinal remnant of the segregation era. To show the systemic nature of this alleged phenomenon, the School Committee leans heavily on the testimony of Dr. William Trent. Dr. Trent, a sociologist, identified teachers' low expectations of African-American and Hispanic students as a significant factor underlying the achievement gap in the Boston public schools.... One difficulty with Dr. Trent's testimony is that it relies on evidence from one locality to establish the lingering effects of discrimination in another.... The shortcomings in Dr. Trent's testimony largely relate to his failure to gather data systematically and point up the pitfalls that the School Committee invited by failing to validate the Policy in advance.... Dr. Trent's reliance on anecdotal evidence fares no better. As a general matter, anecdotal evidence is problematic because it does not tend to show that a problem is pervasive.... Thus, even though anecdotal evidence may prove powerful when proffered in conjunction with admissions or valid statistical evidence, anecdotal evidence alone can establish institutional discrimination only in the most exceptional circumstances.... The remaining evidence upon which the School Committee and the dissent relies—most notably the testimony of BLS Headmaster Michael Contompasis and Dr. Melendez—likewise exemplifies the shortcomings of anecdotal evidence. One cannot conclude from the isolated instances that these witnesses recounted that low teacher expectations constitute a systemic problem in the Boston public schools or that they necessarily relate to the *de jure* segregation of the past....

We do not write on a pristine page. The Supreme Court's decisions in *Croson* and *Adarand* indicate quite plainly that a majority of the Justices are highly skeptical of racial preferences and believe that the Constitution imposes a heavy burden of justification on their use. *Croson,* in particular, leaves no doubt that only solid evidence will justify allowing race-conscious action; and the unsystematic personal observations of government officials will not do, even if the conclusions they offer sound plausible and are cloaked in the trappings of social science....

Our dissenting brother's valiant effort to read into *Croson* a broad discretion for government entities purporting to ameliorate past discrimination strikes us as wishful thinking. The *Croson* Court's own reference to the need for a "searching judicial inquiry," ... suggest[s] an attitude that is antipathetic to those who yearn for discretion. And unless and until the Justices reconfigure their present doctrine, it is the job of judges in courts such as this to respect the letter and spirit of the Supreme Court's pronouncements.

We need go no further. While we appreciate the difficulty of the School Committee's task and admire the values that it seeks to nourish, noble ends cannot justify the deployment of constitutionally impermissible means. Since Boston Latin School's admissions policy does not accord with the equal protection guarantees of the Fourteenth Amendment, we strike it down. The judgment of the district court must therefore be reversed.

NO

Dissenting Opinion of Kermit Lipez

Under the Equal Protection Clause of the Fourteenth Amendment, all racial or ethnic classifications by government actors are highly suspect and will be upheld only if they withstand strict judicial scrutiny. To meet the strict scrutiny standard, a challenged racial classification must serve a compelling governmental interest and must be narrowly tailored to achieve that goal. See *Adarand Constructors, Inc. v. Pena,* 515 U.S. 200, 224–25 (1995). The Boston School Committee argues that the Boston Latin admissions program serves two compelling interests: promoting diversity in the public schools and remedying the vestiges of past discrimination. The majority rejects both arguments. Although I have reservations about the Committee's diversity argument on the facts of this case, I have none about its remedial argument. The district court properly found that the Boston School Committee had a strong basis in evidence for determining that the Boston Latin admissions program serves a compelling government interest in remedying the effects of prior discrimination, and that the program is narrowly tailored to achieve that goal....

In rejecting the district court's conclusion that the School Committee's current admissions program for Boston Latin "appropriately addressed the vestiges of discrimination that linger in the Boston Public School system," the majority asserts that the School Committee failed to present satisfactory evidence of a causal connection between the achievement gap documented by the Committee and the prior *de jure* segregation of the Boston schools. I disagree with this conclusion. In my view, the majority judges the Committee's proof of causation unsatisfactory because the majority misperceives the Committee's evidentiary burden in defending its affirmative action program....

The law is clear that a public entity adopting an affirmative action program to remedy the lingering effects of past discrimination must have a "strong basis in evidence" for concluding that the lingering effects it identifies are causally linked to past discrimination. See *City of Richmond v. J. A. Croson Co.,* 488 U.S. 469, 500 (1989). The more elusive question is what factual predicate constitutes a "strong basis in evidence" justifying action by the public entity. From my reading of the relevant caselaw, I conclude that this "strong basis" requirement is met preliminarily if the public entity whose affirmative action

From *Wessmann v. Gittens,* 160 F.3d 790 (1st Cir. 1998). Notes omitted.

program is challenged in court demonstrates that the entity adopted the program on the basis of evidence sufficient to establish a prima facie case of a causal link between past discrimination and the current outcomes addressed by the remedial program. If this prima facie case is not effectively rebutted by a reverse discrimination plaintiff, the public entity has met its burden of establishing a compelling remedial interest. I now turn to an analysis of the cases....

In the instant case, where there is a long history of court findings of discriminatory acts by the School Committee, there is no dispute about the public entity's responsibility for prior discrimination. Instead, given the time lapse between those court findings of discrimination and the claim that this discrimination still disadvantages minorities, the issue in dispute here is whether the vestiges of that prior discrimination now affect minorities. This showing necessarily requires evidence of the existence of vestiges of the prior discrimination and of a present harm to minorities. It also requires evidence of causal connections between the past discrimination and the claimed vestiges, and between the vestiges and the present harm. Through these connections, the School Committee must show that the need for remedial action was a consequence of the effects of past discrimination. Nevertheless, [the Supreme Court's] strong basis in evidence/prima facie analysis still defines the evidentiary burden of the School Committee in presenting its proof of the causal relationship between prior discrimination and the present effects on minorities....

The majority finds the School Committee's reliance on cases addressing affirmative action plans designed to remedy vestiges of past employment discrimination inapt....

I disagree with this analysis.... [In this case], there is an identifiable barrier to entry that could be challenged by minority applicants in the event the race-conscious aspects of the Boston Latin admissions program were elided. Amicus curiae NAACP makes this claim on appeal; it tried doggedly to intervene below; and its position explains why the School Committee could not, in the context of litigation both current and anticipated, freely admit that composite score ranking may have had a discriminatory impact if used alone. Despite this constraint, the School Committee did allude to the notion of discriminatory impact, as already noted, and there was evidence presented at trial that, for African-Americans and Hispanics, composite score was not reliably correlated with future performance at BLS [Boston Latin Schools]. The Committee also took pains to indicate that its stipulation at trial that [Sarah] Wessmann would have been admitted had a straight-rank-order system been used was not a concession that such an admissions scheme was acceptable.

Although the admissions program challenged here was "voluntary," in the sense of not being impelled by the 1994 order or any other court proceeding or consent decree, the mere act of making a selection among students seeking admission to Boston Latin exposed the Committee to legal action by minority students. As Justice O'Connor characterized the analogous employment situation, "public employers are trapped between the competing hazards of liability to minorities if affirmative action is not taken to remedy apparent employment discrimination and liability to nonminorities if affirmative action is taken."

Wygant, 476 U.S. at 291 (O'Connor, J., concurring). The *Wygant* case dealt with racial preferences in employment, an arena where the shadow of Title VII suits by disappointed minority job seekers inevitably looms over a public employer using selection criteria with the potential to produce an unjustifiable "disparate impact" on minorities. The same considerations apply in the context of a selective public secondary school: the mere act of selection exposes the school system to challenge from minorities based on the disparate impact of the selection criteria used. Here, the relevant provision of federal law is Title VI of the Civil Rights Act of 1964, 42 U.S.C. § 2000d (West 1998), stating that "no person in the United States shall, on the ground of race, color, or national origin, be excluded from participation in, be denied the benefits of, or be subjected to discrimination under any program or activity receiving Federal financial assistance."

There was evidence produced at trial that any exclusive focus on composite score in admissions had a disparate impact on African-Americans and Hispanics. Although the ability of minority plaintiffs to make colorable claims of Title VI violations would not be sufficient to justify a race-conscious affirmative action program (such claims would only be sufficient to force the Committee to find some alternative to composite score rank order admissions), the presence of the disparate impact underlying such claims, when causally related to the history of *de jure* segregation in the system, imposed on the School Committee a duty to ensure that it did not violate the Constitution by using selection criteria that perpetuated the effects of past governmental discrimination. As already noted, the district court in *McLaughlin v. Boston School Committee* was skeptical of the legality of simply reverting to the use of composite score ranking, stating just two years ago that "abandonment of the . . . set aside at the present time *without adopting other remedial measures* would, within the next six years or sooner, convert BLS into an overwhelmingly white and Asian-American school. . . ." 938 F. Supp. at 1008 (emphasis added). The Committee chose a remedial measure for admission to the Boston Latin School in the wake of a long history of desegregation orders and under the threat of Title VI suits by disappointed minority applicants if no affirmative action were taken.

Just as the courts have always encouraged consensual resolutions to desegregation cases, Congress's intent to encourage voluntary compliance with the requirements of Title VI (and VII, for that matter) has always been a backdrop to the scheme of evidentiary burdens the federal courts have placed on litigants pursuant to that legislation. See *Bakke v. Regents of the Univ. of California,* 438 U.S. 265, 336, (1978). Similarly, in cases where there may be a duty to counteract the effects of past government discrimination, the Supreme Court has set evidentiary standards that facilitate a voluntary remedy. A government entity need not admit conclusive guilt for past discrimination's current effects before going forward with a remedial plan. Instead, it must satisfy the court that the evidence before it established a prima facie case of a causal link between past discrimination and the current outcomes addressed by the remedial program. If this prima facie case is not effectively rebutted by a reverse discrimination plaintiff, who always retains the burden of proving the illegality of the affirmative action program, the government has met its burden of establishing a compelling remedial interest under strict scrutiny analysis. With this legal framework in mind, I turn to an analysis of the evidence on the vestiges of discrimination....

The evidence at trial revealed large gaps between African-Americans and Hispanics, on the one hand, and whites and Asians, on the other, in admissions to the exam schools, and in achievement and allocation of resources throughout the system. The most significant of these is the persistent, static gap in achievement between African-American and Hispanic students and white and Asian students. The gap is measured by achievement test scores of fifth and sixth graders on the Metropolitan Achievement Test and the Stanford 9. Expert witness analysis of the test results over a several year period showed a persistent and relatively unchanging gap in achievement in all subject matters which correlated with race: African-American and Hispanic students fared much worse on the tests than whites. The tests also revealed that, in general, Asians fared worse than whites on language skills achievement.

The evidence also demonstrated that African-Americans and Hispanics from the public schools apply to the examination schools at half the application rate of other students in the public schools. Even within the special advanced work classes which are designed to prepare Boston public elementary school students for the examination schools, African-Americans and Hispanics fared worse in the examination schools' admissions process than whites. Finally, there was evidence that African-American and Hispanic applicants to Boston Latin from private elementary schools do much better in the admissions process than their Boston public school counterparts. The existence of these "gaps" was undisputed at the trial....

The Committee presented evidence of a connection between low teacher expectations for minority students and low minority performance on achievement tests. The Committee presented further evidence that these low teacher expectations for minority students are prevalent in the Boston school system, and that this prevalence is a vestige of the long years of segregation in the Boston school system. Given these connections between student achievement, teacher expectations for students, and the impact of years of segregation on these teacher expectations, the achievement gap itself is a current and lingering effect of discrimination....

The majority's criticisms of the Committee's evidentiary case are twofold: 1) the Committee did not establish the presence of differential teacher [expectations] for minority students and 2) the Committee failed to establish any causal connection between prior discrimination and the achievement gap itself; that is, it failed to establish that prior discrimination affected low teacher expectations for minority students and further failed to establish that these low expectations were a cause of the achievement gap....

The majority asserts that [sociologist] Dr. [William] Trent's failure to conduct a survey of the type conducted in Kansas City disabled him from validly establishing that teachers had different expectations for minority students. Specifically, the majority criticizes Dr. Trent's reliance on "anecdotal" evidence about teacher attitudes.... Used pejoratively, the word "anecdotal" describes accounts of isolated instances few in number. Used descriptively, the word describes observational testimony that could embrace many instances of a phenomenon. We should be wary of dismissing as "anecdotal" the extensive observational accounts of experienced school administrators testifying about the prevalence of different teacher expectations in their school systems.…

In the instant case, experienced school administrators and officials, such as Superintendent Payzant and Vice-Chair Gittens, offered their judgment, on the basis of extensive day to day experience with the Boston school system, that there were links between prior discrimination in the system, low teacher expectations, and the achievement gap. Dr. Trent offered his expert opinion on these links without challenge to the admissibility of his testimony. He testified that his conclusions were based on a reasonable methodology in his profession. He evaluated statistics documenting student performance and teacher histories in the Boston school system. He studied the observations of a well-trained administrator in the Boston school system describing teacher performances in the classroom, the impact of these performances on students, and faulty attempts to alter teacher attitudes. He knew the history of segregation in the Boston school system. Seeing statistics and patterns in Boston that he had observed in other school systems where he had found a link between student achievement gaps and prior discrimination, he testified to the probability of such a link in the Boston school system. He had an adequate basis for making that judgment.…

The evidence presented by the School Committee established a prima facie case that differential teacher expectations, grounded in the long history of segregation in the Boston school system, were a substantial causal factor in the undeniable achievement gap found in the Boston school system. In the face of this evidence, Wessmann had the burden of challenging the Committee's prima facie case by disproving the alleged causal linkages between prior discrimination, teacher expectations, and the achievement gap.…

By asserting that the district court erred in crediting the extensive observational testimony of experienced, well-trained school administrators, and by requiring quantifiable data to establish a causal link between past discrimination and present outcomes, the majority would reduce strict scrutiny to a standard that is indeed "fatal in fact." See *Adarand,* 515 U.S. 200, 237 (1995). In my view, the district court properly concluded that the School Committee had a strong basis in evidence for adoption of the Boston Latin admissions program, thereby meeting its evidentiary burden, and that the plaintiff failed to carry her burden of persuading the court that this affirmative action program was unconstitutional.…

To survive strict scrutiny, the School Committee's admissions program must serve a compelling interest in remedying past discrimination and must also be narrowly tailored to serve that goal. "When race-based action is necessary to further a compelling interest, such action is within constitutional constraints if it satisfies the 'narrow tailoring' test this Court has set out in previous cases." *Adarand,* 515 U.S. at 237.…

Fundamentally, narrow tailoring analysis asks whether a program is "overinclusive" or "underinclusive" to serve the purposes of the specific compelling interest on which the program is based.…

[T]he "narrow tailoring" and "compelling interest" requirements serve the same purpose: ensuring that the program in question is not simply motivated by a desire to favor one race. "Narrow tailoring" serves the additional purpose of minimizing inadvertent harms that may result from an affirmative action program, on the basis of a "cost-benefit" analysis. Given these narrow tailoring considerations, I am satisfied that the School Committee has produced a race-conscious admissions program for Boston Latin which is narrowly tailored to address a compelling remedial goal....

The majority characterizes my dissent as "wishful thinking" about the meaning of *Wygant, Croson* and other Supreme Court precedents in this difficult area of the law. Not surprisingly, I disagree. I believe that I am faithful to those precedents and, unlike the majority, apply them accurately to the evidence presented to the district court.

The majority goes awry because it reads *Wygant's* requirement of a "strong basis in evidence" for an affirmative action program and *Croson's* reference to a "searching judicial inquiry" into the justification for an affirmative action program as demands for evidence grounded in quantifiable social science data rather than human judgments. There is no such demand in *Wygant, Croson* or any other Supreme Court precedent. Numbers are not the only source of the requisite degree of certainty about low teacher expectations for minorities and causation. In this case, the extensive observations of experienced administrators in the Boston public schools, supplemented by the testimony of a highly qualified expert who recognized in the Boston public schools a phenomenon he had studied extensively elsewhere, were as probative as the statistical surveys and regression analyses demanded by the majority.

The majority also goes awry because it uses *Croson's* reference to a "searching judicial inquiry" as the basis for disregarding two critical points made by Justice O'Connor in *Wygant*: (1) The strong basis in evidence required of a public entity defending an affirmative action program in court is provided by evidence sufficient to support a prima facie case of discrimination against the favored minority. (2) "In 'reverse discrimination' suits, as in any other suit, it is the plaintiffs who must bear the burden of demonstrating that their rights have been violated."

... The district court followed that teaching, and we should as well.

POSTSCRIPT

Do Affirmative Action Programs in Public School Admissions Policies Violate the Fourteenth Amendment?

In 1954 the landmark civil rights case *Brown v. Board of Education,* 347 U.S. 483 (1954), was decided. *Brown* stood as the culmination of the desegregation stategy of the National Association for the Advancement of Colored People (NAACP), promising the beginning of a new era of equal justice under law for America's racial minorities. For many, the promise of *Brown* was a nation that had overcome the vestiges of past practices of racial discrimination and that stood at the threshold of a truly color-blind society. But that promise has been elusive. Not too long after *Brown* was decided, it became apparent to some that in order to bring about racial justice it would still be necessary to continue to take race into account in many important public policy decisions. The late justice Harry A. Blackmun lent an eloquent voice to this position in his opinion in *Bakke v. Regents of the University of California,* 438 U.S. 265 (1978). There he announced that he yielded

> to no one in [his] earnest hope that the time will come when an "affirmative action" program is unnecessary, and is, in truth, only a relic of the past. . . . At some time, beyond any period of what some would claim is only transitional inequality, the United States must and will reach a stage of maturity where action along this line is no longer necessary. Then persons will be regarded as persons, and discrimination of the type we address today will be an ugly feature of history that is instructive but that is behind us.

For some, race-conscious remedies designed to cure the ills of past discrimination have done nothing to ease racial tensions and have resulted only in creating new problems, such as punishing "innocent" people—Sarah Wessmann, for example—for the sins of others. For others, race-conscious programs have threatened the very integrity of the Constitution, risking one of its most sacred principles: that all stand equal before the law, regardless of race, class, or other personal characteristics. Yet the brute fact remains that, nearly half a century after *Brown,* far too many of America's public schools remain "separate and unequal"—for all intents and purposes, segregated on the basis of race.

Those desiring to read further on this issue might begin with a recent study authored by Derek Bok and William Bowen, former presidents of Harvard and Princeton Universities, *The Shape of the River: Long-Term Consequences of Considering Race in College and University Admissions* (Princeton University Press, 1998). Another important study that should be consulted is Stephan Thernstrom and Abigail Thernstrom's *America in Black and White: One Nation,*

Indivisible (Simon & Schuster, 1997). Stephan Thernstrom, a professor at Harvard University, was the one expert witness called by the attorneys for Sarah Wessmann in her lawsuit against the Boston School Committee. Jonathan Kozol's *Savage Inequalities: Children in America's Schools* (HarperPerennial, 1992) is still an important work in this area as well. In addition, readers might be interested in visiting the Web site of the Center for Individual Rights (CIR) at http://www.cir-usa.org. The CIR is a nonprofit, tax-exempt public interest law firm, which provided legal representation for both Sarah Wessmann in her suit against the Boston School Committee and Cheryl Hopwood in her suit against the University of Texas. Finally, see the NAACP's Web site at http://www.naacp.org, which contains numerous links providing information on affirmative action and other topics.

Contributors to This Volume

EDITORS

M. ETHAN KATSH is a professor of legal studies at the University of Massachusetts–Amherst. A graduate of Yale Law School, his main area of expertise is law and computer technology, and he is the author of two books on the subject, *Law in a Digital World* (Oxford University Press, 1995) and *The Electronic Media and the Transformation of Law* (Oxford University Press, 1989), as well as many articles. He is also active in the field of dispute resolution and is codirector of the Online Ombuds Office (on the World Wide Web at http://www.ombuds.org/center/default.htm), a project designed to assist in the resolution of disputes arising out of online activities. Professor Katsh may be reached by e-mail at Katsh@legal.umass.edu.

WILLIAM ROSE is an assistant professor in the Department of Political Science at Albion College. He has also taught at Bowling Green State University, SUNY at Potsdam, and Mount Holyoke College; practiced law in St. Petersburg, Florida; and taught in prisons. He holds a J.D. from the University of Toledo and a Ph.D. from the University of Massachusetts–Amherst. His research and teaching interests are in the areas of jurisprudence, American legal and political thought, and contemporary political theory. He has articles forthcoming on the politics of legal indeterminacy and on racial profiling, and he has recently completed work on a book-length manuscript, tentatively titled *Legal Modernism and the Politics of Expertise.*

STAFF

Theodore Knight   List Manager
David Brackley   Senior Developmental Editor
Juliana Gribbins   Developmental Editor
Rose Gleich   Administrative Assistant
Brenda S. Filley   Director of Production/Design
Juliana Arbo   Typesetting Supervisor
Diane Barker   Proofreader
Richard Tietjen   Publishing Systems Manager
Larry Killian   Copier Coordinator

AUTHORS

AMERICAN BAR ASSOCIATION (ABA) is the largest voluntary professional association in the world. With more than 400,000 members, the ABA provides law school accreditation, continuing legal education, information about the law, programs to assist lawyers and judges in their work, and initiatives to improve the legal system for the public.

ROBERT R. BEEZER is senior circuit judge for the U.S. Court of Appeals, Ninth Circuit. Before being nominated to the court by President Ronald Reagan in 1984, he served as a judge in the Seattle Municipal Court, and he has also been in private practice with the law firm Schweppe, Krug, Tausend & Beezer. He earned his B.A. and his LL.B. in 1951 and 1956, respectively, from the University of Virginia.

RICHARD BONNIE is the John S. Battle Professor of Law at the University of Virginia School of Law and director of the university's Institute of Law, Psychiatry, and Public Policy. He has written extensively on the legal aspects of mental disability and behavioral health, and he was elected to the National Academy of Sciences Institute of Medicine. He is also a member of the MacArthur Foundation Research Network on Mental Health and the Law.

STEPHEN G. BREYER is an associate justice of the U.S. Supreme Court. He received his A.B. from Stanford University in 1959, his B.A. from Oxford University in 1961, and his LL.B. from Harvard University in 1964. A former U.S. Circuit Court of Appeals judge, he was nominated to the Supreme Court by President Bill Clinton in 1994.

STEVEN B. DUKE is a professor of law of science and technology at the Yale University School of Law in New Haven, Connecticut. He is coauthor, with Albert Gross, of *America's Longest War: Rethinking Our Tragic Crusade Against Drugs* (Putnam, 1993).

WARREN J. FERGUSON is a senior circuit judge for the U.S. Court of Appeals, Ninth Circuit. He was nominated to the court by President Jimmy Carter in 1979, and he has also held judicial appointments on the Anaheim-Fullerton Municipal Court, the Orange County Superior Court, and the U.S. District Court for the Central District of California. He earned his B.A. from the University of Nevada in 1942 and his LL.B. from the University of Southern California in 1949.

DAVID A. HARRIS is a professor of law at the University of Toledo in Toledo, Ohio. Prior to joining the faculty in 1990, he was a public defender in Montgomery County, Maryland. He has also been a Prettyman Fellow at Georgetown University; an associate at the law firm Wolf, Black, Schorr & Solis-Cohen in Philadelphia, Pennsylvania; and a law clerk to federal judge Walter Stapleton in Wilmington, Delaware. Considered the leading U.S. scholar on the issue of racial profiling, he received his J.D. from Yale University and his LL.M. from Georgetown University.

ANTHONY KENNEDY is an associate justice of the U.S. Supreme Court. He received his LL.B. from Harvard Law School in 1961 and worked for law firms in San Francisco and Sacremento, California, until he was nominated by President Gerald Ford to the U.S. Court of Appeals for the Ninth Circuit in 1975. He was nominated by President Ronald Reagan to the Supreme Court in 1988.

ALEX KOZINSKI is a circuit judge for the U.S. Court of Appeals, Ninth Circuit, to which he was nominated by President Ronald Reagan in 1985. He has also served as chief judge in the U.S. Court of Claims in Washington, D.C., and has held positions in the Office of the President-Elect and in the Office of Counsel to the President. He earned his A.B. and his J.D. in 1972 and 1975, respectively, from the University of California.

KERMIT LIPEZ is a circuit judge for the U.S. Court of Appeals, First Circuit. He was an associate justice for the Maine Supreme Judicial Court until his nomination to the court of appeals in 1998 by President Bill Clinton.

JESSICA LITMAN is a law professor at Wayne State University in Detroit, Michigan, where she teaches courses in copyright law, Internet law, and trademarks and unfair competition. She has also taught at the University of Michigan Law School and at American University's Washington College of Law. She has published many articles on copyright, trademark, and Internet law, and she is the author of *Digital Copyright* (Prometheus Books, 2001). She is a member of the American Intellectual Property Association, the Association for Teaching and Research in Intellectual Property, and the National Writers Union, and she serves on the ACLU Committee on Intellectual Property and the Internet.

GREGORY A. LOKEN is a professor of law in the Quinnipiac University School of Law. He received his J.D. from Harvard Law School in 1977.

DONALD W. MOLLOY has been chief judge for the U.S. District Court, District of Montana, since 2001. He was nominated to the court in 1995 by President Bill Clinton. He earned his B.A. and his J.D. from the University of Montana in 1968 and 1976, respectively.

SANDRA DAY O'CONNOR is an associate justice of the U.S. Supreme Court. She worked in various legal capacities both in the United States and in Germany until she was appointed to the Arizona State Senate in 1969. She served as a state senator for four years and served in the Arizona judiciary for six years before she was nominated to the Supreme Court by President Ronald Reagan in 1981.

O. LEE REED is a professor of legal studies at the University of Georgia. The author of many scholarly articles, he is a former editor-in-chief of the *American Business Law Journal,* and he is coauthor of *The Legal and Regulatory Environment of Business,* 12th ed. (McGraw-Hill/Irwin, 2001). He also has served as president of the Southeastern Regional Business Law Association and as president of the Academy of Legal Studies in Business. He holds a B.A. from Birmingham-Southern College and a J.D. from the University of Chicago.

WILLIAM H. REHNQUIST became the 16th chief justice of the U.S. Supreme Court in 1986. He engaged in a general practice of law with primary emphasis on civil litigation for 16 years before being appointed assistant attorney general, Office of Legal Counsel, by President Richard Nixon in 1969. He was nominated by Nixon to the Supreme Court in 1972.

STEPHEN REINHARDT is a judge on the U.S. Court of Appeals for the Ninth Circuit in Seattle, Washington.

JONATHAN ROWE is a contributing editor for the *Washington Monthly.*

ANTONIN SCALIA is an associate justice of the U.S. Supreme Court. He taught law at the University of Virginia, the American Enterprise Institute, Georgetown University, and the University of Chicago before being nominated to the U.S. Court of Appeals by President Ronald Reagan in 1982. He served in that capacity until he was nominated by Reagan to the Supreme Court in 1986.

SIMEON SCHOPF is a writing and research editor for the *Columbia Journal of Law and Social Problems.*

BRUCE SEYLA is a circuit judge for the U.S. Court of Appeals, First Circuit.

DAVID SOUTER is an associate justice of the U.S. Supreme Court and a former judge for the U.S. Court of Appeals for the First Circuit in Boston, Massachusetts. He was nominated by President George Bush to the Supreme Court in 1990.

BONNIE STEINBOCK is a professor of philosophy at the State University of New York at Albany, where she holds joint appointments in the Department of Public Policy in Rockefeller College and the Department of Health Policy in the School of Public Health. She is also a fellow and former vice president of the Hastings Center. Her research interests focus on the intersection of law, medicine, and ethics.

JOHN PAUL STEVENS is an associate justice of the U.S. Supreme Court. He worked in law firms in Chicago, Illinois, for 20 years before being nominated by President Richard Nixon to the U.S. Court of Appeals in 1970. He served in that capacity until he was nominated to the Supreme Court by President Gerald Ford in 1975.

ANDREW SULLIVAN is a former editor of *The New Republic.* He received his M.A. in public administration and his Ph.D. in political science from Harvard University in 1986 and 1990, respectively. His articles have been published in the *New York Times,* the *Wall Street Journal, Esquire,* the *Public Interest,* and the *Times* of London.

CASS SUNSTEIN is a professor of jurisprudence at the University of Chicago Law School, where he is also a member of the Department of Political Science. He has worked as an attorney-adviser in the Office of the Legal Counsel for the U.S. Department of Justice, and he has been the Samuel Rubin Visiting Professor of Law at Columbia University, a visiting professor of law at Harvard University, and chair of the Administrative Law Section of the Association of American Law Schools. His many publications include *The Cost of Rights: Why Liberty Depends on Taxes,* coauthored with Stephen Holmes (W. W. Norton, 1999) and *One Case at a Time: Judicial Minimalism* *on the Supreme Court* (Harvard University Press, 1999). He received his J.D. from Harvard University in 1978.

CLARENCE THOMAS is an associate justice of the U.S. Supreme Court. A former judge on the U.S. Court of Appeals for the District of Columbia, he was nominated by President George Bush to the Supreme Court in 1991. He received his J.D. from the Yale University School of Law in 1974.

JAMES Q. WILSON is the James Collins Professor of Management and Public Policy at the University of California, Los Angeles, where he has been teaching since 1985. He is also chairman of the Board of Directors of the Police Foundation and a member of the American Academy of Arts and Sciences. He has authored, coauthored, or edited numerous books on crime, government, and politics, including *Bureaucracy: What Government Agencies Do and Why They Do It* (Basic Books, 1989).

Index